'PROSPERITY' ROBINSON

The Author

Wilbur Devereux Jones is Professor of History, University of Georgia; he is the author of four previous books, contributor to many journals, and has also appeared on American educational television programs. His special interest is in the Anglo-American political tradition.

'PROSPERITY' ROBINSON

THE LIFE OF
VISCOUNT GODERICH
1782–1859

WILBUR DEVEREUX JONES

PROFESSOR OF HISTORY
THE UNIVERSITY OF GEORGIA

Macmillan

LONDON · MELBOURNE · TORONTO

St Martin's Press

NEW YORK

1967

Published by

MACMILLAN & COMPANY LTD

Little Essex Street London w c 2
and also at Bombay Calcutta and Madras
Macmillan South Africa (Publishers) Pty Ltd Johannesburg
The Macmillan Company of Australia Pty Ltd Melbourne
The Macmillan Company of Canada Ltd Toronto
St Martin's Press Inc. New York

Library of Congress catalog card no. 67–18711

Printed in Great Britain by
R. & R. CLARK, LTD., EDINBURGH

TO THE MEMORY OF

THE LATE DOWAGER MARCHIONESS

OF LONDONDERRY, D.B.E.

Contents

List of Illustrations

Preface

SPENCER WALPOLE in his history of England noted that 'Robinson must have had some qualifications, besides his birth, to win for him . . . rapid promotions, but it is almost impossible for the historian to detect where these qualifications lay'. Observations of this nature regarding Robinson encouraged the present writer to try to solve the mystery of how a statesman with so little to recommend him could achieve, if only for a brief period, the ultimate goal of all ambitious British politicians. The question also arose — why, if Robinson were little more than an amiable nonentity, did Lord Liverpool, Canning, Lord Grey, and Sir Robert Peel assign him to important positions in their Governments? Certain prominent leaders, especially Castlereagh and Peel, seem to have had the greatest confidence in him. What inspired it?

The investigation of Robinson's activities prompted by such questions immediately ran into difficulties. Save for his period of service in Peel's second Government, the Ripon Papers provided only outline information regarding his career; the Castlereagh Papers, despite the close association of the two men, contain few of Robinson's letters, and the Goulburn Papers none at all. So the information for this biography was culled from a considerable number of manuscript collections, and often from comments about Robinson in the letters of his friends and relatives.

While a considerable body of Robinson's letters was finally transcribed, a second difficulty quickly became apparent. Much too often to suit an historian, Robinson directed his pen to trivial matters, and both cautiously and consciously avoided recording his views concerning the important issues of the moment. This characteristic of his correspondence may help to clear up the mystery of why so many of his letters have not survived. They probably ended their existence in waste baskets.

Despite these difficulties, enough information was collected to write a longer biography than the present one, and the writer was called upon to choose certain portions of the whole story for emphasis. Generally speaking, the yardstick employed has been a professional one — what historians might expect to find in a political biography.

The period of his Premiership, and his Free Trade operations — each of which might well be the subject of a monograph — have been natural selections ; beyond these topics, an attempt has been made to clarify his political position at various moments of his career, and to relate him to the reform movement in general. Robinson's almost-forgotten love-story has been introduced only when it is essential to a well-rounded understanding of his political activities and decisions.

It is hoped that Robinson emerges, not as an 'embarrassed phantom', but as a real person who in his own day might have been called an 'experimental philosopher', and, in modern American parlance, an 'egg-head'. He had many of the strengths and weaknesses often associated with this type of personality ; strong in his conviction of doing good, and often weak in his methods for achieving his ends. Regarding the strength of his character, it might be pointed out here that it is one thing to trace weakness to a cowardly nature, and quite another to trace its source to an overscrupulous regard for the feelings and opinions of other people.

The author would like to acknowledge the kindness of the late Dowager Marchioness of Londonderry in making the private papers of the 2nd Marquess available to him, and to express his appreciation to the Duke of Wellington for permission to examine the manuscripts at Apsley House. The author would also like to acknowledge the kindness of the Rt. Hon. the Earl of Harrowby, and of Sir Fergus Graham, Bt., for permission to use certain letters from the Harrowby and Graham manuscripts which were furnished to him by M. G. Brock of Corpus Christi, Oxford. The author also wishes to extend thanks to Commander C. G. Vyner of Fountain's Hall and to his son Henry Vyner ; and to Captain E. R. F. Compton of Newby Hall and his son Robin E. J. Compton for their kindness in furnishing illustrations for this biography. Thanks also go to the Rt. Hon. the Earl of Buckinghamshire for the use of the Buckinghamshire Papers at Aylesbury, and to Professor Asa Briggs for his interest in this project.

WILBUR DEVEREUX JONES

University of Georgia,
Athens, Georgia,
29 April 1966

1

The Amiable Robinsons

==

FREDERICK JOHN ROBINSON was an amiable man. Although both his contemporaries and historians might argue concerning his abilities and other aspects of his character, on this single point they all agree, and such unanimity of opinion would seem to establish this one fact beyond all reasonable doubt. Unless he were some strange mutant, like a sweet apple suddenly appearing on a crab-apple tree, it would be reasonable to assume that an amiable man like Robinson had many good-natured ancestors who brightened British society during the centuries before his appearance.

Accounts of the Robinson family during the late sixteenth century, when they began to ascend the social ladder, are so vague that there is no way of knowing whether or not their amiability contributed to their rise.[1] The William Robinson knighted in 1633 is a passing shadow lost in time, nor is much known concerning his son, Metcalfe Robinson, who acquired the Newby estate, and became a baronet in the year of the Restoration. His nephew and heir, also named William Robinson, married Mary Aislabie of beautiful Studley Royal, and although this property subsequently passed into the hands of the Lawrence rather than the Robinson family, the Aislabies, Lawrences and Robinsons maintained a sense of family unity and eventually the Robinsons were to inherit their combined holdings.

The first of the undoubtedly amiable Robinsons was Frederick's grandfather, Thomas Robinson, a younger son of William Robinson. It may be that his suavity and good nature were partly responsible for his success in the diplomatic service; at any rate

1

his activities first at the embassy in France, and later as Minister Plenipotentiary in Austria won for him a knighthood and the Bath in 1742.   After helping to conclude the War of Austrian Succession, Sir Thomas returned to England and Whig politics. The eccentric Duke of Newcastle bestowed minor posts upon him in 1749 and 1750; and in 1754, while engaged in a temporary quarrel with Henry Fox, made Sir Thomas Secretary of State for the Southern Department.[2]   When Fox made up his quarrel with Newcastle the following year, Robinson obligingly resigned his position in favour of Fox, and Newcastle rewarded his co-operative attitude with a £2,000 pension for two lives, payable from Irish funds.

In 1760 Sir Thomas advanced his claims to the Vice-Treasurer-ship of Ireland, but when Newcastle found it politically inexpedient to comply with the request, Robinson quickly withdrew them, and the following year his reward was a peerage.   He then became the 1st Baron Grantham in Lincolnshire.[3]   Both the new Baron Grantham and his perennial patron, Newcastle, joined the Rock-ingham Government in 1765, but once again the former had to make way for someone else.   When Grafton took over in the following year, he wanted Grantham's Postmaster-Generalship for one of his friends, and the amiable Baron agreed to make way with the understanding that his son, the future 2nd Baron Grantham, should be made a Lord Commissioner of Trade and Plantations.   Certainly few British statesmen could compare with Grantham in the technique of transmuting retirement into advancement.

T. B. Macaulay called Grantham '. . . a dull, harmless man',[4] and another historian dubbed him a 'non-entity' after 'New-castle's own heart'.[5]   Yet when one considers that he had no rotten boroughs to offer, so little landed property that the King hesitated to give him a peerage,[6] and no commanding mien which would overawe his opponents in Parliament, it must be agreed that he made the most of his opportunities and assets, whatever they might have been.   Not only was he a popular man, but he evidently won the confidence of the King, who desired his return to the Secretaryship of State in 1757.

For a wife the first Lord Grantham (then Robinson) chose a descendant of Oliver Cromwell, Frances Worsley of Yorkshire, by whom he had six children. His daughter, Theresa Robinson, married the 1st Lord Boringdon, and their son, the 2nd Lord Boringdon, probably opened some important doors for Frederick Robinson early in his life.

Frederick's father, Thomas Robinson, was born in Vienna in 1738 while his father headed the diplomatic mission there. The 1st Baron Grantham led him along the path which had brought him wealth and prominence — education at Westminster and Cambridge, a seat in the Commons, and specialization in foreign policy. In 1771, the year after his father died, the 2nd Baron Grantham received his first major diplomatic assignment — to go to the Court of Spain as Ambassador Extraordinary and Plenipotentiary, where he was to destroy the 'unnatural alliance' between France and Spain, keep an eye on Gibraltar, and to advance British commercial interests.[7] Like his father, the 2nd Baron approached his tasks with 'diffidence' and modesty as to his own abilities,[8] but not even a Talleyrand could have carried out the assignment successfully. All Grantham's efforts to keep Spain out of the American war proved unavailing, and in 1779 he returned to England a failure. He was then past forty, unmarried, and had done little to advance the interests of his family, and nothing to perpetuate it.

In domestic politics Grantham evidently had no real attachment to any faction or party. Lord North had appointed him to Spain, and later made him 1st Commissioner of the Board of Trade and Plantations, but when Shelburne became Prime Minister, Grantham accepted office from the man who had opposed North in the Lords for a dozen years. This office was the most important that he ever held, and his task the most momentous that he ever performed. Appointed Foreign Secretary in July 1782, he made peace with America. Although he considered himself unfit for the demanding task,[9] he had the confidence of the King, who called him an 'honest Man' who was 'unwarped by connections'.[10]

Considering the difficult position in which Britain was then placed, the terms of peace negotiated by Grantham were not unfavourable. He was satisfied that France, Spain and Holland had gained little from the war, and regarding the future of America he had no opinion. 'America will have acquired independence,' he wrote, 'whether that is a gain or not the wisest man will not pretend to say.' [11] The 'unreasonableness' and 'injustice' with which opposing factions in Parliament greeted his treaty disgusted Grantham,[12] and in scanning the parliamentary incumbents of the day, he found only one man free from the 'old system of corruption', and this was William Pitt. 'He is a most extraordinary phenomenon,' Grantham wrote, '. . . and his character untainted.' [13] But Grantham's peace-making efforts were by no means universally unappreciated. 'Lady Pelham and my Daughter have just drunk your Health,' Lord Pelham wrote to Grantham, 'with thanks for the blessings of Peace.' [14] Shelburne rewarded him with a £2,000 pension.

Shortly after his return from Spain, Grantham's lengthy bachelorhood came to an end. In August 1780, by special licence from the Archbishop of Canterbury, he married Mary Jemima Grey Yorke, younger daughter of the 2nd Earl of Hardwicke and Marchioness Grey. Grantham was then almost forty-two years old, his bride twenty-three, but despite their age differences their letters prove that they were a most devoted couple. Their first son, Thomas Philip Robinson, was born in December 1781, then came Frederick John Robinson on 30 October 1782, and Philip in October 1783.

Lady Grantham's letters provide numerous insights into her character and accomplishments. Although she was strongly patriotic, she wrote frankly: 'I shall not trouble you about politicks, foreign or domestick, as I understand neither.' [15] Lady Grantham loved her garden and the out of doors; attended concerts, ballets, and church. As a devotee of the theatre, she was enthusiastic about Mrs. Siddons; as an amateur painter, she felt qualified to criticize the 'uncertainty' of the colours used by Sir Joshua Reynolds, whom her father wished to have paint the children. As a lover of architectural styles, she spent many hours examining and sketching the fine old castles of England.

Lady Grantham and her husband provided that loving, secure atmosphere in which the tender personalities of children could best develop. At Newby they stayed daily with their family in the Gallery for hours on end, or took them walking around the estate. 'He [Thomas] is grown quite gracious again,' Lady Grantham reported to her father, 'has taken us both into favour & calls upon his Papa to trot about the room with him as he used to.' [16] In addition to providing pick-a-back rides and other amusements, the proud father carefully noted the individual differences among his children. 'The Dear Children improve daily,' he wrote. 'Tom preserves the innate Dignity of his Address. Fred never looks grave for more than a minute & Philip rivals them both in making sounds of all sorts.' [17] The personalities of the first two were thus revealed early in their existences. Poor Philip, however, was fated to die in childhood.

These were no doubt the greenest, happiest years of Lord Grantham's life. On his fifth anniversary he wrote to Hardwicke : 'every Day of the last five years of my Life has confirmed & added to the Happiness of it'.[18] Normally he might have expected that happiness, which had been so long postponed, to have extended for two or three decades, and it may have been the more keenly felt during these too-brief years because of the shadow that hung over it. Lord Grantham had long been ailing ; many of his friends, in fact, had feared his duties in Spain might have been too much for him, but he flourished in the Mediterranean climate and returned to England in fairly good health.

The letters of 1785, however, tell of his 'Astmatick or Gouty' complaints — probably really a heart condition — and during that winter he went through several 'recoveries' and relapses. In late spring Hardwicke loaned Grantham his house in Whitehall Street so he could be near the London doctors, and for a time his son-in-law was well enough to hunt for and find a home of his own — Grantham House in Putney Heath. He disliked boring others with the details of his condition, but one can sense a growing alarm in his letter to Hardwicke of 3 June : 'there is nothing I feel more strongly than the Desire of being restored to perfect health, & that My Dr. Lord, I can assure you not merely on my own Account, but on account of those, whom I love better than myself'.[19]

Coming to Putney Heath was probably a mistake. The London physicians had no more effective remedies for his breathing difficulties than the 'blisters' used by the Yorkshire doctors, and the damp, chill air of a dreary London July seems to have gradually choked the life out of him. His last letter to Hardwicke recalled the balmy atmosphere of sunny, distant Spain: 'I got down to London very well, & am pretty well today, but I who am used to a Southern Climate, do not think this a very genial day.'[20] Two weeks later, on 20 July 1786, he died at Putney Heath. No one who reads his letters can doubt but that he was an upright, moral, modest, kind, gentle, and altogether amiable man.

If Lady Grantham were not left destitute by her husband's death, neither was she inordinately wealthy. She received the house in Putney Heath, and the interest from a £100,000 trust fund set up for the two younger sons. When her mother died in 1797, her properties, which included Wrest in Bedfordshire, the Crudwell estate in Wiltshire, and some holdings in Essex were split between Lady Grantham and her elder sister, Amabel, who also inherited two baronial titles — Lucas and Crudwell. Amabel, whose husband, Lord Hume of Berwick, had died in 1781, was called 'Lady Lucas' in Robinson's letters until 1816, when she resurrected her mother's title and became Countess de Grey of Wrest with the remainder to Lady Grantham and her children. The two young widows lived together, usually at Wrest or Grantham House, for the rest of their lives.

Frederick's elder brother, Thomas, was the chief beneficiary of the many generations of estate-builders who preceded him. At his father's death he became the 3rd Baron Grantham, and received all the landed property other than Grantham House.[21] The death of a first cousin, Sir Norton Robinson, Bt., of Newby, in 1792 brought Thomas a baronetcy and some additional land; and the same year William Weddell, related to the Robinsons through a sister of the 1st Baron Grantham, bequeathed his 'large estates' to Thomas on condition that he adopt the name Weddell.[22] These three inheritances made the 3rd Baron a wealthy man, but he was still not numbered among the real tycoons of the era. The death of his aunt Amabel in 1833 brought him the de Grey earldom, the Barony of Lucas, and the estates which went with them; then when Elizabeth Sophia Lawrence, whose great-great-grandmother had married Grantham's great-grandfather, passed away in 1845, Thomas inherited Studley Royal, Fountains Abbey, and all of her property around Ripon south of the River Ure. By that time he was considered to be one of the wealthiest men in England.[23]

Though only ten months separated Frederick from his brother, those months spelled the difference between great wealth and comparative poverty. Until 1830, when his mother died and the trust fund terminated, Frederick, who then received Grantham House and £50,000, seems to have been landless, and, in his own right, practically penniless. He was dependent upon his mother and brother, his wife, and his income from his governmental positions. From Miss Lawrence he received a share of the Ripon properties — the holdings north of the River Ure — in 1845, but during the major portion of his parliamentary career we must assume that he depended on others to defray his election expenses.

The education of Frederick and Thomas Robinson began early in life under the supervision of their devoted parents. Lady Grantham was teaching Thomas syllables from a spelling book when he was still less than three, and Frederick began to memorize his letters at the age of twenty-five months.[24] The comparative intelligence of the two boys is hinted at in some of their mother's letters. 'Frederick will very probably talk faster,' she predicted in 1783, '. . . but I do not believe that he will ever be so good a crawler on the floor.'[25] This seems to have been the basic contrast between the two in later years — Thomas was the athlete, the man's man; Frederick was the intellectual, and never impressed either sex with his physical abilities. The latter seems to have strongly approved of the home-type education he received, for he later used the same methods, with considerable success, in instructing his own son.

B

Less is known regarding their early formal education. One source noted that Thomas went to a private school under a Dr. Glasse; another states that Frederick went to Sunbury, in all probability the same school.[26] Thereafter Frederick went to Harrow, and for this period in his life there is a description :[27]

He was an excellent scholar for his age, and shone particularly in composition, his exercises being not less remarkable for the ease with which he dispatched them, than for their brilliancy. The pride and favourite of the masters, he had likewise the singular good fortune to be popular among his school-fellows, with whom his gaiety served as an antidote to the jealousy which, even at schools, often attaches to superior merit. Without being at all handsome, his countenance had an ingenious and pleasing expression, his blue eyes beaming with intelligence and good humour. His future attainment of very high distinction in public life was confidently predicted by the general voice of the school.

Popularity — intelligence — amiability, these characteristics he seems to have had in abundance, and perhaps explain why he never lost a friend.[28]

Like many of his generation, Robinson was something of a classical scholar. In 1798 he delivered an address on Galacus by Tacitus. At St. John's College, Cambridge, which he entered in 1799, he won Sir William Browne's medal for the best Latin ode, a piece called *Melite subacta* ('Malta Surrendered to the British'), which he recited at the Senate House in 1801. The poem traced the history of the island down to Horatio Nelson's conquest of it in 1799 — 'But now, fair Isle! shall bliss be thine,' he concluded.[29] Robinson evidently liked the iambic foot and the octosyllabic line; at any rate, he was still using them in a poem written in 1840. His poem of 1801, although it has some of the fire of the Romantic Age, hardly justifies him a niche in the distinguished halls of English literature.

The letters of Lady Bessborough, a Foxite Whig whom Robinson came to know through Viscount Duncannon, Lord Althorp, or Lord Boringdon, provide a few glimpses of Robinson during this period in his life. She mentioned him as dining with her in 1798, and the sophisticated, thirty-six-year-old social luminary and her sixteen-year-old escort seem to have been close friends. 'The latter [Robinson] carried me to Ly. Melbourne's to supper,' she wrote, 'and made me very angry by cutting off some of my hair as a pattern for his wig.'[30] Two years later Robinson seems to have formed a rather serious romantic attachment for some unidentifiable young lady, which was followed with interest by the Melbournes and his other friends.[31]

Robinson paid Lady Bessborough a fairly extended visit in 1802, and he was frequently mentioned in her letters at that time. She noted that he wore his new 'wig à la Brutus', a short head-piece currently fashionable in France, and considered in England as the mark of a liberal individual who followed the fashions. But the impression left by some of her references was that of a scholarly young man who lacked the vivaciousness which usually made him such a pleasant companion. 'Robinson answers me in the moon', she complained, 'and talks to me of Cassandra, Cleopatra, or the siege of Troy.'[32] In another letter she pictures Robinson as 'grumbling' over one of Voltaire's works, and talking entirely too much about scholarly subjects, which bored some other visitors.

At Easter time in 1802 Robinson matriculated at Cambridge, and received his M.A. degree shortly thereafter. This was a traditional step — his father and brother had taken similar degrees at the university before him. In May of the same year Robinson was admitted to Lincoln's Inn to begin his study of law. Later he was fond of recalling that the family coachman had once predicted that he would become Lord Chancellor,[33] but, although he remained a member of the Inn until 1809, it is unlikely that he ever intended to become a lawyer, let alone advance to the top of that profession. His studies at Lincoln's Inn were merely an adjunct to his political career.

In 1802 the Peace of Amiens opened France once again to British tourists, and one of the first to go there was Lord Boringdon.[34] Lord and Lady Bessborough went in December, and Robinson was a member of their party. In her letters he is mentioned as walking with the girls in the Tuileries, dining with the Second Consul of France, and gratifying his 'gourmandise (his chief passion)'.[35]　She mentioned that most of the English were presented to Napoleon on one occasion, but whether or not Robinson met the man whose career he followed with a mixture of fascination and distaste is unknown.

From such references it would seem that Robinson received an excellent education, and was a superior scholar, with an interest especially in the classics and in eighteenth-century literature. 'An intercourse with distinguished men was eagerly sought and fully appreciated by me', he wrote later in life,[36] and it is clear that his 'connections' gave him contacts with most of the important political leaders in contemporary Britain.

In physical appearance he seems to have been a blue-eyed blond, with a fair complexion, and a face that was plain, if not actually homely, which faithfully reproduced his reactions and emotions.　He was probably one of the least inscrutable men ever to enter British public life, optimistic, jolly, and forward without being aggressive.　Robinson's interests seem to have been wholly healthy and normal.　He evidently fell in love once, and perhaps more often. Although he loved poetry and flowers, he also hunted with considerable enthusiasm.[37]

To use modern terms it is clear that Robinson led a 'sheltered existence' in his youth ; he lived in the eye of the political, social, and economic hurricane which was sweeping the continent of Europe, and had little contact with the unpleasant facts of contemporary life.　His was a genteel background, a babyhood and childhood filled with a complete satisfaction of his spiritual and material wants, one designed, indeed, to create the amiable individual that he turned out to be.

Both Robinson and his brother, Lord Grantham, embarked on their careers in the same year — 1803.　In the newly expanded militia Grantham found a place as Lord-Lieutenant of the Yorkshire Hussar Regiment of Yeomanry Cavalry, a post he was to hold for forty years.　He gave Robinson a captain's commission which he retained until 1814 and perhaps longer.　Originally it had been planned for Robinson to tour Europe that autumn, upon his coming of age, but the renewal of the war made such a visit impracticable.

Grantham, who had plenty of employment himself in his new job and the management of his estates, sent his brother to visit their cousin (once removed), the 3rd Earl of Hardwicke, who had become Lord-Lieutenant of Ireland under Addington. In a letter from Grantham conveyed by Robinson his brother explained that it was necessary to find him some 'proper occupation' pending the next election, when he would be returned to Parliament, and that he hoped '. . . some situation under you might present itself, which tho' at present rather subordinate, might be an extremely proper situation, for one with an inclination, and I can say without vanity with abilities to appear in [the] future in a higher one.' [38] Hardwicke lived up to his family obligations and made an opening for Robinson as a confidential secretary.

Although Robinson must have been gratified to have found gainful employment, he probably regarded Ireland and the Irish with considerable distaste at this time. As a patriotic Englishman who had lived through the rebellion of 1798, he must have regarded the people there with profound distrust, and, as he admitted later, his 'early impressions' and 'hereditary prejudices' had steeled him against Catholic Emancipation because he had been 'taught to believe that the papal faith was always connected with arbitrary power'.[39] The events in Ireland during his employment there could hardly have improved his opinion of things Hibernian.

When he arrived, the Government was still investigating the roots of the Robert Emmet conspiracy of 23 July 1803.[40] Then, towards the end of the year, a suspicious calm settled over the island,[41] which was induced, the Government learned in February 1804, by the anticipation of the arrival of two French squadrons staging at Brest, which would support a general insurrection.[42] The island was almost in a state of siege. Additional troops were raised, and a system of warning stations was established along the coasts. Spies and informers told the Government that the French were expected early in July.[43]

The French, of course, did not arrive, but in January 1805, there was a flurry of excitement when a jittery lieutenant at one of the warning stations gave signal number '5'—enemy transports steering east — and neglected to rectify his mistake. The report that the French fleet had joined the Spanish at Cadiz caused further uneasiness in May, and there was no relaxation of the tensions until news arrived of the crushing British victory at Trafalgar.

The highlight of Robinson's period in Ireland, however, was his special mission to London. Hardwicke was involved in a continuing quarrel with Sir Evan Nepean, the Chief Secretary, who had returned to England late in 1804 and was very influential in determining Irish policy. The Lord-Lieutenant therefore sent Robinson to London in early 1805 with a letter to William Pitt, demanding that Nepean be replaced, preferably by an individual with a Yorke connection. Two other matters were also called to Pitt's attention — the honour of the Garter, and the activities of a certain individual who planned to release some embarrassing documents relating to the Act of Union.[44] But the Nepean affair was the important item — if a satisfactory Secretary were not appointed by 12 March, Hardwicke would leave Ireland.

On arriving in London Robinson first had a conference with Hardwicke's brother, Charles Yorke. Although Yorke expressed doubts as to the wisdom of delivering a letter penned in a moment of annoyance, Robinson nevertheless applied for an interview with Pitt. A week passed before he was able to talk with Pitt's secretary, and still another before he secured his interview with the Prime Minister. All that is known of this interview comes from one of Hardwicke's letters in reply to Robinson's account of it : [45]

So far as depended upon you, nothing appears to have been omitted, and though Mr. Pitt seems to have been more communicative and unreserved upon some topics than could have been expected, yet . . . the affair remains in as undecided a state, as it was in the month of November . . . I am therefore sorry that Mr. Pitt should consider it as a mere difficulty between Sir Evan and myself . . . I am really much obliged to you for the manner in which you have executed my commission, & for the satisfactory and clear manner in which you have detailed the substance of what passed at your interview.

Although Robinson carried out his instructions with precision and aplomb, the Prime Minister kept putting off Hardwicke, and when he replaced Nepean in March, it was with one of Sidmouth's supporters, Nicholas Vansittart, and not with a friend of Hardwicke's.

The Home Government, in fact, paid little attention to the advice of its Lord-Lieutenant, and he finally was driven to resign when Pitt disbursed some Irish funds without his consent. The Prime Minister then kept postponing the question of his replacement, and he died before the matter was settled. Hardwicke therefore continued in Ireland until the Grenville–Fox Ministry sent the Duke of Bedford to take over the administration. 'We shall not', Robinson wrote Charles Yorke on 24 March 1806, 'be quite at liberty till the end of the week'.[46]

Robinson thus spent more than two years in Ireland at the outset of his career, and he spent them working for a man who, despite his connection with the conservative Addington Administration, was liberal by nature. Hardwicke avoided coercive measures in Ireland whenever possible, fought for Irish trading interests, and on one occasion removed an Irish official because of his violent anti-Catholic expressions.[47] Although he opposed Nepean's stirring up Emancipation sentiment at this time, he eventually came to favour that reform himself. The quarrel between Nepean and Hardwicke, the charges against Hardwicke of revenue frauds in connection with the manufacture of liquor, brought by a disgruntled revenue officer,[48] these were unpleasant features of his stay, but, by and large, the years were richly rewarding and gave Robinson an insight into the practical problems of a rather enlightened administration.

When he returned from Ireland Robinson had passed his twenty-third birthday, and his age no longer barred him from a seat in Parliament. The questions naturally arose — which constituency would he represent? To which political party, or faction within a party, would he ally himself? In his day it was natural for the scion of a prominent political family to secure a seat through one of his 'connections', or, failing this, to buy a seat. Robinson was forced to accept the second alternative.

The 3rd Earl of Hardwicke controlled a Reigate constituency, and also a seat for Cambridge County, but his brother, Charles Yorke, occupied the latter, and the other does not seem to have been available in 1806. Another of Robinson's powerful 'connections', the 1st Earl of Malmesbury, had once controlled Christchurch (Southampton), but he had given it up, and therefore had no constituency to offer. Grantham in 1805 had married a daughter of the 1st Earl of Enniskillen, a powerful Orange leader who controlled seats for Enniskillen and Fermanagh, but these seats were apparently also unavailable.

Some mystery, then, surrounds Robinson's acquisition of Carlow, an Irish borough near Dublin, which was under the patronage of the Earl of Charleville. A quarter of a century later he told the Lords that he had once purchased a seat in the Commons, and later noted that £8,000 was the price of a parliamentary seat. While there is no doubt that the seat was bought for him, just how much was paid, and who footed the bill remain unanswered questions. As Carlow returned a different representative at each of the five elections between 1801 and 1812, it may be that the burgesses who had voting rights looked upon the seat as an ordinary source of income. Be this as it may, Robinson appeared in the Commons in December 1806 as another product of the rotten-borough system.

How he should vote in Parliament seems at the moment to have been decided as much by his family and his 'connections' as by himself. Lord Hardwicke had once been a follower of Fox, but he transferred his support, probably for patriotic reasons, to Pitt in 1794. Although George Rose still included him in his list of 'Pitt's Friends' in early 1806,[49] the late Prime Minister had thoroughly exasperated him, and he was becoming increasingly friendly towards Lords Grey and Grenville. Lord Malmesbury, called the 'Lion' because of his shock of white hair, had also been a Foxite, but once he enlisted under Pitt's banner in 1793, he thereafter considered himself one of the purest of all Pittites. When Pitt died in 1806 Malmesbury resolved that he would thereafter exert such influence as he had in furthering what he considered to be Pitt's policies.[50] His interpretation of those policies made him an enemy of the Government in power.

The split between Hardwicke and Malmesbury goes far toward explaining the ambiguity of Robinson's political position in 1806–7. His first vote, in favour of the elimination of the slave trade, does not in itself provide evidence of his political position, as the project found support on both sides of the House, but it might indicate that Robinson, left to his own devices, would follow a liberal line. A division of February, however, had more political significance. A Treasury secretary, William Fremantle, was charged with using the influence of his office in the Hampshire election, and Robinson joined Canning, Castlereagh, Perceval, and George Rose in a losing vote against the Government on this issue. Save for these votes, and his appointment to one of the many election committees, the closing weeks of the Grenville Government, which fell in March 1807, were uneventful ones for Robinson; but he was finally launched upon a political career, and was following in the footsteps of his amiable father and equally amiable grandfather, both of whom had found fortune, if not much fame, in that profession.

2

---◆---

The Alfred Club Set

THE formation of a Government by the Duke of Portland in 1807 caused the split between Robinson's family 'connections' to widen considerably. Neither Hardwicke nor his brother, Charles Yorke, was on good terms with Portland, and the former had entered into confidential communications with Grenville.[1] When the Portland Government was finally formed, however, Hardwicke and Yorke regarded themselves as 'not obliged or pledged to any party'.[2] Lord Malmesbury, on the other hand, regarded the Portland Government as an extension of Pitt's Ministry, and he worked hard for its success.

Because of his connections Robinson achieved a considerable position of prominence in the factional struggle of the time. This is evident from the offer made to him on 30 March, an offer undoubtedly engineered by Malmesbury, who wrote of it as follows : [3]

> In the morning I spoke to Fred. Robinson about his accepting the Admiralty ; he doubtful, with no good reason, but influenced by the Yorkes, and his own family. Spoke to Lady Grantham ; she irresolute, and, though not saying so, manifestly against his taking office, under an Administration she did not think would last.

The following day Robinson rejected the proposal, and probably for the reasons noted by Malmesbury. It is, in retrospect, a pity that he did so, for it would have strengthened his claim, if he had accepted, to having held more different Cabinet positions during his career than any other British statesman.

16

If he did not seize this opportunity for participation in official life, Robinson was able, during the elections of May 1807, to secure a permanent seat in the Commons. This was for Ripon, a borough and market-town near Studley Royal in Yorkshire, whose 146 burgage voters sent two representatives to the Commons. In this instance his means of acquiring the seat are quite clear. At the moment the representation was controlled by Elizabeth Allanson and her niece, Elizabeth Sophia Lawrence, the same distant relative of the Robinsons who was to divide her properties between Thomas and Frederick in 1845. A rather romantic story which had some currency at the time traced Elizabeth's failure to marry to her enduring love for the dashing, handsome Grantham, but as she was born in 1761, and Grantham in 1781, she would have been a seemingly confirmed spinster long before he reached maturity. Be this as it may, the two brothers were extremely attentive to Elizabeth Lawrence during her life, and were richly rewarded at the time of her death.

The previous occupants of the Ripon seats had all been classified as Tories, and Robinson was generally considered to belong to that party upon assuming his place in the representation. To some extent he had to assume the political attitudes of his patroness, who was well known for her Church and charitable work. Although she might favour measures of a humanitarian nature, she was a strong 'Protestant' on the Emancipation question, and so were the burgesses of Ripon. From what is known of his attitudes, Robinson in 1807 could accept these views without doing violence to his own convictions, and thereafter his re-election was fairly certain, if not absolutely so. At every election thereafter he would circulate through the borough and answer all the questions put to him by the freeholders.[4]

Although Malmesbury had been defeated in his first attempt to tie Robinson and his 'connections' to the Government, he was not easily discouraged, and was more successful in his second try. Austria, in April 1807, was thoroughly defeated, and advised Britain that she proposed to mediate an end to the war on the Continent; but Canning, at the Foreign Office, decided to send a mission to Austria with the offer of a large sum to stay in the war. Canning talked over the situation in May, and finally chose Malmesbury's close friend, Lord Pembroke, to head the mission. Under these circumstances, it was an easy matter for Malmesbury to secure a place for Robinson in it. 'A'Court goes with him as Secretary of the Embassy,' Malmesbury wrote, 'Douglas [Sir Andrew's son] as Private Secretary, and Frederick Robinson as a friend.' [5] This was probably Robinson's first contact with Canning, the man who was to play for a brief period an enormous role in his political future.

Before the Pembroke Mission could accomplish its purpose, Russia had been badly mauled at the battle of Friedland, and there was no hope that Austria would continue the unequal struggle alone. So the disappointed diplomats proceeded to Trieste and then to Malta — which must have been thrilling for Robinson in view of his poem — where they received instructions to return home. By and large, it was mainly a tourist experience for Robinson, but in a modest manner it prepared him for the vital diplomatic mission of 1813, when next he went to the Continent.

All parliamentary fledglings, such as Robinson, had one day to face their moment of truth, when they presented themselves for the first time to the sophisticated, easily bored, fellow members of the Commons. The first speech attributed to him in *Hansard* was dated 11 April 1808, and it was on the budget, the area in which he was later to rise to fame. A speech of 15 April 1807, attributed to John Robinson in the index, may possibly have been his first effort. Francis Horner noted that a 'great many new orators' spoke during this debate; [6] and Charles Abbot recorded that 'several young members', including 'Mr. Robinson' presented themselves to the House.[7] As John Robinson had been in Parliament since 1802, the adjectives 'new' and 'young' probably would better fit Frederick, but perhaps the best evidence of his ownership is the style of the speech itself.

The pattern was one which Robinson was to follow faithfully throughout his parliamentary life. This particular speech was made in opposition to a motion which stated that the late change of Government (the overthrow of Grenville) was to be regretted.

At the outset Robinson lauded the creditable manner in which the motion had been made, and expressed his conviction that the mover had the highest motives in bringing it forth, all of which was preliminary to a rather mild criticism of the late Administration. Then toward the end of the speech Robinson admitted that he regretted the late changes on 'general grounds', which seemed to support, up to a point, the motion he was opposing.[8]

A contemporary observer later made the following observation about Robinson's speeches: [9]

> One leading characteristic of his speeches is the want of anything decisive as to the opinions he holds on the subject under discussion. If he means to vote against the question before the House he commences by urging arguments against it; but before he has gone half-way through he is sure to make so many admissions in favour of the opposite side, that . . . you cannot possibly see how he can, with any show of consistency . . . vote for either.

This characteristic, which involves absolute integrity in the consideration of a question, is one of the most striking evidences of Robinson's intellect. Normally such fair consideration of the views of the opposition was neither expected, nor required in debate, and this supererogation on Robinson's part won for him unusual respect, and even admiration in some quarters. 'His voice and countenance are in the highest degree prepossessing', another observer wrote. 'Before he utters half-a-dozen sentences, the auditor finds himself involuntarily exclaiming, "This must be a scrupulously honest man."' [10]

The 'scrupulously honest man'! This is the public image which Robinson created for himself — the detached arbiter among different points of view, the honest broker urging compromises among clashing interests, the statesman-intellectual who sought truth in a field usually ruled by emotion and self-interest. To foster and maintain this image, Robinson had to play the role both inside and outside the House of Commons. At the same time he achieved a posture which was not only inoffensive to others of lesser integrity, but one which resulted in his general popularity on both sides of the House.

How did Robinson happen to choose this role? Had he been inspired as a youth by the family's admiration for William Pitt, whose 'untainted' character his father had been so quick to notice? Had he decided that the image of the untainted states-man was of practical value to his career in an era which tolerated considerable corruption? The first is possible, and the second, which would seem to require posing, is doubtful, for Robinson was remarkably free and natural in his relations with others.

Perhaps the safest conclusion is that the honest man was the natural Robinson, created by the demands of his mind, body, and spirit. Intellectually he was never able to be a violent partisan because he could understand so perfectly both sides of an argu-ment. Physically he shrank from violent clashes with stronger personalities, and during this period there were many such. Spiritually he was a deeply religious person who took the Golden Rule quite seriously.

Although Robinson had accepted a place in the Pembroke Mission in 1807, he still did not consider himself to be a regular supporter of the Government. The Malmesbury connection, and the sponsor of his seat, both pulled him in that direction, but he seems to have followed the general lead of Charles Yorke, who hesitated to ally himself with the Tories in opposition to his brother. Yorke became increasingly conservative as the months went by, but Lord Hardwicke, during the period 1807–12, opposed the Tory Governments on every major test of strength, and was as steady an opponent as Lord Grenville, and even more so than Lords Holland and Grey, who sometimes missed divisions.

Yorke and Robinson sat on the Government side of the House during the 1808 session, and supported the Ministers on the Copenhagen division, and in their opposition to Catholic claims. Robinson spoke on two occasions, but neither effort is worthy of notice. He was still very much an unknown quantity at the time, and he was often referred to as 'Lord Grantham's brother', which implied he was noteworthy chiefly as a member of an aristocratic, politically-minded family.

At the end of the year the Ministry was seeking someone with just such qualifications to undertake the thankless task of moving the Address. The day after Christmas, Spencer Perceval wrote Robinson a letter asking him to speak for the Government at the opening of Parliament in 1809. He explained that the Government was seeking someone who could 'launch our debate, with good effect from the ability with which he wd. open it', and asked to be excused for taking the liberty 'in applying to you'.[11] It was a formal letter, indicative of the slight acquaintanceship existing between the two men.

The letter was delivered to Robinson at Newby Hall, where he was visiting his brother, and his acceptance was probably approved by Grantham and the rest of the immediate family. Replying in the same formal tone in which the offer was made, Robinson feared that he might 'prove a disappointment to you', but nevertheless acceded to his request.[12] George Canning warmly approved the selection. 'Mr. Robinson', he wrote, 'is the best possible choice.'[13]

Acceptance meant a firm commitment to the Portland Government, and Robinson realized that this was unlikely to meet with Hardwicke's cordial approval. He waited several days, then broke the news to his powerful 'connection' with the observation 'this step may possibly not meet with your entire approbation', and begged for indulgence.[14] Hardwicke's reply is not available, but he continued to correspond with Robinson in a cordial manner in 1809, and it is clear that he carefully avoided the domineering attitude that once brought tragedy in his family.

Robinson faced this major ordeal on the afternoon of 19 January 1809. His task was to defend the military operations in Portugal and Spain, which meant praising the Convention of Cintra, which had permitted the French to extricate their army from Portugal, and to minimize the importance of their occupation of Madrid. In other words, he had to show there were gleams of hope in a grim situation. Whether he carefully prepared and memorized his speech, as his friend Robert Peel was to do in a somewhat similar situation, or spoke extemporaneously, as he always did later,[15] we do not know. Nor do we know if his

voice had its 'singing' quality on this occasion,[16] for about all
we know of it is embodied in the cold print of *Hansard*.

Britain, he declared, would never desert her allies no matter
how hopeless the military situation might seem, and he singled
out one of them — Spain — for special praise. But being Robinson he admitted that 'speculative men might differ on points
relating to internal reforms and regulations' — which was his
way of stating that he was well aware of the shortcomings of the
former listless, corrupt, ineffective, and bigoted Spanish monarchy. The bravery of the British troops in Portugal drew from
him an encomium, and the British economy was declared to be
'superior to all the opposition and schemes of deterioration the
tyrant could devise'.[17] Only in matters relating to the war was
Robinson strongly partisan, and, by and large, it was the type
of speech called for by the situation, full of hope and national
pride, and the optimism of youth, which is always refreshing.
Stephen Lushington, who followed Robinson, noted his 'ability
and eloquence': Castlereagh described it as an 'able' speech.
Following the ordeal Robinson would be satisfied that he passed
this test in a creditable manner.

The session of 1809 might aptly be described as a rather un-
savoury session, which was highlighted by exposés and charges
of a sensational nature being brought against prominent individuals. Shortly after the debate on the Address, the Peninsular
Campaign and other vital problems were pushed aside while the
Commons investigated the alleged peccadilloes of the Duke of
York, and his mistress, the wily and intelligent Mary Anne
Clarke. Charles Yorke called the investigation a 'conspiracy of
the most atrocious and diabolical kind against his royal high-
ness . . . founded on the Jacobinical spirit which appeared at
the commencement of the French Revolution'.[18] The more
cynical Malmesbury called the charge 'infamous, not because
entirely groundless', but because its instigators held 'level-
ling principles'.[19] During the lengthy investigation Robinson
asked two minor questions which seemed to strengthen the
Duke's case, then put one regarding Mary Anne Clarke's use
of the Duke of York's credit which was later taken up by

one of the Duke's chief opponents, the Whig Radical, Samuel Whitbread.

The investigation of corruption in high places moved much nearer to home when some legislators sought to involve certain members and former members of the Irish Government in something like a bootlegging racket. Hardwicke, who had been charged with dealings of this nature back in 1805, evidently lived through some trying days in April, but his name did not arise in the debate of 17 April. 'It is not improbable', Robinson assured him the following day, 'that they are sensible of the absurdity of bringing forward such cases as those which refer to you'.[20]

Attempts were made to put still others on the investigatory rack. Castlereagh was charged with using Government patronage to secure a certain seat in the Commons, but Canning, who was shortly to break with him, carried a resolution which cleared his colleague. In May both Castlereagh and Perceval were charged with corrupt election practices, and Charles Yorke, who now appeared as a staunch supporter of the Ministers, fended off the attack.

That spring, Castlereagh, then Secretary for War and the Colonies, began his close association with Robinson. They had apparently met earlier, possibly through Hardwicke, who was on intimate terms with Castlereagh,[21] or through Malmesbury, who also knew him. Whoever brought them together could hardly have imagined what the association was to mean to Robinson. Castlereagh was to be the most important 'connection' established by Robinson throughout his career.

At the moment Castlereagh needed an Under-Secretary in his office to replace his intense and emotional half-brother, Charles Stewart, who was to join the British military forces in the Peninsula. Castlereagh wrote to Robinson on 27 April that his feelings of 'much personal regard' would be gratified if he would accept the vacant position.[22] Robinson's reply is not available, but Castlereagh wrote to Stewart the following month : 'Robinson has accepted and promises to be an acquisition — his appointment was much approved in all Quarters'.[23] Frederick, whom nature had not fitted for a military career, was nevertheless deeply

C

interested at the moment in military strategy and tactics, so we may assume that he was eager to accept an appointment which would give him some contact with the military campaigns.

The half a dozen or so available letters written by Robinson during the next five months provide some insight into the strictly routine nature of his new position.[24] He obviously made no decisions — though he probably sat in on discussions of logistical problems — but he relayed the orders and suggestions of his superiors to the field commanders, including General Sir Arthur Wellesley, in the Peninsula. The pay scale for officers, the embarkation of military units, the despatch of small craft — these are the subjects discussed in his letters.

Robinson was at this post when the ill-fated Walcheren Expedition was sent out during the summer of 1809, and he approved unreservedly of the invasion attempt. 'Undoubtedly the appearance of so large a British Force in that quarter could not fail to be sensible to Austria', Robinson confided to Yorke, 'if she were willing and able to continue the contest, and my view of our operation was, that if it were successful *in toto* all the better for us; if it failed, it could only fail from drawing a very large Force from other points to oppose it, and thus operate as a diversion . . .'[25] But the well-laid plan went awry, and like many other military débâcles looked bad in retrospect. Austria did not stay in the war, and disease broke out among the British expeditionary force.

The tragic failure led to the dissolution of the Portland Government. Since the preceding March, Canning, who was convinced of Castlereagh's incapacity for his position, had urged the Duke to replace him, but the ageing Portland postponed any action until 6 September, when Canning resigned. The Duke also tendered his resignation, and in the explanations which followed, the story of Canning's attempts to replace Castlereagh came to light. Convinced that Canning had conspired against him, and that his colleagues had been patronizing him for several months, Castlereagh concluded that his personal honour was involved.

Robinson may have suspected earlier that all was not well between the two statesmen, for Canning at times avoided direct contact with Castlereagh by relaying messages through Bagot and Robinson.[26] A letter in the Hardwicke Collection shows that Castlereagh advised Robinson, Grantham, and Yorke of his intentions before issuing a challenge to Canning — if, as is not certain — the following letter by Robinson to Hardwicke refers to the duel :[27]

Pepys noted that you regret I did not communicate to you the letter from Lord Castlereagh, which I sent to Mr. Yorke, and I want to explain this. When Castlereagh sent me that letter it was with instructions to show it to my brother and to send it to Mr. Yorke. Without his authority, I would not even have shown it to my brother, as it was highly confidential, and it was a long time before I communicated the particulars of the case to Lady Lucas and my mother.

This letter displays a trait of Robinson's — the absolute ability to keep a confidence — that probably endeared him to Castlereagh, Canning, Peel, and others, as it was rather rare in this age of rumours and gossip in high places.

When Spencer Perceval took over the disorganized, dispirited, and crumbling Government, he gave Robinson the opportunity to stay on as Under-Secretary, or to take a seat at the Treasury or Admiralty.[28] Malmesbury supported Perceval, and would have liked to have Robinson stay on, but Hardwicke regarded the Government as a 'feeble remnant of the late Ministry' and strongly opposed it.[29] Robinson, who wanted to avoid an election at that time,[30] doubted that Perceval could carry on, but in effect accepted Yorke's advice at this juncture in his career. 'I will not . . . give a definitive answer to Perceval till I hear from you,' he wrote. 'There is no present member of it [the Government] with whom I have any personal connections.' *

---

* Robinson to Yorke, 5 Oct. 1809. HSP, B.M. 45036. This categorical statement would seem to rule out any political intimacy between Robinson and any individuals in the Cabinet at that moment, which would include Earl Bathurst, Earl Camden, Lord Eldon, Lord Liverpool, Viscount Melville, Lord Mulgrave, Spencer Perceval, Richard Ryder, and the Earl of Westmorland. Some biographical sketches have tried to associate his early career with Lord Eldon. This is obviously an error.

Yorke counselled refusal of office, but not opposition. 'Between support and office the case is widely different,' Robinson agreed. 'The one I could cheerfully give, the other would, I am persuaded, be a source of perpetual disquiet.' [31]

Robinson's conduct at this moment is open to criticism, even censure, depending upon the reasons assigned for it. If he refused Perceval primarily because of the Government's weakness and uncertain prospects, Malmesbury was right in calling this a narrow and selfish attitude; but if Robinson believed that the successful conduct of the war required a strong coalition Government, then his motives are defensible. The only evidence that this second consideration may have influenced him is a sentence in one of his letters to Yorke that October. 'It would be a matter of great satisfaction to Grantham and myself', he asserted, 'if any circumstance should lead to the re-establishment of the political union between the various branches of the family, which events have unfortunately tended to destroy.' [32] Such a reconciliation could have been accomplished only through union among the Pittites, so dear to Malmesbury, and Grey and Grenville, the choices of Hardwicke. This coalition, of course, was never accomplished, and Robinson was to remain with the Tories. But during the next few years he was to move closer to the liberal path followed by Hardwicke.

Robinson spent the entire autumn of 1809 with his brother and his 'transcendently beautiful' sister-in-law at Newby. Contemporaries describe the mansion as a comfortable place with heating facilities in the hallways as well as the rooms, with fine furniture, amusing books, and an art gallery. Robinson undoubtedly enjoyed this ancestral home the more because of its great flower garden. A few years later a visitor recorded that the mignonette, sweet peas, and jessamine brought into the house by the children during the day provided such a heavily sweet aroma that they had to be taken out at night. [33] When the recess ended, Robinson stopped at Wimpole to visit Hardwicke while *en route* to London and the opening of Parliament.

The conference between Robinson and Hardwicke obviously

had no political significance. The latter immediately joined
Grenville in an unsuccessful attack in the Lords, while both
Robinson and Yorke helped the Government stave off a similar
assault in the Commons. Shortly thereafter the formation of a
committee to investigate the ill-starred Walcheren Expedition
sheds further light upon Robinson's intimate political relationship with Castlereagh. The Government wanted Robinson
placed on the committee not only because he was a political
'neutral', but because he would sit as 'the friend' of Castlereagh,
one of those deeply involved in the investigation.[34] George
Tierney remarked that 'full justice' was done to Castlereagh's
interests by the nomination of Robinson.[35] Following the investigation, the Ministers, and former Ministers, escaped censure
by the comfortable margin of fifty votes.

Yorke maintained the fiction of his political neutrality for a
few months, but when it became apparent that Perceval's chances
for survival were good he quickly accepted, first a sinecure worth
£2,700 per annum, and then in April a post in the Cabinet as
First Lord of the Admiralty. Immediately upon accepting office
he offered a seat at the Admiralty, worth £1,000 a year, to
Robinson, who, like himself, was a needy younger brother.
Robinson wrote to Hardwicke that his acceptance stemmed 'from
a desire to comply with a wish of Mr. Y. . . .'[36] In making this
decision Robinson placed his foot on the bottom rung of a ladder
which, during the next eighteen years, was to lead, one after
another, to higher-paying and more important positions, until he
reached the highest rung of all.

It was a modest enough start. Later, after the war, when there
was a strong movement for the abolition of sinecures, Robinson
was called upon to defend the duties of Admiralty Lords, and the
case he presented was not a very convincing one. The only
important task he mentioned was their jurisdiction, along with
the Lord High Admiral, over capital cases arising in the navy.
'This duty', Robinson declared, 'is nothing of a sinecure, either
in labour or feeling. . . .'[37]

Although the position brought him into contact with the most
effective and important branch of the British armed services,

there is nothing in Robinson's speeches or letters to suggest that he ever took a deep interest in naval affairs. As late as 1812 he seemed to be unaware that corporal punishment, long a crying abuse of the service, was practised intensively,[38] and his views regarding the practice of impressment, a continuing major irritant in Anglo-American relations, were vague and even immature.[39] Even though he was associated with the navy, his chief interest during 1810–12 lay in the army operations, and especially the Peninsular Campaign.

That same year there appeared a short pamphlet entitled *A Sketch of the Campaign in Portugal*, which, according to John Croker, was 'written chiefly by the Honable. Fred. Robinson. Some passages were by another hand.'[40] The collaborator may have been one of any number of people, especially Charles Yorke. The purpose of the pamphlet was to defend Viscount Wellington from the 'sarcastic censure' and the 'obloquy' of his enemies, and the whole defence was based on the supposition, which later proved quite correct, that the French army in Portugal would encounter logistic difficulties and be forced to retreat. Like his speech of 1809, the tone of the sketch was strongly optimistic and patriotic. Through the darkest days of the war Robinson never wavered in his dedication and optimism, and, when the clouds began to clear, his country rewarded him with a full measure of confidence and respect.

For Robinson, Wellington personified his country's ascent *de profundis*. So in 1810, while the war was still going badly, he strongly defended the Government's resolution to reward Wellington's services with a £2,000 annuity against opponents who called his recent victory not a victory, but a 'piece of ministerial foppery'.[41] The military situation had improved somewhat by 1812 when the Government decided to award the now Marquess of Wellington some £100,000 worth of lands and tenements. 'If ever there were a case which called for an expression of national gratitude,' Robinson declared, 'it was the case of the marquis of Wellington.'[42]

This theme of patriotism, used so often by Robinson during these years, inspired one of the greatest speeches of his career on

27 February 1812. Defending the necessity of the war, Robinson declared that it had been forced on Britain, and he called for offensive rather than defensive measures — 'a war of hope against a war of fear'.[43] Britain must stand firm, he insisted, as the 'protectress of the liberty of the world', and from this high position she could never resign — *et propter vitam vivendi perdere causas*, for the sake of life to lose one's reason for living. This speech, made months before Napoleon's débâcle in Russia, was so effective that the Opposition leader, Samuel Whitbread, paid Robinson his warmest compliments.[44] This same leader time and again attested not only to Robinson's abilities, but to the fairness and intellectual tone of his presentations.

This strong patriotism displayed by Robinson was not unique in contemporary political life, but was shared by many others, and especially a group of young statesmen who might be called the 'Alfred Club set'. Early in his career Robinson had had many friends among the Whigs, and as late as 1808 he was described as Lord Althorp's friend, even though that statesman, since Pitt's death, had identified himself with the Whig cause. Although Robinson never severed completely his social connections with those on the other side of the House, the politics of the day brought him increasingly into contact with statesmen who were to form the backbone of the Tory Party after the war.

Among the friends of Robinson was Lord Palmerston, whom he had known since their days at Harrow. Another was Henry Goulburn, who recalled later:[45]

In looking back at my career & thankfully acknowledging the many advantages which . . . I derived from it, I cannot omit recording the friendships which I formed there at St. John's with Mr. M. Perry & Mr. F. Robinson, the former since Bp. of Carlisle & the latter the Earl of Ripon, both of whom I still number among my dearest friends.

Further, Goulburn noted that, on coming to Parliament in 1807, he found there many of his college contemporaries, Viscount Palmerston, Charles Manners Sutton, Frederick John Robinson, and Robert Pemberton Milnes, as well as William Vesey

Fitzgerald, Marquess Wellesley, Henry Drummond, and John
Wilson Croker. He continued : [46]

> Those that I have mentioned lived very much together. We usually
> dined together at the Alfred Club on a Wednesday, and being joined
> a short time afterwards by Mr. Peel . . . formed a Society intimately
> united in political sentiment & literary tastes.

The text of Goulburn's memoir is somewhat ambiguous. Among
the Alfred Club set, Robinson and Milnes entered Parliament in
1806 ; Croker, Goulburn, Manners Sutton, and Palmerston in
1807 ; Fitzgerald in 1808 ; Peel in 1809, and Drummond in 1810.
Wellesley, of course, sat in the Lords, and belonged to an earlier
generation of statesmen.

There is little cause to wonder at the members of the set having
common interests and tastes. All were aristocrats or wealthy
commoners and had similar economic interests. Drummond,
Fitzgerald, and Peel were products of Christ Church, Oxford ;
Palmerston, Robinson, and Goulburn had gone to St. John's,
Cambridge, and Milnes and Manners Sutton to Trinity College
of the same university. Croker, an exception, had attended
Trinity College, Dublin. They all owed their introduction into
Parliament to the rotten-borough system. Croker (Downpatrick),
Drummond (Plympton Earls), Fitzgerald (Ennis), Goulburn
(Horsham), Manners Sutton (Scarborough), Milnes (Pontefract),
Palmerston (Newport, I.W.), Peel (Cashel), and Robinson (Car-
low) had been elected from boroughs with constituencies ranging
from 12 burgesses (Ennis) to 650 voters (Pontefract), and owed
their seats to influence or purchase. They also represented an
age group. Croker and Manners Sutton (1780) were the oldest,
then followed Robinson (1782), Fitzgerald (1783), Goulburn,
Palmerston, and Milnes (1784), Drummond (1786), and Peel
(1788). They were therefore part of a war generation, and, save
for the period 1802–3, probably only Croker, Manners Sutton,
Robinson, and Fitzgerald could remember when their country
was at peace ; none had a clear impression of English life prior
to the revolutionary period. Thus they could hardly appreciate
what was meant by a return to 'normalcy', such a state of affairs

being known to them largely from the descriptions of their elders.

Their outlook was undoubtedly conditioned by the military events of the past two decades. Although Britain had achieved striking naval successes at the battles of the Nile and Trafalgar, the land contests with France had been marked by continuous defeats, if not of British forces, of those of her allies. It is therefore to the credit of the Alfred Club set that they were in no sense defeatist in their outlook. To use one of Robinson's expressions — 'On the contrary, quite the reverse.' They displayed unshakeable confidence in the destiny of their nation.

In this patriotism and confidence, the Alfred Club Tories form a parallel to the contemporary American 'War Hawks'. Like their British counterparts, these young Republicans, including statesmen like John C. Calhoun, Langdon Cheves, Henry Clay, Felix Grundy, Richard M. Johnston, William Lownes, and Peter B. Porter had entered political life between 1806 and 1811. As a group they regarded Britain in much the same light as the young Tories regarded France — as a traditional enemy with whom war could hardly be avoided. Because of the different electoral systems in the two countries, however, their average age was about five years older than the members of the Alfred Club set.

Representing as they did the ruling classes, the Alfred Club set faced serious problems beyond the war and national survival. The revolutionary attacks on class privileges, and political and ecclesiastical monopolies, were a challenge to the 'Establishment', not only on the Continent, but in Britain itself. During their lifetimes, first the Foxite and later the Burdett Radicals had kept up steady pressure for greater freedom and reform, and while the national emergency could contain the movement during war-time, no intelligent young man could expect it to languish once peace returned.

Faced with both international and domestic questions of the gravest nature, it was perhaps appropriate for the young Tories to gather at the Alfred Club. While the faro tables at White's or Brooks's might establish and disestablish fortunes, and Watier's

offered a haven for dandies and gourmands, the Alfred Club provided a quiet background for serious discussions. 'A duller
place than the Alfred does not exist,' a member wrote a few years
later. 'You hear nothing but idle reports and twaddling opinions.
They read the Morning Post and the British Critic. It is an
asylum of doting Tories and drivelling Quidnuncs. But they are
civil and quiet.' [47] Perhaps the place was somewhat more exciting
during the war years, for, despite their *gravitas*, the young Tories
loved humour and even horseplay, but Peel, Goulburn, Robinson,
and Drummond especially contrasted sharply with the young,
aristocratic wastrels of their generation.

The Alfred Club set contributed their share to the debates in
Parliament. Milnes's speeches especially glow with the warm
spirit of the Romantic Age. Croker spoke more often, too often
for his own reputation. Manners Sutton drove home his points
with legalistic finality, and Peel reasoned with his audience.
Robinson was not a frequent speaker, but on some Members his
speeches made a deep impression. Robert Plumer Ward wrote
after hearing Robinson's speech of 27 February 1812 : [48]

Robinson highly distinguished himself in the best young man's
speech I ever heard in the Parliament. Peel, when he has spoken, has
been more flowery, and with more classical allusion ; but in readiness,
in clear, forcible, and demonstrative language, and in the appearance
of an old and able debater, Robinson beat him, and indeed all his
contemporaries.

Robinson evidently also impressed the members of his set — at
any rate, they seemed to accept his promotions as well-deserved,
and as a matter of course.

Goulburn in his memoir noted that the Alfred Club set was
'intimately united in political sentiment', and a study of the
divisions between 1807–12 would confirm this statement. Croker,
Fitzgerald, Goulburn, Manners Sutton, Milnes, Palmerston, and
Robinson all eventually gave their support to the Portland
Government, and, save for Milnes and Wellesley, they were also
friends — in the cases of Palmerston, Manners Sutton, and
Robinson, members — of the Perceval Government. The first
serious split in their ranks came on Canning's motion of 22 June

1812 for an early consideration of the Catholic claims in the next Parliament.

The details of Robinson's conversion to the liberal view are not known. Lord Grantham voted for the Catholics in the Lords as early as 21 April 1812, much to the consternation of his father-in-law, Malmesbury, and Lady Lucas. Robinson faced not only their opposition, but that of Elizabeth Sophia Lawrence, and his constituents, who opposed not only Catholic Emancipation, but the repeal of the Test Act.[49] In anticipation of Canning's motion, Robinson explained his changed views in a lengthy letter to Miss Lawrence of 16 June, which, he said had arisen 'solely from the sincere and conscientious conviction of my understanding'.[50] His main argument was that Emancipation would conciliate Ireland, and yet would not 'endanger the perfect security of the Protestant establishment'. At the same time he promised not to vote for a measure that did not provide for the latter. Robinson's attitude seems to have been thoroughly pragmatic — the important object of conciliating Ireland could be gained at no cost to the religion of which he was a member.* Elizabeth Lawrence, and the Ripon constituents, continued to give Frederick their confidence, even though they did not agree with him on this issue.

When Canning's motion came to a vote, Robinson, Croker, Fitzgerald, and Palmerston voted for the Catholics, but Drummond, Goulburn, Milnes, and Peel took an opposing view. Thus the unanimity of the Alfred Club set was broken, and the outlines of the Liberal Tory movement appeared, but this one issue, despite its importance, by no means interrupted the harmony of the group during the war years, or for some time thereafter.

Robinson was present in the Commons that tragic 11 May

---

* 'I cannot forget', Robinson said in 1813, 'that the principle of our constitution is jealousy. It is jealous of the Crown, jealous of the aristocracy, jealous of the democracy, and the Roman Catholics have no right to complain, if it is jealous of them.' *Hansard* (1st ser.), xxiv. 962–5. For him the constitution was a limiting and balancing of contending forces — a thoroughly pragmatic attitude.

1812 when Spencer Perceval was assassinated. He collected as much information as he could regarding the murder, and dispensed it to his aunt, the Hon. Mrs. Robinson, and her guests at dinner that night. Fear and even panic followed on the heels of the event, and there were rumours that the murder might have been the first act of a major revolutionary disturbance. Mrs. Robinson recorded that her dinner was not a 'gay or regular one'.[51]

The following day Richard Ryder, who was scheduled to present a motion to provide funds for the late Prime Minister's family, was so moved that the task had to be carried out by Lord Castlereagh, who had joined the Government the previous February. Castlereagh himself was unable to finish. When he came to speak of Perceval's family he was 'so much affected that he was obliged to sit down amidst the loud cheers and strong sympathy of the House'.[52] Tearfulness was later to plague Robinson, and it is interesting to note that his closest political friend, following Yorke's resignation in 1811, was not immune from such attacks. Robinson's own reaction to the death does not seem to have been highly emotional. 'I felt very sincerely for the loss of Perceval', he wrote to Peel, 'and I never knew anyone more universally regretted'.[53]

Long and complex negotiations followed before the reins of government were entrusted to Lord Liverpool on 8 June, and in this Government Castlereagh was to play a major, even dominating role. In the various adjustments that followed, the Foreign Secretary was careful to provide for the interests of his 'élève', as Brougham termed Robinson.[54] For a time it appeared he might have the Treasurership of the Navy, one of the choicest financial plums available, but in the end Robinson secured the working position of Vice-President of the Board of Trade, and two sinecures, a Lordship of the Treasury — worth £1,000, and a Joint Paymastership of the Land Forces — worth £2,000. He apparently only drew the emoluments of one, however, and it was probably the latter.[55]

In the summer of 1812 Robinson took up the duties of the Board of Trade, and set foot on the path which was to win him transient fame. This was the winding, often obscure path of economics, a study still very much in its infancy, but which became increasingly important as the complex industrial structure of the state in Britain developed. How well he was prepared for his task, we can only guess. Probably he had read Adam Smith, though he rarely appealed to that authority in his speeches. Much later he acknowledged the merits of David Ricardo and Thomas Malthus, but, save for Ricardo's work on bullion and currency in 1809, the works of these economists were still in the future. If Robinson had had a deep interest in the field early in life, evidence for it is lacking; though the first undoubted speech made by Robinson in Parliament concerned the budget of 1808. 'I plunged . . . into all the mysteries of trade before my holidays began,' Robinson wrote to Peel in 1812, which implies the field was not familiar to him.[56] Croker noted that 'Robinson is overwhelmed with business, & grown as cross as fifty cats.'[57]

His new post forced Robinson, who still did not relish doing so, to speak in Parliament when trade questions arose. While controversy may continue as to just who was the father of Free Trade in Britain, the fact is clear that Robinson was a trade enthusiast from the start, and realized the two-way nature of trade. For example, he defended the continued importation of American cotton into Britain after the War of 1812 began,[58] and observed in connection with the West Indian trade: 'It was impossible . . . to carry on long a trade when all the advantages of exportation were on one side; and it ought to be considered, that America took our manufactures in exchange for her raw materials, and we were in a manner compelled to that advantageous exchange, for she had nothing else to give.'[59] He squirmed under the restrictive legislation which Britain had adopted to combat Napoleon's Continental System. 'Nothing could be worse', he wrote to Peel, 'than the restrictive system which Buonaparte compels us to adopt, and which obliges us to make as much fuss about importing twenty pounds of truffles as if it were an army.'[60]

A long letter written by Robinson in 1813 to Peel, then Chief Secretary for Ireland, asking for the repeal of the export duty on foreign linens, which depressed the Prussian linen trade, shows that he looked clearly into the future, and tried to make provisions for inevitable changes in the trade patterns. 'The wit of man cannot in the present circumstances of Europe devise a reason which should [keep] Prussians from finding out (& very shortly too)', he wrote, 'that if we check, by retaining this duty, the export of foreign linens from here, they may go *direct* from home to the Continent of America . . . and get the market from us.' [61] While Robinson had a sympathetic understanding of the export needs of other countries, his urgings to loosen up the British restrictive system were almost invariably based upon arguments that such revisions would be beneficial one way or another to Britain herself.

The problems of trade, however, did not draw Robinson's attention away from the land war, and some years later Croker was to look back on those days 'when once a week at least we found solace and diversion in coffee and Quintilian, buttered toast and General Robinson'.[62] When Napoleon invaded Russia, Croker predicted a French victory, but Robinson correctly prognosticated a 'tremendous scrape' for the French.[63] This remarkable forecast, however, was rather spoiled by his hope that the Russians would stand and 'fight it out'.

These discussions of tactics among the Alfred Club set were aided by the possession of classified information by Goulburn, Croker, Peel, and Robinson, but they were by no means always grave in tone. Late in 1812 Croker wrote to Peel : [64]

I have just put a rare quirk on Robinson today. We have had news from Russia & America ; so I took an American bulletin with its cursed crackjaw names, and applied them to supposed transactions of Napoleon's and Alexander's armies. Robinson has printed all the maps, but cannot find one 'point d'appice'. The Ottawas, he concludes, are southern cossacks, & he thinks he remembers the name of General Cass, and he has some recollection that one division of the 7th corps *was* at Winnebago. In short, it was excellent.

There are other numerous evidences that Robinson would enjoy a joke on himself as thoroughly as when someone else was the butt.

The victories of 1813, and the steadily improving appearance of the war in Europe, were greeted with the greatest enthusiasm by Robinson. That August he gleefully informed Charles Yorke that Austria had entered the war, swelling the ranks of the Allied armies. 'What a tremendous crash it will be!' he predicted. 'But I do hope that the righteous cause will be protected & suffered to effect its grand object of the deliverance of Europe.'[65] Later that year, when Soult was encircled, Croker wrote to Peel: 'Robinson is in raptures at this moment & swears, yes, swears, that "*from this position Soult must depart*".'[66]

Heretofore the Continental war, which had dragged along during most of his life, had been for Robinson a murky reality, imagined on the basis of printed reports and verbal descriptions, but in December 1813 his chance came to view the battlefields of Europe in person. Writing to Yorke, he explained that Castlereagh has just asked him to accompany him on his trip to the Continent, adding:[67]

. . . I hope that whatever may be the result of our proceedings that at least they will be such as to secure the Government the sanction of all reasonable and thinking people. If I had had an opportunity of conversing with you, I might have talked over public affairs with less Reserve than is possible to do by letter . . . I think I may venture to say that up to this moment nothing has been done by Government with reference to the complicated State of Europe, which could have *been* otherwise, or perhaps even *wished* otherwise.

The usual Robinson caution is much in evidence in this letter. Yorke's reply, on the other hand, recorded his views of a just peace in detail, and many were similar to the provisions of the later peace treaties.

The grave tone Robinson adopted in writing Yorke reflected only one side of his mood at securing this unexpected assignment. Croker's letter of 24 December to Peel had the following remarkable conclusion:[68]

Robinson comes in & *swears* that Lord W. has given Soult a *most infernal licking*.

He goes on Monday to Frankfurt where the French will give him a *most infernal licking*.

They snatch the pen from my fingers.   They make a devil of a noise. Robinson owns he is prepared — to run away.   JWC
Quite the reverse !
These fellows are highly absurd.   FJR
Alas Poor Soult.—F.

In this holiday mood, General Robinson at last went to war.

3

From Paris to Old Burlington Street

FEW periods in Robinson's life are so well documented as those months in 1813–14, when he accompanied Castlereagh to Europe as an assistant with the rank of Minister Plenipotentiary. On the night of 27 December Robinson, together with Joseph Planta and William Montagu, left London for Harwich through a fog so dense that the post chaise had to proceed by torchlight. They travelled all through the night, and after seventeen hours finally reached their destination shortly after noon the following day. Castlereagh's party, including his wife, Lady Emma Edgcumbe and General Pozzo di Borgo, made even slower time, and did not reach the port until evening.

Their departure depended upon the caprices of the winds, and it was Sunday, six days after the party left London, that their ship, the *Erebus*, finally ventured into the choppy North Sea. 'Many of us seemed off our food at breakfast', Montagu recorded, 'and the muster of dinner eaters was extremely small'.[1] The ladies remained in their cabins throughout the voyage, but 'Lord Castlereagh seemed to thrive most amazingly, devoured broiled bones, and rather laughed at the sick ones'.[2] A swift trip took them across the sea, and that night they anchored off what seemed to be Scheveningen near The Hague.

The events that followed seem scarcely credible when one considers the international importance of the mission. Not an officer on board was familiar with the coast of Holland, and when they sent a small boat ashore to learn the position of their ship, it was found to be floating in a cul-de-sac between a shoal and Schouwen

Island.[3] A Dutch pilot came aboard to help them, but the wind
was blowing in the wrong direction, and it took them the entire
next day to find their way out of the inlet.   Unfavourable winds
the following day again immobilized the *Erebus*, and they spent
another night at anchor upon a 'tremendous swell'.   'A night's
rocking at anchor . . . reduced him [Castlereagh] to the level of
the rest', Montagu recorded, 'and the next morning he kept his
cabin.' [4] By that time the entire mission was temporarily out of
action.   But the next day the ship managed to push on to Helle-
voetsluis, and on 5 January — nine days out of London — the
party finally set foot on Dutch soil.

The following day Robinson, clad in his Ripon Yeomanry
jacket, set out with the rest of the party for The Hague, which
they reached on 7 January.   The next day he went with Lady
Castlereagh to the Maison de Bois, where the Prince of Orange
welcomed the Princess of Orange amid great, popular celebrations.[5]
The Dutch were extremely friendly towards their British visitors,
and properly hostile towards their recent occupiers, so Castlereagh
and Robinson could leave the country on 9 January with the
knowledge that it was friendly, independent and monarchical.

From The Hague to Frankfurt-am-Main the Ministers spent
six days in what Castlereagh called 'an Ice House' — meaning
their carriage and its perpetually frosted windows.[6] 'Nothing',
Robinson wrote, 'could be more detestable than the Roads about
Münster and Paderborn.' [7] They remained at Frankfurt for only
a day, and on 16 January pushed on for Basle through the Rhine
Valley, which, Frederick regretted, was not 'clothed in its summer
dress'.   *En route* they had a brief brush with the shooting war.
A pocket of French troops still held out near Hüningen, and
commanded the road over which they had to travel.   Though
local people assured them that the French 'seldom fire at Carriages passing singly along the road', Robinson — without
recording his own feelings — noted that the servants were
frightened out of their wits during the passage.[8] On reaching
Basle they found that the headquarters of the Grand Army had
already moved to Langres in France, and the weary travellers
had to go on to that town.

Although Castlereagh confided his innermost thoughts, hopes and theories to Robinson during their journeys together,[9] the latter's letters are singularly uninformative as to the diplomatic situation. At Langres he was in daily association with the monarchs of Austria, Russia, and Prussia, as well as their Ministers, Metternich, Count Nesselrode, and Prince Hardenberg, and thus had access to a wealth of facts and rumours. But his letter of 28 January to Charles Yorke merely revealed there was a two-way division of opinion as to the next move; some — he did not say whom — wanted to go on to Paris, others to offer a peace to Napoleon on Allied terms.[10] As to the terms of the peace, he merely stated that Castlereagh agreed with Yorke on 'essential points', whatever that might mean in terms of territorial exchanges. The most definite attitude to be gleaned from the letter was Robinson's own — standing near the field of battle he had become more cautious, and agreed with those who wished to try negotiations with Napoleon from their position of strength.

His letters, on the other hand, are a valuable source of information regarding the last days of Napoleonic Europe. The French people, with defeat staring them in the face, like the Germans in 1945, blamed everything on their arbitrary ruler.[11] 'The people did not scruple to express the greatest abhorrence of Buonaparte', Robinson recorded, 'but *there* it appears to me to *end*. They seem quite à battue. . . .'[12] He often asked himself the question, which many others were pondering at the time, after Napoleon — who? — what?

Early in February there was a serious difference of opinion between Castlereagh and the Russians as to the next move. Russia wanted to go on to Paris, set up a Russian governor, and call an assembly of notables to create a new government for France; Castlereagh favoured negotiations. During a discussion the Russians produced a letter from their ambassador in England, which indicated that the Government strongly opposed peace with Napoleon. Castlereagh replied that he must be guided by his own judgment, and thereafter sent Robinson back to England with an indignant letter requesting the united support of the Home Government.[13]

On 18 February Robinson collected his things, including some eau-de-Cologne he planned to smuggle through Customs, and went off under the escort of a French official. 'We were very sorry to part with Robinson,' Montagu wrote, 'as you may well suppose, and miss him extremely.' [14] The French made his trip as expeditious as possible, but Robinson still did not arrive in England until 24 February. There — for the first time in his career — he found himself the centre of national attention, a rather mysterious figure bearing, it was believed, information of the greatest secrecy and importance.

Little information is available regarding Robinson's three days in London, save for an interview he had with his aunt, to whom he described the personalities of the men then planning the future of Europe — the Tsar 'very deaf, talking very loud in a sputtering unpleasant way'; the monarchs of Austria and Prussia 'rather silent'; Armand de Caulaincourt 'rather melancholy and quiet'.[15] Robinson, on his return, crossed over to Calais in four hours, then went on to Paris and to Chaumont, where Castlereagh was staying.

When he arrived at headquarters around midnight of 4 March, Robinson found Castlereagh deep in the study of a tactical problem. He concluded that troops should be taken from the Crown Prince of Sweden and sent as reinforcements to Blücher and Schwartzenberg, but some of the Allied leaders feared that such a move might offend the Crown Prince and cause diplomatic complications. 'The plan must be adopted', Castlereagh insisted, 'and orders given immediately.'[16] The Foreign Secretary had his way, and the troops were sent. Robinson considered this to have been the most vital tactical decision in the closing phase of the war.

While at Chaumont Robinson enlivened the British headquarters 'with good jokes, good humour, and fuss', and continued to predict the outcome of important battles, sometimes with remarkable accuracy. This won him several nicknames, one of them 'General B. of Irradowitz', but the one which caught the fancy of his companions was the 'Grand Duke of Phussand-bussle'. When he returned to headquarters after an absence,

Robinson was in the habit of rummaging through the papers on the desk like a general going through important despatches. One day a member of the mission left a letter on the desk addressed with the sobriquet noted above, and Robinson often found himself called the 'Grand Duke' thereafter.

Following a French defeat at Laon, the British mission took heart and went from Chaumont to Troyes, nearer Paris. Perhaps for the first time Robinson saw the horrors of war along the way, which were described by Montagu as follows : [17]

In our journey from Chaumont to Troyes we had a pretty striking view of the horrors of War. All the villages were deserted and the houses vacant or pulled down — dead men and dead horses in abundance. The dead men were scattered about in various places most of them entirely stripped, and probably had not been touched by anyone since their death . . . The French prisoners I have seen are in a wretched state — without clothes and dying of fatigue . . . with so large an army and so many straggling troops, a great many excesses are of course committed, yet there is more discipline kept up than I expected.

The move turned out to be premature, and, due to the movements of Napoleon, the mission retired south-east to Bar-sur-Seine and then Bar-sur-Aube, which they reached on 21 March. Two nights later they learned that the advanced guard of Napoleon's army was only three leagues outside the city, and, as Robinson put it, 'it became absolutely necessary for us to decamp forthwith'.[18] They did not cease their withdrawal until they had reached Dijon in the south. This was a most unfortunate occurrence, for at Dijon they were cut off from the Grand Army, and were virtually isolated from developments during the final phase of the war. 'We have been going on very quietly here,' Montagu reported in April, 'eating, drinking, riding, going to the Play, shopping, joking and laughing. Meanwhile the Armies and the Emperor of Russia have made a triumphant entry into Paris.' [19]

We can be sure that Robinson had no influence over the course of events during this final phase of the war — but did he offer Castlereagh any constructive suggestions previously, or in any way contribute to the making of British policy? This we will probably never know because Robinson was so completely un-informative in his letters. 'Whatever you may think in England,' he wrote to his aunt in March, 'I am still *confident* that we acted right throughout; and I am equally satisfied that but for *our mission* all would have gone wrong.' [20] On reading this cryptic conclusion, his brother wrote: 'I suppose he means that the Emperors and the King would have been cheated, or cheated themselves with a disgraceful Peace, or that Great Britain would have been left in the lurch, if Ld. Castlereagh had not been sent in time to stop the mischief.' [21] As no other individual was as familiar with Robinson's vagaries as was Grantham, this inter-pretation must be given serious consideration, but Robinson must also have had in mind Castlereagh's decision to reinforce Blücher and Schwartzenberg, and his masterful work in creating the Treaty of Chaumont, which welded together the splintering coalition. If Robinson had a hand in either, there is no evidence for it, save for the increasing confidence that Castlereagh placed in him as an adviser and a friend.

The sights and sounds of France and England in that trium-phant year of 1814 could not have failed to have made a lasting impression on Robinson. In some of the great, colourful moments of April–May 1814 Robinson was not only an interested observer, but an unobtrusive participant. One such moment occurred on 11 April, when the Comte d'Artois entered Paris, and personified the return of the old order to the country. Robinson described the scene as follows: [22]

About Eleven O'clock Castlereagh & I . . . mounted our horses and joined the Cavalcade that went to meet him. The streets were crowded to the greatest degree & lined by the National Guards. At a little distance . . . we drew up by the road side to wait for his arrival. He was on horseback surrounded by Officers of the National Guard, and some of his personal attendants. As soon as he saw Castlereagh he called him up & we proceeded with the procession close to him. He was soon after met by the French Marshals Kellermann, Moncey, Ney, Marmont etc. etc. which (altho' somewhat awkward from various cir-cumstances) went off very well. The procession then proceeded to the Church of Notre Dame, where Te Deum was rung. No words can describe the joy & enthusiasm of the innumerable crowds who literally *paved* the Street. The Women in particular showed the liveliest marks of interest. I saw many on the Windows & in the Street who were absolutely overcome & fainted from excess of feeling, in that it exceeded all demonstrations of joy that I ever saw.

Another observer declared that the enthusiasm was limited chiefly to 'a superior class of society',[23] which would indicate that the swooning females were probably ladies of quality. Probably the exhilarating experience made Robinson a somewhat less reliable observer than usual.

The scene changed later to a place whose sights and sounds possessed a natural interest for a member of the Commons. This was Luxembourg Palace, where the Senate which had decided to recall the Bourbons was holding its sessions. Robinson was unimpressed with that quasi-deliberative body, so unlike its powerful counterpart in England. 'The Senators met (for they never debated)', he wrote, 'in a very handsome hall of a semi-circular shape, in which speaking must be abominable, so that it was not a great misfortune to them to hold their tongues. What they may do now, I know not, but they are a very motley lot & ought to be weeded before they are assm'b to make laws.'[24] Robinson was conscious that Freedom, the particular ward of his own country, had returned to the Continent with the destruction of Napoleon's empire, and he evidently assumed that the French parliament would thereafter play a major role in the law-making process.

Whether or not Robinson ever came face to face with the former master of Europe during these weeks is uncertain, but he frequently picked up and reported gossip about him then current in the highest circles. One curious and interesting sidelight appeared in a letter to his brother in mid-April: [25]

Buonaparte sets off I believe today for his new empire in the island of Elba . . . He is said to be very low and I really believe would upon the whole have preferred an Asylum in England, where he says he should be quite at his ease, and could enjoy himself without molestation . . . His great fear at present is that he should be taken in passage or carried off after his landing by an Algerine Corsair, and '*Les puissances*

Barbaresques ’ haunt his imagination more than the coalition of all
Europe did before. I think he has put himself in a very ridiculous
position, and it was extremely difficult to know what to do with him.

Robinson, like some others of his time, evidently regarded
Napoleon as slightly deranged. On viewing two portraits of the
former Emperor, one made early and one later in life, Robinson
observed : ‘There is however the same expression of genius and
malignity, and I think an air of madness, particularly in the
latter.’ [26]

The scene which probably impressed Robinson more than any
other occurred on 4 May, just before he and his friends departed
for a party being given by Charles Stewart. Uninvited, un-
heralded, and unidentified a man in civilian dress suddenly
appeared, and announced himself quite simply — Lord Wellington ! For half a dozen years he had conducted his own private
war against Napoleon, and he was not even acquainted with the
generals on either side who had fought the war in central Europe.
At the ball Robinson watched curiously as the English hero was
introduced to Marshal Blücher, whom he was to meet again at
Waterloo, and to Marshal Ney, former staff officer to Napoleon.
‘He . . . compleatly cut out the Emperor of Russia,’ Robinson
wrote feelingly. ‘I confess that when I rode home in his train . . .
I felt proud of being his countryman.’ [27]

There were many other interesting and stimulating sights in
the capital of the fallen nation. Robinson often visited the art
galleries, and his critical comments regarding the paintings he
saw indicate that he inherited his mother’s enthusiasm for pic-
torial art. The shops sold products, such as clocks and china,
which he bought for himself or as presents for his many relatives.
‘The head of the Board of Trade’, Montagu charged, ‘is the
greatest smuggler of the Mission.’ [28] Certain other traditional
objects of the city of Paris did not escape his attention. ‘The
women . . . are not at all pretty and dress themselves detest-
ably,’ Robinson wrote to Peel, a fellow bachelor. ‘At a small
party the other night . . . they all looked like House Maids
turned out of a stage coach. . . . if Women in England adopt

the present fashion of Paris, it will become absolutely necessary to forswear the sex.' [29] Some Parisian women wore head-dresses a yard high — 'the most ridiculous thing you ever saw', Robinson commented disgustedly.

This pleasant interlude in his political life was brought to an end by appeals from Lord Liverpool. As early as 9 April the Prime Minister wrote to Castlereagh regarding the meeting of Parliament, and the necessity of having someone on hand to assist Bathurst and Vansittart in answering questions, if any should arise. 'Could you not spare Robinson?' he asked.[30] Castlereagh evidently felt that he could not do so at the moment, and later that month the tone of the Prime Minister became more exigent : [31]

We begin to feel it of the utmost importance in the event of your absence being further prolonged (as will probably be the case for a fortnight longer) that you should send Robinson back to us . . . If you could let us have Robinson, I should feel perfectly at ease, and I should be under no apprehension of his presence provoking discussions, which are much more likely to take place when they think that they could embarrass Government by bringing them forward.

But Castlereagh, who was busy drawing up the Treaty of Paris, evidently felt Robinson's assistance was necessary ; at any rate, he kept him in Paris until after the treaty was signed, and did not release him for more than two weeks after Liverpool wrote his second plea.

Robinson left Paris on 14 May and arrived in London four days later. One of the first to speak with him at length was his aunt, the Hon. Mrs. Robinson, who left a memorandum which recorded Frederick's account of the end phase of the war, and the position of the restored monarchy at that time : [32]

Intelligence had been received by the Allies just after the battle of Arcis sur Aube that a Royalist & constitutional party courted at Paris, and that the Allies had only to beat Buonaparte in the field & leave the French themselves to restore the Bourbons & settle their own Government for they would never suffer the *Allies* to subjugate & bring back the Bourbons. . . . Had Buonaparte got there he would have fought & the French with him in Paris till it had been quite destroyed & to the last . . . That the Marshals supported the Bourbons as their own consequence is now attached to their cause, but the rising officers have very different feeling[s], & the Army is still endor'd (attach'd) to Buonaparte. That the Bourbons are in a delicate & difficult situation, which requires great circumspection, patience & judgment.

Robinson once more brought up the reinforcing of Schwartzenberg and Blücher, but if he discussed such vital questions as the futures of Saxony and Poland, his aunt did not record the conversation. Probably he did not.

One of his main purposes in returning to London was not so much to answer questions in Parliament, as to help make preparations for the visit of the crowned heads of Europe, who were coming to Britain in June. Whether or not anyone fully realized it at the time, this visit probably marked the beginning of the British ascendancy over Europe, which was to continue down to World War I, and even longer. The Tsar's tendency on this visit to play up to the Opposition party in the Parliament embarrassed the Tories, and deepened Castlereagh's suspicions of Russian intentions in Europe.

Little information is available regarding Robinson's part in the official ceremonies which were so much a part of the visit, but a glimpse of him is caught during a barge ride on 12 June, which carried the royal visitors on a round trip from London to Woolwich. Various governmental officials were assigned to the barges to oversee the comfort of their guests. 'Amidst others,' his aunt wrote, 'the great Duke of Fussingbustle, alias Frederick Robinson.' [33] She added that it was a 'gay and beautiful scene'. Another gala event of the visit was Lady Hertford's ball, where the amorous Tsar of Russia lived up to his reputation for appreciating, feminine beauty by selecting Lady Grantham for a dancing partner.[34] Just what Robinson's reactions were to all these festivities, we do not know, save that he expressed boredom on one occasion.

Robinson was now past thirty, a bachelor, and somewhat uneasy as to the effect of his sedentary life upon his constitution. At some time during this warm, eventful, summer of 1814, he decided to seek *la vita nuova*, to leave the ranks of the unwed, and to embark on the traditionally choppy sea of matrimony. Thereafter an intense, strange, and often pathetic love-story unfolds, a little-known story, but one which ran parallel with that of his political life, and impinged upon it at almost every important juncture.

If Robinson's ancestors were moral and amiable, those of his wife-to-be, being much less conventional, inspire a somewhat different quality of interest. The 3rd Earl of Buckinghamshire had been a musician, and before his accession to the title in 1793 had conducted operas. From a financial standpoint, he married very well. His wife was Albinia, daughter of Lord Vere Bertie, a son of the Duke of Ancaster, and she brought with her a very large income, as well as a disposition to follow her fancies in various directions. Those fancies in time made her name well known, even slightly notorious. Albinia was especially addicted to faro, then popular among the faster set, and the parties at her home lasted into the small hours of the morning. A contemporary periodical referred to her, rather sanctimoniously, as one of the 'Faro Dames'.

With a musician for a father, a gambler for a mother, and reared in the free-and-easy moral atmosphere of the later eighteenth century, the 4th Earl of Buckinghamshire likewise followed his fancies, and at age seventeen became a father. His natural son, Henry Ellis, grew up in the Buckinghamshire household, and though his father treated him with kindness and concern, he was excluded from the inheritance because of his extra-legal status, and was first the charge of his father, and later of his half-sister and Robinson. Later the 4th Earl married twice. His first wife was Margaretta, co-heiress of Edmund Bourke of Urrey, by whom he had two children : a daughter, Sarah, born in 1793, and a son, John, who died in infancy. After Margaretta's death, the 4th Earl married Eleanor Agnes Eden, the eldest daughter of the 1st Earl of Auckland, in 1799, and, although she provided no further children for him, she undertook the task of rearing his previous offspring.

In politics Robert Hobart, the 4th Earl, formed an unshakeable connection with Addington, and when his leader, then Lord Sidmouth, joined Perceval's Government, the Earl received the Board of Control. Following Perceval's untimely death, his successor, Lord Liverpool, gave Hobart the Duchy of Lancaster. He was fairly intimate with Liverpool — the two sometimes imported their Madeira wine together [35] — and thus had political influence beyond that which his personal abilities, which were mediocre, would have given him.[36] The 4th Earl also had a family connection with Lord Castlereagh, who, in 1794, had married Amelia Anne Hobart, a daughter of the 2nd Earl.

As there was no eligible male heir to the Buckinghamshire fortunes, the generations ended with Sarah Albinia Louisa Hobart, who was due to inherit, upon the death of her father, all of the unentailed estates of the Hobart family. In her grandfather's time, the family's annual income had been £16,000, which was comfortable enough, but did not establish the Hobarts among the richest families in Britain. The 4th Earl no doubt added to that income through his marriages, positions in the Government, and possibly inheritances — if he did not, it is impossible to account for the very large income of the Robinsons after her father's death.

A mundane question is a poor beginning to a story of romance, but in Robinson's case one can hardly avoid asking it, for it is certain to go through any interested reader's mind. Did he marry her in anticipation of her very considerable inheritance? Certain known facts would lend possibility, at least, to such an interpretation. Robinson, of course, was impecunious, dependent on his governmental salaries and the gifts of his brother and mother, and he watched money carefully. 'There is no Salary', he wrote to his brother at the time of the 1813 mission, 'but our Expenses are paid.' [37] Time and again he complained of the high cost of his purchases in Paris. Yet there is no evidence of his having been miserly — his great popularity would seem to rule that out. Other facts which would substantiate an economic interpretation of Robinson's marriage, however, include the bride's physical appearance, and her personality — no contemporary described her as attractive in either respect. All of these facts would seem to establish the pattern of a thirty-two-year-old, penniless bachelor, despairing of finding a more suitable mate, suddenly deciding that Sarah would provide the economic security he so much desired; but one other fact would seem to overturn them all, and wipe away the unattractive picture. What existed between Robinson and his Lady Sarah was not a mere liking based on mutual adaptation, or even an average sort of love, but an abiding devotion as intense in him, or even more so, as it was in her.

The origins of the romance are unknown. During the five months of his mission in Europe that year Robinson wrote seventeen letters to his family, and these are for the most part available. Although his mother, Lady Lucas, the Hon. Mrs. Robinson, and Lord and Lady Grantham all appear in them frequently, there is not a single mention of 'Lady Sarah', nor does she appear in his letters to his friends. It would seem possible that Castlereagh introduced Robinson to the family, including Lady Sarah, but the mystery remains why she was ignored early in the year, then, three months after his return to England, the wedding plans were being made. Croker wrote to Peel on 4 August: 'Imagine Robinson's fuss — about to be married — the Lady very tender; her father very jocose; the writings very long; the lawyers very dilatory; the board of trade very exigent, Castlereagh's movements very doubtful & the thermometer at 84 in the shade.' [38] Both the 4th Earl and Lady Sarah were obviously very happy with the arrangement, with which the 'writings' and the 'lawyers' seem to have had some connection.

The arrangements for the wedding and the wedding itself give rise to further unanswered questions. Lady Sarah's trousseau consisted of 'five beautiful sattin gowns all covered with lace, and twelve high gowns all covered with lace, and nineteen more low gowns all covered with lace — thirty-six in all'.[39] The Archbishop of Canterbury himself presided at the nuptials, but the number of guests was very small. The bride's father and stepmother (by then the Dowager Countess of Buckinghamshire), Robinson's mother and brother, Lady Lucas, and four others completed the party. There was apparently no reception after the wedding.

Because of Lady Sarah's puzzling personality, and the lack of facts concerning her save for a few brief periods of her life, every bit of evidence must be carefully weighed. Why the very elaborate trousseau, when they went on no honeymoon, and had no reception? Robinson was one of the most popular men in the Commons — where were all his friends? We know from later incidents that Lady Sarah had a profound sense of insecurity, and, knowing this, we might interpret the elaborate wedding preparations as one expression of this feeling, and the smallness of the wedding party and lack of a reception as another. She wanted a wedding in the highest style, but feared crowds.

After the ceremony the couple set off in an 'elegant chariot and four' for her father's estate, called Fitzroy Farm. They remained there for a time, and then made Robinson's annual autumnal visit to Newby together. 'It must be an amusing sight to see Sarah scolding the post-boy for not driving fast enough', Emily Eden wrote, 'or calling to the hostler for "a pair of horses to St. Albans immediately"', or adding up the inn-keeper's account, and giving him something for the scoundrel that drove. That is the style she must now adopt.' [40] This observation, and their two visits, give some insight into the financial status of the new couple, who, down to the death of the 4th Earl in 1816, seem to have lived off Robinson's salary and the contributions of their relatives.

The Robinsons remained at Newby until early November, when Frederick received a summons from Lord Liverpool to repair forthwith to London. Robinson replied that he would leave immediately, but probably could not reach the capital over the bad roads until the following Monday — 'and', he added, 'if Lady Sarah should be tired, I may not perhaps be able to reach London till Tuesday morning.' [41] There was some reason for his caution at this time, for Lady Sarah was already pregnant, but this was to be merely the first in a long sequence of excuses Robinson was to make on her account. Thereafter his life had to be accommodated constantly to her health, moods, and feelings.

One of the first visitors to call upon Robinson when he reached

town was Robert Peel, who called at the Board of Trade and
found Robinson immersed in his work. He thereafter described
their mutual friend to Goulburn : [42]

He has made more rapid progress to acquiring a certain steadiness
of demeanor & portliness peculiarly befitting the marriage state than
anyone I ever saw — talks of 'We' — and 'Lady Sarah' in a sort of
tone which I should have taken 3 years at least to acquire. He gives,
however, as no small proof of increasing vivacity that he lost his
umbrella some time since and has not bought a new one. I thought him
grown thinner — but could hardly judge, as he was walking — when
I observed it — with Warrender — and it might be the effect of
contrast.

Robinson was not only married, but very much married.
Aside from the dry humour in Peel's letter, there was a suggestion
of sadness for the break-up of the Alfred Club bachelors.

Robinson, who was in Europe at the time, had nothing to do
with the remote origins of the corn measure. Corn prices, which
had fluctuated between 60*s*. and 120*s*. per quarter during the
period 1800–13, took a sharp downward turn in 1813, and the
agricultural interest in the Commons secured the appointment of
Sir Henry Parnell's committee in 1814 to consider the Corn Laws
in general. The law of 1804 then in operation placed a prohibitory duty on corn when the price was under 63*s*., but permitted its importation at a 6*s*. rate when the price reached 66*s*.,
which indicated that this last figure was considered a fair,
remunerative price-level the year the law was passed. Parnell's
committee, however, noted that wheat had sold for 53*s*. during
the reign of Charles II, and calculated that, with inflation, the
price should be 105*s*. in 1814, but they recommended that 84*s*.
be adopted as a price-level fair to all.

During the debates that followed, the Government in effect
accepted the reasoning of the Parnell Committee, and offered a
number of resolutions. These resolutions would permit the entry
and free warehousing of foreign grain in Britain at all times, and
no duty was to be paid unless the corn were introduced into the
British market. If the current market price were 87*s*., the grain

would be assessed at only 6*s*. a quarter, but, if the price fell to 84*s*. or below, the duty was prohibitory. A preferential tariff, however, was suggested for corn grown in British colonies. So many petitions on the subject poured into the office of Nicholas Vansittart, the Chancellor of the Exchequer, that the whole matter was referred to a select committee, and no corn measure, save for a very minor piece of legislation, was passed that year. It is important to note, however, that Robinson had nothing to do with the 84*s*. figure, which was adopted by the Government probably without any reference to him.

How did Robinson come to be so closely associated with the measure? We know that back in April 1814 he had hoped to be sent home to defend the Government's foreign policy. 'I shall press him to send me,' Robinson wrote, 'because I think it would be the finest opportunity in the World for me to get an hold of the House of Commons.' [43] He added that he could do the job as well as Vansittart, but, on second thought, he crossed it out. After his return in May, the opportunity to defend the Government's policy had passed, and Robinson was so idle that Liverpool later complained about his failure to participate in the debates. [44] So Robinson eagerly sought an opportunity to tackle the Commons, and Liverpool wanted to put his talents to work; the nominal President of the Board of Trade and member of the Castlereagh faction, the Earl of Clancarty, obviously could not take charge of the corn measure. Under these circumstances, it was almost inevitable that the Bill should be assigned to Robinson. George Rose, the Treasurer of the Navy, would have been well qualified from his knowledge of economic affairs to have guided it, but he was feeling his years, and probably wanted someone else to bear the tedious burden of the inevitable debates.

Many years later Robinson recalled that Lord Liverpool had asked him to take charge of the corn measure, and that he had accepted the task with the greatest reluctance. 'I took the liberty of expressing to him', Robinson stated, 'that I had a great objection to the principle of any Corn Law whatever.' [45] If his memory thirty years later did not play tricks on him, this would imply that Robinson stood for Free Trade in 1815, or even earlier. Be this as it may, the first positive evidence available of his connection with the Bill of 1815 is a letter Robinson wrote to Hardwicke, who had served on the Lords committee on the Corn Laws the previous year, on the subject of the difficulties in taking the corn averages.[46]

The next question which arises is — who drew up the resolutions, and the final measure? Were they Robinson's work? Speaking in 1827, Robinson noted that he had 'matured and prepared' the measure of 1815,[47] but it is not clear whether he meant both the resolutions and the Bill, or simply the latter. It seems probable that the latter possibility is the correct one, and that the resolutions were the work of the whole Cabinet, which had on hand the report of the Parnell Committee, the findings of two later committees, and a mass of statistics gathered by George Rose.

George Tierney is the source of one account of the origins of the resolutions. He stated that the Cabinet met at Lord Liverpool's home one Tuesday, and drew up the resolutions with complete unanimity; then, the following Thursday, they called in a prominent member from London, Sir William Curtis, to discover what might be the urban reaction to a Bill designed to help the rural interest.[48] A newspaper, in February 1815, noted that the 80s. figure had been agreed upon at Lord Liverpool's meeting,[49] and this would seem to substantiate Tierney's account. But if they consulted Curtis, his reaction must have been highly discouraging, for he voted against their measure at every stage.

The nine resolutions which were probably drawn up by the full Cabinet represented a liberalization of those of the previous year, which practically prohibited the introduction of foreign grain into the British market if the price per quarter were 84s. or less. It is probable that Rose's statistics had shown that this level was too high, for Rose himself believed that 75s. would be a 'sufficient protecting price'.[50] The Cabinet therefore selected a sort of median between the figure of 1814 and Rose's level, and adopted 80s. in their resolutions. The other provisions — the admission of foreign grain, and a preference for colonial produce followed the outlines of the 1814 resolutions, and there was only one other

E

major difference. The resolutions of 1814 had called for a sliding scale of duties between 84*s*. and 87*s*.; those of 1815 did not establish a price area in which a sliding scale would function. In so far as the general public was concerned, the resolutions represented an attempt by the Government to fix the price of corn at 80*s*. per quarter, or higher.

On 17 February, Robinson moved that the House resolve itself into committee to discuss the Government's resolutions, but, before it did so, a member asked if the Government planned to ask for a renewal of the Income Tax that year. Vansittart replied that he would not ask for such a renewal, which was good news to the agriculturists, who were taxed heavily under Schedules *A* and *B*, and also to the urban members, who were interested particularly in dropping Schedules *C* and *D*. No announcement could have given the restrictive corn-legislation a more favourable send-off.

Robinson's speech in support of the resolutions is most interesting today for the light it sheds upon his views regarding trade in general, and Free Trade in particular. Was he a Free Trader, or a Protectionist at this time? In some respects this particular speech represents a model of Robinson's characteristic ambiguity, and his listeners were left to interpret certain parts of it to suit themselves.

Robinson called upon the members to be guided by reason, rather than emotion, in considering this question, and he spoke philosophically of the 'public mind' at the moment. His initial recommendation of the resolutions was certainly a left-handed one : [51]

He had never disguised from himself, and he was not at all ashamed to confess it, the extreme difficulty, as well as the extreme importance of this question. He never had disguised from himself that it was a choice of difficulties. The committee were not called upon to enter on a plain path ; there was, in fact, a certain evil to be apprehended either from adopting or rejecting the principles he was about to submit to the committee . . .

He then went on to insist that Britain at the moment really had no freedom of choice in this matter because the country had long ago committed herself to restrictive principles : [52]

It is not, therefore, a question between restriction and non-restriction — but how they were to apply principles, which had been long called into action by the existing circumstances of the country. This was the only ground on which he would now recommend the measure he was about to submit to their consideration.

It is quite clear, then, that Robinson did not support the Bill because it was right in principle, or because trade restrictions were good in themselves, but only because at the moment there seemed to be no alternative to it. The scholarly Francis Horner later commented on this part of Robinson's speech, noting that Robinson 'fully recognized the great principles, which . . . ought to regulate our commercial policy . . . and that the House had only to balance between difficulties — between the nature of the necessity, and the deference that was due to the great radical principle of free trade'.[53] Horner, however, disagreed with Robinson as to the necessities of the moment.

Robinson then proceeded to establish the necessity, as he saw it. The restrictive system, he declared, could not be abandoned without a 'frightful revulsion', and he stressed particularly the most valid justification for the protection of agriculture — the dangers of depending upon foreign nations for a food supply. Yet even in these statements he hedged. Bolstering the price of grain artificially tended to bring more and more land under cultivation, much of it ill-adapted to agriculture, and this meant that high prices for grain naturally followed higher production costs. Still it was absolutely necessary to keep this sub-marginal land under cultivation so that grain would be available in times of deficiency following poor harvests. Britain could never rely upon an unlimited supply of foreign grain to make up for such deficiencies — 'on that impossibility he founded the present measure'.[54] If one could prove, then, that such a supply of grain would be available year after year, Robinson's whole argument would fall to the ground.

Robinson, however, also feared that foreign competition might

ruin native farmers and throw them out of business, and, once
this occurred, the exporting nations could raise prices about as
they chose. This line of thought led finally to his rather strange,
but interesting, *laissez-faire* defence of the contemplated restrictions : [55]

He thought the final effect of the system would be, to give such a
powerful support to our own agriculture as would greatly increase the
produce of the country. It would excite a strong competition between
the different parts of England and Ireland ; so that the growth of
Corn, if Providence blessed us with favourable seasons, would be sufficiently large to afford an ample supply for the people of the country,
and would enable them to be fed at a much cheaper rate, in the long
run, than could be effected by the adoption of any other system.

Later in the debate Robinson asserted that he would abandon
the measure instantly if he thought it would raise the price of
bread, but he anticipated that it would be calculated 'to lower
the price of corn, and to reduce the high rents'.[56] This proved
to be correct. The farmers, greatly encouraged by prospective
high prices, produced an abundance of grain, and, save for the
year 1817, the trend of grain prices was downward.

Because of the importance of this particular measure in Robinson's career, it might be appropriate to trace its passage through
the Commons, and to analyse the support and opposition to it.
The first three resolutions were passed quickly, and the opposition centred on the fourth, which established the 80*s*. price-level
for the admission of foreign grain. Alexander Baring made an
unsuccessful effort to substitute 72*s*. for the original figure. On
27 February an attempt was made to prevent bringing up the
Report, and, when this failed, the opponents the following night
tried to deny leave to Robinson to bring in a Bill, but were again
beaten. Robinson was therefore able to introduce his corn
measure, based on the resolutions, on 1 March, when it had its
first reading. After a fairly spirited contest, the Bill had its
second reading on 3 March, and the House went into committee
on it three nights later. At this stage, on 8 March, another
unsuccessful attempt was made to reduce the 80*s*. level, and
thereafter its opponents gave up. The news of Napoleon's return

from Elba arrived in Britain on 10 March, and the Corn Bill was quickly forgotten.[57]

The debates reveal how little Free Trade sentiment existed in the Commons in 1815 ; if the Government had lowered the import figure to 76*s.*, it would have won over most of the Opposition, and, if they had gone down to 72*s.*, the measure would have been passed almost unanimously. Francis Horner and George Philips were the only members to speak strongly and effectively on behalf of the principle of Free Trade, and the nucleus of the opposition were Sir Robert Peel sen., Charles Barclay, and Thomas Babington, manufacturers who based their objections on practical, rather than philosophic, considerations.

Most opponents of the Bill recognized the principle of Protection, and were concerned merely with its degree. Sir James Graham, father of a more illustrious son, wanted a 72*s.* maximum. The manufacturer, Kirkman Finlay, also considered it a question of degree, and so did John Calcraft, whose wealth came from the land. Samuel Whitbread would have supported the resolutions, if a better method could have been found for taking the averages, and he correctly predicted that the measure would neither keep up rents nor help the farmer.[58] The Radical, Sir Francis Burdett, who was interested in the land, was accused by a contemporary periodical of absenting himself from the debates in order to conceal his support of the measure.[59]

Support for Protection was very widespread, and none of the divisions was even close. Sir Frederick Flood, Henry Grattan, and Sir John Newport acknowledged the importance of the measure to Ireland, and so did Robert Peel, who stressed emphatically the need for Protection there.[60] Some of the Scottish members were also strong proponents of the Bill.[61] Even the Opposition leader, George Ponsonby, supported the measure both with his voice and his vote.

William Huskisson, who later became associated with the Free Trade movement, deserves a moment of special attention. He spoke a number of times during the debates, and on every occasion in strong support of the measure. No one defended the 80*s.* level more consistently, and he declared 'less than 80*s.* as a protecting price would not remunerate the farmer'.[62] On 3 March he followed Robinson, who predicted that the Bill would lower the price of corn and diminish the rents, and declared that the measure would eliminate the fluctuations between 55*s.* and 125*s.*, and cause the price of corn to fluctuate between 70*s.* and 80*s.*[63]

Alexander Baring was another whose view of the effects of the measure was foggy in the extreme. Calculating on the assumption that it would establish an 80*s.* per quarter price for grain, he charged that the Bill would add £14,000,000 annually to the 'tribute' paid by the city consumers to the agricultural interest. As it turned out, the worst that opponents could say against the Corn Act of 1815, once it was in operation, was that it kept corn prices somewhat higher than they would have been if Free Trade had been established. By 1822 the most decided opponents of the measure were not the townsmen, but the farmers, who had waited in vain for the onset of parity prices.

When the corn resolutions were first presented to the Commons in February, they did not attract much attention out of doors until a member from London, where bread prices were always higher than in other places, argued on 24 February that the pending Bill would raise bread prices still further. Sir James Shaw's statement at once brought the argument down to the level of the mass of people in terms which they could readily understand. They listened to the theme time and again from street orators, and even heard it sung by ballad minstrels in the streets. Its impact upon a people already feeling the effects of the post-war depression was enormous.

The rising tide of popular resentment reached a flood on 6 March, when the Commons was to consider the 80*s.* provision for the measure, and during the afternoon of that day a huge crowd assembled around Parliament, blocking all avenues of approach to it, and all entrances to the lobbies. The huge demonstration, following the usual pattern, became more menacing as the hours went by. Hooting and hissing greeted some of the Members who reported early, but they were permitted to enter the building. Those who appeared later encountered increasing difficulties, and when John Wilson Croker's carriage drew up, he was dragged from it, struck a number of times, and forced to promise he would vote against the corn measure.[64] Sir Frederick Flood was also seized about the same time, and bandied about by the crowd 'like a basket of mackeral at Billingsgate'.[65] Although the entire metropolitan police force, and fifty constables, were on duty in the area, they were powerless to aid Croker and Flood, who were finally permitted, shaken and fully impressed as to popular sentiment regarding the Bill, to proceed into the Commons. Some other Members also suffered indignities, but no one was injured seriously.

William Vesey Fitzgerald, who had been unable to rescue his Alfred Club friend, went to the Speaker, Charles Abbot, and demanded that means be found to protect the Members. Abbot then brought some infantry and cavalry units into the area, and created the unusual, and potentially dangerous, situation wherein the Members debated in a building surrounded by the military. Castlereagh explained that the situation could be considered regular, as the troops were under the authority of a civil magi strate, and Abbot continued to give explanations until all Members were satisfied.

The arrival of the troops broke up the demonstration outside Parliament, and many small parties detached themselves from the crowd, voicing their intentions to attack the houses of Robinson, Darnley, Eldon, and Ellenborough, all of whom were connected with the hated Bill. Darnley's house had its windows broken ; soldiers aided Eldon in the protection of his home, while Ellenborough, an orator of note, used his talents to good effect, and dispersed the demonstrators from around his home.

Robinson was then living in a rented home in Old Burlington Street. On Monday, 6 March, he learned from 'common report' that there would be demonstrations that night, and therefore took Lady Sarah to her father's house for safety. In his testimony later, Robinson said he had expected his windows to be broken, and noted that this was one of the hazards a politician who brought a controversial measure forward had to face.[66] Either at Lady Sarah's request, or by his own decision, he also moved in with Lord Buckinghamshire, and so the defence of the establishment was left to the servants, reinforced by some troops which Lord Sidmouth sent at Robinson's request.

The soldiers had not yet arrived when the mob attacked the house for the first time. They smashed the windows and iron railing in front of the house, then went inside and destroyed some furniture, and terrorized the servants. 'The mob threatened to murder the servants', Robinson asserted, 'if they did not say where I was to be found.' [67] As the Buckinghamshires' house was not attacked, we may assume that the servants withheld information regarding their master's whereabouts. Presumably the soldiers arrived, dispersed the mob, and stayed there all night. Perhaps the most important fact from a legal standpoint arising from the 6 March foray was that the demonstrators actually entered the house and threatened the lives of the servants.

After the soldiers departed the following morning, the mob returned again, broke into the house, chased the servants upstairs, and again threatened them with grievous bodily harm. Although none was injured, the servants were evidently thoroughly frightened, and the footman, William Sutton, went to Lord Buckinghamshire's house to report and seek advice. Just what Robinson told him to do is not too clear. There were actually two considerations involved — the protection of the servants' lives, which were presumed to be threatened, and the protection of Robinson's property. Later Robinson denied specifically that he had told the servants to arm themselves, but had simply assured them that a permanent guard would be stationed in the house until the crisis had passed.

The three servants, Sutton, James Ripley, the butler, and William Smith, the coachman, were left with the problem of defending themselves in case the soldiers departed again. Some pistols were on hand, or hastily secured, but they had no ammunition. Some swan shot was secured, under circumstances not explained, by Sutton when he went to Buckinghamshire's. Therefore on the evening of 7 March both soldiers and armed servants were on hand to greet the mob.

The soldiers were stationed, at Robinson's order, inside the house, where they were not only given their dinner, but a 'horn of liquor', which was something less than a half-pint. So long as the horse guards patrolled Old Burlington Street in pairs, the gradually collecting crowd did not attempt to raid the house, but the guard rode off around nine o'clock and the attacks began. The soldiers at first fired blank charges at them through the windows and the fan-light, but after a time, possibly on Ripley's orders, one or more of them began to use swan shot.

Many of the details — the size of the crowd, and what they were doing at the time of the fatalities — were never clearly established. Sutton later testified that two shots, and no more, were fired almost simultaneously at the time the front windows were broken open. One of the shots was fired by Ripley. Smith said that a soldier fired first, followed by two or three other shots, while the crowd was throwing things into the house. Amelia Davis, a witness who was outside walking with Jane Watson, testified that there were only about fifty people on hand, and that they were doing no more than throwing an occasional rock at the building. Not one of the three witnesses placed the demonstrators inside the house at the moment of the fatal firings.[68] As a result of the blasts of swan shot, a midshipman named Edward Vyse was killed immediately, and Jane Watson, a twice-married widow and mother of one child, was mortally wounded.

Sir Francis Burdett, the leading Radical agitator in Parliament, brought up the shootings on 10 March, when he charged: 'No man knows whether he is safe in going along the streets, if people are to be placed in ambuscade, and allowed to fire through doors and windows.'[69] Robinson then 'rose under great agitation' and told his story of the tragic incident. This brief speech must be considered one of the most important of his whole career, not so much for what he said, but for his emotional condition at the time he said it. 'Mr. Robinson's speech was interrupted by tears,' a periodical reported, 'which testified the grief of which he felt, as a man of humanity.'[70] There is no evidence that he ever had given way to such emotions before in the Commons, and the experience seems to have left a permanent scar on him. Having lost control once, he seems to have lived in dread of repeating the performance, and this fear, in turn, gave rise in the future to the very result which he wished to avoid. From this time forward he was never able to speak on a subject which moved him deeply without giving evidence of his emotions. This caused his friend, and later enemy, Charles Stewart, to refer to him as the 'Blubberer'. After his exhibition, and a sharp exchange with Castlereagh, Burdett apologized to Robinson : 'I did not attach any blame to him personally, but to the soldiers who were employed.'[71]

A coroner's inquest was held almost immediately after the shootings to determine the cause of the death of Edward Vyse, but no formal charges resulted from its hearing. In the case of Jane Watson, however, a coroner's jury in Middlesex launched a more thorough investigation, and during the course of its hearings Robinson insisted that he be allowed to take the stand. His appearance, which probably arose from a desire to help his servant, James Ripley, did not make much of an impression on the jury, largely because his evidence was hearsay in nature. The result of the inquest was to bring formal charges of 'wilful murder' against Ripley and three of the soldiers, but they were subsequently exonerated of the charge at a formal trial.[72]

The Old Burlington Street incident gave rise to another situation, beyond Robinson's tearfulness, which was to have a most far-reaching effect upon his subsequent career. Lady Sarah, who was naturally neurotic, was pregnant at the time of these events, and, according to an individual who knew them, reacted in a most extreme manner. 'Her fears were so excited', the friend explained, 'that it was alleged the precautions she took to insure the Minister's personal safety, sometimes interfered with the discharge of his imperative duties.'[73] Lady Sarah's fears seem to have grown gradually from morbid anxiety to positive obsession during the next decade, haunting, nagging fears, destructive to her own peace of mind, as well as to that of her husband.

4

Economics with a Heart

Robinson continued as Vice-President of the Board of Trade, under its President, the Earl of Clancarty, until 1818, when he assumed full control. As Clancarty had never taken an interest in the Board, this delay in Robinson's promotion was not due to his occupancy of the Presidency, but to certain financial considerations. Neither of the positions then carried a salary, and it was necessary to attach sinecures to them, if the President and Vice-President were to be remunerated for their labours. Liverpool's plan, probably urged on him by Castlereagh, was to attach the Paymastership of the Navy to the Presidency of the Board, but George Rose, who held the former position, twice refused to give it up, and the promotion was impossible until his death in January 1818.[1] Probably urged by Lord Melville, Liverpool planned to give the Vice-Presidency to Thomas Wallace.

Not only did Robinson become President of the Board of Trade in 1818, but he received also a seat in the Cabinet. 'Mr. Robinson's standing in the house of Commons, his character and talents,' Liverpool explained to the Prince Regent, 'appear fairly to entitle him to such a mark of distinction.'[2] The Prime Minister also explained the reasons for the promotion to Robert Peel, who was seeking a higher office for his friend Fitzgerald at this time. 'Upon Robinson's claims, his Talents & his Character,' he wrote, 'it is unnecessary for me to say anything to you.'[3] One contemporary observer, apparently unaware of Robinson's close friendship with Castlereagh, traced Robinson's advancement to his talents, and popularity with the Navy Board,[4]

65

which indicates that it was not regarded generally as a mark of political favouritism.

The promotion of Thomas Wallace seems to have been based on political expediency, rather than his personal qualifications for the position. 'With respect to Mr. Wallace,' Liverpool wrote, 'he has been 28 years in Parliament, has *invariably* followed the same Political Line as myself.'[5] Wallace accepted the offer gratefully, the more so, he wrote, because it gave him contact 'with a description of business I am far from disliking'.[6] His interest in trade affairs, however, does not seem to have been important, and his advancement was due to party services.

These facts about Wallace are of some importance because both in his own time and later some observers endeavoured to trace the Free Trade movement to him, rather than to Robinson. Charles Arbuthnot, a consistent detractor of Robinson, later noted that Wallace's work at the Board had reduced Robinson to a 'cypher'.[7] In making this statement, he was probably re-peating a rumour he had heard, but there seems to be no real basis for it. All available evidence indicates that Robinson managed the Board himself between 1812 and 1818, and that during the next four years he turned over the routine work to his new and able subordinate. Later Robinson told Parliament that both Nicholas Vansittart[8] and Wallace were Free Traders, and that the latter had furnished 'the most valuable assistance in all those commercial measures which have originated with myself'.[9] In other words, Wallace was merely his assistant, and not a policy-maker.

The great depression which settled down upon Great Britain at the end of the Napoleonic Wars lasted almost without inter-ruption during Robinson's term of office at the Board of Trade. Even less was known then than now regarding continued periods of economic stagnation, and Robinson's analysis of it was prob-ably as accurate as could be obtained at the time, and was at least partially sound. It was caused, he believed, by the cessation of the artificial economic demands created by the long-continuing conflict, which caused widespread economic dislocations.[10] His belief in the soundness of the *laissez-faire* system is evident in his reluctance to sanction governmental interference with the free play of economic forces, which would, he was convinced, eventually restore prosperity. Unsound businesses created by unnatural war-time demands must go to the wall; uneconomic farms must be abandoned; the vital iron and textile industries must simply wait out the depression, and hope for the better days a revival of world trade would bring. Although Robinson undoubtedly possessed a mercantile mind, his heart was filled with a kind of bourgeois liberalism which would not permit him to apply this chilly economic philosophy uniformly and without reference to the human suffering that might be involved.

Even if Robinson had sought to sit out the depression without action, there were powerful and vocal interests in Parliament which, through plea and pressure, could force the Government to take cognizance of their plight. The agricultural interest was quickly disenchanted with the Corn Act of 1815. Although the bad harvests on the Continent briefly raised the price of corn to 90*s.* late in 1816, this was merely a small acclivity on a price path which led steadily downward.

The farmers knew they were suffering, but were none too clear as to the measures necessary for their relief. Some wanted an ever-normal granary system under which the Government would buy up surplus grain in bumper years; some wanted a bounty on corn exports; but most of the agricultural agitators wanted a fixed duty on foreign grain which they thought would make their monopoly of the home market complete.

The pressure began in 1816. Robinson was forced to agree to the formation of another parliamentary committee on the agricultural distress, but he opposed proposals to abandon the warehousing of foreign grain in England, or to grant a bounty on grain exports. 'His conviction', he explained, 'was that no trade which could stand by itself needed the assistance of a bounty, and that no bounty would uphold a trade which required artificial support.' [11] The revival of agricultural prosperity in 1817–1818 temporarily removed the pressure of the agricultural interest, but the price collapse in the latter year brought its return. Between 1819 and 1821 some twelve hundred petitions were sent to Parliament calling attention to the distress, and the agricultural lobby finally opened an office near Parliament so that they could work more effectively in their cause.

In January 1819 Robinson bluntly refused to reopen the question of the Corn Laws, which, as the events of 1815 had shown, was a sensitive and dangerous one in the extreme.[12] The following year, however, he agreed to a committee of inquiry on the vexed subject of taking corn averages with a view to eliminating the frauds which sometimes marred the system;[13] and in 1821 he agreed that a committee might examine the tax burdens on agriculture. But all along he took a firm position against making the Corn Laws even more restrictive than they were under the Act of 1815.

In view of the fact that the agricultural interest was one of the mainstays of the Tory Government, this continued resistance to their pleas and demands was politically heroic, but in 1822 the Liverpool Government yielded to the steady pressure. The Act of 1822 created a graduated scale of tariffs between 70s., when the duty was 17s., and 85s., when the duty on foreign corn dropped to 1s. It is perhaps significant — perhaps because positive information on the subject is unavailable — that Robinson neither introduced, nor took much part in the defence of this measure, which he considered useless. His view probably is embodied in a remark he made that same year : 'He would admit that restrictions upon the trade in corn were not in themselves desirable, and that a new system, of which such restrictions would form no part, might not afford relief to agriculture.'[14]

While the Corn Laws formed the main battle line between the Government and the agricultural interest during these years, certain special groups within the body of the latter staged their own forays on the flanks of the Board of Trade. 'Butter and cheese have had a high duty imposed on them,' Robinson explained many years later, 'forced upon the Board of Trade after the War by Lord Western and Sir John Newport together with a host of Irish Merchants & managers in the counties of Waterford & Cork.'[15]

Stagnant Ireland with its highly volatile population presented demands which in 1816 could not be ignored. The Irish butter interest wanted a 30*s*. per hundredweight tariff upon foreign, especially Dutch, butter; merchants concerned with the importation of the latter pleaded for a 10*s*. maximum. Caught between two fires, Robinson split the difference, and adopted a 20*s*. duty, if the butter were imported in British ships, and 25*s*., if imported in foreign craft. At the same time he yielded to the Irish cheese interest, and laid down tariffs of 16*s*. and 20*s*. per hundredweight.[16] These proved to be highly remunerative duties, and they were therefore protective and not prohibitive — the revenues from them were so large that it was difficult to remove the duties at a later date.[17] When the butter interest in 1822 sought to raise them further, and eliminate Dutch competition, Robinson gave them a lecture : 'If, on every occasion like this, we were to put restrictions on trade, we might as well declare at once that on principle we would have no commercial intercourse with foreign states. If this country sent goods abroad, it was proper that other countries should be allowed to transmit their products in return.' [18]

The hides and tallow segment of the agricultural interest fought much less successfully to secure concessions from the Board of Trade. Shortly after the war Robinson successfully resisted an increase in the duties on these items, which he believed would mean 'an utter end of the magnificent prospects opened . . . in South America'.[19] Although he turned the initial demands aside, when the nations of Europe began to export tallow to Britain in significant quantities, the British interest demanded that the duties on that item be quintupled. Once again Robinson was able to resist their pressure, and on the ground that this was one of the few items that the European nations could sell in Britain. 'Now that one article was found on which they could make a profit,' Robinson continued, 'the state was to step in and take it in the shape of a tax. If this was to be our rule of commercial policy, we might as well shut up shop at once.' [20]

The weakest of all the Canadian colonies, Newfoundland, presented the Board of Trade with a continuing problem. Its economic existence depended on the fish trade, which, during the war, was flourishing, but which collapsed after peace returned. Those interested in the fishing trade asked the Government to remove a large number of people from Newfoundland to Canada, and to place a bounty on Newfoundland fish for those who remained. Robinson opposed the bounty on the ground that it would merely complicate the problem in the long run.[21] A Government offer to provide a year's subsistence to a thousand settlers in Canada, if the merchants would remove them, was rejected. So the Newfoundland problem remained, and became ever more acute.

Robinson was not completely deaf to the pleas of that poverty-stricken colony. His Act of 1819 rigidly enforced the rights of Canadian fishermen, as against those of Americans, in the area, and, on learning that France and the United States were providing bounties to their fishermen, he was ready to grant a year's bounty so that the British colonists could get a fresh start in their trade. When it was discovered that the report of the American bounty was inaccurate, however, Robinson quickly withdrew his approval of the project, and the colonists were left to fend for themselves unassisted by the Board of Trade.[22]

Under the influence of the lingering depression, the British manufacturers, many of whom were opponents of the Government, were interested primarily in protecting the interests of their particular products, and, at least until 1820, Free Trade sentiment was still weak on the opposite side of the House. Robinson carried on a number of battles with them, but his difficulties might be adequately illustrated by describing briefly only one — his unsuccessful attempt to repeal the linen duties. As early as 1813 he had advised Peel of the desirability of repealing, or modifying, the transit duties on foreign linens, but the Irish linen interest would have none of it. 'Pray ask Robinson what he thinks of the 15 per cent duty on foreign linen', Peel wrote to Goulburn, probably in 1815, '& tell him in confidence that Dennis Browne is coming over and that he has declared "as a Privy Counsellor" that he will impeach the man who attempts to repeal the duty.'[23] When it became known that Robinson had such a project in mind, he was 'burned in effigy in half the towns in the north of Ireland'.[24]

The linen interest was much too strong for Robinson and he agreed not to modify the duty unless both the English and Irish manufacturers would agree to a plan for abolition, and this they did not do. When the Latin American market began to open up, it was discovered that the people there simply did not like Irish linens, and wanted to buy assorted lots which would combine British linens with those manufactured on the Continent. Exporters to Latin America then began to complain, and demanded the right to import Continental linens for re-export to Latin America without payment of duty. Fearing this would cut down on the percentage of Irish linens included in the lots, the powerful Irish linen board would not agree, and the exporters often changed Irish labels to German labels in order to sell their lots to the Latin Americans. Robinson tried to find a solution to this impasse, but in this he was unsuccessful.

In 1817 Robinson, in his most effective speech since the defence of the Government back in 1812, explained his difficulties to the Commons : [25]

Many of the observations respecting the foreign commerce of the country . . . had his entire concurrence. But he felt more than the hon. and learned gentleman [Brougham] seemed to do, the infinite difficulty which there was in extricating ourselves from that system. . . . In all the communications which he had had with persons engaged in trade, he had never heard the general principle denied, but he never could get the individual to allow that the general principle ought to be applied in his case. . . . He was convinced . . . that every proposition of that nature [commercial agreements] would be overcome by the hostility of the great mass of the manufacturers . . . The hon. and learned gentleman asked why there was such a heavy export duty on coals ? But if the hon. and learned gentleman were to come to the House with any proposition to this effect, he would immediately have the half of the manufacturers of the country in arms against him. Only last year he had proposed to take off the export duties on small coals. Immediately the manufacturers of glass came forward and said the measure would be enabling foreign manufacturers of the article to undersell and ruin them . . . The people of the continent had capital, skill and industry — there was nothing mysterious about machinery. At present we might be somewhat better in constructing the machinery, and have more skill in working it ; but if the peace should last . . . he

F

did not see what there was to prevent the people of the continent from rivalling us, if not in countries where no manufacturing were established, at least in their own countries.

This ability to see beyond Britain's immediate advantages, and to visualize the spread of the Industrial Revolution into many other countries, attests to Robinson's intellectual stature. Probably much of his anxiety to open up new trade channels for British goods stemmed from the realization that the day would come when Britain would face stiff competition in the export of manufactured goods from the more advanced nations of the Continent.

Alexander Baring's presentation of a petition signed by some London merchants to the Commons on 8 May 1820 is sometimes considered to have symbolized the epoch of Free Trade. This petition opposed duties which protected against competition, called for the loosening of trade restraints, and cited the economic axiom of buying in the cheapest market and selling in the dearest. Baring concluded the presentation with a warm compliment to Robinson: 'He was convinced that no gentleman was more anxious to see the sound principles to which he had alluded carried into operation than the right hon. gentleman in whose hands at present the regulation of trade was placed.' [26]

This was the cue for Robinson to make a brilliant reply, but he did not quite rise to the occasion. 'He had always given it as his opinion', Robinson said, 'that the restrictive system of commerce in this country was founded in error and calculated to defeat the object for which it was adopted.' [27] He then complained about the difficulties he had encountered in trying to liberalize the trading system, but to indicate that his efforts had not been entirely fruitless, mentioned that about three hundred duties had been repealed over the past two or three years. Two of those to which he was alluding were probably Acts of Edward IV and Richard III, repealed in 1816, which prohibited the importation of wrought iron goods. The fact that such an impressive number of tariffs were removed without much altering the restrictive system would seem to prove Robinson's statement concerning the breadth, depth, and complexities of the trade system which existed when he came to office.

No summary of Robinson's views on economics would be complete without some reference to his attitude toward labour, which was suffering at this time under the extreme application of the *laissez-faire* doctrine. In 1819 a member named Peter Moore asked leave to bring in a Bill to establish a standard regulation for the pay of the ribbon and silk weavers. In his Coventry constituency there were five classes of such workers, each working 96 hours a week, whose pay varied from 10s. to 1s. 6d. a week, and the lower-paid workers were forced to accept relief.[28] Robinson opposed the Bill on the ground that 'it was inexpedient to allow the wages of labourers, of whatever denomination, to be settled by any other means than by the natural demand for their labour. Indeed, he was almost ashamed to use so trite and acknowledged a principle. . . .'[29]

This rigid application of economic principles did not in Robinson's case, however, extend to children. When Sir Robert Peel in 1818 proposed to limit the work of children under sixteen years of age, Robinson pointed out: 'If the bill went directly to interfere in the labour of adults, he thought it would be objectionable; but it would be going too far to say, that by protecting the children the adults might be incidentally interfered with and that therefore the children should be left as they were.'[30] It should be added that Robinson — in full knowledge that the Act of 1815 would not raise corn prices — had lowered the rents paid by his wife's tenants after the war, and in this area under his personal control, he followed a liberal course.

One sequence of events during Robinson's term at the Board of Trade deserves separate treatment, not because it is necessarily the most important, but because it is the best-documented, and helps clarify his relations with Castlereagh. This is the story of the Anglo-American negotiations on a great variety of complex questions, some diplomatic and territorial in nature, others primarily economic.

The story actually begins back in 1783, when the United States found that independence brought with it exclusion from the British colonial trade system. To be cut off from the trade privileges

she had enjoyed since early colonial days came as a severe
economic jolt, and her cherished hope thereafter was to re-
establish by treaty with Britain the commercial privileges she
had lost — that is, to secure the right to pick up and discharge
goods where she pleased within the Empire. Great Britain, on
the other hand, was wedded to the mercantilist system of monopoly, which was thought by many economists and business men
to underpin British economic strength.

The Americans tried to project a commercial treaty during the
Treaty of Ghent negotiations, a most unpropitious moment, for
feelings on both sides of the Atlantic were still very raw. 'We
never, before or after leaving Ghent,' one of the American negotiators wrote to Henry Clay, 'received the slightest disposition on
the part of Britain to enter with us into a commercial treaty,
although *repeatedly* assailed by us on that subject. Lord Castlereagh . . . expressed himself very explicitly against the expediency of commercial treaties in general . . .'[31]

This was Britain's position late in 1814 — when Robinson was
on his honeymoon and was unavailable to advise Castlereagh.
Yet not many months later, when the Americans broached the
subject of a commercial treaty, together with the negotiation of
such irritating questions as impressment, neutral rights, and
blockades, Castlereagh had changed his position completely, and
welcomed them. As early as 11 May 1815 Robinson was ready
'to receive with great attention any propositions concerning
the general commerce which they were prepared to make'.[32]
Was Robinson the moving spirit in bringing about this
change? Evidence is lacking, but once the conference opened,
his liberal and generous attitude proves that he was ready to let
bygones be bygones, especially when the nation's business was
concerned.

At the conferences of 1815 Robinson, the senior member, was
assisted by Dr. William Adams, and Henry Goulburn; while
America was represented by Henry Clay, Albert Gallatin, a
statesman with a Continental background, and that New World
aristocrat, John Quincy Adams. There were a number of points
at issue.[33] The Americans wanted to navigate the St. Lawrence

River as far as Montreal; the British desired to trade with the Indians in American territories. Both propositions involved sovereign rights, and neither country was ready to concede the privilege requested. Britain sought some 'equivalent' concession for the American indirect trade with India, while the United States insisted that this trade, which brought specie to India, was its own equivalent. Britain largely conceded this point. Britain wanted to end discriminatory American tariffs, and to equalize port charges in trade between the United States and British ports in Europe; the United States wanted to extend these provisions to the entire British Empire. The United States conceded these points.

The procedure was slow and laborious. The Americans first submitted their project; then on 16 June the British negotiators sent copies of their counter-proposals both to the Americans and the Foreign Office, which may indicate that the latter played a passive role in the negotiations. At times it appeared as though a stalemate would result. 'I expect from what passed between us & the Americans this morning', Robinson wrote to Castlereagh on 19 June, 'that our negotiations will end in smoke.'[34] But at the same time the usually optimistic Robinson advised the passage of a Bill through Parliament which would permit them to put the proposed treaty into effect without having to wait for the next session.

Shortly thereafter the negotiators concluded that they were wasting their time in continuing the conferences, and Robinson reported the results to Castlereagh with the following observation:[35]

You will therefore have to decide whether it is worthwhile to sign a Treaty (omitting always as I think they will the Canadian article) for two, three or five years, which shall for that period regulate the intercourse between our dominions in Europe & the United States and shall for the same period give them the *indirect* voyage to the East Indies, without any equivalent from them.

Castlereagh decided it was worth while. From his point of view the treaty symbolized the restoration of friendly relations with America; for Robinson, it was the beginning of the reciprocal trade movement in which he was to have a lifelong interest.

It was due largely to Robinson's friendly attitude that the otherwise disappointed Americans were sent away in a better frame of mind. The Treaty of Ghent had on both copies mentioned the King before the President, and had carried the British signatures above the American. Adams, for permitting this, had been rebuked by his sensitive and watchful superiors, and he tried to have the names and signatures transposed on the American copy of the Commercial Convention of 1815. Goulburn and Adams were reluctant to concede the point. 'Mr. Robinson finally said he believed we were right,' Adams recorded. 'At least it had been so at the Treaty of Chaumont, which was the only treaty he had been before concerned in writing.' [36] After the final signature of the convention, Gallatin remarked to his colleagues: 'Well, they got over the transpositions very easily, but you would not have found it so if Dr. Adams had had the reading of your copy, instead of Mr. Robinson.' [37] This would indicate that Robinson had concealed this concession from at least one of his colleagues.

Not only did Robinson agree to the transposition of the signatures on the American copy, but he agreed to call it a convention rather than a treaty, as the Americans wished. Minor points? — in retrospect, perhaps. But for the United States, then seeking some slight admission of the equality from Great Britain which she had so dramatically declared back in 1776, they were major ones. 'Now the only thing of any value that we obtained by this convention', John Quincy Adams confided to a friend, 'was a formality.' [38]

The Commercial Convention of 3 July 1815 consisted of five articles. The first declared a 'reciprocal liberty of commerce' between Britain and America; secondly, it was stipulated that American tariffs on British goods brought to her ports, and British tariffs on American goods brought to British European ports would be no higher than those charged on like articles from other foreign countries, and it also equalized the port charges on American and British ships in each other's ports. The third article permitted American vessels to pick up goods at Indian

ports on a 'most-favoured-nation' basis, provided such ships
returned directly to American ports. The fourth article permitted the establishment of consulates in each other's territories,
and the fifth limited the duration of the treaty to four years from
the date of signature.

Once the treaty came into force — over the protestations of
some of the members of the Commons [39] — Adams discovered
that it contained more than a mere formality. Three years later
he noted that it not only had had a 'great moral effect' on improving Anglo-American relations, but it had aided the American
carrying trade, and expanded intercourse with British and European ports.[40] Britain also received some benefits. She was protected against discriminatory American tariffs on her exports to
America, and was now able to carry American goods profitably
to her West Indian possessions.

Robinson further displayed his goodwill during the ensuing
years by interpreting the provisions of the convention in a
manner favourable to the United States. One dispute involved
the carrying of Irish emigrants to America; British regulations
permitted one passenger for every two tons register, while those
of the United States permitted one person for every five tons.
Britain could have regarded this as an immigration-control provision beyond the scope of the convention, but Robinson nevertheless passed an Act in 1816 which placed the nations on an
equal footing in this business.[41] Some British merchants contended that the Indian article did not give American ships the
right to pick up cargoes in British ports for trade in India, but
on 20 June 1816 Robinson passed an Act which established the
American right to this type of trade.[42]

Those observers who have looked upon Robinson as a nonentity
are faced with a large number of proofs of his activity at this
time which wholly contradict such an interpretation. John
Quincy Adams, who remained in Britain as Ambassador, on one
occasion complained to Lord Liverpool regarding a discriminatory duty on American cotton, and was 'asked if I had spoken
on the subject with Mr. Robinson'.[43] When he brought up
certain objectionable auction duties on American goods in a

conversation with Castlereagh, the Foreign Secretary replied:
'I agreed with Robinson before he left town . . . that this
should be remitted. . . .' [44] When Adams inquired at the
Foreign Office about the Bill to equalize the Irish passengers, an
official there 'sent me to Mr. Robinson to enquire what the intention of the bill now before the House of Common was . . .' [45]
These references would indicate that Robinson acted as the
principal economic adviser of the Government at this time, and
that he worked in the most intimate association possible with
Castlereagh, who displayed an increasing interest in economic
affairs.

Although the Convention of 1815 had had some salutary
results for both nations, the United States still found itself
knocking on the gates of the British Empire, and on 25 January
1816 she sounded out the British Government on the subject of
further negotiations. The British Government proved receptive,
but cautious. The United States was particularly anxious to
trade with the British West Indies, and they sought an understanding on this subject — or at least some encouragement —
before sending their delegation. Such encouragement was very
long in coming. Adams brought up the West Indies in a conversation with Castlereagh in July, and although the Foreign
Secretary seemed conciliatory, he added 'I cannot now be prepared to enter upon the particular points of the question, owing
to the absence of Mr. Robinson.' [46]

It seems probable that both Robinson and Castlereagh were
convinced that the British restrictive system was self-defeating,
and that the correct policy was to expand trade in every direction.
When Castlereagh brought the West Indies matter before the
Cabinet in August, however, there were many in the Government
who did not agree with him, and on 21 August he explained to
Adams that the colonial system might be wise or unwise, but that
the Government was committed to it. He then made a statement
of great importance: 'he said it was understood by this Government that the United States would be perfectly free to adopt any
countervailing regulations, either of prohibition or of additional
duties that they might think advisable. That Britain would

have no right to complain of them.' [47] This was an open invitation to America to take such retaliatory action, and it was to be repeated by both Castlereagh and Robinson to the Americans during the next few years. Did they actually seek such action from America so that they might have an additional reason for amending the colonial system? While proof is lacking, it was just such a measure by the United States in 1818 that broke the impasse, and brought about the second of the commercial conferences.

John Quincy Adams did not remain in Britain long enough to participate in the second conference, but went home late in 1817 to become Secretary of State. Although he had failed to secure any major concessions from the British during the two years of his ambassadorship, he left with a high opinion of Castlereagh, who was always 'gentlemanly, conciliatory, and obliging'.[48] Adams described Robinson to his successor, Richard Rush, as a 'perfectly fair and candid mind; and of a conciliatory and obliging disposition'.[49] The magnitude of these compliments can be appreciated only when they are compared with his opinions of Canning — 'invariably noted for the bitterness of his inveteracy against the United States' [50] — and of Croker — 'an inveterate and rancorous enemy to America'.[51]

When Richard Rush arrived in London, he brought up two matters which again illustrate Castlereagh's dependence on Robinson not only in economic, but in diplomatic affairs. Rush broached the subject of certain American slaves purloined by the British during the recent war, and Castlereagh 'promised to keep the whole subject in mind, and see Mr. Robinson . . . in relation to it'.[52] On the subject of certain tariff refunds, the Foreign Secretary 'gave no opinion in reply, but promised . . . to converse with Mr. Robinson, and prepare himself for an answer'.[53] Evidence like this suggests that Castlereagh and Robinson were such intimate friends that their conversations would range over wide areas of problems.

Rush had only been in Britain a short time when, on 11 February 1818, an exchange took place in Parliament, which had repercussions in the United States. After hearing William

Henry Lyttelton complain of Spain's prohibitive tariffs on British goods, Castlereagh observed that Spain was acting on principles 'now quite exploded in the politics of this country'. 'Even we ourselves', he continued, 'were still a good deal embarrassed by the restrictions of our own commercial regulations.'[54] Robinson then pointed out that Britain was also guilty of laying heavy tariffs without even including a grace period which might cushion the blow to nations affected by them.[55] On reading an account of this debate, John Quincy Adams concluded that it meant a major change in British commercial policy, and he did not hesitate to act on the hints Castlereagh and Robinson had given to him while he was still in Britain.

A period of economic sparring set in. Congress, by an Act of 18 April 1818, closed American ports to British ships coming from colonies from which American vessels were excluded, a blow to Britain's carrying trade between the West Indies and America. Britain countered with a clever device. On 8 May 1818 she opened, with some restrictions, the ports of Halifax and St. John's to American ships, hoping that her own vessels could then sail from the West Indies to American ports via these Canadian harbours; but the American Government refused to relax her restrictions, and the plan did not work. This commercial situation was one of the factors which brought about the Anglo-American negotiations of the late summer and early autumn of 1818; and, despite these economic manœuvrings, Albert Gallatin, one of the American negotiators, concluded that the attitude of the British Government was more favourable towards the United States than ever before.[56]

A month before the formal negotiations began in Robinson's office on 27 August, Castlereagh and Robinson met with the other American negotiator, Richard Rush, and expressed the hope that 'some modification of that [colonial] system mutually beneficial might be the result of frank and full discussions'.[57] This was a reversal of Britain's position of 21 August 1816, and for the first time some hope was held out to the United States that some parts of the British Empire might be opened to her.

The negotiations which followed on this subject were so complex and far-reaching that the Americans were at times uncertain as to their instructions on some of the points at issue. Rush and Gallatin demanded 'perfect reciprocity', which embraced a number of ideas.[58] British vessels operating between the West Indies and the United States could carry such American and West Indian products as American ships were permitted to carry in the same trade; the charges on ships, and duties on cargoes, would be the same for British and American vessels in this trade; the duties on items imported into the West Indies and the United States would be the same for circuitous as for direct voyages; British ships coming from the West Indies to American ports had to leave from harbours open to American ships; American and British vessels operating in the West Indian trade were to be of the same description. The United States desired, under this system, to carry naval stores, livestock, provisions of every description, tobacco and timber to British ports in the West Indies and Latin America; and to pick up cargoes of sugar, rum, molasses, coffee, salt, and other products for sale wherever she could find a market. The United States also sought a similar arrangement with the British North American colonies.

While Britain was ready to accept these conditions, she would do so only if she could interpret them in her own way. Without restrictions upon the products involved in the trade, American timber would compete with Canadian timber; American provisions would take some of the market from provisions grown in Britain and Canada; and the United States ships would compete with British vessels in carrying and distributing West Indian products. Britain, therefore, wanted to put restrictions on American shipments of timber, provisions, and fish to the West Indies, and to force American carriers to pick up cargoes of West Indian sugar and coffee at Bermuda, Halifax, or St. John's. She also insisted on charging lower duties on produce of her West Indian and North American colonies than on the same products brought from America.

Some insight into the futile efforts to resolve the British and

American points of view on the subject of this trade is provided by a report Gallatin made to Adams : [59]

the Ministry will go as far as public opinion permits them. Mr. Robinson was very explicit on that subject, and almost complained of our insisting on an unlimited intercourse, which we must know could not at once be opened, even if the Administration was precisely of the same opinion with ourselves. And he intimated that such unlimited intercourse (with the exception of salted provisions) would be the ultimate result of its now being partially opened. He added that, considering our proximity, and that the West Indies could have no shipping of their own, the greatest part of the carrying trade in the direct intercourse must necessarily be done by American vessels ; and that, in order to restore the equality, it was absolutely necessary that a portion of that intercourse should be carried through the medium of Bermuda and Halifax.

Robinson's conciliatory plan for limited intercourse could not be reconciled with American demands for 'perfect reciprocity'. The Americans would not budge an inch. 'We thought it safer to err on our own side of the question', they reported, 'and to ask for more than perhaps under all circumstances, we expected to obtain, rather than to limit our demands to less than might be intended by our government.' [60] Negotiations on the subject, therefore, broke down, but the discussions were carried on in the friendliest of manners, and no hard feelings were left behind.

Despite this failure, and that also of Castlereagh's project to solve the impressment issue,[61] the negotiations of 1818 had some tangible results. American fishing rights in Canadian waters were closely defined ; a boundary was drawn between Canada and the United States from the Lake of the Woods to the Rocky Mountains ; a joint occupation of the disputed Oregon territory was agreed upon; Britain accepted arbitration of American claims for slaves taken during the War of 1812, and the Convention of 1815 was renewed. These were solid achievements, and represent the most important Anglo-American *entente* prior to the Webster–Ashburton Treaty.

The failure of trade negotiations by no means led to shelving that subject during the next few years. Robinson's proposals were sent to the American Government, and they provided matter for Cabinet discussions during the spring of 1819. They objected to the limitation of articles in the West Indian trade, and even more to the duties proposed by Robinson to protect the commerce between Canada and the West Indies.[62] Their views were embodied in counter-proposals, but these were flatly rejected by Castlereagh in September 1819.[63] The Foreign Secretary and Robinson had told the American negotiators in 1818 that, if their talks failed, they would not take offence at any future 'restrictive measures' on America's part,[64] so it came as no surprise when Congress, on 18 May 1820, closed American ports to British ships coming from Canadian harbours, which stopped shipments of West Indian goods to America via Canada.

Thereafter Robinson did not again attempt to solve the trade question by formal negotiations with the United States, but, instead, resorted to unilateral action, which resulted in his Acts of 1822, the most impressive edifices erected by him while at the Board of Trade. Although American economic pressure was a factor in producing these Acts, it was by no means the only one. Two other considerations were in his mind — the success of the Free Port Act of 1805, and the triumph of the revolutionary parties in what are today Argentina, Chile, Colombia, Venezuela, and Mexico.

The Free Port Act of 1805 had been designed to make the ports of Bermuda and Turk's Islands collecting and distributing points for the goods of many nations, filling a function akin to that of Malta in the Mediterranean. Under its terms, the ports of these islands were opened to European vessels, and early in 1817 the same provisions were extended to American ships. One of the purposes of Robinson's legislation was to grant the same privileges to ships of the new Latin American nations.

Robinson evidently believed that an extension of the free port system would greatly increase the volume of New World trade, and that Britain would secure a fair share of the increase. He was further encouraged to modify the navigation system by the rise of Free Trade sentiment in Parliament in and after 1820, and by the petitions of the West Indian colonies, which complained that excessive regulations were stifling their trade, and bringing about economic stagnation.

Thus many factors led Robinson to ask Parliament, on 1 April 1822, for permission to bring in two Bills to modify existing colonial trade legislation. In a very effective speech he established precedents for his request by noting that India, Ceylon, Mauritius, and the Cape of Good Hope had had their trade restrictions removed, and that trade in the whole Far East was comparatively free. The purpose of his first Act, he said, was to establish a large number of free ports in the New World, and to draw up a list of trade items which could be imported into them and exported from them on equal terms by ships of all nations. A few products, however, were to be subject to a small tariff for the benefit of the North American colonies. In return for these concessions, Britain would demand reciprocal privileges for her ships in the ports of participating foreign nations. The second Bill was to remove restrictions on British ships operating between European and West Indian ports; instead of being required to funnel West Indian produce through ports in England, they could be carried directly to the areas of ultimate consumption. Under its terms British ships would also be permitted to pick up enumerated items in European and African ports, and carry them direct to the West Indies. Robinson concluded his address on a high note, such as was to be often heard during the next few years: [65]

> Those who have studied the history of commerce, who have watched its expansive and penetrating qualities, its imperceptible, but almost equally certain tendencies to increase, are well aware that when its chains are once broken, there is no calculating to what an extent it may ultimately be carried. . . . Give it but the light of reason for its guide, and enterprise will never be wanting to convey it to every quarter of the globe.

'We may hope', Rush mused after reading this speech, 'that such sentiments as these will . . . complete the overthrow of that old-fashioned system upon which Mr. Robinson's bill will have made the first serious attack.' [66]

Although Free Trade sentiment had increased in Britain, the interests affected by Robinson's measures quickly submitted their petitions against change. Non-resident West Indian planters feared Americans would become distributors of sugar in Europe; Irish and Scottish sugar-refiners feared American competition in their field; Canadian timber and fishing interests feared America might take over their West Indian markets; British and Canadian corn-producers feared Americans might take over the West Indian grain market; the 'Saints' feared that trade expansion would lead to the smuggling of slaves into the West Indies.[67] Not all of these fears were entirely baseless.

One of the main arguments advanced by the opponents of the Bills was that the United States could not be depended upon to relax its laws in favour of British ships. Robinson took up this matter in a conference with Richard Rush in April, and thereafter the two had a series of meetings on matters connected with the pending legislation. As Rush was unable to assure Robinson that America would relax her laws, Robinson told him he must introduce a clause 'to suspend by an order in council its operation as against all foreign states which did not accede to its enactments'.[68] Rush assented to this, and wrote to his Government: 'as far as his own intentions can prevail, which seem to me to be always liberal, the bill may therefore be expected substantially to embrace them'.[69] During these conferences Robinson stressed to Rush that the duties laid would be 'fair and moderate', and designed not to preclude competition, but to promote it.[70] Robinson's views were reported by Rush to his home Government, and by an Act of 6 May 1822 the President was empowered to open American ports to ships coming from ports in the West Indies which might be opened to American ships. This aided Robinson in his battle with the Opposition in the Commons.

Robinson's two Acts of 24 June 1822 by no means created Free Trade in the Western Hemisphere, but they established a large number of harbours as Free Ports,* and provided a list of

---

* Direct trade was permitted with Jamaica, Grenada, Dominica, Antigua, Trinidad, Tobago, Tortola, New Providence, Crooked Island, St. Vincent, Bermuda, the Bahamas, Barbados, Demerara, Berbice, St. Lucia, St. Kitts, Nevis, Montserrat, Quebec, and ports in New Brunswick, Nova Scotia, and Newfoundland.

items, subject to small tariffs, which might be traded in them. Important items, such as sugar, coffee, and tea, were excluded, but there were a large number of provisions for and products from the port areas which could be traded profitably. Under the new arrangements, British vessels were permitted to pick up certain enumerated items in any port in Europe or Africa, and carry them directly to any of the West Indian and North American ports. The system created a large number of possibilities for expanding British trade, and might be expected to give new life to the ports involved.

The initial reaction of the American Government was favourable. Robinson had not only made the protective duties very moderate, but he had long before hinted that the Americans might circumvent them by laying export duties on the affected items when British ships picked them up in American ports — an idea which Gallatin had relayed to Adams back in 1818.[71] Under these circumstances, the American Government passed an Act of 1 March 1823, which suspended non-intercourse with all ports mentioned in Robinson's acts.

Robinson's term of office at the Board of Trade, and Castlereagh's at the Foreign Office, ended with Anglo-American relations on a friendlier basis than at any time since the Revolution. Richard Rush, who was much more of a radical democrat than Adams, considered that Castlereagh was dangerous to 'all the remaining liberties of England', but at the same time called him the British statesman who was most interested in promoting Anglo-American goodwill.[72] 'We are amongst those who think very favourably of Lord Goderich,' Rush wrote some years later when Robinson had acquired that title. He called Robinson a 'clear-headed, diligent and efficient man of business', and especially noted his 'fine education' and 'admirable temper'. Robinson seemed to Rush like an intellectualized version of Lord Liverpool.[73]

The new era of good feeling ushered in by Castlereagh and Robinson was, unfortunately, not long-lived. Canning and Huskisson, who were in charge of many of the later negotiations, were not regarded as friends of America, as their predecessors had been,[74] but there was more to the breakdown of cordiality than Huskisson's jealousy, or Canning's dislike, of the United States. Many Americans in high places harboured the same sort of 'rancour' toward the British that Huskisson and Canning were accused of cherishing, and, in an atmosphere of mutual distrust, the arrangements of 1822 could not even be maintained, let alone enlarged and expanded.

Robinson and Castlereagh, like Lord Aberdeen at a later date, understood perfectly the importance of dispelling the impression of superciliousness which Americans so keenly resented then in British statesmen, and were therefore able to conduct negotiations in a wholly friendly manner, even when they led to nothing. If this arose from any special affection Robinson had for the United States, evidence for it is lacking; on the other hand, he liked people in general, and the Americans he met were certainly included among them. Possibly he had a special interest in America because his father helped bring that country into existence back in 1783. No British family, indeed, has a stronger claim to being the pioneers in the Anglo-American understanding than the Robinsons, who, in three successive generations were responsible for the Treaty of 1783, the Convention of 1815, and the Treaty of Washington of 1871.

Commercial policy was not Robinson's only concern during his years at the Board of Trade. With the death of his father-in-law, Lord Buckinghamshire, in 1816, all of the unentailed Hobart properties fell to Lady Sarah, and with them the family's political interests. John Quincy Adams noted in May 1817 that Robinson and his friends were very pleased that the Hobart interest had defeated the Coke interest in Norfolk County.[75] Robinson's letters to Lord Liverpool show a considerable interest in practical party politics. In 1818 he asked which side the Prime Minister desired him to take in the Lincolnshire election;[76] and the same year he worked hard to bring in his brother-in-law, Henry Ellis, for Boston.[77] Adding these new interests to his old ones — Hardwicke, Malmesbury, Grantham, and Castlereagh — Robinson appears as a rising statesman with many powerful connections.

G

Certain other attitudes, in addition to his advocacy of Free Trade and Catholic Emancipation, and opposition to slavery, added to Robinson's growing image as a Tory liberal. One of his speeches of May 1821 is worth quoting to illustrate this point : [78]

there never was a time when the direct influence of public opinion was so all-powerful as at the present moment. He did not complain of this change ; he respected the wishes — he respected the feelings of the people, and he trusted he should always endeavour to consult their interests. He did say, however, that it was the duty of the government, in whosoever hands it might be placed, not to consider every particular expression of public opinion as a necessary law by which they were to be guided. If they had not the firmness to look at the right and the wrong side of a question . . . it was impossible that the government could be conducted efficiently or beneficially, with a view to the interests of the people themselves. When he said this, he did not wish it to be supposed that he thought lightly of public opinion. On the contrary, no man respected it more ; and he believed that in this country, above all others, when public opinion was once fixed and deliberately entertained, there did not exist a power, either in the Crown or the parliament to resist its operation.

This last statement is as clear an expression of popular sovereignty as could be desired, but what made Robinson more 'liberal' than many of his Tory colleagues was his interpretation of the bounds of the 'discretionary area' which always lies between popular opinion and the elected representative's sense of duty and of right. For Robinson this area was much smaller than many of his contemporaries considered it to be — in other words, he was more responsive to the 'public mind', or public opinion. Lord John Russell in 1822 called Robinson 'the most liberal member of his majesty's cabinet, one who I believe really takes an interest in the progress of liberty'.[79]

The post-war years were difficult times for one of liberal inclinations, and more especially if that person were a member of Liverpool's strongly conservative Cabinet. One can only understand the adamant attitude of some of its members by recalling that the events of the French Revolution, which did so much to link republicanism and terror, were not long past, and that there were genuine fears that revolt might actually break out in Britain.

Such a possibility was strengthened by the wretched conditions created by the Industrial Revolution, and on top of these — depression.

In such a situation, it was easy to argue that the time was not right for the extension of freedom, and from this argument one could pass with ease to the curtailment of traditional liberties. Robinson, who certainly was convinced of the necessity of extending freedom in many areas, was appointed to a parliamentary committee in early 1817 to investigate the nature and causes of unrest in Britain. The hearings of this committee convinced him that the Spencean movement was subversive, and that the Government needed extra powers to cope with it. Particularly distressing to him were the binding oaths taken by members of the society, which prevented defections, and the coercion allegedly applied to individuals to force them to join it; considerations which led him to speak in favour of the Habeas Corpus suspension Bill in February 1817. 'He was far from wishing to speak against those societies', Robinson added, 'which honestly met for the purpose of seeking by constitutional means, to redress what they regarded as evils in the state . . .' [80] Whether or not the state was justified in resorting to extraordinary measures to cope with the Spenceans depended ultimately upon one's assessment of the nature and seriousness of the threat they presented; and Robinson's speech at this time would place him with those who were convinced a threat existed, but certainly not in the ranks of the reactionaries.

The following year Robinson defended the use of spies and informers by the Government as a means of locating agitators, but his alarm did not reach sizeable proportions until after the 'Peterloo' incident, when he compared conditions in England with those preceding the French Revolution. He declared that the right of assembly had been subjected to 'frightful abuse', and that the object of the agitators had been to force through their demands by weight of numbers.[81] Yet even at this moment when he seemed most perturbed, Robinson wrote to Hardwicke :[82]

We got thru the seditious meetings bill last night, and I hope your Lordships will find it effectual to its object. The like respecting the Press are I think more difficult, and more doubtful as to their efficacy, and I am inclined to think may be less favourably received in the House. It is certainly no easy matter to devise a measure sufficiently strong to meet the evil of the seditious press, without at the same time operating upon that part of the press which is of a very different character. In endeavouring to protect the latter, we may throw away the means of curbing the former.

Robinson was also ready to put some restrictions on aliens in 1822. But, in supporting all of these coercive or repressive acts, he evidently did not think British freedoms were really in danger from them. Speaking on the Aliens Bill, Robinson gave his support 'not for the purpose of arresting the progress of liberty — an object which, if it were even entertained by his majesty's government, it would be impossible, in the present state of knowledge and civilization, to effect.' [83]

In supporting the coercive legislation of the Liverpool Government on these occasions, and in defending sinecure positions on others, Robinson could not wholly escape the reactionary stigma which was attached to it during the post-war years. But no Member achieved such popularity as he did in the Commons, where Members on both sides of the aisle seem to have had a genuine liking for him. Part of this liking was probably due to an absence of fear of an intelligent, modest, and diffident individual who carefully avoided hurting anyone's feelings. Once in 1816 he corrected Alexander Baring and caused the latter some mortification; [84] and on two occasions he crossed swords rather determinedly with Brougham, [85] but these were exceptions. Most of his contacts with the Members were made in the lobbies and not in the arena of partisan debate.

Robinson's reluctance to present himself to the House more often led to rumours of laziness, or indifference. One Member complained in 1821 that Robinson rarely assisted the Government, save for answering an occasional question on trade. [86] The most extended analysis of Robinson's strengths and weaknesses in 1822 was made by his friend, Croker, who was probably a reliable witness: [87]

I shall put out of the question . . . Vansittart and Bragge Bathurst, because they are inefficient for general debate. There remain Robinson and Charles Wynn. Our friends say that Robinson must work, and some even are of opinion that he would, with a little practice, become an excellent and powerful debater . . . if Robinson will boldly throw himself into the stormy current of debate, I think he may possibly be found to swim very well; but I doubt his making the effort. . . . As none of those I have mentioned, except Robinson, are looked to even to play second fiddle, many persons have turned their thoughts to Palmerston, who they think as powerful in intellect as Robinson, and much more to be relied on in readiness and nerve. I agree in the latter part of this opinion, but not in the former. He himself was yesterday expressing great expectations from Robinson's acuteness of mind and great natural eloquence of expression, if he could be induced to take heartily to the work.

This observation is another testimonial to Robinson's superior intellect, which may, in itself, provide a key to his taciturnity and his timidity. Utterly unable to resort to pretences, and always aware of the powerful arguments on his opponent's side of a question, debating was simply not his forte. Speaking — he could do that well — but arguing a question, sometimes against his own private convictions, this he could not do.

Robinson's failure to live up to the expectations of his friends in this area of political life after more than fifteen years in the Commons was the single count against him in the eyes of party leaders. Only once had he really risen to the occasion — in his defences of the British war effort, which he interpreted as vital to the preservation and extension of freedom, and during the dreary post-war years no inspiring theme arose to stir his imagination enough to overcome his natural timidity. One such theme was to arise in 1823, which stirred the artist in Robinson, and called forth his maximum oratorical abilities; then, for a time, his earlier failures were forgotten.

In Kent some sixteen miles from London lay North Cray, the country seat of Lord Londonderry (Castlereagh). To this retreat, with its clear-water river and sweet-briar hedges intermingled with roses, a tired, feverish, Foreign Secretary came in 1822, following the rising of Parliament, to live out his last few days within a cloud of mental confusion. On the morning of 12 August, he committed suicide. 'Temporary derangement incidental to a bad state of bodily health' was the verdict of Robinson, Sir Henry Hardinge, Wellington, and Joseph Planta, men who knew him intimately, and thus were able to make an accurate diagnosis of his condition prior to the terrible tragedy.[88]

On 20 August, Londonderry was interred at Westminster Abbey, and among the bearers of his remains was his protégé and friend, Frederick Robinson. A large gathering of townspeople watched the funeral, not sorrowfully, but curiously, and the ceremony of his passing was dignified by the tears of only a few relatives and his friends. His monumental accomplishments in the field of war-time and post-war diplomacy buried under the reactionary image created for him after the war, the architect of the Concert of Europe was laid away quietly, while the statesmen both in England and abroad pondered the readjustments which would arise from his passing.

George Canning was called in to fill the vacancy at the Foreign Office, but this was merely the first of a series of shifts designed to strengthen the Liverpool Government. Toward the end of 1822 Lord Bathurst, for reasons of health, decided to resign from the Duchy of Lancaster — 'in many respects the most desirable office within the patronage of the Crown', Liverpool called it.[89] The Prime Minister offered the Duchy to Vansittart, who, in turn, would vacate the Exchequer, which would be given to Robinson. After consulting Sidmouth, Vansittart decided to accept, provided that Robinson, and no one else, should succeed him at the Exchequer. Vansittart wrote to Liverpool on 16 December: [90]

I am aware that, though nervous, he is not without ambitions, & I know (tho' not immediately from himself) that he has had the feeling of being superseded, which this offer, whatever may be its result, must of course remove; but I do not think the Exchequer is the object he aims at, for I have occasionally talked with him in a loose way on the subject, & he has always expressed a great dread of the labor & confinement of the situation. . . . much may depend upon the mode of making the overture to Robinson, who will be very apt to be nervous when it is first stated to him . . . Peel's opinion will have great weight with him.

The 'supersession' noted by Vansittart probably referred to the changes of 1821–2, when Peel went to the Home Office, and Charles Wynn, to secure the support of the Grenville faction, was given the Board of Control.

As Robinson had applied to Liverpool for advancement, possibly to the Foreign Office,[91] after the death of Londonderry, the Prime Minister was less uncertain as to his acceptance of the Exchequer than Vansittart, but nevertheless two days later he wrote letters both to Robinson, and Peel, whom, by favourable coincidence, he was then visiting. The letter to Peel merely stated that he hoped 'no nervousness nor apprehension of his own supposed Deficiency' would prevent Robinson from accepting the position.[92] To Robinson he wrote : [93]

> I will confess to you that I consider this arrangement as important, not only as regards yourself, but on many other views, particularly as it will effect a purpose, which our poor friend Londonderry had very much at heart, & which Canning must for many reasons strongly anticipate, the Promotion of Huskisson in a way which will be satisfactory to all his Friends, as well as to every branch of our Political connection.

Liverpool then enjoined secrecy, as the changes had not yet been discussed with the King. No hands were safer in which to entrust a secret. Robinson did not even tell his mother about it for a full month ! [94]

The Chancellorship brought with it a £5,300 annual income, a house, and a small amount of patronage, concrete attractions which Robinson was not one to overlook.[95] No offer, indeed, was more readily accepted. 'I cannot hesitate a moment in accepting the offer . . .', Robinson replied, 'and I entirely approve the arrangement which you propose with respect to Huskisson.' [96] The Exchequer was regarded as a particularly 'arduous' office, and one in which Huskisson admitted 'I should not be able to survive a second Session'.[97] There was, indeed, amazement both among Robinson's friends and his few enemies, such as the Arbuthnots, that he had displayed no nervous hesitation whatsoever before accepting.

Although it would seem that appointment to the Exchequer

would be a natural step upward from the Board of Trade, this reason was not among those offered by contemporaries for Robinson's promotion, which, like the others, was regarded in a narrowly political light. Liverpool said it fulfilled Londonderry's wishes, which meant that it would please the Londonderry faction, and it would also please Vansittart, the man who had to make way. The King, on being informed of the promotion, noted that it would give 'great satisfaction to the country gentlemen'.[98] Sidmouth obviously gave his blessing, and so did Bathurst, while Lord Eldon merely stated that the arrangements were what one would have guessed they would be.[99] Peel probably strongly urged Robinson to accept.

George Canning may have been one of the original promoters of the whole system of arrangements.[100] But there was a notable lack of enthusiasm for Robinson at this time among the Grenville group. Wynn regarded him as simply an improvement over his predecessor, which was not high praise, considering Vansittart's unpopularity.[101] William Henry Fremantle did not consider Robinson the 'fittest man' for the job, but, like Wynn, noted that he was very popular in the Commons.[102] Some other contemporary statesmen were more critical. Lord Colchester wrote that 'nobody' thought Robinson could be a successful Chancellor,[103] and Bootle Wilbraham wished someone with 'less general benevolence' had secured the job.[104]

It is clear from these reactions to his appointment that Robinson was popular, and that most statesmen wished him well, but that he had still not won the confidence of his contemporaries. Only his faithful old friend, Charles Yorke, stated that the '*sound* part of the Publick', rather than Robinson, was to be congratulated on the appointment.[105] In most minds there was doubt — would he sink or swim, survive or perish? Not even Yorke caught a glimmer of the startling success Robinson was to achieve at the Exchequer.

While Liverpool and the King considered Robinson's elevation a tribute to Londonderry's memory, the members of the former Foreign Secretary's political faction were by no means all well satisfied with the new political arrangements. The identity of many of the members of the political clique can be established from the private correspondence of this period, and it included : the 3rd Earl of Clanwilliam, once Castlereagh's private secretary ; the 1st Viscount Clancarty, often associated with Castlereagh in diplomatic matters ; Joseph Planta, also a former secretary to Castlereagh ; Sir Henry Halford, the King's physician ; the 2nd Earl of Mount Edgcumbe, who had also married into the Buckinghamshire family ; the Earl of Ancram, a 'connection' of Castlereagh's wife ; and Charles Stewart's friends, Lord Burghersh of the Westmorland family, Sir Henry Hardinge, a career soldier now serving in Parliament ; and finally, the new Lord and Lady Londonderry, who, with an income estimated at £80,000, could afford to back as many as ten candidates at a general election.[106]

Lord Londonderry, formerly Charles Stewart, and his brother's widow were particularly affronted at the appointment of Canning to the Foreign Secretaryship, even though its late incumbent had long since given up his old feud with Canning. For a time in 1822 they actually hoped to create a party of their own, but the project was quickly given up. Londonderry wrote his sister-in-law in December : [107]

I have considered a great deal the Purport of Your last letter with regard to a Third Party. Had those persons who ow'd so much to our Sainted Angel relinquished Office on Canning's app't, and shew'd a disinclination to have him as Their Leader, a party might have been form'd and in time have become strong. But with Fredk. Robinson, Clancarty, Halford actually in office with the Govt., and with all our other connections as well as (I believe) Yours, the Mt. Edgecumbes, Ancram etc. etc. more inclined to support the ministers than even to stay away, I hardly see the possibility of such an Idea as you mention being carried into effect.

He was particularly bitter about Robinson's and Clancarty's decisions to stay on.

Some of the group were unwilling to accept Robinson's appointment as a settlement of Liverpool's political obligations to them. Sir Henry Hardinge took his case to Robinson late in January ;[108] in 1823 Londonderry sought a £2,000 pension, then the command of the Londonderry militia, and later a position at court — but all were refused to him. Thereafter he increasingly identified himself with the Duke of Wellington, an obvious leader for one of his military background, but his chief purpose in political life thereafter was to defend the name and ideas of the half-brother whom he so much admired.

The Cabinet changes of 1822–3 were not wholly satisfactory to some others who were intimately involved in them. One of these was 'that pretty, neat-dressed, smooth-faced, soft-spoken gentleman William Huskisson', as Cobbett once described him.[109] Twelve years the senior of Robinson, an intimate associate of Canning, Huskisson was, according to his biographer, a member of the 'Inner Cabinet' at Fife House which advised Liverpool on financial matters.[110] If he were, indeed, a member of such a cabinet, its leader showed very little interest in bringing him into the Government, and in 1821 had passed him over in favour of Charles Wynn.

In 1822 Liverpool and the King both opposed enlarging the Cabinet with the inclusion of Huskisson, and Robinson's offices were tendered to him without this further mark of distinction. 'I can tell the world why I do not put myself into competition with Robinson to succeed Vansittart,' Huskisson wrote to Canning, 'but they must be left to guess . . . why the President of the Board of Trade is excluded in my person from a Cabinet . . .'[111] At first Huskisson rejected the offer, but was at length persuaded by Canning to accept it with a promise that his elevation to Cabinet rank would not be long delayed.

Even more wroth than Huskisson at the arrangements was Thomas Wallace, Robinson's former assistant at the Board of Trade. His chief 'protector' at the time was apparently Lord Melville, the First Lord of the Admiralty, but a much less influential member of the Government than Canning. During the summer of 1822 Wallace told Robinson he expected to become President of the Board of Trade, if Robinson gave up that position, and requested that Robinson present his case to the Government. Although Robinson did so, he assured Liverpool that Wallace's claims were inferior to Huskisson's, and thus cast his own veto against Wallace.[112] If, as has been sometimes claimed, Robinson was indebted to Wallace for his Free Trade programme, he was singularly ungrateful in his treatment of Wallace at this time, but, from what we know of Robinson's character, this was not his way of behaving. In presenting Wallace's claims, Robinson mentioned 'his services as Chairman of the Foreign Trade Commission, and as head of the committee of enquiry', but did not stress any special talents Wallace had for handling trade problems.

When the bad news was broken to Wallace, no amount of soothing could close the wound. Early in 1823, he wrote to Liverpool: [113]

Had Mr. Huskisson possessed any peculiar aptitude for the situation, had any mark'd accession of political weight to the Government been obtained by his appointment, I should have acquiesced with cheerfulness . . . but neither of these can be fairly assigned, when nothing but personal consideration for the individual is even brought forward, I cannot but feel that justice has *not* been done me in the preference given. It is not the appointment to the Treasurership of the Navy to which I am now disposed to offer the least objection — it is to placing him in a position of *my direct superior* at the Board of Trade . . .

Wallace, rather than serve under Huskisson, resigned, and was out of the Government until he returned as Master of the Mint. His supersession at this time probably was a mistake, for it gave the office to an individual inexperienced in the tariff manipulations, and one who lacked background knowledge of the Anglo-American trade negotiations. In both areas, Wallace might well have served better than Huskisson, who owed his appointment to his faithfulness to Canning.

Robinson had little experience with the problems of national finance before he took over the Exchequer in 1823. Although he had been a Lord of the Treasury, and had served on the finance committee of 1819, which had studied the currency situation, down to the time of his promotion he had rarely addressed the House on financial affairs. On one occasion, in 1821, he deprecated any attempt to abrogate the bank payments of 1819, and appeared in the role — in today's terms — of a 'sound money man'.

He was by no means alone in that role, for the nation had officially adopted it in the Act of 1819, which placed the country firmly on the gold standard. This Act had been deflationary in its effect, the opposite of the remedies used in the twentieth century to fight business depressions, but the best statistics now available indicate that the bottom of the economic cycle was reached in 1819, after which there was a gradual upswing until a peak was reached in 1825. Robinson was therefore fortunate in taking office in the middle of the climb, while his predecessor, poor Vansittart, had waded through the business troughs of 1816 and 1819.

The Act of 1819 was counteracted by certain inflationary measures taken by the Government, possibly at the urging of Castlereagh who seems to have been an advocate of cheap money.[114] In 1822 it arranged with the Bank of England an enormously complex transaction familiarly known as the 'Dead Weight', under which the Bank undertook to pay pensions of armed forces personnel in return for a set annuity from the Government. At the time everyone traced the scheme to Vansittart, but a note in Mrs. Arbuthnot's journal indicates that Castlereagh was its real father.[115] The same year the Government asked the Bank to purchase the five per cent navy stock from holders who had refused to convert it into stock with four per cent interest, and also introduced a plan for a sizeable public works programme. They also decided to permit the country banks to issue notes of less than £5 beyond the deadline of 1825, which had been fixed in 1819. The Dead Weight arrangement gave temporary relief to the National Exchequer; reconversion of the navy stock made that type of investment less attractive, and encouraged the investment of capital in the private sector of the economy; the public works programme put money into circulation, and the revision of the deadline encouraged the issue of small notes by the country banks. The effects of these inflationary measures were being felt when Robinson took office.

The budgetary situation in 1823 still bore strong reminders of the long and exhausting war. Pitt had at first financed the war by short-term loans, and the National Debt, only £239,000,000 in 1793, had grown to £846,000,000 in 1816, and interest charges accounted for half of the annual expenditure. As the war lengthened, Pitt and his successors had had recourse to a huge variety of excise taxes, and the Income Tax as well. Although the Income Tax had been abolished in the post-war years, the excise taxes remained as a fairly important source of national income.

It was Robinson's task to maintain and possibly increase the Government's income through a manipulation of the taxes and tariffs then in force. Whether or not he had help in constructing his first budget, as some authorities assume,[116] we can glean from his speeches the general principles upon which Robinson acted while Chancellor of the Exchequer. He believed in what some economists today call the 'filter down' theory of tax relief — that tax benefits granted to the upper classes would stimulate business activity, expansion, and spending, and thus help general prosperity. Taxes which raised the prices of British goods to the point of injuring their competitive position were bad taxes; so, too, were taxes with high collection costs, or which fluctuated from year to year to the point of unpredictability. Taxes or tariffs which encouraged smuggling were also bad taxes. He seems also to have understood thoroughly, both in the fields of tax and tariff revision, that there were certain levels of such charges which brought maximum income to the Treasury, and that too-high taxes or tariffs were self-defeating. Probably none of these principles or ideas originated with Robinson, some, in fact, date to Adam Smith, but he made them his own, and put them into effect.

Preparing his speech on the financial situation must have been a considerable ordeal for Robinson, who, novice that he was in the field of finance, had to face David Ricardo, John Maberly, Edward Ellice, and Joseph Hume, experts who had made life miserable for Vansittart. Modest, distrusting his own abilities, and probably afraid of appearing incompetent, the anticipation of that great and fearful moment may have made Robinson ill. At any rate, late in January a newspaper noted that he was again absent from a Cabinet session because of 'severe indisposition'.[117]

Robinson's hour — probably the finest in his career — came on 21 February 1823, when he arose before the Committee of Ways and Means to explain the financial situation of the country. He explained very lucidly the anticipated income and expenditure for the coming year, and the probable surplus to be anticipated; but, before revealing the secret of who would be benefited by the disposal of this surplus, he described Britain's enlarging trade opportunities in a sentence of considerable length: [118]

If we look to the extensive and populous countries now opening to British commerce in almost every quarter of the globe; — if we consider the facilities which commerce in general has derived from the liberal system of policy which this country has recently adopted, by sweeping away the useless lumber of antiquated prejudices and restrictions; if we advert to the growing disposition of other countries to follow our example and to benefit by our experience; — if we admit to be true in theory, that no trade can be permanently beneficial to one party unless it is equally so to the other; — and if we find that in fact, foreign demand for our manufactures has kept pace with our consumption of the produce of other states, and that in all the great branches of our industry we compete successfully with all our rivals, who can say I expect too much, when I anticipate a great and gradual increase (not the less valuable because it is gradual) in all those items which constitute our revenue of customs.

While his audience waited to hear the good news, Robinson prolonged the suspense a little longer, and expressed the sentiments which were to give him his new nickname of 'Prosperity Robinson'.[119]

Looking forward, then, to the result of this state of things, as connected with our commercial interests, I may confidently say, 'The wide, unbounded prospect lies before me' without being compelled to add, with the poet, that 'shadows, clouds and darkness rest upon it.' We have seen the opening of a brilliant dawn, and we may anticipate without hesitation the steady and glowing splendor of a meridian sky.

Although Robinson's verse might often read like doggerel, he was perhaps the only statesman of the century to turn an economic report into literature.

The Dead Weight arrangement had helped Robinson to create a 'surplus' of £7,147,214, but £5,000,000 of this had to go into the Sinking Fund — a Tory fiscal manipulation related to the National Debt and he thus had only a little more than £2,000,000 for tax reductions. All of the assessed taxes in Ireland were removed, and a large number of those in England were also wiped away.* Robinson frankly admitted that his reductions were beneficial chiefly to agriculture, the only area of the economy still in the doldrums, but noted further that 'no diminution of taxes that gives to the more wealthy increased means of employing those who are poorer, can fail of being beneficial to the latter'.[120] So it was primarily a rich man's budget, especially thoughtful of estate owners, and only a few savings, such as the diminution of the window tax, helped the tradesmen.

The new Chancellor, his message delivered, sat down 'amidst loud cheers'. It was more than a budget speech. It was a striking personal triumph and vindication of Robinson as a parliamentary figure. John Maberly, who sometimes spoke for the distilling interests, would have desired more tax-cutting, and less attention to reducing the Debt, but others were warm in their praise. Alexander Baring, of the great banking family, thought 'it impossible for anyone to have given an explanation more clear or satisfactory'.[121] David Ricardo, whose death that year was to prevent his hearing Robinson's later budgets, remarked that 'the science of political economy had never before had so able an expositor as it had now found in that House. He thought that there never yet had been in that House a Minister filling the situation which was held by the right hon. gentleman, who had in that capacity delivered sentiments so candid, so wise and so excellent.'[122] Praise, indeed, when one recalls that both Pitt and Perceval had held that position during his lifetime. Even Joseph Hume was complimentary.[123]

This favourable reception encouraged Robinson to speak more often during the session, and his reputation grew apace. 'Robinson

---

* These included taxes on windows, male servants, wheeled vehicles, occasional house servants, occasional gardners, certain ponies and mules, horses and mules engaged in agriculture and trade, on clerks and shopmen of traders, and some other items of a similar nature.

has risen during the session in an extraordinary degree,' the Radical, Hobhouse, noted in his diary. 'His manner of speaking is fervid and displays an appearance of manly candour, whch. predisposes his auditors in his favour.' [124] Fremantle wrote to Buckingham : 'The complete ascendency which both Robinson and Peel have acquired over him [Canning] in the House of Commons, but more particularly the former, must weaken his means of playing us a trick. . . .' [125] 'The King spoke highly of Mr. Robinson,' the hostile Mrs. Arbuthnot recorded in her journal, 'but said Peel *had not heart enough for him* ! ! !' [126] When Robinson gave his year-end summary, even Maberly had come over to his side, and declared he had 'never heard such an open, fair, or candid statement'.[127]

To make the golden year 1823 even better, corn prices began to fluctuate upward, and by the end of it all segments of the British economy were in a flourishing condition. The loss Robinson had expected from the cut in excise taxes proved excessive, and increasing business activity brought enlarged revenues from the stamp tax and the Customs. The Treasury also received a £2,200,000 'Godsend', as Robinson later called it — the repayment in part of a British loan to Austria which had been practically written off as a loss. Austria paid this loan in stocks, which the British Government did not want, but the banking firms of Messrs. Reid, Rothschild, Baring & Company bought up the stocks at a discount and paid the Government in cash. Quickly and miraculously the stocks rose to par value following the transaction, which gave the bankers a tidy profit, and everyone was happy as a result of it.

Robinson therefore had a nice surplus at his disposal early in 1824. To secure even more, he proposed to convert Government 4 per cent bonds to bonds bearing $3\frac{1}{2}$ per cent interest, which would save the Treasury £375,000 annually, and to remove the bounties from whale fishing and the export of Irish linen, which would save £50,000 and £100,000 respectively. The first of these operations, like the reconversion of the 5 per cent bonds in 1822, tended to channel investment capital into private enterprise, and this money helped stimulate the boom already in progress.

On 23 February 1824 Robinson delivered his second great financial address to the Commons. No further reductions in direct taxation were part of the new budget. 'It is my intention', he declared, 'to propose that we should make use of the surplus which has accrued, and which will accrue, as a means of commencing a system of alteration in the fiscal and commercial regulations of this country.' [128] Reaching a higher note, he explained : 'It is time to cut the cords which tie down commerce to the earth, that she may spring aloft, unconfined and unrestricted, and shower her blessings on every part of the world.' [129] This, then, was his first Free Trade budget, but Free Trade in his time did not mean a complete removal of trade barriers, but an ending of prohibitive tariffs.

Continuing, Robinson pleased the West Indian interest by reducing the tariff on rum to that on other British spirits. The Aldermen of London were probably happy to learn that the restrictions on the shipping of inland coal to London were to be eased, and that the duties on sea-borne coal would be reduced. The wool interest, however, listened with mixed emotions to his plan to abolish the tariff on foreign wool, and to permit the free exportation of British wool. Robinson estimated that these changes would cost the Treasury £500,000.

His proposals affecting the silk industry cost just about as much. Some of Robinson's restrained humour was displayed during his discussion of his silk plans. Only last year, he noted, a Member of the Commons had 'produced his Bandana handkerchief, even in this place, and having triumphantly unfurled the standard of smuggling, blew his nose in it'. Robinson continued : [130]

Everyone who has been on the coast and has watched the arrival of vessels must have frequently observed females step out of them, apparently in a state of the most uncomfortable corpulency, who in time however, and without surgical aid, were safely delivered of their burthens, and returned to the natural slimness and grace of their own figures.

To help eliminate such smuggling, Robinson proposed that the prohibitory laws on foreign silk be replaced by a 30 per cent

H

ad valorem duty on most silk goods. He also proposed that the duties on East Indian, Chinese, and Italian raw silk be cut so that those areas might acquire exchange with which to buy British goods.

Unlike the proposals of 1823, those of 1824 were pointed primarily at increasing trade, so much so that a disgusted representative of the agricultural interest complained his group were 'neglected by gentlemen who were led away by their love of spinning jennies'.[131] But some other provisions of the budget found more favour on the Tory side of the House — to earmark £500,000 for the building of churches, £150,000 for the repair of Windsor Castle, and an additional sum to found a National Gallery. All of these, not inappropriately, were to be paid for from the 'Godsend' received from Austria.

Once again Robinson scored a triumph, and resumed his seat amid loud cheers. A newspaper the following day called his speech 'one of the most luminous and gratifying financial statements it was ever, perhaps, the lot of a Minister to submit'.[132] Robinson's theme — 'the country is in a state of unexampled prosperity' — could not be denied, and the success of his previous financial changes seemed to point to a dazzling future. But in 1824 Robinson brought Free Trade out of the realm of theory, and its reduction to practice gave rise to complaints from those directly or indirectly affected.

In March the Barings presented petitions against the admission of foreign silks, and Robinson, always a compromising individual, postponed the date of the tariff reductions from 5 January to 5 July 1826; but when Fowell Buxton presented a petition from the parishioners of Bethnal Green begging that their 'day of destruction' be advanced again to 1829, he refused to agree. With the support of the manufacturers of Manchester and Derby, Robinson was able to stand firm. A Free Trader, Agar Ellis, warned Robinson that the 'slightest check' to the coarse-linen trade would be fatal to the infant industries of Tipperary, and, in response to his pleas, Robinson agreed to repeal the linen bounties at the rate of 20 per cent a year, beginning in 1825. This concession was exclusively for the benefit of Southern Ireland, for the North Ireland manufacturers, as well as those of Scotland, were prepared to give up the linen bounties immediately.

Some manufacturers feared that the exportation of long wool, a particularly British product, would be too much of a boon to their German competitors, but Robinson was able to carry this part of his plan with the support of the yarn exporters. His plans for coal placed Robinson in the position of umpire between the 'inland' coal suppliers of Staffordshire, who brought their coal to London via the Grand Junction and Paddington Canals, and the 'northern operators' of the Tyne and Wear River region, who shipped their coal by sea and the Thames to the capital. The inland suppliers were restricted to shipments of 50,000 tons annually, and paid heavy freight charges; the northern operators were charged an extra duty at London, which they complained violated the principle of equal taxation. Robinson proposed to lower certain inland duties so that the inland operators could actually ship 50,000 tons to London and to equalize the coal duty at the port of London with the coal duties at other ports — this for the benefit of the northern operators. His plan was carried with the cordial support of the London Members, whose constituents could see warmer winters in prospect.

During this period of readjustments of the 1824 budget two letters are available which indicate how the decisions on such matters were reached during these years. Due to Huskisson's illness in March, he exchanged letters with Robinson on current concerns. Huskisson had apparently done a good deal of negotiating with the silk manufacturers, and Charles Grant, who was to succeed Huskisson at the Board of Trade, was working on a fishing bounty Bill. But it was Robinson who was formulating the proposals, and Huskisson merely gave his reaction to them; for example, with respect to Robinson's plan for hemp, Huskisson commented: 'I like your proposal very well.' [133] With regard to wool, Huskisson observed: 'I think you have decided in the best manner making the export and import duties two pence.' Sweeping conclusions can hardly be based on such meagre evidence, but these documentary proofs of Robinson's control of financial and trade matters must be given due weight in deciding

which of them should be considered as the father of the Free
Trade movement of the period.

It was a highly successful session for Robinson. The duties on
rum, coals, wool, and silk were all reduced, and the Union Duties
were repealed as a gesture of goodwill to Ireland. The law stamp
tax was also reduced. For these boons, Robinson, following his
speech of 7 May 1824, received the thanks of the Free Traders.[134]
Many in the Opposition were more than satisfied with the new
Tory Chancellor. John Cam Hobhouse, a Radical, declared that
Robinson had 'enlightened even his political enemies by some of
the sound views of commercial policy he had opened'.[135] The
ageing Whig leader, George Tierney, contrasted Robinson's
brilliant administration with the work of his predecessor, and it
was on this occasion that the latter refused the compliment at
the expense of his friend, who, he said, had been 'strongly impressed with the soundness of the principles of free trade', but
had been unable to put them into effect.[136]

Although Robinson might deny that his predecessors were
hostile toward revisions of the trading system, the public, as
always, sought to personify the new system in his period. 'I
should have liked to see the faces of your clerks', the 2nd Earl
of Minto wrote to Robinson, 'who had imbibed their liquors of
wisdom in the school of George Rose & Vansittart when you first
ventured to broach your abominable heresies.'[137] Free Trade
was momentarily triumphant, and its prophet, Robinson, was
supported on a wave of prosperity.

Robinson's financial proposals of 1825 were a continuation and
combination of those he had submitted during the previous two
years. Work on them evidently went on over a considerable
period of time, for the reduction of the hemp duty, which was
projected in 1825, was one of the subjects Robinson mentioned
to Huskisson in his letter of March 1824. Wholesale tariff reductions, which formed an important part of the financial scheme of
this year, were probably the work of Huskisson almost exclusively.

The constantly strengthening boom rushed to its peak in 1825
with such force that many of Robinson's calculations regarding
tax receipts proved much too conservative. He had anticipated

a surplus of £1,050,000 at the end of 1824 but, despite tax reductions of £630,000 more than he had expected that year, the increased income from the Customs and Excise taxes not only cancelled out this loss, but gave him a surplus of £1,437,744.

Under these circumstances one can understand why Robinson should have stated, as a beginning to his financial address of 28 February 1825, that Britain's prosperity had 'nothing hollow in its foundation, artificial in its superstructure, or flimsy in its good result'. Then he went on to philosophize on the subject of the expanding nature of human wants : [138]

there is a principle in the constitution of social man which leads nations to open their arms to each other, and to establish new and closer connexions, by ministering to mutual convenience ; a principle which creates new wants, stimulates new desires, seeks for new enjoyments, and, by the beneficence of Providence, contributes to the general happiness of mankind. This principle may, it is true, be impeded by war and its calamities ; it may be diverted by accident from its natural channel ; it may be counteracted (as we well know in this country) by the improvidence of mistaken legislation ; but it is always alive, always in motion, and has a perpetual tendency to go forward ; and when we reflect upon the facility which is given to its operation by the recent discoveries of modern science, and by the magical energies of the steam-engine, who can doubt that its expansion is progressive, and its effect permanent.

Acting on this belief, Robinson tried to predict the surpluses for 1825, 1826, and 1827, a very rash endeavour, especially in those times.

Much of the surplus in hand had been consumed by an arbitration award the Russian Tsar had made in favour of the United States, and by an increased budget for the army, which rarely in any country misses an opportunity to exploit moments of prosperity. Cutting the tariffs on iron and hemp, and lowering the wine duties took up part of the remainder, and so did the equalization of taxes on Scotch, Irish and English spirits, which was expected to end smuggling and to permit devotees of Scotch whisky to drink with good conscience. A cut from 30*s*. to 15*s*. of the tax on cider was proposed, and when a Member shouted out '10*s*.', Robinson replied : 'Well, sir, I will not squabble about 5s.; let it be 10s.' He then resumed his attack on the assessed taxes, the House Tax and the Window Tax.* The last two projects were notable concessions to the lower income groups.

For the third successive year Robinson scored a triumph. Some would have wished to dispose of the surplus in a different manner, others desired deeper cuts in the assessed taxes, but the overwhelming majority would have agreed with an editorial in the *Morning Chronicle*, which observed : [139]

> It has, indeed, been objected to the Chancellor of the Exchequer that his principles are excellent, but that his practice is not always in accordance with his principles . . . we admit the justice of the objection. But when we consider that the principles of Mr. Robinson are his own, but that he is obliged, in many cases, to square his practice with the principles of others, we are more disposed to thank him for the good he does than to find fault with him for the good he does not do. When he began his career, he was considerably in advance of the greatest part of the House . . ., and he had no doubt a very difficult task in extorting assent from minds beset with the most opaque prejudices, to a system beyond their comprehension . . . Mr. Robinson therefore was under the necessity of demonstrating to men unable to comprehend his principles, by a gradual reduction to practice, that they would not be productive of ruin to the country.

The editor in this case probably exaggerated if he stressed Robinson's difficulties in winning over the Cabinet, but underestimated them in the areas of budget balancing and formulating a programme which would receive wide support in the Commons.

Robinson had promised in his address that William Huskisson would shortly introduce a plan for a general reduction of prohibitory tariffs, and the latter made his statement on 25 March. Lest the House think he was poaching on Robinson's preserve, he assured them : [140]

---

* Robinson repealed the assessed taxes on four-wheeled carriages drawn by one pony, and those on occasional waiters, coachmakers' licences, carriages sold by commission, mules in mining districts, husbandry labourers who sometimes performed domestic services, and carts. All houses rated under £10 were exempted from the House Tax ; all houses with fewer than seven windows were exempted from the Window Tax.

He [Robinson], I am sure, will allow me to consider myself, however humble, as a fellow-labourer with him in the same vineyard. Whilst I am pruning away the useless and unsound branches, which will bear at best, but a scanty and bad crop, my object is to draw forth new and vigorous shoots, likely to afford better and more abundant fruit ; the harvest of which, I trust, it will be his lot hereafter to present, to his applauding country, in the shape of further relief from taxation.

Huskisson thus informed the House that, although a part of Robinson's general plan, the tariffs adjustments were his own. The rates he proposed ranged between 30 per cent and 10 per cent, rape seed alone being admitted free of duty.

By 1825 Robinson's comprehensive economic programme had been completed. A large number of assessed taxes, the heritage in many cases of the Napoleonic Wars, had been wiped away ; protective tariffs had replaced prohibitive duties, which, by permitting the sale of foreign goods in Britain, provided exchange for the exporting countries to purchase British manufactured goods. The burdens on both the upper and lower classes had been to some extent lightened, some of the causes of smuggling had been removed, and he established a new efficiency and economy in tax collections. Whether Robinson in 1825 — as he insisted in 1846 — planned to take the next long stride and throw out the protective duties in favour of Free Trade can, in the absence of evidence, be neither proved nor disproved. Probably he thought about it, but the budgetary realities of the moment would have been an insuperable obstacle to such a plan.

These three years, a unit in Robinson's life, formed the public image of 'Prosperity Robinson'. Some later used the term in a derogatory fashion, but it perhaps provides the key to another of Robinson's contributions to British economic history. Most economists today will agree that optimistic leadership helps generate prosperity, while pessimism within the business community will intensify and lengthen depressions. Robinson did not have consciously to act a part. His cheerful optimism sprang from a strong faith in the soundness of the British economic system, and this faith, imparted to others, undoubtedly played its part in the economic buoyancy of these years.

———◆———

The Broken Idol

'FRED ROBINSON is not a bit spoiled by his popularity & success,' a relative wrote in 1825.[1] All sources confirm this observation — the Robinson of the golden years 1823–5 was still the modest, cheerful, unassuming, and obliging individual that he had always been, and one who listened patiently to the requests of the veritable flood of Members who visited his home during the sessions.[2] Sir Thomas Baring wanted a pension for John McAdam, the road engineer;[3] Lord Palmerston sought aid for a steamship inventor, who was '*aground*' even though his ship was 'afloat'.[4] Robinson was always ready to consider the merits of deserving individuals, and to respond sympathetically.

No one received more concentrated attention than the King — and the King was rarely without some project in mind. In 1823 Robinson provided funds for the purchase of a property at Kew;[5] the following year he arranged for appropriations to repair Windsor Castle, Buckingham Palace, and Carlton House. In his zeal to be of service to the Royal Family, Robinson arranged to lease certain mines in Nova Scotia to the Duke of York in 1825, but his failure to advise the King of the project at an earlier stage in its development brought royal displeasure, rather than gratitude.[6] This experience probably made him more cautious in his future relations with the monarch.

Robinson's sense of humour and personal idiosyncrasies often provided amusement to his friends. 'I rather flatter myself (as Robinson would say),' Peel had written back in 1815;[7] and in 1826 Palmerston wrote: 'Well, Heavens & earth, as Robinson would say. . . .' [8] Croker related an incident which occurred in 1826 as follows : [9]

Everyone knows the story of a gentleman's asking Lord North who 'that frightful woman was?' and his lordship's answering, that is my wife. The other, to repair the blunder, said I do not mean *her*, but that monster next to her. 'Oh!' said Lord North, 'that monster is my daughter.' With this story Fred. Robinson, in his usual absent enthusiastic way, was one day entertaining a lady whom he sat next to at dinner, and lo! the lady was Lady Charlotte Lindsay — the monster in question.

Robinson himself often related how he one day sat beside Lord Lyndhurst in Chancery Court while two lawyers argued their cases, and, before leaving, whispered to Lyndhurst : 'Well, I don't know how the case may be decided ; but, in my opinion, Mr. Hart has so completely answered Mr. Bell that he has not a leg to stand on.' Lyndhurst whispered in reply : 'I am sorry I cannot agree with you, for — they are both on the same side.' [10] Only those who thought about the story an extra moment would realize that it was something more than a joke on Robinson, but his cheery, guileless manner evidently gave him the leading role in many a humorous anecdote of the period. These qualities of his personality also made him the recipient of numerous sobriquets. One of the most famous of these — 'Goody' — was apparently in use as early as 1821,[11] long before it could form an alliteration with his title.

Despite his popularity, Robinson had to pay the price of all successful men who rise to the top of their profession — some contemporaries, for reasons of envy, jealousy, or difference of opinion on specific issues, were bound to become critical. At the outset in 1823 the members of the Cabinet were a harmonious group, and, according to the Duke of Wellington, each thought for himself, and no attempt was made to form a faction within it.[12] This harmony, however, was not long-lived. With a great national hero of more conservative opinions on one side, and a brilliant, experienced statesman like Canning with more liberal opinions on the other, the lesser members gradually found themselves pulled in one direction or the other.

Robinson never entered into a close relationship with Canning, yet he could not escape his influence. At a gathering in 1823, Canning chose Robinson rather than Huskisson, who was also present, to be his partner in the game of 'Twenty Questions', which he enjoyed very much.[13] Whether this was a recognition of Robinson's intelligence, or merely a trivial incident in a continuing campaign to win over Robinson, we cannot even guess. In July of the following year, one observer noted that Robinson 'moves with Canning',[14] which might indicate that Canning's efforts had been to some extent successful. The same year Wellington was reported by the hostile Arbuthnot to have called Robinson 'a shallow fellow'.[15] Whether or not any individual willed it, the split in the Cabinet was already beginning to take place, and the Cabinet meetings of 1824 were less harmonious than those of the preceding year.[16]

The basic issue dividing the two sections of the Cabinet was the Catholic Question, which, in 1825, with the formation of Daniel O'Connell's National Association, became of extreme urgency. When Henry Goulburn introduced a measure to curb the activities of the Association, Robinson spoke and voted for it, and the other members of the 'Catholic' group in the Cabinet also gave it their support; but this show of unity was short-lived, and the later debates of that year found the members of the Cabinet speaking and voting against each other. Robinson tried desperately to play the role of peace-maker, and evidently believed that the support of the Catholic clergy was necessary if Ireland were to be restored to tranquillity. He therefore made some sort of agreement, without the prior approval of either the Cabinet or the King, to pay the Catholic priesthood. Wellington was seriously considering such a move himself, and Peel was later to adopt such a device, but Robinson's adopting the plan on his own caused much consternation. Liverpool told him that an attempt to pay the priesthood would result in his impeachment,[17] and later in the year Wellington wrote that Robinson's plan would have brought the King and the Commons into collision, and broken up the Government.[18] Even without this divisive issue being raised, it appeared that the Cabinet might be dissolved in 1825.

Liverpool, Peel, and Canning all threatened to resign at one time or another, and Robinson announced in May that he would withdraw from the Government, if his doing so would further the cause of Catholic Emancipation.[19]

Toward the end of the session the 'Protestant' members of the Cabinet were in favour of a dissolution, hoping that the activities of O'Connell's Association, which were resented in England, might strengthen their voice in the Commons. Canning, of course, opposed this, for fear that a dissolution might weaken the Emancipation forces. Robinson, according to Croker, was 'of both opinions' — in other words, he attempted to occupy a middle ground which was indeed narrow, if it existed at all.[20] In the end, Canning promised to restrain the Emancipation group during the next session, if the dissolution project were given up,[21] and, as it turned out, this proved an easier task than might have been expected. That autumn, public attention was abruptly diverted to an even more pressing concern, and it was one in which Robinson was intimately involved.

After the resumption of gold payments in 1821 Great Britain was using gold, or paper backed by gold, as its circulating medium. Although it managed the National Debt, the Bank of England was a private firm in competition with other banks, and so long as its charter was not coming up for renewal, it could accept or reject the advice of the Government with respect to its policies, or not consult the Government at all. As the source of the gold reserve for the other banks, it was the main prop for commercial credit in England, and its ability to pay gold on demand was absolutely necessary for the functioning of the whole credit system.

As the Bank of England did not open branches in the areas outside London, local credit was supplied by country banks. Such banks rarely kept much gold on hand, and, when they needed such currency, they would rediscount their paper through London banks, which would act as their agents with the Bank of England. Thus the Bank of England was subject to calls upon its gold supply at times and for amounts which could not be predetermined, and if, for any reason, the Bank could not respond to their requests, the country banks would collapse.

Under normal conditions the Bank could provide gold as requested, but the period between 1823 and 1825 was not a normal one. There was a tremendous investment boom in progress, fed by the inflationary policies of the Government, and the easy credit policies of the banks. Many of these investments were made in the new, unstable, Latin American republics, from which financial returns might be long in coming, if they came at all. These accounted for some of the bullion outflow from Britain during this period, and still more went overseas through the loans of Baring's, Rothschild's and other British banks. So long as the exchanges were favourable, these gold exports in the form of loans and investments provided no cause for worry, but, once the exchanges turned against Britain, then the Bank was potentially, or actually, in trouble. The corner was turned in November 1824, and the outflow of gold began.

What, if anything, did Robinson do to anticipate a credit crisis? In so far as the Bank of England is concerned, he did nothing but watch. 'Robinson tells me', Peel wrote in 1823, 'that the Bank of England has undertaken the lending of Money on mortgage entirely of their own free will, and without any suggestion or expression of a wish on the part of the Government.' [22] This controversial plan, under which loans were made on landed estates with suitable yearly incomes, put £1,500,000 into circulation before the practice was given up in 1826. The policies of the Bank during this period, then, appear to have been strictly their own, without suggestions or supervision by Robinson.

Only one of Robinson's measures might be considered as a hedge against a financial stringency. He helped assimilate the Savings Bank laws of England and Ireland in 1824. Under Robinson's plan these banks were limited to small depositors, and their safety was to some extent guaranteed. The trustees of the Savings Banks were made financially liable up to £50 each, and the Treasury was granted the authority to issue Exchequer Bills to them to aid them in case of runs. It was a wise measure for the protection of the lower income groups.

Early in 1825 the business horizon in Britain began to cloud. The public optimism which had fathered the speculations had lost its edge, stock buying slowed down, and the values of stocks — many inflated far beyond their values based on earning power — began to sag. As the banks in many instances were 'loaned out', credit became increasingly difficult to obtain, and a growing scarcity of fluid capital appeared. All that was needed to turn this business stagnation into a financial panic was some incident, and this occurred in June 1825, when Parliament debated whether or not a certain individual was justified in refusing Bank of England notes, and demanding gold. That gold was becoming increasingly scarce in Britain (and in October the Bank began to ration its discounts) meant financial stringency. Business men could not secure money to meet their payrolls; banks were unable to secure gold to redeem their notes. On the black day of 12 December, Pole, Thornton and Company, the agent for forty-seven country banks, closed its doors, and during that dark December, bank and business failures multiplied. The golden years were over; Robinson's prosperity was lost in a mountain of frozen assets.

Then began the clash between economic theory and economic fact. Robinson was a theorist, and experimental philosopher, who seems to have believed that theory without practice was like faith without works. His attitude anticipated that of Herbert Clark Hoover, who announced in 1929, following the United States stock-market collapse: 'The fundamental business of the country, that is, production and distribution, is on a sound and prosperous basis.' A month later, he insisted: 'Economic depression cannot be cured by legislative action or executive pronouncement'; and, as the Great Depression deepened, he tried to popularize the slogan 'Prosperity is just around the corner.' This was Robinson speaking again over a distance of three thousand miles, and a century's time.

The sources regarding the workings of the Government during the December crisis are unusually scanty. It appears that, when the crisis set in, Liverpool and Canning called all Cabinet members to London except Huskisson, who was so distrusted by the

financial world, they thought it best to keep him 'out of sight'.[23]
The main problem at the moment was the Bank, which appeared
to be on the verge of insolvency. According to Mrs. Arbuthnot,
Huskisson rather hoped the Bank would break, so that the
Government could revise its charter; Liverpool floundered
around; Robinson offered no plan whatsoever; but Wellington
by his mere presence buoyed up the Bank directors. All that
the Government advised was for the Bank to pay out notes and
gold up to the bitter end,[24] and in the end the financial community saved itself by a collective self-help. Some gold was
secured from abroad, partly through the efforts of Rothschild;
the Directors kept the printing presses busy turning out notes,
and scoured every nook and cranny for exchange media. The
Bank proved its qualities for survival in a most difficult *laissez-
faire* situation.

Once the immediate crisis had passed, the chief concern of
Liverpool and Robinson was to prevent a repetition of it in the
future. Accordingly, on 13 January 1826, they sent a joint
memorandum to the Bank, which embodied their views on the
causes of the panic, and provisions for the future.[25] They blamed
the débâcle on the 'rash spirit of speculation' fostered by the
country banks, and regarded the £1 and £2 notes, held by small
holders who were easily frightened, as a contributing cause.
They recommended the withdrawal of such notes, and asked the
Bank to surrender its exclusive privileges in the matter of part-
ners, save in the London area, which would permit the development of sound joint-stock banks elsewhere. They also wanted
the Bank to open branches in other parts of the country. These
suggestions were based on the theory that big banks would be
strong and safe banks.

After a short correspondence with Liverpool and Robinson,
the Bank Directors finally agreed to permit the establishment of
joint-stock banks outside the London area, in return for their
receiving the same sort of monopoly around the capital as the
Bank of Ireland enjoyed around Dublin.[26] The ideas presented
by Liverpool and Robinson at this time were not new, and Vansittart evidently discussed them some years before with the Prime

Minister; only the wording of the first memorandum, which called monopolies 'out of fashion' sounds much like Robinson. Thereafter Liverpool and Robinson split the labour of carrying out the agreement with the Bank. The Bank Charter Amendment Bill was introduced into the Lords by Liverpool, and Robinson undertook to guide the Promissory Notes Bill through the Commons.

When Parliament met in February, Robinson assured the House: 'Although the leaves and branches of the tree have been shattered, its roots were firmly fixed, and they would shoot forth again with fresh beauty.' Then he gave his views on the function of the Government in the economic world: [27]

it was in vain for any man who had observed the progress of the late events to deny, that, looking at the cause of the late shock in the pecuniary transactions of the people, that there was no legislative precautions that could have averted the mischief. It was quite impossible to expect this virtue from public enactments, with the view of effectually controlling or directing the speculations of individuals in so great a commercial country as this. . . . It was quite impossible to govern the speculations of individuals of such a country as this, without doing far more mischief than good. . . .

Robinson therefore, like Hoover, acted on the assumption that business cycles were inevitable, and one merely had to wait for the inevitable economic readjustments which would start the wheels turning again.

The business men, of course, could see nothing cheerful in the situation, for many of them had large stocks of high-priced, unsold goods on hand, which represented a fair portion of their financial assets. Back in 1793, during war-time, the Government, as an exceptional measure, had advanced loans to business men on the security of their goods, which helped tide them over. Throwing the *laissez-faire* theory to the winds, many of the business men now wanted the Government to act on this precedent and rescue them. Thus the temper of the House was bad when Robinson introduced the Promissory Notes Bill on 10 February. The business men were interested in their present solvency, not in preventing future panics.

A formidable phalanx of country bankers, country gentlemen, and city merchants formed to oppose the Promissory Notes Bill, which they believed would be bad for business and deepen the depression,[28] and after a week's struggle Robinson announced a compromise whereby the Bank of England, but not the country banks, could continue to issue small notes until 10 October. According to Greville, Robinson was forced to modify the earlier plan by the country banker, Hudson Gurney, who declared that he and the other country bankers would all demand gold from the Bank at once, if Robinson did not consult their wishes.[29]

On 23 February, the hard-pressed merchants, with the sympathetic interest of the Bank, presented their demand that the Government issue Exchequer Bills, which they could cash at the Bank. Robinson believed that Government loans to merchants with their goods as collateral would 'offer a bonus to extravagant speculation', and refused to adopt the war-time expedient in time of peace.[30] Once again the pressures were too strong for him, and the best he could do was to compromise — the Government would fund part of its debt to the Bank, and the Bank would then loan money to the merchants on their goods. This method avoided direct Government aid to the merchants.

There was an obvious principle involved in Robinson's refusal to aid the merchants at this time, and to rescue them from the hazards of their business. Had the country been at war, the Government might recognize some special obligation because their hardship would be an indirect result of a political decision, but little would be left of the *laissez-faire* concept if the merchants could secure special treatment whenever they encountered trouble. In defending this position, Robinson stood virtually alone that night. Canning muttered a very short paragraph; Huskisson, Peel, and Herries were all silent.

After a thoroughly unpleasant February, Robinson faced the task in March of making his first financial statement against a background of depression and commercial stagnation. Despite the financial crisis, Robinson would have had a £714,000 surplus which might have been used for tax reductions, if Huskisson had not erroneously omitted a one-shilling tobacco duty when he drew up the tariff schedule, and thus dissipated the anticipated surplus. According to Herries, Huskisson 'had made such gross mistakes that almost every item in his tariff would be obliged to be altered'.[31] Be this as it may, due to Huskisson's blunder, Robinson was a lonely figure the night of 13 March — deserted both by his prosperity and his customary surplus.

Yet — it was a good speech. 'The violence of the storm has passed away . . . the clouds which impended over us have begun to disperse,' he said, and insisted there was nothing in the present state of affairs to cause alarm and despondency.[32] Obviously having heard references to himself as an impractical philosopher by 'practical' men, he called for the union of theory and experience, and stressed the favourable consequences of mass education. The body of the speech was devoted to a defence of his financial operations, which had resulted in the repeal of £8,000,000 of taxes and tariffs; and he pointed out that the increased consumption of many articles on which tariffs had been reduced proved the theory of Free Trade. Only two concessions were made which could stir any enthusiasm in the House. He promised next session to recommend that the Sinking Fund be used to reduce the unfunded as well as the funded debt; and to reconsider the Dead Weight arrangement, which many financial observers had deemed objectionable.

The cheering which followed the speech was considerably fainter than it had been in recent years, but it was by no means wholly absent. Maberly followed with some critical remarks, and Hume launched a general attack upon Robinson's financial operations. Alexander Baring, as in the past, bestowed his compliments, and, had he not done so, Robinson would have been left virtually undefended. Huskisson rose towards the end of the debate to make some observations on the soap duty, but Canning, Herries, and Peel were once again silent.

It could hardly be expected that the panic could come and go without the Opposition seeking to make political capital out of it, and Robinson was perhaps the natural target for partisan attacks because of his position in the Government. The heavy artillery in these forays were John Maberly and Joseph Hume, aided

I

occasionally by the rapier thrusts of Henry Brougham, and some occasional puffs from that formerly active volcano, Sir Francis Burdett. The first attack was made on 10 March by Maberly, who moved a series of resolutions critical of Government financing in general and the Dead Weight in particular. This time Herries hurried to Robinson's support, but on this third occasion Canning, Peel, and Huskisson had nothing to say.

Maberly's attack proved to be merely a reconnaissance for Hume's attack on 4 May. Hume had evidently spent the last two months studying Robinson's financial statement and collecting statistics of a sort to refute it; but it was more than an attack on Robinson — it was a blanket condemnation of Tory finance since the time of Pitt. To examine the charges in detail would require at least a monograph. Among other things, Hume declared that Robinson had overstated the reduction of the National Debt, and was in error in tracing the reductions to the Sinking Fund. He also complained that the reductions should have been larger, and that the Sinking Fund and Dead Weight were responsible for financial losses. Some of the other forty-seven resolutions he moved noted that exports were decreasing, the consumption of malt, wine, and spirits had decreased, and pauperism and crime were on the increase.

Robinson complained that Hume's resolutions were not given to him until almost noon, so that he was unable to prepare a detailed defence of his policies, but it is almost as difficult to evaluate his answer as to weigh the truthfulness of Hume's statements. Certain points, however, are obvious. The two men used different years or periods to support their generalizations, and thus arranged their statistics. Hume failed to take into consideration the growth of the Empire and the British population when he declared that governmental expenses and crimes were increasing; yet he was careful, when it helped to support his charges, to postulate the rising consumption of certain items on the basis of the population growth, and to make adjustments between the values of paper and hard currency. Many of his shots were really fired at William Pitt, father of the Sinking Fund, and at Vansittart and Castlereagh, who instigated the Dead

Weight arrangement. Robinson's only responsibility as Chancellor was for retaining the first, and putting the second into operation. In so doing, Robinson was probably wrong, and his only defence was that the Sinking Fund was an article of Tory financial faith, and that he could not reject the Dead Weight without repudiating his immediate predecessors.

The rest of Hume's attack was against the Free Trade principle. If the consumption of malt, spirits, wines, and the rest had actually decreased following the reduction of taxes and tariffs, then Free Trade was a failure, and the economic history of nineteenth-century Britain proved it was not. When the smoke of Hume's attack cleared, certain facts stood out clearly — Robinson had reduced taxes, cut tariffs, and loosened up the whole commercial system, and in so doing had laid new foundations for British prosperity and commercial expansion.

Hume was not alone in making the attack. Brougham joined in stressing the decreases in consumption, and the increases in the crime rate, and Maberly made a general attack. At this moment, when Free Trade was in trouble, it should be noted that never a word was spoken in its defence, or in support of Tory finance, by Canning, Huskisson, Herries, or Peel. Robinson stood alone in the lists, and was the only statesman to break a lance in defence of these principles.

There are no descriptions of Robinson's emotional state during the trying verbal contests of 1826. His speeches read logically and lucidly, and the records of the debates do not indicate that he broke down at any point. A contemporary noted that, if a perplexing question were asked of Robinson during a debate, his face would register his confusion, and he would underline it by wiping his brow with a handkerchief. Probably during these debates such evidences of his emotional state were in evidence, but he never seems to have been at a loss for words.

Robinson's ordeal was considerably mitigated by the kindnesses of his opponents. At the opening of the session, he invited the support of the Members across the aisle, and it was often forthcoming. 'We shall have a division on Robinson's plan,' the Earl of Sefton wrote to Creevey. 'Most of the Oppn. will vote for him.

I certainly shall.' [33]   Between his pleas for aid to the merchants, and criticism of the Promissory Notes Bill, George Tierney sandwiched the following statement : 'He gave the Chancellor of the Exchequer all possible credit for his recent policy. The right hon. gentleman might depend upon him for support. So long as the right hon. gentleman stood by himself, he would stand by him like a good and faithful soldier.' [34]   Alexander Baring, a consistent opponent of the Dead Weight, always said kind things about Robinson, when he voiced his criticisms against it. Even Hume was careful to point out that his resolutions were not intended as an attack on Robinson.[35]

Although Free Trade in 1826 was something of a broken idol, and the aura of prosperity had departed from Robinson, he had personally weathered the financial panic in good shape, and his popularity on both sides of the House continued unabated. This popularity, rarely matched by any Member before or since, was the reward not only for his liberal policies, but for the essential kindness, honesty, and integrity of his character, which made of him a sort of special person whom the customs of the House protected from personal invectives.

If the roseate years of his political life had been followed by a trying year in the Commons, the year 1826 in Robinson's domestic life was extremely worrying for him. Although the earlier years of his married life are almost unreported by contemporaries, the letters of Emily Eden, a close friend of Lady Sarah, permit a fairly detailed look into Robinson's trials and troubles during 1826. This is most fortunate, otherwise history would simply record that he tried to resign at the end of it, and this attempt would be interpreted — as many uninformed contemporaries interpreted it — as a sign of weakness, or even cowardice.

A first child was born to the Robinsons on 22 May 1815, and they named her Elinor Henrietta Victoria — the first name in honour of Lady Sarah's stepmother, Eleanor Eden, and the second for Grantham's wife. A second child, Hobart Frederick, was born in September 1816. As Grantham had already appropriated the name 'Frederick' for his own son, born in 1810, they gave the boy Lady Sarah's family name, and his father's was placed in the middle. They hardly got to know Hobart Frederick. He died within two days, and was buried at Nocton.

Only a few scraps of information concerning Elinor are available. She was supposed to have said, upon observing the discomfort of her mother during pregnancy, that she would 'have all her children before she married, and enjoy herself afterwards'.[36] There is no reason to doubt that she made such a remark, but, if so, it was a child of sixteen months speaking, and it therefore seems probable that she observed Lady Grantham, rather than her mother, a year later. Be this as it may, we know from another source that Elinor's 'mind and its functions . . . were certainly very singular'.[37] The Robinsons had no more children during Elinor's lifetime, and we may assume that their ample store of paternal and maternal love was concentrated on this little girl, on whom nature had played one of its cruellest tricks.

A few glimpses of the Robinsons' domestic occupations are scattered through the correspondence of the period. Late in 1815 Robinson was working on a poem, inspired no doubt by the battle of Waterloo, in which Napoleon played a central part. 'It appeared to me not to be unlike him', Robinson explained, 'to attribute his failure to fate & not to the courage of his opponents.' [38] This ode does not seem to have been published, but from Robinson's letters describing it, the verse must have been in sharp contrast to those he wrote a quarter of a century later, when he had entered his Victorian Period, and had become a mere rhymer. His known interest in literature and learning was to bring him the honour of the Presidency of the Royal Society of Literature in 1835.

A family tragedy occurred in 1816, when the 4th Earl of Buckinghamshire fell from his horse in St. James's Park, and died at the early age of fifty-six. Death did not immediately follow the accident, and the earl attempted to carry on his duties as President of the Board of Control while labouring under the greatest 'affliction', according to Robinson, in which he had ever seen a man.[39] This lingering death of her father may have had a morbid psychological effect upon Lady Sarah, who was pregnant

at the time, and loved her father very dearly, but proof of this
is lacking. The estates which fell to her as a result of the earl's
demise must have been considerable, for in 1825 Robinson, who
had only a salary in his own name, was described as 'too rich'
to compete for a pension.[40]

The most important estate to fall to the Robinsons was Nocton
Hall, seven miles south-east of Lincoln, which had been much
improved by the 4th Earl, and was very productive. In 1820
Robinson told the Commons that there were no signs of agricultural depression on his estates — no tenants were abandoning
their farms, no rents were in arrear, and there had been no
increase in the poor-rates. The death of the 4th Earl also bequeathed to the Robinsons the problem of Henry Ellis, whose
circumstances of birth made him a sort of charge on the estates.
Robinson secured temporary employment for him as secretary
during the Anglo-American negotiations of 1815,[41] and in 1824
Ellis was made Clerk of the Pells, a fairly secure position.

Between 1816 and 1825 Robinson's domestic life seems to have
followed a pattern normal for one of his class and profession. In
London they lived in the Somerset House quadrangle, and one
visitor noted the 'striking view' of the great illuminated bridges
crossing the Thames, as seen through a back window. But Lady
Sarah did not consider the town atmosphere healthy, and some-
time during this period they also acquired a residence at Blackheath. Following the rising of Parliament, the Robinsons would
leave London to stay for a while at Nocton, then they would pay
their autumn visits, perhaps to Sophia Lawrence at Studley
Royal, the Hardwickes at Wimpole, the Peels at Lulworth Castle,
or the Granthams at Newby Hall.

The annual visit to Newby brought Robinson into contact with
a large number of his brother's friends, for it was the Granthams,
rather than the Robinsons, who made a mark in society. Lady
Grantham, or 'Nette', as Robinson called her, was a strikingly
beautiful and gracious hostess, whose only social fault was
loquaciousness.[42] But there are a few references to entertain-
ments given by Lady Sarah, both for relatives and political
figures, so she was by no means wholly inactive in the social

sphere. In 1820, for instance, she had Vansittart, Bathurst, Lord Mulgrave, and the American ambassador to dinner.[43] Yet the number of times the Robinson names are omitted from gatherings which one might expect them to attend is impressive. Richard Rush's diary contains a large number of references to parties given by Castlereagh, and, from the regular absences of Robinson's name, one might conclude he and Castlereagh were only slightly acquainted.

There are only a few references to Lady Sarah's health before 1826. Three of these mentioned her affliction of mumps in 1819,[44] which may be the merest coincidence, or, on the other hand, evidence that she was already magnifying minor disorders into major ones. The Cato Street Conspiracy does not seem to have unnerved her, and she simply complained that the wives of the intended victims had not been notified of the danger, which involved her husband.[45] During the winter of 1824–5, stronger evidences of her illness begin to appear. 'Mr. Robinson has been making Visits this Christmas', Lady Lucas (now de Grey), wrote to Hardwicke, 'but Ly. Sarah has been troubled with some tezing Complaints that Originate in Bile.'[46] The next reference dates to July 1825, when Robinson told Charles Wynn that Lady Sarah was 'very unwell yesterday morning',[47] and she was apparently not with him when he visited Lord Henley in August, and some other friends the following month.[48] Lady Sarah, however, accompanied her husband on a visit to Gorhambury in January, 1826.[49]

Lady Sarah's collapse seems to have taken place in March 1826, when Robinson was defending his economic programme in the Commons. So far as we know, there was really nothing wrong with Lady Sarah, but she was convinced that she could not walk, and was on the threshold of death. 'She talks and thinks of nothing but her health,' Miss Eden recorded.[50] The reasoned opinions of her physicians might bring relief for a few precious moments, but, in her agonies of mind, Lady Sarah sought solace from another source. 'She professes the degree of religious feeling that is seldom met with,' wrote Miss Eden. 'The *quantity* of her religion it is impossible to deny, but I doubt its *quality* being

right . . .' [51]   The last observation probably referred to Lady
Sarah's arbitrary treatment of her friends and relatives during
this period. She refused to see either her stepmother [52] or Henry
Ellis or Grantham,[53] people usually near and dear to her, which
indicates further the mental confusion into which she had fallen.

Robinson thought it decorous to have his wife stay at Blackheath during this trying period, so she would be away from the
observation of the Treasury Clerks, but worry over her condition
did not interfere with his efficiency as a Minister. In August his
major concern was the state of the Corn Laws, which he wanted
to change. He wrote to Peel : [54]

> What we can do in respect to the defective crops of oats and potatoes,
> I do not very well see. I am satisfied that stopping the distilleries
> would give very little real relief, and would be liable to every imagin-
> able objection. I am much disappointed that the Ports have not opened
> for oats ; but that must now wait till Novr., an additional proof of the
> extreme evil that may arise from the present state of the Corn Law,
> even to Ireland where it is so strongly maintained to be indispensable.

One of Peel's letters written nineteen years later was to have a
similar ring to it, but Robinson's plan to meet the potato short-
age, which brought distress to Ireland, was a revision, not an
abolition, of the Corn Laws.

Under Robinson's plan for the Corn Laws in 1826, barley, oats,
rye, peases, and beans were to be admitted under a variety of fixed
duties, and wheat was to be subject to a sliding-scale of tariffs.
This sliding-scale adopted a principle which he called 'intermediate rest'. If the price of wheat were 55s. or below, the duty
was to be 25s. ; between 55s. and 75s., it would be 15s. ; between
75s. and 80s., it would be 5s., and from there on it would be
nominal. 'It is clear', he pointed out, 'that fraud would be much
less easily practiced where the variation between the high and
intermediate duty would not exceed 10s., and where the latter
would attach upon a range of prices so broad as the difference
between 55s. and 75s.' [55]   Years later Robinson wrote to Gladstone : 'Many years ago I proposed such an arrangement (before
Huskisson's sliding scale was brought forward), but at that time
it was supposed to give too much facility ; but I have continued

to think that it is the best mode of arranging a variable scale.' [56] Robinson's plan was therefore rejected subsequently because it gave more encouragement to imports than the one finally adopted, which obviously was the work of Huskisson.

Robinson made a new scheme for emigration, a reviving issue because of the business stagnation, part of his general plan for the revision of the Corn Laws. He hoped that the corn tariffs would provide sufficient funds to ship an estimated 40,000 paupers abroad each year, half of them to Canada, and the rest to Australia and the Cape Colony. This plan seems to have foundered on the objections of the Duke of Wellington, who believed that such yearly quotas would merely encourage the paupers who remained to fill up the vacuum created by the departed. He traced Britain's population problem to the Poor Laws, which encouraged people to marry early, and to be idle.[57]

Although neither of Robinson's proposals was adopted by the Government, they are in themselves evidence of a deep and intelligent interest in his governmental position, and the state of the country. There is no suggestion whatsoever at this time that he planned to quit his job, despite the difficulties created by his domestic situation. He had made an adjustment to his problems, and might have carried on without a thought of resignation if Fate had not prepared for him a second blow, which was even heavier than the first.

Robinson remained at Blackheath with Lady Sarah until October, when he went to visit his mother and Lady de Grey at Wrest. This visit was cut short when he received word that Lady Sarah was dying. He therefore returned to Blackheath with the greatest haste, only to find that the report had been exaggerated, and that his wife was out for an airing. Lady Sarah evidently used this device to bring back her husband, whom she preferred to her stepmother as chief attendant.[58]

On or about 23 October little Elinor fell ill. Regarding the immediate cause of the illness, we are ignorant, but Emily Eden blamed Lady Sarah for it. 'All her fears I can excuse', she wrote, 'with the death of her child from mismanagement constantly

weighing on her mind.' [59] What the nature of this mismanagement was, she did not say, and we are left to wonder whether it
might have referred to a home accident, or simply neglect.

Hydrocephalus has several forms. The chronic type may be
either hereditary or acquired, and, if the disorder is present in
infancy, the individual rarely reaches puberty ; but there is also
an acute form, arising from an inflammation of the meninges,
which is usually tubercular in origin. The only description of
Elinor's condition appears in a brief note by Hardwicke : [60]

The poor child's disease was one that could hardly have been expected, & the account given by the Surgeons is very extraordinary.
They state that the brain was as large as that of a person of five &
twenty, and the skull was beginning to grow thin. It is probable that
this extraordinary circumstance had some influence on her mind and
its functions which were certainly very singular.

From this description, it can hardly be determined whether it was
acute or chronic hydrocephalus, or even hydrocephalus at all.
There is no evidence of mental retardation — the hints about
her, indeed, point in the opposite direction.

While it might be decorous to leave the topic of Elinor's death
at this point, one can only understand Robinson's state of mind
in late 1826 by providing some of the grim details of the circumstances that surrounded it. When Elinor lapsed into unconscious-
ness, two doctors, Warren and West, were called in, and they
immediately pronounced the case hopeless, but differed regarding
what should be done. 'He [West] was right from the first',
Emily Eden wrote, 'and perhaps that is the painful feeling, to
think that all the misery he saw, might have been spared, if he
had not been thwarted.' [61] What he had in mind might have
been anything from heavy sedation to mercy killing. 'She has
had a most wretched night,' Miss Eden wrote on 30 October,
'constantly screaming and groaning without one moment's
quiet.' [62] Yet she lingered until 31 October. 'To the last the
poor child's sufferings were dreadful,' Emily Eden observed, 'and
she never had one moment's consciousness.' [63] Even men accustomed to watching human pain and agony were touched by the

child's agony. When Elinor finally passed away, Dr. West broke down, and 'cried like a child'.

During these terrible days of late October Robinson seems to have retained his composure. 'Nobody can tell what he goes through,' Miss Eden noted, 'and he is, I think, as nearly angelic in his feelings and conduct as it is possible for man to be. The doctors speak of him with tears in their eyes.' [64] Although Grantham joined his brother the morning after Elinor died, Robinson seems to have given way completely, and to have suffered a complete emotional collapse.

Rather strangely, Lady Sarah rose to the occasion. One night she actually sat up with the child, and in the morning had 'several fainting fits', but after this momentary weakness, she became a tower of strength. She cried a 'good deal' on learning of her daughter's death, but was perfectly reasonable in her grief, and kept repeating she was fortunate in having her husband left to her.[65] 'Lady Sarah seems to have forgot her own complaints in making exertions to support Mr. Robinson,' a distant relative wrote, 'who is overwhelmed with grief.' [66]

Three days after Elinor's death Robinson wrote a letter to the King, requesting permission to be absent from the 'approaching *early* Session of Parliament', which would not take up business of any importance, so that he could take his bereaved wife to Nocton.[67] The King responded warmly in the affirmative.[68] His colleagues were also thoughtful of him — Croker even offered his house, if the Robinsons wanted a change of scenery.[69] In replying to a letter from Huskisson, Robinson said if it had depended on his own feelings, he would have met Parliament, but that Lady Sarah needed him. He continued : [70]

I cannot help flattering myself that Hume & Maberly (who are the great financial questioners) will be disposed to hold their tongues when they find that they cannot get answered ; and I am quite satisfied that under the present circumstances of our money affairs, the less that is said about them the better. We could say nothing positive & nothing very satisfactory. In short it seems clearly to be the policy of the Governt. to say & do as little as possible before Xmas. Pray let me hear a little what you are all saying and thinking in Cabinet about Corn.

Robinson evidently assumed that no one but he could answer the questions on finance, and hence, in his absence, they would not be asked.

Huskisson replied on 20 November with an explanation of the sliding scale the Cabinet had adopted, the object of which was to make the import price prohibitive until the price of corn reached 60s. per quarter.[71] Although the plan did not adopt the principle of intermediate rest, and the tariffs were higher than those in Robinson's plan, he gave it his support, and hoped that the Government would unite behind it.[72] Robinson also advised Liverpool of his acceptance of this plan, and the Prime Minister, in reply, told him that the proposal embodied the wishes of 'some of our Country Gentlemen'.[73]

Meanwhile Robinson had gone with Lady Sarah to Nocton, and she had borne the journey 'extremely well'. Little Elinor was still very much on their minds at Nocton, and they carefully gathered up all of her toys and placed them in a box marked 'To be saved first in case of fire'. Two children had been born, and two had died — the Robinsons, accustomed to being parents, now faced a long and lonely future by themselves. Lady Sarah was then only thirty-three years old, and it was probably she who decided that their direct line would not die out, that they would have another child upon whom they might bestow their parental affections. Whatever might be said against Lady Sarah's disposition, at least she was a woman, female in all of her instincts and interests.

In a letter which probably dates to early December, Hardwicke wrote to Yorke : 'Lady Sarah I am sorry to hear has not retained the energy she exerted for some time after their misfortune, and is again beginning to subside into her former nervous state.'[74] Emily Eden again provides some details of Lady Sarah's illness of early December 1826 : [75]

the folly she is betrayed into, her fear is responsible for ; but as she knows that her mind is beyond her own control, the provoking thing is that from the moment she begins to be ungovernable, she refuses to see anybody except servants who cannot contradict her. As long as Mr. Robinson is forthcoming that does not signify, as to a certain degree he prevents her from doing anything outrageously foolish. . . . You must see her to understand the state she is in ; but she is not unkind to anybody, and never finds fault with anybody she speaks of. She very seldom speaks at all, unless she is excited to defend some religious point. She sometimes smiles when Mr. Robinson and I have been talking nonsense, but does not say anything.

This seems to have been a rather strange, new turn in Lady Sarah's personality, for she is often described at other times berating people (but never her husband) in no uncertain terms.

Lady Sarah's morbid fears now came to be centred also around her husband ; this is clear from a number of incidents recounted by Miss Eden. One morning Robinson, having arisen with a headache, took some medicine and retired to his room ; Lady Sarah immediately sent for three doctors, who, when Robinson arose shortly and came downstairs in perfect health, had to be met along the roads and turned back. It was an expensive fit of nerves, for one of the doctors charged a hundred guineas to make the trip. 'Mr. R.', Miss Eden concluded, 'is all smothered up in her dressing room . . . and I do not know when he will be allowed to call himself well again.' [76] Lady Sarah also feared that her husband's tendencies towards corpulency might be dangerous. 'The poor man is starving', Emily Eden observed, 'as Sarah will not allow him to dine except in her dressing-room at two o'clock, because, as she does not dine down with the family, she says she cannot trust him not to eat more than is right. . . .' [77] On another occasion, Lady Sarah would not permit Robinson to go to the stables without having his mother-in-law along to take care of him.[78]

It was after this stables incident that Robinson wrote Lord Liverpool, in part, as follows : [79]

You are aware how much during the whole of the last Session of Parlt. . . . the state of Lady Sarah's health kept me in constant anxiety. . . . What has occurred since to Lady Sarah and myself is certainly not calculated to give me greater confidence in my own power to do my duty . . . and altho' Lady Sarah knows too well what her own duty is, but to strive to the utmost . . . to overcome the pressure of the calamity which has befallen us, I cannot but foresee that the return to Downing Street and the inevitable solitude arising from my constant absence in the House of Commons may be more than her bodily health and strength would be equal to withstand. It is not unnatural that this should be the case, and it is the fear of this which has forced upon me the consideration of what means may best enable me to consult her feelings, health and comfort, without producing embarrassment to the King's service. It has occurred to me . . . that this object . . . could be attained if my situation in the Government could be transferred from one in the House of Commons to one in the House of Lords . . . considering how efficiently Canning, Peel and Huskisson represent the Government in the H. of C. . . . I do not think that a change which would leave it to them exclusively could be any practical inconvenience to the Government . . . I should add that if such a change should be felt by you to be desirable . . . I should not think myself justified in making difficulties by being particular as to the specific office, as the change would take place for my convenience and at my request, *your* convenience ought to determine the mode.

Liverpool replied: 'Be assured the Government hangs by a thread. The Catholic question, in its present state, combined with other circumstances, will, I have little doubt, lead to its dissolution in the course of this session.' [80] Himself ill, Liverpool was evidently convinced that even he could not restore unity to the increasingly dividing Government, but he did not want it to fall over the details of a Cabinet shift.

The outcome of Robinson's negotiations with Liverpool is recorded in a letter written by Robinson to Peel some months later.[81]

Had I consulted nothing but my own wishes and my domestic comfort and happiness, I should have been out of office when Parliament reassembled in February; but when I expressed to Lord Liverpool in December last my anxiety to be relieved from my situation in the House of Commons . . . I ceased to press my wishes, upon his earnest representation that any change in my situation would infallibly precipitate a crisis . . . I yielded to the representation in order to avoid embarrassment either to the King or to my colleagues; but I told him . . . if at the end of this session he should not have found himself enabled to make any arrangement such as I sought, I should necessarily have retired — a step which I should have taken without a moment's regret, as far as regarded myself individually.

Robinson, then, obviously did not add to Liverpool's burdens by pressing for the change at this time.

Now, in his letter of 14 December to Liverpool, suggesting the change, Robinson asked him to keep the matter '*entirely confidential*'. Yet the same day that Liverpool turned down Robinson's request, he revealed that Robinson 'is evidently most anxious to get out of his present situation' to Robinson's arch-enemy, Charles Arbuthnot.[82] He might as well have published it in *The Times*, for Arbuthnot, who called Robinson 'the most frivolous, chicken-hearted, poor creature he had ever met with',[83] circulated the story of Robinson's attempt to abandon the Exchequer wherever it would do him the most harm. As a deficiency was in prospect, this charge of desertion under pressure might receive credence among those unacquainted with the details of Robinson's domestic situation. Liverpool's breach of confidence, so completely unnecessary and weakening to his own Government, is difficult to explain, and impossible to justify.

Put in chronological order, the facts of the situation were these. The deficiency, reported to be at least £3,000,000, was anticipated by the *Morning Chronicle* as early as 17 October,[84] and, if a newspaper knew about it, certainly the Chancellor of the Exchequer would also; yet in none of his letters written at that time, or in November, after the death of his child, is there the slightest suggestion that Robinson intended to resign. The idea occurred to him in December, after Lady Sarah's illness had entered a new, and acute stage, and this was likely to be aggravated by the pregnancy that they hoped was in prospect. Robinson broached the idea of changing his situation in the Government, but immediately — and this is very important — agreed to stay on during the difficult session, and to face Hume, Maberly, and the others, alone, just as he had done in 1826. His resignation was to come after the present financial difficulties had been resolved.

Arbuthnot and his friends, who probably included the Duke of Wellington, put the worst possible interpretation on Robinson's motives, whether from conviction, or for partisan reasons, each observer must decide for himself. Robinson was a 'Catholic' stalwart, close to Canning, whom many statesmen hated and feared, and a strong factor in the Commons because of his popularity. Any discrediting of him would mean a weakening of the Liberal Tory group of which he was a member. All the evidence shows that Robinson, harassed by his domestic difficulties and anticipating even more in the future, was quite ready in December 1826 to virtually abandon his political career for the sake of his wife's peace of mind. How ironic a twist of fate, then, that the end of the next session would not find him in retirement, but at the very threshold of Downing Street!

6

How a Premier was Made

===

ROBINSON returned to his work early in January and, due to the illness of Canning and Huskisson, there was plenty of it on hand. The Duke of Wellington needed funds for the relief of certain Spaniards ; [1] the King was seeking aid for a new project. [2] Both matters were important enough to deserve Liverpool's personal consideration. Robinson also aided in drawing up the agenda for the coming meeting of Parliament, and arranging especially for the most important debates in prospect — on the Corn Laws and Catholic Emancipation. [3]

But his main concern was the financial condition of the country. The deficit created by the falling revenue was increased by an unexpected draft by the armed forces to cover the costs of troops despatched to Portugal to support the constitutional government there. Once Parliament opened, Joseph Hume demanded a financial accounting immediately, but Robinson put him off, and a few days later he also disposed easily of an attack by Maberly. He did not, however, refuse to admit that financial affairs were not prosperous, and he provided some of the details of the deficits. 'The fact was', he stated candidly, 'that he had been too sanguine. It was, perhaps, the error of his character.' [4] The tone of these debates was actually more friendly and less urgent than during the previous year, and Robinson filled his role gracefully and effectively. As it turned out, he was never called upon to make a financial statement in 1827.

Lord Liverpool fell victim to a stroke on 17 February, but seven weeks elapsed before it was absolutely certain that he could never return to his post, and during the interim the most complex negotiations among individuals and sections of the parties took place. Two excellent accounts furnish the general details of these negotiations,[5] but neither of them provides a specific account of Robinson's part in them. While a large number of references about him are available, letters written by him during this period are scarce.

Robinson at first showed initiative, and the day after Liverpool's stroke he wrote to Huskisson and Peel, suggesting that the members of the Cabinet in the Commons should hold a meeting. Peel decided to consult Wellington, and it was agreed instead to hold a meeting of the whole Cabinet,[6] where it was decided that Liverpool should not be replaced until it became absolutely clear that he would be unable to resume his office. Following this initial show of leadership, Robinson faded into the background of political affairs, hoping, but hardly believing, that the Cabinet could be reconstructed from its present elements, and toying with the idea of retirement.

Time and again Robinson's name arose in discussions as a possible successor to Liverpool. Lord Colchester mentioned him as one of seven possibilities on 21 February;[7] the Canningite, Lord Thomas Binning, on 23 February, thought of Robinson as First Lord with Canning as 'Viceroy' over him;[8] Sir James Mackintosh, a prominent Lansdowne Whig, on 21 February, suggested Robinson as Prime Minister with a peerage.[9] Binning also mentioned the possibility of Robinson going to the Lords as Foreign Secretary, a project which John Wilson Croker suggested to Wellington, with little response, on 18 February.[10] There was unanimity that Robinson should hold a high position in the next Government, but doubts in some quarters as to his ability to fill the highest place in it.

Most authorities agree that Canning had some hopes of being able to form an Administration which would include most of his former colleagues in Liverpool's Government. Acting at the request of the King, he contacted Peel in late March to sound him out on the subject of co-operation, but, as is true in some other instances, the reports of this conference do not tally at all points.[11] Canning probably suggested the possibility of Peel's taking a peerage and the lead in the Lords, a project which Peel refused to entertain, and he intimated to Canning that he might not be able to serve in his Government because of the Catholic question.

On 2 April, not long after his unsatisfactory interview with Peel, Canning had an even more important conference with the Duke of Wellington, in which Robinson's name came up for discussion. Just what was suggested by Canning was clear neither then, nor now. Canning, recalling this conference, quoted himself as saying that he was willing 'to remain where I was, Mr. Robinson going to the House of Lords, with the Department of First Lord of the Treasury'.[12] In other words, he would be Prime Minister with the office of Foreign Secretary. Wellington understood him to say that 'Mr. Robinson should be called to the House of Lords, and be made First Lord of the Treasury'; [13] that is, they would serve under Robinson as Prime Minister. This part of the conversation may not have been a lengthy or detailed one — at any rate, Wellington did not mention it when he reported this interview to his friend, Mrs. Arbuthnot.[14]

If Canning's suggestion is a matter of controversy, so, too, is Wellington's reaction to it at the time. A memorandum by Lord Ellenborough stated: 'The Duke when he saw Canning last had heard Canning propose Robinson as the person under whom both could serve, to which the D. did not disagree, only saying he thought R. hardly of calibre enough.' [15] Colchester quoted a statement made later by Wellington as follows: '"Canning had told me two days before, that Robinson was to be head of the Government; and then he writes me word that *he* [Canning] is to be the head. I had no objection to serve under Robinson; but after this duplicity, I would not serve *under* Canning".' [16] Whatever may have been Canning's exact statement, and whatever may have been Wellington's exact answer, the Duke apparently came away from the conference under the impression that Robinson would be Prime Minister, and he had not declined to serve under him. The Duke, however, was convinced that great difficulties would arise if Robinson were Prime Minister, and some of the 'late innovations' sponsored by Robinson and Canning would make it difficult for one who disagreed with them to continue very long in a Government headed by either of them.[17]

As Canning told the King on 28 March that he wanted the 'substantive power of First Minister',[18] it seems probable that he toyed with the idea of making Robinson the nominal head of the Government, if he could retain thereby the services of Liverpool's followers. The plan was abandoned, according to Canning, because Robinson as First Lord of the Treasury would have either wanted to act the part — which was unacceptable to Canning, or would feel degraded at having the office and not the powers that normally went with it.[19] Robinson did not even know that such a plan had been afoot until 2 May,[20] and this lack of communication on Canning's part would indicate that Canning never gave the project really serious consideration.

On 10 April Canning sent out invitations to join his Administration. The one to Robinson was conveyed by his old friend, Joseph Planta, then Under-Secretary for Foreign Affairs. According to his later explanation, Robinson believed that the new Government would leave the Catholic Question open, and that it would be, in substance, a continuation of Liverpool's Government; so, without consulting anyone, he consented to serve.[21] The sources are silent as to whether or not the peerage was offered this early; certainly the Colonial Office could not have been, as it was still filled by Earl Bathurst.

Robinson anticipated Peel's rejection of the offer, and on 12 April he received a letter from his former Alfred Club associate, which attests to the close friendship between the two men. 'My retirement from office — would have nothing half so painful in it', Peel wrote, '— as the interruption of that cordial Regard and Esteem which I believe we have mutually felt for each other — which I am sure I shall ever feel for you.'[22] This was more than an affluence of sentiment inspired by the moment of parting; the later relations between the two proves the truth of the last phrase. Robinson, a much more emotional individual, replied in a similar tone.[23]

Peel's defection was only one of many. Wellington refused, Bathurst resigned the Colonies, Westmorland the Privy Seal, Eldon the Lord Chancellorship, Melville the Admiralty, and, had not the King persuaded him to stay on, Bexley would have given up the Duchy of Lancaster. Two at the lower levels had once been among Robinson's intimates in the Castlereagh faction — Lord Londonderry gave up his office of Lord of the Bedchamber, and Sir Henry Hardinge quit a clerkship of the Ordnance.

In so far as Robinson was concerned, these wholesale desertions put an entirely new face on the matter. He told Parliament that he had not been prepared for others, aside from Peel, refusing to serve under a 'Catholic' Prime Minister,[24] and he found the situation 'most distressing'. 'I cannot', he wrote to Peel, 'bring myself to add to the King's embarrassment by retracting my acquiescence.'[25] If anything, Robinson had understated his feelings and doubts in describing the new situation as 'distressing'. 'I saw enough of Goderich [then Robinson] during the anxious moments of the formation of Canning's administration', Granville wrote later, 'to prevent my feeling surprise or disappointment at his shrinking from the duties of a responsible situation in Times of Difficulty.'[26] We may be sure that he not only did not encourage Canning in the formation of his experimental coalition, but that he tried — at every step — to discourage it.

There was little intimacy between Robinson and Canning. 'Mr. Canning was not a personal friend of mine,' Robinson recalled later. 'My intercourse with him was purely official. . . .'[27] It seems probable, then, that Robinson knew little or nothing about his new leader's plans until their lengthy interview of 14 April, when Canning, apparently for the first time, told Robinson that he meant to create a coalition with the Lansdowne Whigs, and that he would be Leader in the Lords and Colonial Secretary in the new Government. Despite Canning's strong personality and consummate powers of persuasion, Robinson left the interview fearful and unconvinced.

The following day he wrote one of the most informative letters

of his political career in which he foresaw the collapse of the
coalition which Canning would create : [28]

I am convinced that the means do not exist of forming a neutral
Government with any prospect of success in the result, or of satisfaction
in the attempt. Can any such Government as could now be formed
upon that principle be really neutral upon the Catholic question ? . . .
The result then is that in my opinion such a Government cannot now
be formed with any well-grounded hope of success ; and I think that
the King ought to be told so. As little do I see the possibility of forming
a Government to which adequate support will be given . . . unless the
Whigs form a part of it . . . An admission of the Whigs being thus
become by the mere force of circumstances . . . inevitable, the whole
question assumes an entirely different aspect. I have no personal
objection to Lord Lansdowne and to others of that party ; but they are
as a body committed upon many points upon which I cannot concur
with them, particularly Parliamentary Reform and questions connected
with the Church in Ireland, that before I could join in Cabinet with
them, I should deem it indispensable to know distinctly how far the
body of the Whigs are prepared to adopt our notions upon these subjects, and whether they would require freedom of opinion and action.
To the latter I could not consent. I have had enough of Cabinets
divided upon *one* subject ; and it would be almost madness to apply the
principle to *other* questions. I lay no stress here upon the separate
difficulty as between Lord Lansdowne and myself in the House of
Lords, saying only that I fear it would turn out to be insuperable. . . .
If . . . we are to establish new political connections with persons
hitherto opposed to us, I am sure that you will not think that I am
doing anything more than what is necessary for my own vindication
. . . if I urge the indispensable necessity of some definite understanding with these connections (be they few or many) as to the principles
upon which they would be prepared to act, and I feel that I am the more
enabled to seek for explanation and satisfaction upon these points,
because, having no desire whatever to remain in office, a sense of duty
alone has led me not to take the opportunity of Lord Liverpool's
retirement to retire myself from public life.

Upon receiving Robinson's advice, Canning sent Joseph Planta
to tell him that he was physically unable to enter upon a written
discussion of 'hypothetical cases of difficulty', but that he did
not share Robinson's apprehensions.[29] When he made a definite
offer to the Whigs on 19 April, however, Canning stated the posi-

tion of his Government on Catholic Emancipation, the Test Act, and Parliamentary Reform, and a copy of this letter was probably sent to Robinson in an effort to quiet his fears.[30] Then he went on to form the divided Government which Robinson was sure would not last.

The lead in the House of Lords for a time was contested not by Lansdowne, but by his followers, who believed that he should hold that position for reasons of party prestige. Lord Holland noted that Robinson 'stickled and insisted upon the lead',[31] but Granville recorded that Robinson shrunk 'from the duties of a responsible situation' — which could only mean the leadership in the Lords.[32] Granville wrote that Canning 'having pledged himself to Robinson, [would] have abandoned the hope of any junction' if the Whigs had not indicated they would accept Robinson in that position.[33] It is probable that Robinson had this position forced on him by Canning, who was determined that a thoroughly reliable personal follower should have it; otherwise his influence in the Upper House would have been small indeed. Even when Robinson assumed the title there, most of Canning's Whig allies continued to look to Lansdowne for leadership in the Upper House.[34]

The coalition Government was a triumph for Canning's political artisanship, brought about by the force of his determination and personality. Lord Granville, who was later so critical of Robinson's nervousness during this crisis, would not accept a Cabinet position for fear of having to speak in the Lords. William Sturges-Bourne reluctantly agreed to take the Home Office with the understanding that it would be held on a temporary basis; Viscount Dudley and Ward went to the Foreign Office with the understanding that he could retire at the end of the session. William Huskisson remained at the minor post of the Board of Trade because he wanted to defend his trade policies in the Commons, and to avoid an election. Certainly none of these Canningites could be said to have given much encouragement to their leader at this moment.

The real courage Robinson displayed in assuming the leadership in the Lords can only be appreciated when his difficulties

there are considered.   In following Canning, he had made enemies,
and none of them more bitter than the members of the old Castlereagh faction, such as Lord Londonderry and Lord Clancarty,[35]
and these had to be added to the sizeable number of Lords who
had nothing against him personally, but cherished a deep dislike
and distrust of Canning.   To aid him were his new Whig allies,
whom he did not know, but who looked to Lansdowne rather
than to himself for leadership.   Both his position and the
House were utterly new to him, and there were pitfalls he
could not discover until he fell into them.   He undertook the task
of guiding a Corn Bill through this House which did not embody
the principles and ideas that he had suggested, and he did this
as a member of the type of Government, neutral on the Catholic
Question, which he was sure could not last.

When one stands at the base of Robinson's mountain of difficulties, one is more apt to wonder, not why he was fearful of the
position, but why he undertook it at all.   What, indeed, is the
nature of cowardice?   Most individuals who express an opinion
on the subject will answer that it is not to fear, but to run away.
How easily and even gracefully could Robinson have run away
by pleading the desertion of his friends, or his wife's health,
or his opposition to a neutral Government!   But in this crisis
Robinson not only did not desert Canning, but accepted from
him the most difficult assignment the new Prime Minister had
to offer.

On 28 April Robinson was gazetted as Viscount Goderich of
Nocton, County Lincoln, a title formerly held by a maternal
ancestor.   The name 'Goderich' was derived from Goodrich
Castle in Herefordshire, but there was something rather 'un-
English' about the name, which was pronounced in two syllables
with a long 'o', and it was mispronounced and misspelled on
numerous occasions.   Some contemporaries rendered it as 'Goodrich', or 'Godriche', or even 'Goodrick'.

During April Lords Londonderry and Ellenborough were busy
trying to arrange a hostile reception for this new addition to the
peerage, the former motivated by bitterness, the latter by personal

ambition. Londonderry sought to enlist certain Tory Lords, especially the Duke of Wellington, the Duke of Newcastle, the Marquess of Hertford, and the Duke of Rutland ; Ellenborough worked among the Whigs. Their object was to form a coalition of those excluded from the Government for the purposes of systematic opposition, and had they been completely successful, they would have formed an enormously powerful combination indeed.

Wellington recommended, to Londonderry's disappointment, 'a measured and moderate conduct', and deplored any attempt by Londonderry to raise the false issue of Canning's treatment of Castlereagh.[36] The Duke of Rutland wanted a Wellington Government, and so did the powerful Earl of Lonsdale, but although Londonderry found the former 'violent' against the Government,[37] he would obviously take his cue from Wellington. The Duke of Newcastle was also described for a time as 'violent', but by the time the Lords met, he opposed any 'hasty and intemperate' move that might drive the King into a closer alliance with his Ministers. Lonsdale was opposed to violent opposition to Canning, and the Marquess of Hertford, regarded as 'uncertain' by Londonderry, at length accepted a mission to Russia from the Government.

Londonderry's failure to organize an opposition among the Tories was matched by the results obtained by Ellenborough. Lord Grey, the most powerful of the non-coalition Whig leaders, agreed not to join Canning's Administration under any circumstances, but he did not want to attack it prematurely. This was also the attitude of his followers, Lords Lauderdale and Rosslyn. So Londonderry and Ellenborough failed to create a solid bloc which would oppose the 'sergeants and corporals of the old Tory party' which the former called the members of the new Administration.[38] In the light of the beating Goderich took without such an organized opposition, one can only speculate regarding his fate had they been successful.

The disorganized state of contemporary parties was vividly illustrated by the appearance of the House of Lords when it opened on 2 May:[39]

The ex-Ministers took their seats on the cross bench; the new Ministers took theirs in the usual front row above the fireplace; Lord Lansdowne in the back row behind them, and Lord Holland near him; Lords Grosvenor, Caernarvon, Darlington etc. also on the Ministerial side. On the usual Opposition benches, Lords Grey, Lauderdale, Ellenborough, Rosslyn, and Londonderry, with Lords Kenyon, Mansfield, Winchilsea, the Duke of Newcastle, and the Marquess of Salisbury.

Thus, with Whigs and Tories on both sides of the House, with 'Protestant' and 'Catholic' members likewise split, and the former Ministers in an ambiguous position, the House certainly had a 'singular' appearance, to use Lord Colchester's adjective.

Lord Goderich made his explanation, during which he held out the olive branch to the seceders, described to some extent his own part in the recent changes, and — for reasons not entirely clear — made one of his most explicit claims to having launched the Free Trade movement in Britain.* Ellenborough also spoke. 'It is notorious', he asserted, 'that the whole system upon which the government subsequently proceeded was laid down by Mr. Wallace. . . .' [40] This was merely the first pin-prick, a harbinger of the more deadly thrusts to come. All in all the first night was successful. Goderich had spoken 'very well',[41] and the temper of the House did not seem to be too hostile.

At the moment there were few issues upon which the opponents of Canning could attack his Government in the Lords, but two of a sort rapidly emerged. One was Canning himself; the other

---

* Goderich said : 'I readily admit, my lords, that I am the individual, who of all others, whether in his majesty's government or out of it, am peculiarly to blame for the introduction of these measures into this country — if the measures be in themselves blameworthy.' *Hansard* (2nd ser.), xvii. 477. The preceding March, he had told the Commons : 'But the truth was, that as to that free trade . . . if any individual member of his majesty's government was liable to the censure of the hon. baronet, he was that member.' *Ibid.* xvi. 1047. These statements appear to be explicit, and, if the historian traces the origins of the Free Trade legislation during this period to Huskisson, Wallace, or Liverpool, they must be regarded as falsehoods. It should be added that no contemporary statesman had stronger claims to absolute honesty than Robinson.

was the obviously unfinished state of his Government, which was not yet fully formed. On 4 May Lord Londonderry formally opened the period of harassment by a bitter attack on Goderich :[42]

> When he looked at the building which had been erected, he found it divested of all its main pillars, and that it was composed now of a sort of rubbish. The artificer had certainly been dexterous in forming the building, but he questioned its durability. Could he have found out such a mass of rubbish in any other quarter, formed as it were by the two parties. The artificer had made a dexterous endeavour to un-Whig a part of the Whigs, and un-Tory a part of the Tories. . . . That his noble friend . . . who had in early life walked hand-in-hand with him, under an individual who had carried the glories of this country to a higher pitch than any other minister . . . should at this moment find those individuals, to whom he had been opposed for the last twenty years, now supporting the government, and quietly contemplate such a state of things, he could not understand.

The attack may have been even more personal and brutal than it now appears in the records of the debates because Lord Salisbury, an opponent of the Administration, explained apologetically that it had been prompted by one of Harrowby's remarks. Goderich's reply was inadequate, possibly even tearful. Lord King, a Whig peer, made the best retort by observing that those who knew anything about building realized that the materials which were sent away were the rubbish. This word 'rubbish', however, was used sometimes thereafter by its opponents in describing Canning's Government, but not in the debates.

Although the House of Commons settled down to an orderly routine by 11 May, Goderich was quite unable to control the Lords. On 10 May Newcastle made a bitter personal attack on Canning, and hostile speeches were delivered by Harewood, Salisbury, Lauderdale, Falmouth, and Ellenborough, but the climactic speech was delivered by Lord Grey, whose polemic against Canning must have been prepared in advance. This debate left the impression of concert between the Tory and Whig opponents of the Government. Goderich demanded that they move a vote of no confidence in what Colchester called a 'flourishing speech',[43] but his opponents had no wish to clear the air by adopting such a forthright approach, which would have spoiled their game of discrediting Goderich, and, through him, Canning's Government in their House.

On 14 May Londonderry made another speech, which warmly praised Grey's recent denigration of Canning. 'The present period', Lord Dudley, who followed him, observed, 'presented the only example to be found in the history of this country of an Opposition founded on no public principle, but merely on personal antipathy to the prime minister.' [44] These remarks set off another general discussion of the Government and its head, and illustrated again Goderich's powerlessness to deal with the situation; but the following night Lord Redesdale, a stalwart opponent of the Government's Corn Bill, moved some resolutions which permitted Goderich to speak at length on Free Trade.[45] On reading this speech one feels that Goderich was walking a familiar path with confidence, but two days later he was again lost in the underbrush.

Londonderry's blunt attacks undoubtedly hurt Goderich emotionally because they involved a charge of unfaithfulness to the memory of a close friend, but it was the oratory of Ellenborough that had the most devastating effect upon him. The debate of 17 May was another disorderly affair in which various members proclaimed their lack of confidence in Canning, and it featured another speech by Ellenborough in support of Grey's opinions of the Prime Minister. 'If they are to be told that they did not deserve the confidence of the country,' Goderich replied emotionally, 'for God's sake let a motion be brought before the House for that purpose. . . .' [46] Confident that the leader in the Lords was highly vulnerable, Ellenborough delivered a final, devastating thrust at him several nights later: [47]

If the noble viscount had known this House better; if he had been better acquainted with its quiescent nature, its sedative habits on all subjects, he would have known that, on no occasion whatever was the acrimony of party feeling allowed to interfere with the discussion of momentous topics, and that his deprecation of such acrimony was altogether unnecessary. But if, in this respect, he had shown himself to be a young peer, he had in other respects proved himself to be a young statesman . . .

While Ellenborough was thus undermining Goderich in the Lords, William Huskisson was unintentionally preparing to add to his troubles. The Corn Bill of 1827 was based upon a series of resolutions adopted by the Cabinet before the secession, and Goderich might therefore expect to have it supported by Wellington and the others when it came before his House. But Wellington — probably influenced by Goderich's letter to him on corn and emigration — seems to have come to the conclusion that the measure was designed primarily to raise revenue, and not to secure a fair price per quarter for British agriculturists.

Wellington on 24 May wrote to Huskisson suggesting an amendment which he said would make the measure more acceptable to the Lords — that foreign corn warehoused in Britain should not be allowed into the domestic market until the average reached 66s.[48] To this suggestion Huskisson wrote a careless reply : [49]

Had your proposal been, that no corn bonded after the passing of the present bill should be allowed to be entered for home consumption till the average price had reached 66s., and that, thenceforward, all corn so bonded, or thereafter imported, should come under the regulations of the bill, individually I should not object to such a proviso.

Huskisson meant to write 'before', rather than 'after' in the first line — otherwise the communication did not make sense — but the error permitted the Duke to claim later that he had agreed to the amendment.

The corn measure gave the Lords something substantial to talk about, and provided some relief to the harassed Goderich. He made an effective speech in support of it on 25 May, and, although opposed by his close 'connection', Lord Malmesbury, he secured a two-to-one majority for going into committee on it. Just before going into committee, on 31 May, Goderich learned that the Duke would propose an amendment. 'I am told that you have agreed to a clause to be proposed by the Duke of Wellington!' Goderich wrote to Huskisson. 'Is this so?'[50] Huskisson sent him a copy of the Duke's letter and amendment, but not his reply, so Goderich could not spot the error in it. He was more opposed to the proposition than Huskisson had been, and would have preferred to change the effective date of the Bill, rather than to block the release of the corn then in bond.[51]

When the Lords went into committee on 1 June, amendments flew thick and fast, but Goderich secured the rejections of those offered by Lords Stanhope, Bathurst, Ellenborough, and Rosslyn before the Duke rose to drop his bomb, 'that foreign corn in bond should not be taken out of bond, until the average price of corn shall have reached 66*s*'.[52] Many Lords believed that this would exclude foreign corn from the British market when the price was under 66*s*., but this was actually not the case, for speculators could warehouse foreign corn in Ostend, Flushing, or Antwerp, and introduce it from there into the British market at any time under the terms of the Bill. The effect would be to undermine the warehousing system in Britain — one which Goderich had always tried to build.

The Lords, anxious to accept Wellington's leadership, rallied around him with great enthusiasm. 'He was of opinion', Goderich announced, 'that if the clause of the amendment were adopted, its introduction must, as a necessary consequence, lead to a rejection of the bill altogether. [Cries of 'no, no' and laughter from the Opposition benches.] He was somewhat at a loss to know what noble lords intended by these expressions of merriment ; but this much he would say, that those noble lords should not laugh him out of his opinions.' [53] His protestations only provoked laughter, and the Lords carried the Duke's amendment by a 78–74 margin.

The downcast Huskisson, whose agreement to his amendment the Duke asserted, explained to Goderich that he had written a 'hasty reply',[54] and his friend later explained and defended Huskisson in the Lords ; but the problem of the moment was to secure strength for an attempt to remove the provision on the Report, scheduled for 12 June. Goderich tried unsuccessfully to secure the support of Earl De La Warr, a Lord of the Bedchamber, who, instead, turned in his resignation.[55] On receiving a note from the Duke on 5 June, Goderich sought to conciliate him by adding a provision designed to prevent fraud in taking the averages,[56] but the Duke turned it down and suggested another designed to fix the 66*s*. price, which Goderich was forced to reject.

In his letters to the Duke at this time, Goderich laboured under a serious disadvantage. 'If we are in earnest in respect to the duties,' the Duke observed, 'as I conclude we are, we do not lay them to obtain revenue, but we mean they should act as a prohibition.'[57] Goderich would not admit this, but he undoubtedly hoped that the new measure would loosen up the system, and increase the importation of foreign grain. Thus, the two men were arguing from two different points of view, which could not be reconciled. 'What more can I say to you?' Goderich asked in his final letter to the Duke on the subject. 'If my view is erroneous, it is at least a sincere one . . .'[58] Negotiations having failed, the two could only commit their forces to battle on 12 June.

In his speech that day, Goderich played his last card — an appeal on behalf of the people. 'I think', he said, 'we ought to pause before we consent to a measure which would, in times of scarcity, have such a ruinous effect upon the mass of our population.'[59] Wellington countered skilfully with an offer to withdraw his amendment if the Government would adopt a system, established in 1791, which laid certain restrictions on taking corn out of bond, and this the Government could not accept. Although Hardwicke, and even Grantham, appeared for the division, the Duke won the day by a 133–122 margin. There could be little question regarding the leader who possessed the confidence of the Lords — it was not Goderich, despite his nominal leadership, but the Duke of Wellington.

In victory, the Lords who had followed Wellington were by no means wholly satisfied, for the time had passed when the wishes and interests of the aristocracy were paramount in the country. There was little British-grown corn on hand, and, if the next harvest were poor, prices would rise sharply, and cause unrest among the manufacturers and labourers. While the Lords might secretly agree with Redesdale that the landed interest had a right to the increased profits which accrued to them in time of scarcity, the events of 1815 were still not wholly forgotten, and they wanted some sort of Bill which would protect them against a charge of selfishness later.

As of 13 June, the Government was not decided as to its next step, and Goderich simply announced that it was not his intention to proceed with the Corn Bill. Lord Ellenborough asked that the Act of 1822 be brought into operation, but Goderich declared it was too much opposed to the principles of the Government measure. No doubt he realized the nervousness among his fellow peers, and for a fleeting moment punished them by offering no escape from their uncomfortable position. This attitude, according to Lord Seaford, provoked a 'most violent speech from Lord Grey'.[60] Grey stated that he did not think any noble Lord would abandon the Bill merely to excite the country, but that he would 'never consent, under the influence of fear, to give way to clamour'. 'If there should come a contest between this House and a great portion of the people,' he continued, 'my part is taken . . . I will maintain to the last hour of my existence, the privileges and independence of this House.' [61] Grey's 'last hour', as it turned out, was to come sooner than he thought.

Goderich's attitude on 13 June may have been dictated by Canning, whose first impulse was to make political capital out of the situation by appealing to the 'popular party'; but a second thought caused him to reject this hazardous course.[62] Goderich later explained that he had decided not to offer another comprehensive corn measure, but merely to deal with the grain now on hand. To what extent the decision was his, we do not know; but his speech in the Lords indicated that the substitute measure was his own. The new Bill passed through the Commons, and came to the Lords on 25 June, where, with the support of Grey and Wellington, it was easily passed. Grey noted that Goderich had adopted a tone of 'moderation — if not apology' in his speech; Goderich denied this, and Grey said he was sorry he had used the term. So the session ended.

The opinion of contemporary observers regarding Goderich's performance in the Lords was, in many cases, unfavourable.[63] Neither he, nor Lansdowne for that matter, had much weight or

Frederick John Robinson

Lady Sarah Robinson

Thomas Philip Robinson, 2nd Earl de Grey

Some members
of the
Alfred Club Set

John Wilson Croker

Henry Goulburn

Richard, 2nd Earl of Mornington, afterwards the Marquis Wellesley

Charles Manners Sutton, 1st Viscount Canterbury

Henry John Temple, 3rd Viscount Palmerston

Admiral Sir Edward Codrington

Arthur Wellesley, 1st Duke of Wellington

authority there.[64]   But certain sections of the Press were not ready to turn their backs on him.   'If the main business of government hereafter', wrote the *Globe and Traveller*, 'be not to shame or to silence a brawling aristocracy, but to devise measures for the public good, and to consult on them calmly, we have no doubt he will not be found wanting.'[65]   To the *Edinburgh Review*, Goderich was still a leading 'experimental philosopher'. 'His devotion to liberal principles of policy have gained for him deserved popularity', it commented, 'and given him a still more enviable place in the esteem of reflecting, rational men.'[66]

Towards the end of the session, Goderich seems to have acquired more self-confidence, and, if Canning had lived, he would probably have continued to lead the Government in the Lords.   But this raises the interesting question — could Canning's Government as a whole have gone on?   In view of the fact that Goderich was to be his successor, this question is of the highest importance to any interpretation of later events, even though there is no way of knowing just what an improviser of Canning's skill would have done to strengthen himself in the face of specific threats.

The lack of a division in either House in which confidence in the Government was directly involved makes it impossible to estimate the strength of Canning's following.   The adverse vote on the Corn Bill, after the Government exerted a major effort to win the division,[67] must be taken as strong evidence of weakness in the Upper House, even though Canning tried to minimize the importance of that vote.[68]   On the other hand, it is quite clear that the forces of Wellington and Grey, who administered the defeat, had not formed anything approaching a coalition at the time of Canning's death, nor was such a combination in prospect.

Lacking the direct evidence of a vote of confidence, Canning's strength must be estimated from the state of the coalition itself. Lansdowne was uneasy in his new place, and, if Canning had lived, he probably would have come under pressure to add Lord Holland to his Cabinet.   On the other side, the 'Protestant' Tory, Herries, wrote in July: 'I am getting out of my trammels; but using my best endeavours to do so without creating inconvenience or embarrassment to anyone.'[69]   Lord Lyndhurst,

L

according to Mrs. Arbuthnot, 'will be quite sure to rat to us the moment he thinks his present house is falling down'.[70] Lords Anglesey and Bexley, however, seem to have been stable enough members of the Government.

Opinions as to the Government's prospects were various, but most observers doubted its stability. Goderich had not believed that a Government supposedly neutral on the Catholic question could survive, and there is no reason to believe that he changed this opinion. Huskisson, on the other hand, believed that they would 'weather all our difficulties' if Canning's health held out. Herries did not think the coalition could be maintained, even if headed by a healthy Canning. 'If he had lived till the next session of Parliament', John Cam Hobhouse observed, 'it is by no means unlikely that he would have been driven from his post.'[71] Two important authorities on his Government have also expressed some doubts as to Canning's ability to continue.[72]

Early in August the ill and harassed Prime Minister completed a long paper on the situation in Portugal. 'Send it to Goderich and Robinson,' he told his secretary, 'and desire them to cut it up and not to spare it.'[73] Then he realized the slip and corrected the order to Goderich and Dudley; but the fact that it was made at all might be further proof of the high esteem in which he held Goderich and his opinions. On 7 August a bulletin described Canning's condition as very serious, and at 3.50 a.m., he died.

The Cabinet was not caught wholly unprepared by Canning's death. They met on the afternoon of 6 August and unanimously agreed to carry on if their leader passed away.[74] When Lansdowne, as Home Secretary, officially informed the King of that event, the monarch decided to send for Goderich, Canning's closest political associate, and Sturges-Bourne, his most intimate friend.[75] The two therefore went to the palace on 8 August.

The interview was fairly brief. The King desired Goderich to replace Canning at the headship, and to make Sturges-Bourne the Chancellor of the Exchequer; he expressed a disinclination to take any more Whigs into the Cabinet, and promised to send his views in a written communication.[76] This document, dated

8 August, bound the Cabinet not to consider the Reform question, and, as to Catholic Emancipation : 'If the question were at any time forced upon the Government, from that moment the Cabinet was to be considered as dissolved.' [77]

Shortly after noon on 9 August, the Cabinet considered the King's conditions. They readily agreed not to take up Reform, but the provisions regarding Emancipation were more restrictive than those imposed on Canning — which had made it an 'open question' in the Cabinet — and the Cabinet demurred. So Goderich, in his reply to the King, asked that the conditions imposed regarding this question should be the same as those accepted by Canning,[78] and to this the King agreed.[79] Thus the new Government, from the standpoint of the conditions upon which it was based, was merely an extension of Canning's.

Goderich discovered almost immediately that royal initiative was to restrict sharply his freedom to reorganize the Government. The King from the start ruled out the addition of more Whigs, and on 10 August Goderich received a list of 'suggestions' regarding the distribution of Cabinet positions — Lansdowne to have the Colonial Office; Sturges-Bourne (who would not take the Exchequer), the Home Office; the Duke of Portland, the Presidency of the Council; and Lord Wellesley was to replace Dudley, if he retired from the Foreign Office.[80] Herries was the King's second choice for the Exchequer. If this plan were carried out, it would involve the addition of a Tory–Catholic — Wellesley; and a Tory–Protestant — Herries, to the Cabinet.

Goderich was able to secure the Duke of Portland the following day,[81] but his immediate worry was John Charles Herries, one of the few Tory–Protestants in the Government. He therefore visited Herries, and asked if he were 'with him', to which Herries replied that Goderich might consider 'my letter addressed to Mr. Canning as being addressed now to himself'.[82] Herries thus committed himself to continue in the Government without the Exchequer or any other position having even been mentioned to him.[83]

The first major reorganization problem arose for Goderich on 11 August, when George Tierney, a member of the Whig branch

of the Government, called upon him. Tierney pointed out —
with considerable truth — that the Government needed reinforce-
ment in the Lords, and suggested that Lord Holland be taken
into the Cabinet. Goderich replied that the Government's
stability depended 'essentially upon its being composed out of
existing materials; and that I was not prepared to undertake
any other system'. [84] So it was to be Canning's Government also
in the matter of its personnel. Later that morning Croker warned
him that without Wellington and Peel, he would never meet
Parliament, but Goderich replied that he doubted if Peel would
act under a Prime Minister pledged to the Catholics.[85] In this
assumption he may have been wrong — Peel might have accepted
his invitation,[86] but Goderich felt he could do nothing to alter
the structure created by Canning.

That same day, 11 August, Goderich also took up the twin
problems of Sturges-Bourne and Dudley, two Canningites with
little confidence in their own abilities. Dudley wished to give up
the Foreign Office, but Goderich achieved a minor victory by
persuading him to stay on. Sturges-Bourne, however, resolutely
refused the Exchequer, on grounds of incapacity for the position,
and nothing that Goderich said could make him change his mind.
He therefore let Bourne advise the King of his refusal, having
no idea at the time of the acute embarrassment that Bourne's
refusal would ultimately cause him.[87]

Toward the day's end, Goderich had only one major worry —
the Whigs' demand for the admission of Lord Holland. So that
evening he wrote to Lansdowne, asking whether Holland's support depended on his admission to the Cabinet, and whether or
not his admission had to be immediate.[88] In reply, Lansdowne
explained that Canning had promised Holland would be admitted
when 'an occasion' presented itself, and that the present moment
seemed to be such an occasion; but he agreed to a 'short delay',
if the question were definitely settled.[89] Goderich, then, could
retire that night fairly well satisfied with the events of the day.

Goderich did not see the King on 12 August, which was a
relatively uneventful day, but he must have broached the subject
of Holland in a letter to the monarch, who replied: 'The King

has no personal objections to Lord Holland, but, the King has the very strongest objections . . . that the present Govt. should bear either the name, or even the semblance of a Whig Administration.' [90] The King then submitted his second list of Cabinet selections. This time Huskisson, who had been ignored in the earlier list, was shown at the Colonial Office, and Herries was placed at the Exchequer. The importance of this second suggestion lay in that Herries — a Tory–Protestant — would be admitted into the Cabinet at a time when Holland — a Whig–Catholic — was being excluded. The King also wanted Thomas Wallace to have the Board of Trade, *vice* Huskisson.

After studying the list, Goderich visited the King on 13 August and explained that the admission of Wallace — a Tory–Protestant-seceder — into the Cabinet at a time when Holland was denied admission would cause objections among the Whigs, and the King acknowledged this, and accepted Charles Grant (then Vice-President) as President of the Board of Trade. This was a victory for Goderich, who also received a promise from the King regarding Holland which read : 'So whenever the time shall arrive, which can only be determined by experience, the King shall have no objection to consider the wishes of Lord Holland's friends.' [91] 'Nothing particular' was said about Herries, and Goderich 'had no reason to suppose that the King attached any peculiar importance to his appointment.' [92] After the discussion, Goderich kissed hands, and formally became Prime Minister. Even before this — according to rumour — he had taken steps to secure a £3,000 pension upon retirement.[93]

After this successful interview with the King, Goderich visited Herries, who did not give a positive answer, but did not seem to want the Exchequer.[94] At the moment Goderich does not seem to have attached much importance to the appointment of Herries, and certainly did not consider it in the same light as the inclusion of Wallace in the Cabinet. 'On the following morning, Tuesday the 14th,' Goderich recorded, 'I received a letter from Mr. Herries, stating his inability to undertake the office, and declining it.' [95] This left him free to offer the position to his old friend, Lord Palmerston, who, as early as June, was describing himself

as a Whig,[96] and thus should have eminent qualifications for the
coalition Cabinet. But Goderich did not contact Palmerston
immediately.

Instead he talked with Lansdowne, and communicated the
rather indefinite promise of the King regarding Holland's admission ; at the same time, he mentioned that Herries had been
offered the Exchequer. At the moment Lansdowne made no
comment on the latter proposition, and simply discussed the
Holland matter,[97] but that night he wrote to Goderich and
indicated he meant to bring up the Herries' question at the next
Cabinet.[98] In reply, Goderich noted that the appointment had
been settled 'between the King & Myself', a customary procedure
because the Exchequer was so intimately connected with the
Treasury Department.[99] The same night Goderich wrote to
Huskisson, asking him to become Secretary of State, and to
assume the lead in the Commons, noting :

> The task which I have undertaken is not to remodel by getting
> materials from without, but to reconstruct with materials from amongst
> ourselves, and I . . . flatter myself that my colleagues are sincerely
> disposed to aid me in this attempt. . . . I regret . . . your absence
> upon the present occasion, whereby *I* lost the benefit of your advice
> and assistance ; but all would have been confusion if we had waited.
> Every variety of intrigue would have been at work, and we should have
> fallen to pieces in the conflict.[100]

The day following, 15 August, Goderich looked forward to
putting the finishing touches to his Administration. Advising
the King that Herries had declined the Exchequer, he suggested
that it be given to Palmerston, while Herries would take the War
Office without a seat in the Cabinet.[101] Palmerston was then
called in, and informed of this tentative arrangement.[102] Next
he informed Lansdowne he had reason to believe that Herries
would not take the Exchequer, and the Whig leader indicated
he would not press Holland's claim. 'I flattered myself', Goderich wrote, 'the whole difficulty was over.'[103] The same day
both Goderich and the King wrote letters to Wellington, asking
him to take the Horse Guards, and these were given to Lord
Anglesey for delivery.[104] Goderich also wrote a courtesy letter

to Wellesley in which he admitted his 'own inadequacy' for the headship, but declared he could not shrink from a task given him by command of the King, and with the 'confidence and support' of his colleagues.[105]

This brief narrative of the events between 8 and 15 August shows Goderich at his best. Acting virtually alone, he had set about filling the Cabinet offices with diplomacy and skill, and seemed to have accomplished the reconstruction of what he called 'Canning's Government' with a minimum of friction. From a number of sources, he received votes of confidence. Among the newspapers, the *Globe and Traveller* was warmest in its praise; [106] the pro-Wellington *Morning Post*,[107] and *The Times* [108] (whose editor, Thomas Barnes, received confidential information from Greville and Brougham), were less enthusiastic, but not hostile. Lord Wellesley gave Goderich his confidence; [109] and Lords Grenville and Buckingham eventually tendered him their proxies.[110] 'The intelligence of Lord Goodrich's [*sic*] commission', Colonel Meyrick Shawe wrote, 'gave great satisfaction to Ireland.' [111] Thus on or about high noon on 15 August, the new Administration had arrived at its most flourishing condition, but the moment proved as illusory as the prosperity of 1825.

To understand the extraordinary events of 17 August, it is necessary to clarify as much as possible the sources of opposition to the new Government. The fragmented condition of political parties at the moment makes this an exceedingly difficult undertaking; Lord Londonderry, for instance, recognized the existence of six 'parties' at this time — Goderich's, Lansdowne's, the 'Old Whigs', the 'Old Tories', the 'Tail' of the Whigs, and the 'Tail' of the Tories.[112] Even this is an oversimplification of the political reality then existing, for the classification ignores the factions operating within the groups.

The only one of these six groups which was thoroughly dependable was the 'Goderich party', and one has to range far and wide to locate its probable members. Certainly it included Lord Grantham and Lord Hardwicke, and his other family connections, the Earls of Malmesbury and Enniskillen and the Duke of

Buckinghamshire, would be expected to support him on most issues. The Duke of Portland and Lord Francis Leveson-Gower, who often expressed personal attachment to Goderich, should probably be listed among his followers, and also the members of the old Grenville group — Lord Grenville, the Duke of Buckingham, and Charles Wynn.

By the 'Tail' of the Tories, Londonderry probably meant those who had been closely identified with Canning. Chief among them were William Huskisson, the Earl of Dudley, and Sturges-Bourne, whose allegiance to Goderich was based not on friendship or social intimacy, but merely upon similarity of views, and reverence for the memory of their departed leader. 'I could not be in a Cabinet with those who had worried Canning to his doom,' Huskisson wrote later, 'and . . . if my own feelings would admit of it, I should be of no use, as I should be abandoned by everyone of Canning's personal and political friends.[113]

These two groups — Goderich's 'party', and the 'Tail' of the Tories were the most dependable political factions supporting the new Government. The Lansdowne 'party' was less so because their motive in joining the Government was basically one of a partisan nature. Lansdowne wrote to Brougham on 11 August : [114]

I quite agree with you that under the present unfortunate circumstances, all sacrifices must be made to keep things in a right direction. I can give no stronger proof of it than by consenting for some time at least to keep my present office *under* Goderich, & acquiescing in any other arrangements whatever they may be which can give effect & stability to the Govt. to which however I wish to belong for no other reason than its occupying the ground which the enemy is still ready to take up . . .

By the 'Tail' of the Whigs, Londonderry probably meant Lord Holland and Henry Brougham, among others, Whigs who supported the Government out of office. Their general attitude was probably much the same as Lansdowne's. Brougham, for example, wrote to Lord Grey on 13 August that his 'game' was to see a 'weak government' in power.[115]

The attitude of the 'Old Whigs' was generally unfriendly to-

wards the Government, but not extremely so. 'I have personally
no ill-will to any of them', Lord Grey wrote on 24 August, 'but
collectively they do not inspire me with the confidence which is
necessary to my declaring myself the supporter of any Government.' [116] 'Lord Goderich seems to be a good-natured and good-
humoured man', the Duke of Bedford wrote, 'but totally unfit
for a Prime Minister.' [117] Some of the Old Whigs believed that
if Lansdowne had remained aloof, the Canningites would have
been forced to take office under a Whig Premier; [118] and most
of them probably followed Grey's formula — their support would
increase with the extension of Whig power in the Cabinet.[119]

Of the six different groups named by Londonderry, there remains for discussion the most important of all — the 'Old Tories',
which included the Tories, other than the Canningites and members of Goderich's 'party' in and out of the Government. Some
of these were close friends of Goderich, and could bear him no
ill will even though they might not approve his political activities.
Peel certainly belonged in that category, and so, too, Bexley,
Lord Melville,[120] and Westmorland.[121] Others were more extreme
opponents of Goderich than any that could be found in the Whig
camp. Londonderry,[122] Arbuthnot,[123] the Duke of Rutland,[124]
and Lord Eldon were all anxious for the overthrow of the 'remnant
of Canning's Administration', as Rutland termed the Government.

But by this time the Old Tories looked to the Duke of Wellington, an obvious candidate for the Prime Ministership, for advice
and leadership. In a memorandum the Duke compared Goderich's position with that of Canning, and revealed his own attitude
toward both Prime Ministers. Against Goderich, he did not find
the 'personal objections', such as temper, spirit of intrigue, and
hostility toward the great landed aristocracy that obtained in
Canning's case. Then, there was the Catholic question espoused
by both of them. 'I believe', the Duke wrote, 'that Lord Goderich has been more in earnest upon this question than Mr. Canning ever was. But there can be no mistrust of Lord Goderich's
intentions; there may be of his talents and fitness for his situation.' [125] The Duke objected — as Goderich himself had done

— to an overwhelmingly 'Catholic' Cabinet pretending to be neutral on that question, and he predicted that Goderich would secure Radical support as the friendly successor of Canning, which, of course, alienated him from the Tories.

Unlike the other Tory seceders, Wellington was shortly called upon to adopt a more definite attitude toward the Goderich Government. Lord Anglesey arrived on the morning of 17 August with the letters offering the Horse Guards to the Duke, and Wellington spent an hour drafting replies which would make clear that his acceptance did not tie him to the Government. 'I have never thought', he informed Goderich, 'that political differences of opinion ought to prevent me from commanding his majesty's army at the Horse Guards, equally as an army in the field . . .'[126] Aware that his motives would be misinterpreted by a part of the political public, the Duke emphasized his detachment from the Government by treating Anglesey with obvious coldness.[127]

Wellington found that many of his friends, such as Westmorland and Peel, readily admitted that he had no alternative but to take this non-political position,[128] but others adopted a different view. Mrs. Arbuthnot argued the question with him until he became angry and '*swore* (which he never does)',[129] and promised to 'keep entirely aloof' from the members of the Government.[130] It is indicative of Goderich's thoughtfulness and gentlemanly character that he made no attempt whatsoever to involve the Duke in governmental affairs outside the military department. Neither he nor his colleagues made the slightest approach to Wellington, who, in September, felt that they might be carrying the policy of aloofness a bit too far.[131]

Certain facts seem to emerge from this brief survey of the six political units mentioned by Londonderry. The base of the Government, formed from Goderich's 'party', the 'Tail' of the Tories, Lansdowne's 'party', and the 'Tail' of the Whigs, was exceedingly shaky because a genuine coalition among them had not been formed, and it was the more so because of the enforced exclusion from government of such powerful leaders as Wellington and Grey. Although Goderich had many more friends than Canning, there was a feeling among many of them that he was too amiable an individual to be Prime Minister during a period of political chaos, and, as Westmorland put it: 'As the asperity respecting Canning may not operate so strongly against him, on the other side the fear of him will not bring so many supporters.'[132] Goderich had hoped that a certain *esprit de corps* had developed during the brief Canning Administration which would carry the Government through the difficult period of reorganization, but by 17 August the remnants of that spirit, evident to a certain extent on 8 August, had disappeared, and a severe blow was dealt to his Government — one from which it never completely recovered.

Following Sturges-Bourne's refusal of the Exchequer, Goderich, knowing that he would have the approval of the King, suggested Herries for that position.[133] This proved to be a major blunder, which seemed to be repaired when Herries rejected the offer on 14 August, and Palmerston expressed his willingness to undertake the office. But on 15 August, Sir William Knighton, the King's physician, visited Herries and convinced him that the Whigs were scheming to increase their influence in the Cabinet,[134] and Herries thereafter seems to have regarded himself as the protector of the 'Old Tory' interest in the Cabinet.

When Goderich visited him on 15 August to discuss the War Office appointment, Herries announced a willingness to accept the Exchequer, if he could have an 'immediate temporary absence' to improve his health. Goderich was not in a position now to renew the offer because of his commitment to Palmerston, and statement to Lansdowne that Herries would not accept the appointment, and he seemed 'delighted' when Herries told him he could do as he chose about the Exchequer.[135] That night, however, the King, probably convinced by Knighton that he should extend his authority in the new Government, drew up a letter to Herries, demanding that he take the Exchequer, and he sent it to him — open — through Goderich.

Goderich received this letter the morning of 16 August, the day of Canning's funeral. He mentioned this new difficulty to Palmerston, just before they went to Westminster Abbey, and his friend agreed to accept or not to accept the Exchequer, as might suit Goderich's convenience.[136] It was evening before Goderich was free to go to Windsor and impress on the King the 'difficulties wh. might arise out of the affair', but the monarch remained obdurate. This was a moment of the greatest importance in Goderich's career as Prime Minister. He was convinced that the Herries appointment should not be made, and, as the King's adviser, he should have insisted on his advice being followed, or have given up his position. This he did not do, but instead tried to induce Herries, who visited him later that night, to resist the King's wishes when the Cabinet assembled at Windsor the following day. Whatever might be said about Herries's activities throughout this crisis, he was undoubtedly right in pointing out that to resist the King's demands was Goderich's job as Prime Minister.[137]

So the stage was set for the strange occurrences of 17 August. Charles Greville, who was not aware of the difficulties confronting Goderich, left an account of the goings and comings into and from the Throne Room on that day.[138] Four times Goderich spoke with Lansdowne, and between each conference, visited the King. Lansdowne, Carlisle, and Tierney based their objections to Herries on three grounds — that he would have the lead in the Commons whenever Huskisson was absent; the objectionable 'manner' of his appointment; and the fact that it violated the principle of forming the new Cabinet out of existing materials.[139] Only the second would seem to bear scrutiny, for Herries had been in Canning's Government, and was ready to make any arrangements concerning the lead that might satisfy the Whigs. The Whig leaders contended that the King had already engineered the appointment of the Duke of Portland, and should not be permitted to dictate in the matter of Herries. In his four conferences with the Whigs, Goderich located only one escape hatch — they would permit the matter to be shelved until Huskisson returned,[140] and the harassed Prime Minister made this suggestion in his second interview with the King. There were two reasons for the postponement — the appointment concerned Huskisson, who was the leader in the Commons, and it was the only way out of the impasse.

Herries had two interviews with the King.[141] The King assured him that the opposition to his appointment was a 'Whig trick', inspired by their hatred of his Tory–Protestantism. At one point he threatened to make Lord Bexley Prime Minister, if this were necessary to retain Herries, and at another, he tried to force the seals of office into Herries's hands. Herries was obviously in a tight spot — risking royal displeasure on the one hand, and a most extraordinary violation of constitutional procedures on the other; but he followed Goderich's plea to resist, and at length a compromise was arranged. Herries was sworn into the Privy Council — with or without Goderich's consent — but he did not receive the seals. Until he actually took his oath at the Court of Exchequer, he was not Chancellor.

Lansdowne had only one interview with the King, which was prefaced by some whispered instructions from Goderich as he passed through the door. Goderich may have emphasized the need for delay, and Lansdowne, who was in no position to secure a sympathetic hearing of his real objection to Herries — the addition of a Tory–Protestant, while Holland was excluded — no doubt was ready to take that way out. Just what passed between him and the King is not known; nor is information regarding the King's interview with Lord Bexley available.

All in all, it was a thoroughly frustrating day. The King was frustrated because he could not have his way immediately, the Whigs because they could not exclude Herries, and Herries because he remained suspended in mid-air. Goderich's frustration must have been unique in the history of Prime Ministers — he could induce virtually no one to follow his advice.

During the period of waiting, before the arrival of Huskisson on 28 August, Lansdowne found that Brougham, who had first urged him to resist the appointment of Herries, had changed his mind, and advised against breaking up the Government over the issue.[142] While his position was somewhat weakened thereby, that of Herries was strengthened by a journalistic battle that raged late in August. On 24 August the *Morning Chronicle* printed a rumour that Herries's appointment had been held up because of his connections with the Rothschild banking interest, which Goderich tried to quash by publishing a categorical denial of it in another paper. *The Times* and the *Courier* took up the story, the former attacking, and the latter defending Herries, and, although the *Chronicle* apologized to Herries on 27 August, the damage was done. Herries could now argue that he had to take the Exchequer lest his failure to do so would add colour to the rumour.

Meanwhile, Huskisson had arrived in Paris on 20 August, having heard the news of Canning's death while *en route*, and there he received a long letter from Joseph Planta describing in detail the development of the present Cabinet crisis.[143] Huskisson, who felt he owed it to Canning's memory to keep the coalition Government alive,[144] quickly wrote two letters to Goderich, one to be shown to the King, the other as a strictly private communication. The private letter was warm and hopeful.

Upon arriving in London on 28 August, Huskisson immediately visited Goderich, and went from him to Lansdowne and Carlisle. 'Their minds are quite made up to immediate resignation', he reported to Goderich, 'if the King persists in putting the Ex. Seal in Herries' Hands.'[145] Later that evening Lansdowne offered a way out which was unacceptable to Huskisson — that Huskisson himself should be Chancellor.[146] The next morning he received a brief note from Goderich announcing that the King would see him at noon that day. 'God knows how it will all end,' Goderich wrote. 'Pray let me see you as soon as you return from Windsor.'[147]

Huskisson suspected that the King was trying to control the Government, and the interview verified his suspicions. The King complained that he had to act as Prime Minister, as Goderich had no nerves, and seemed ready to attempt a coalition with the seceders. It was then that Huskisson stated he could not sit in a Cabinet with those who had 'worried Canning to his doom', and the subject was dropped.[148] In the end Huskisson was able to secure a major concession from the King — Sturges-Bourne might receive the Exchequer, and Herries some other position, if it were agreed that Herries would eventually succeed him.[149]

A ray of hope now shone through the clouds, and on 30

August, Goderich, Huskisson, Herries, Lyndhurst, and Sturges-Bourne met for a general conference, which was an exercise in futility. Without waiting to hear Herries's views, Bourne immediately rejected the compromise.[150] So Huskisson and Lyndhurst took him to see Lansdowne, and, as a result of this conference, Bourne's attitude softened. Then came Herries's turn to balk — his acceptance of any other office would be an act of 'self-condemnation and degradation'.[151] Goderich then undertook to change Herries's mind, and had nearly won him over when Bourne raised his objections again, and nothing Huskisson could say would remove them. After the conference Huskisson was bitter that Bourne had caused the failure of their hopes, but Goderich, in his understanding way, wrote: 'I really feel for him, and can hardly blame him; but it is a sad thing when all seemed within our reach.'[152] He then suggested that Huskisson take the Exchequer seals, to which the latter replied: 'It is my duty to lose no time in informing you that before I allowed myself to go into the difficulty which had so unfortunately arisen respecting the Exchequer Seal . . . my mind was unalterably made up in no case to accept the Seal myself.'[153]

The same group forgathered at the Royal Lodge on 31 August to make a final decision regarding the Exchequer. After a conference with Goderich, the King declared they must act on the Prime Minister's advice — an unusual turn — and persist in the Herries appointment, but what would be done if Lansdowne and the Whigs resigned from office? Lyndhurst observed they would be able to procure strength enough to go on, but failed to identify the source of it; Huskisson stated that the secession would hurt in the Commons, but would help in the Lords. 'Goderich was nervous and not very intelligible,' Huskisson recorded, 'but anxious to do his best to prove his devotion to the King.'[154] It was finally decided that the King himself should break the news to Lansdowne at a special conference.

Rather strangely, after the die was cast, Goderich seems to have been calm about prospects. 'I feel with you all the importance of keeping them and all the difficulties consequent on losing them,' he wrote to Huskisson, 'and altho' more sanguine upon the subject, it is a most anxious moment.'[155] He wrote to Lansdowne and begged him not to break up the Administration over 'this single and isolated point',[156] and, at Huskisson's suggestion, wrote a letter to the King, asking him to be kind to Lansdowne at the interview. 'He is most sanguine in his expectation', Goderich wrote to the King in his tantalizingly vague manner, 'that the kindness and condescension with which your Majesty treats all those whom your Majesty invites to approach your Majesty, will lead to a satisfactory result of this harassing business.'[157]

Huskisson, on the other hand, after his show of confidence at the Royal Lodge was deeply perturbed, and spent a sleepless night. 'The more I reflect,' he wrote to Goderich, 'the more I tremble at the difficulties you will have to encounter in supplying the loss we shall sustain in a manner adequate to the occasion.'[158] Before Lansdowne went to the King, Huskisson played their last card. To reward the Whigs, the peerages for Lord Darlington and Lord Cawdor would go through without delay; Edward Stanley, scion of the wealthy Derby family, would be made Under-Secretary for the Colonies, and Sir James Mackintosh would be placed at the India Board. He also indicated that Lansdowne's future demands for patronage would be treated with sympathy.[159]

The *dénouement* of this whole affair on 1 September was placid compared with the stormy scenes that had preceded it. The King asked if Lansdowne were prepared to break up the Government on a personal question, which was not one of principle, and when Lansdowne said he wished to retire on personal grounds, if the service admitted of it, the King replied that it did not. Lansdowne then agreed to stay on if he were permitted to state that his decision was based on the King's express desire that he should do so, and the King agreed.[160]

After leaving the King, Lansdowne, fearful of the manner in which Herries might use his victory, wrote to Huskisson that he depended on 'your friendship & to Lord Goderich's' to put his conduct 'in its proper point of view'.[161] When he learned of Lansdowne's fears, Goderich wrote to Herries immediately: [162]

We must forget all that is unpleasant in what has occurred, and act cordially and frankly together. If we do, and start well, depend upon it the country will support the King in his resolution to support us, particularly if we exert ourselves *bona fide* to get rid of, or at least to nullify, the odious distinctions of Whig and Tory . . .

Herries replied: 'I hope we shall all endeavour to act strictly upon this principle of subduing all distinctions of parties on which you desire your Government to be conducted. I espouse that principle heartily, and I am prepared to maintain it constantly and cordially.' [163]

So at long last, on 1 September, the Goderich Government was finally established, but the events of those two weeks in August had not increased confidence in the Prime Minister's qualities of leadership. Brougham accused him of mismanagement, assuming, quite wrongly, that Goderich had persuaded Herries to reconsider his initial refusal of the Exchequer.[164] George Tierney told Greville that the Whigs believed in Goderich's integrity, but his 'deplorable weakness' had made him unfit for the position he held.[165] Even Huskisson was at times critical of Goderich.

But the tendency after the crisis was over was for most of the members to forget the past, and to pull together. 'Goderich & I shall go on . . . perfectly together,' Huskisson wrote. 'He is the very best choice the King could have made.' [166] In mid-September Fremantle wrote to the Duke of Buckingham: 'I hear the different members of the Government are perfectly satisfied with one another; that is, I mean that Lord Lansdowne is content with all that was done by Lord Goderich.' [167]

It is difficult, in going through the statements made by individuals during this period, to distinguish between resentments of the moment, and settled feelings. If, as his letter to Brougham early in the crisis indicated, Lansdowne had no interest in the coalition Government save as it would advance Whig interests and keep out the Tories, he could hardly be expected to act on the principle of obliterating party distinctions within the Cabinet. Herries, on 31 August — just before his great victory — wrote to Bexley that the Government 'should, if possible, be maintained for some time at least, even if it be not calculated for any

M

considerable duration.'[168] Yet the following day he gave Goderich his categorical promise to help obliterate party distinctions.

Whatever might be concluded regarding Lansdowne's and Herries's intentions toward the Government, the activities of William Holmes, Treasurer of the Ordnance, are indefensible. He sent a list of the new Cabinet to the Arbuthnots before it was publicly released, provided them with inside information regarding the Herries dispute, and predicted to Mrs. Arbuthnot on 6 September that the Government would blow up long before Parliament met.[169] Holmes appears to have been little better than a spy for the Old Tory interest — how many more like him there were at the lower echelons, it is impossible to say.

Even if Goderich did not inspire confidence, he had a right to expect that members of his Government would keep confidences on subjects important to his Administration, and that information and rumours should not be leaked to cause suspicion and uncertainties. Observers today might have wished that he had adopted a firm position, and weeded out of his Government all those whose primary loyalties were to other political groups, but this raises the question — if he had done so, how many Members would have been left? The political situation being as it was, one might even conclude that, if led by a firmer man with a stronger policy, Canning's Government could not have been reconstructed in August 1827.

7

How a Government Fell

═══

NOT only did Goderich, the rational man, the man of goodwill, have to contend with the irascible King, the scheming Knighton, the legalistic Herries, the worrying Huskisson, and the restless Whigs during these months, but the vagaries of his pregnant wife continued to be a source of concern both to him, and to his step-mother-in-law, who lived with them temporarily in Downing Street. 'Sarah', Emily Eden reported in July, 'is worse than ever',[1] and a little later: 'It is a shame to let anybody see the abject slavery in which she and Mr. Robinson live. It is quite a Fowell Buxton case.' [2] Spinster Emily's sympathies, which for a long time had gone out to the harassed husband, were perhaps diluted with a species of envy at the attentions received by Lady Sarah, and, on learning that he had become Prime Minister in August, she wrote: 'All the poor little children who read History 100 years hence will come to the Goderich administration, and . . . they will not have an idea what a poor creature he is. . . . But it is so like her luck! She has always all her life had what she wished, even to a child.' [3]

Miss Eden's letters give only fleeting glimpses of Goderich's domestic trials — a tantrum brought on by some sort of difficulty with a house at Knightsbridge; the administering of laudanum to quell Lady Sarah's excitement; [4] poor Lady Buckinghamshire staying in Downing Street, and not permitted to leave, even though Lady Sarah refused to see her.[5] On 29 August, when Huskisson was having his first conference with the King, Lady Sarah fancied her hour had come, and, disturbed by the noise, had her husband send away some construction workers employed in the vicinity.[6] How many such dress rehearsals took place before the actual performance, we can only guess. There was another on 3 September, when Goderich returned home to find his wife 'in a very precarious state'.[7]

But Lady Sarah confounded her female detractors, some of whom refused to believe she was actually pregnant,[8] by not only giving birth, but presenting her husband with a son and heir, who was named George Samuel Robinson. The middle name was taken from 1 Samuel i–xx, as both Frederick and Lady Sarah had been deeply impressed by the biblical accounts of Sarah and Hannah, who had given birth to sons after hope for such issue had been abandoned. The King sent warm congratulations,[9] to which Goderich responded in kind. 'He is in tip-top spirit,' Robert Wilmot Horton reported to Huskisson of Goderich.[10]

The birth of a son to the Prime Minister was popular in Britain, and at this moment the Goderich Government was in a most flourishing state. Yet both his professional and domestic tranquillity proved to be short-lived, and a letter by Emily Eden gives some insight into Lady Sarah's post-natal state of mind : [11]

Such a mess ! She is crosser than ever, now she has all her wishes gratified. In short, all the stories that we have all known of her are nothing compared to what we might know now. Sister will not hear of her being crazy, though I have proved to her how advantageous it would be to Sarah's character . . . it is extraordinary the number of good stories the Opposition letters bring of Lord and Lady Goderich. However, all those of her meddling in Politics are perfectly unfounded. Her attention to her own self is never disturbed for a moment, and she does not ever ask for any public information. Gooch is appointed her third physician in ordinary and she was unusually cross on Friday because he had not called before two. She had had Clarke and Pennington, but as she observed with the sweetest resignation, 'Physicians, I believe, always neglect their dying patients.'

Early in December, she reported a story concerning the physicians : 'They all met to consult a few days ago, and Pennington stood by the fire soliloquizing and was heard to say : ''Well, this is the first time, I suppose, that we four ever met to consult when there was no complaint to consult about." ' [12]

There is some evidence to show that Lady Sarah's demands had by the end of the year reached a point where they interfered seriously with Goderich's professional activities. By then she was so absorbed in her imaginary disorders that she paid no attention whatsoever to her baby.[13] Emily Eden once called her character 'cross-grained', and this is probably the best adjective that could be used to describe it. She longed for their new son, then paid no attention to him; she wanted Lady Buckinghamshire near her, but often would not see her for days on end; she hated living in Downing Street until she came to leave it; and she did not want her husband to be Prime Minister until, partly because of her antics, his retention of that position was impossible.

Lord Goderich's Government was from the standpoint of personnel merely an extension of that of Canning, the only changes, save for one, having been occasioned by Canning's death, or had been planned by him.* Goderich became First Lord, and Huskisson, Colonial Secretary *vice* Goderich, while Charles Grant took the Board of Trade *vice* Huskisson. Canning had planned to replace Lord Wellesley as Lord-Lieutenant of Ireland at the end of the year with Lord Anglesey, and this arrangement continued in effect. The Duke of Clarence, as First Lord of the Admiralty, continued to function outside the Cabinet. The only other change was to replace Lord Harrowby, as Lord President of the Council, with the Duke of Portland, which had been suggested

* The Goderich Government was composed as follows : First Lord of the Treasury, Lord Goderich ; Foreign Secretary, Lord Dudley and Ward ; Home Secretary, Lord Lansdowne ; Lord Chancellor, Lord Lyndhurst ; Lord Privy Seal, the Earl of Carlisle ; Board of Control, Charles Wynn ; Master of the Mint, George Tierney ; Duchy of Lancaster, Lord Bexley ; Woods and Forests, Sturges-Bourne ; Secretary at War, Lord Palmerston ; Lord President of the Council, the Duke of Portland ; Board of Trade, Charles Grant ; Lord-Lieutenant of Ireland, Lord Wellesley ; War and the Colonies, William Huskisson ; Chancellor of the Exchequer, J. C. Herries ; Master General of Ordnance, Lord Angelsey.

by the King, but which had the cordial concurrence of Goderich. Under Canning Portland had sat in the Cabinet without portfolio.

Goderich lacked both the prestige and force of personality to give unity to Canning's Government, and, as a result, the Cabinet tended to break into interest groups. Herries, Lyndhurst, Anglesey, and Bexley, being the only 'Protestants' in the Cabinet, tended to form a clique; Tierney and Carlisle, having been Whigs, looked to Lansdowne for leadership; Lord Dudley and Sturges-Bourne, who had been 'pure Canningites', tended to regard Huskisson as Canning's real successor; and this left Goderich, Wynn, Palmerston, Grant, and Portland as a group outside the others. Contemporary sources stress the major role played by Huskisson in the direction of the Government, which resulted from the force of his personality, rather than from experience, or parliamentary ability.[14] Late in the year there were some rumours that Huskisson sought to become Prime Minister himself,[15] but these appear to have been wholly baseless. His assumption of leadership on so many occasions, however, seems to have irritated Herries, who never had had much admiration for him.[16]

Despite the disunity within the Cabinet, and the lack of strong leadership, there were a number of factors which brought its members together, and gave the Government some semblance of strength. Canning's memory and his former supporters in Parliament, in the industrial community,[17] and in the Press gave the Government some internal unity and solid backing. The self-interest of its members also provided a motive for pulling together. Goderich, Herries, and Huskisson all enjoyed a prominence in the coalition Government, which they could not have attained in any other combination; Lyndhurst, if the seceders returned, would have been probably replaced by Lord Eldon, and, if the Whigs took power, his position would go to Sir James Scarlett;[18] Lansdowne had staked much of his political prestige on the success of the experiment;[19] while Tierney was much in need of the income he derived from his job. Then, as of September 1827, there were a number of negative factors operating in the Government's favour. No real issues on which to attack them were then apparent, and, although Londonderry stated that the 'great aristocracy of both of the great parties' was against them,[20] no real opposition was to appear until December.*

Although divided by their political backgrounds, the members of Goderich's Government could agree upon most issues, and their measures of domestic policy would have provided excellent materials for a Speech at the opening of Parliament. The financial situation of the country had improved during the past nine months. Exports to the United States and Europe had recovered, and there had also been a considerable increase in imports ; and, although the armed services made new demands on the budget for operations in Portugal and around Greece, the financial outlook was not menacing.

The Goderich Government seems to have adopted a project during this period which would have cut the Gordian knot of British finance, and permitted further experiments with Free Trade. Much later Herries recalled : 'Fifteen years ago . . . when I held the office of Chancellor of the Exchequer, I had come to the determination, in entire concurrence with Huskisson and Lord Ripon, to propose a Property Tax by way of commutation of some of the existing indirect taxes, which were more obstructive to the industry of the country.'[21] That the Government did more than toy with the idea is confirmed from two other sources. Mrs. Arbuthnot, late in December, stated that the Government

* In November Huskisson recognized a 'frondeur' section within the Government which included Sir George Warrender, and probably William Holmes and Herries. Huskisson to Binning, 28 Nov. 1827. HUSP, BM 38752. Among the Whigs, Lord John Russell, Viscount Milton, the Duke of Grafton, Earl Cowper, Viscount Althorp, the Earl of Carnarvon, Viscount Duncannon, and the Marquess of Tavistock might be called 'Watchmen' ; i.e. they were waiting to see the direction of the Government. Moore to Russell, 31 Oct. 1827, in Walpole, *Russell*, i. 137. The Tory aristocrats the Marquess of Hertford, the Duke of Rutland, the Earl of Lonsdale, the Earl of Shaftesbury, and the Earl of Powis, who controlled 30 seats in the Commons, and Whig aristocrats, such as Earl Grey, the Earl of Rosslyn, Earl Fitzwilliam, the Duke of Bedford, and the Earl of Lauderdale were undoubtedly among those Londonderry had in mind.

meant to propose such a tax,[22] and Greville noted that the Government had unsuccessfully sounded out the Marquess of Tavistock to move the Property Tax in the Commons. It would appear, then, that the Property Tax was to be the keystone of a new Free Trade budget.

The principle of economy in government was strongly espoused by Goderich's followers.[23] Goderich himself had established such a tradition both as Chancellor of the Exchequer,[24] and as Colonial Secretary,[25] and he helped Palmerston negotiate army reductions with Wellington, who finally submitted a memorandum on the subject.[26] Although the enlisted strength of the army was cut, the Duke shielded the officer corps from the economy knife.[27] Lord Lansdowne suggested that the Yeomanry forces be reduced from 24,000 men to 6,000 men, which would effect a saving of £90,000, and in the agricultural districts they were virtually dissolved. 'I regret much', Hardwicke wrote later, 'that Lord Goderich when he was in office dissolved all the Yeomanry Corps.'[28] Gone therewith was one of Grantham's chief interests.

Wellington suggested how savings might be effected by the local purchase of rations for troops in Mauritius, Ceylon, and the Ionian Islands, and by approving the use of colonial troops for public works, but his hint that the settlements on the African Coast, used in connection with the anti-slave trade operations, might be cut down could not be acted upon, as Goderich, like his predecessor, was committed to abolish slavery. Huskisson, in adopting the economy programme in his own department, tried to cut down the expenses in the Ionian Islands.[29]

The most pressing question of domestic policy — Catholic Emancipation — had been tacitly shelved when Canning came to power, and the following statement indicates that Goderich, had he retained power, might have continued in this way for the balance of King George IV's reign : [30]

A few days before Lord Goodrich [sic] resigned the Premiership, Lord Brougham wrote to Mr. Bennett to sound out the leading Catholics, and ascertain if they were disposed to postpone their question, in favour of a liberal Government. This was done & Mr. B. sent him an answer stating that they were content to abandon their claims during the life of George the 4th upon an understanding that they would be brought forth when the present King came to the Throne, provided their doing so would keep that Ministry in office.

This letter was sent to Goderich by a Dublin barrister, Richard Newton Bennett, in 1832. Whether or not the Catholic question could actually have been postponed that long, it is evident that the Irish Catholics were well satisfied with the measures taken by Goderich during his months in power.

Goderich's Irish policy was pacific and conciliatory. In November Palmerston wrote to William Lamb, the Chief Secretary in Ireland, that he hoped Lamb would 'make us a present of your Irish Yeomanry, the disbandment of which would probably be a good measure both in economy and in politics'.[31] For a time the Government planned to ask for a renewal of the Association Act, but late in November they were 'of a mind' to let it expire, and to enforce the ordinary powers of law.[32] The same conciliatory spirit motivated their appointments of governmental officials in Ireland. For the position of Chancellor of Ireland, the more ardent 'Catholics' wanted William Conyngham Plunket, while the 'Protestants' backed William Saurin.[33] Both were rejected in favour of the Vice-Chancellor of England, Sir Anthony Hart, who turned out to be one of Goderich's best appointees.[34] In early October the Government decided to pension off the Under-Secretary to the Lord-Lieutenant in Ireland, William Gregory, who was *persona non grata* with the Irish Catholics.[35]

William Lamb worked tirelessly to establish rapport with the Irish people, and during the autumn he busied himself with a great variety of legislation affecting Ireland — a jury Bill, a general paving and lighting measure, a Bill for the registration of deeds and others pertaining to customs and tolls, grand jury presentments, tithes, and sheriffs.[36] When he suggested trimming the annual grants to the Kildare Place Society and the Society for Discountenancing Vice (two Anglican organizations which spread Protestant education among the Irish poor), the Government agreed to their diminution.[37]

The Government's foreign policy was, in general, an extension

of Canning's, save that the new head was probably more isola-
tionist in his outlook, and less inclined to intervene in the affairs
of other nations, than his predecessor had been. Goderich's views
in 1827 were probably the same as they had been back in 1823,
when he said : [38]

He thought the result of the events of the last five and twenty years
had given rise to a state of things on the continent, from which it was
clearly our interest to keep aloof. There were contests now going on
in Europe — not like those of former days, when the matter in dispute
was the possession of some paltry province — but contests between
revolution on the one hand, and the exercise of power on the other. . . .
The House must perceive that they could not consistently embark in a
war with power against freedom ; but they ought, at the same time,
to take especial care that they did not side with revolution against
existing establishments.

To say that his policy was one of non-intervention in favour of
freedom might sound confusing, but it would probably describe
what Goderich had in mind.

The United States hoped, when Goderich came to power, to be
able to settle both the West Indian trade question and impressment, through a new treaty with Britain, but all that was accomplished was an indefinite extension of the Treaty of 1818. Dudley
in his note on the trade question told Gallatin that Britain preferred that municipal regulations, rather than treaties, govern
her commercial intercourse with other nations ; [39] Huskisson left
the impression in his talks with the same statesman that the
Government was too weak to take up impressment.[40] Yet two
years later Goderich made a strong speech in favour of reciprocal
trading agreements, and at the same time stressed the enormous
importance of American trade.[41]

What caused the failure of the Anglo-American talks in 1827?
Ellenborough, early in 1828, noted that 'Huskisson, to my great
surprise, expressed great dislike of the Americans'.[42] One might
reason from this that Huskisson's dislike was transformed into
Government policy, but this explanation is probably incorrect.
The reply received by the United States on the trade question
was merely a restatement of Canning's position, and, as Goderich

was determined to carry out Canning's policies as well as to retain his personnel, it seems probable that he was unwilling to deviate from them even in this instance, when his own views would have dictated a different course.

There were a few successes in foreign affairs, the most important being the seeming success of Canning's intervention in Portugal, which had given the regency there to Dom Miguel. 'All accounts lead us to believe', Goderich explained to Lord Wellesley in October, 'that Dom Miguel is much improved in character & disposition; and the Emperor of Austria & the Austrian Govert. seem increasingly disposed to give him good advice & to urge upon him the importance . . . of abiding by the oath which he swore to the constitution. . . .' [43] The following year Miguel became a tyrannical usurper, but at the moment British Iberian policy seemed to be prospering.

Considering all of these things together, it can hardly be said that Goderich's Government lacked materials for a Speech. They could have announced that the commerce of the nation had revived, that their Property Tax would permit further progress toward Free Trade, that notable economies in Government had been instituted, that Ireland was and probably would continue to be quiet, and that the intervention in Portugal had been successful. As corn prices were reviving, they could have avoided that vexing problem altogether, or simply mentioned the fact of their recovery. Such a Speech might have been received by both Houses, if not with enthusiasm, with acceptance at least, but as it turned out, the Speech was never delivered. The year 1827 had brought all sort of strange shifts and political developments, but nothing could have been more unexpected than that a brilliant British naval victory should accomplish the overthrow of the Government.

When the vassal state of Egypt in December 1825 came to the rescue of the Turks in the Greek war for independence, the Great Powers of Europe, which had hitherto done little to further the Christian cause, became interested. In order to save Greece, Canning, after some brilliant diplomatic manœuvrings, secured the signatures of France and Russia to a pact of 6 July 1827, which called for an armistice in the war, and, by a secret provision, pledged the three powers to interpose themselves between the contestants if either refused to accept the armistice. It was at this point that the Goderich Government took over. Stratford Canning was then Ambassador to Constantinople, and Sir Edward Codrington, an experienced admiral, commanded the British fleet in the area.

The first news of importance received by Goderich came in September. 'The Turks *positively* reject our propositions', he wrote to Huskisson on the 20th, 'and the thing is now brought to a crisis.' [44] The Government was now faced with the problem of how to 'interpose' their naval forces, and to separate the contestants so that a type of armistice would go into effect; but, even though Goderich called it a 'crisis', he did not assemble the Cabinet until 28 September. By that time the Egyptian fleet had already come to Navarino Bay.

At this Cabinet meeting there was general agreement that a moderate course would be followed, and that a limited blockade would be established around Greece. After this decision had been reached, Huskisson and Lansdowne left town again, and were apparently not present when Lord Howard de Walden, the Under-Secretary for Foreign Affairs, raised serious objections to the instructions to be sent to Codrington — as the Egyptian vessels often flew Austrian colours, it would be impossible to create an effective blockade if ships flying neutral flags were permitted to proceed through it unmolested.[45] So the instructions were held up until Huskisson, and probably others, could consider de Walden's objections.

Before this problem of total versus limited blockade could be settled, the Cabinet learned on 8 October that Stratford Canning had taken it upon himself to order a total blockade, and the question now before the Government was — should they approve his action, or order the more moderate course. Dudley was uncertain what to do; [46] Goderich wanted to adhere to their original plan for a limited blockade.[47] The morning of 9 October, Goderich, Bexley, Wynn, and Grant met for a discussion of the instructions, and it was decided to let the original instructions stand, and to inform Canning that they did not intend to disavow his interpretation of the rights of neutrals ; but that the blockading force should proceed with caution and avoid any collision with them.[48]

After these conclusions had been reached, the instructions were again held up by the arrival of a memorandum from Huskisson, who recommended that the blockade should be applied only to belligerents, and to neutral ships in convoy. Goderich talked the matter over with Dudley, and advised Huskisson that the instructions would probably be modified to incorporate his idea.[49] Having decided to make this change, Dudley next sought the approval of Lansdowne, who probably sent his views to Goderich on 12 October.[50] The final instructions contained the following paragraph : [51]

> The instructions which go out to you with this letter are calculated to save you from what is most painful in the discharge of an important public duty — any doubts as to the limits of it. The principle I should recommend you to bear in mind, as the key to any difficulties that may still present themselves to you, is that we are not at war — that we do not desire to be at war — but that what we aim at is to part the combatants.

These instructions were finally sent on 16 October, four days before the Battle of Navarino, and Admiral Codrington did not receive them until 8 November. If the same delivery schedule were followed, it would seem that Codrington would have received the limited blockade instructions before 20 October, and that the battle, in consequence, would not have taken place. It is clear that Goderich from the first wanted to send the original instructions, and that his only responsibility for the Battle of Navarino was permitting Dudley and de Walden to insist on consulting Huskisson and the others. It is clear, however, from their letters, that Dudley especially looked to Huskisson for leadership, and the same to some extent was true of de Walden.

As so often happened before the advent of rapid communications, the policy of the Government was actually determined by the British representatives in the crisis areas, and not by the Cabinet. 'The Allied Governments desire to avoid anything that

may bring on war', Canning advised Codrington, 'yet the pre-
vention of supplies is ultimately to be enforced if necessary, and
when all other means are exhausted, by cannon shot.' [52]   Codrington, on the basis of these instructions, issued his general
order of 8 September : 'All other means should be used to maintain the blockade, and cannon only as a last resort.' [53]   Had
Codrington been a young admiral, concerned with the trim
appearance of his ship, Canning might have used the term
'cannon shot' with impunity, but to a battle-hardened veteran
like Codrington, who found the smell of powder exhilarating, it
sounded like a call to arms.

During September and early October the admiral maintained
the blockade, and watched helplessly as the frustrated Moslems de-
vastated the Morea, but, as winter neared, both he and the French
admiral agreed it would become increasingly difficult to maintain
the blockade. Codrington decided that a show of force might
cause the Turks to accept an armistice, and on 20 October sailed
his fleet into Navarino Bay, near the Turkish and Egyptian fleets.
Someone fired a shot, and after a full-scale engagement which
lasted four hours, the Ottoman forces were completely smashed.
'I am sanguine enough to think that the victory of October 20th,'
Codrington reported to Dudley, 'instead of creating a war, will
prove the only means of preserving peace. Here again you will
smile at my maritime diplomacy.' [54]

The news of the Admiral's maritime diplomacy reached Goderich on 10 November, and he wrote immediately to Huskisson : [55]

The Turkish Fleet and the Agyptians are destroyed in the harbour
of Navarino. . . . This brings the question to a point, and the next
step to be taken is of vital importance . . . the action arose from the
allied Fleets going into the harbour at Navarino & taking up a position
exactly opposite to the Turkish line & close to it. *We* say that the
Turks fired first. The justification of the Admirals in taking up so
threatening a position, which (it must be owned) almost inevitably led
to a contest, rests with the violation of his engagement by Ibrahim
Pacha in the beginning of Oct., & upon the subsequent cruelty with
which he prosecuted the war. We must, I think, have a Cabinet
tomorrow of those who are accessible. . . . I do not suppose however
that we could *decide* anything in one cabinet, but there are to be con-

sidered 1st Calling of Parlt. 2nd explanatory declaration. 3rd course to be pursued with respect to the Porte, particularly whether we ought not instantly to instruct the Ambassadors, supposing them to be still allowed to remain at Constantinople, to renew the offer of *mediation*, more correctly speaking, of a negotiation for the pacification of Greece, in the war between whom & the Turks, we are almost become parties. These are very large and serious questions.

This letter is proof that Goderich, when left to himself, did not panic, and that he thought clearly and constructively in an emergency. He was ready to call Parliament immediately, and this step might have saved his Government.

But the Prime Minister lacked the force of personality to bring into motion the creaky political machine that Canning had created. Huskisson suggested that they wait until French intentions became known before they decided on their own course,[56] and another delay took place, during which the Duke of Clarence, as First Lord of the Admiralty — without receiving the sanction of the Cabinet — recommended Codrington for the Grand Cross of the Bath.[57] The Duke of Wellington strongly advised the King not to bestow the honour without consulting his Ministers, but his advice was ignored.[58] So the Government found that official approval of the Battle of Navarino had been given, and it was up to them to defend it in Parliament.

Huskisson returned to London for the Cabinets, and Goderich's letters to him, one of the best sources of information during this period, therefore ceased. Palmerston wrote that the Cabinet seriously considered calling Parliament at their 13 November meeting, but decided against it. 'The mere circumstance of our having made a bonfire of the fleet of our good ally at Navarino', he wrote, 'is not deemed a reason for assembling Parliament because this was not a declaration of war, but only a slight act of remonstrance struck parenthetically into an unbroken friendship.' [59] Just who favoured, and who opposed, the calling of Parliament, he did not say.

The Cabinet also decided to try to uphold the provisions of the 6 July 1827 treaty, and to bring an end to the fighting in Greece, but at the moment they had to wait until they learned

the Turkish reaction to the destruction of their fleet, and the
Turks pursued a policy of delay. The Government hoped that
the Turkish supplies for their forces in Greece would run out,
and this would force them to withdraw, but as of 4 December, the
Cabinet was in a state of 'uncertainty'.[60] Later that month they
learned that the Egyptians planned to withdraw from the Morea,
and a despatch was sent ordering that every assistance be given
to convey Ibrahim and his troops back to Egypt.[61] Otherwise,
there was little that the Government could do, save to hope that
the Navarino disaster would discourage Turkey, and bring about
negotiations.

Much of the Cabinet's time seems to have been devoted to
working up a defence of Codrington's action. Late in November
they sent the Admiral a memorandum which asked certain questions : his instructions were to use force only to maintain the
blockade, so why did he sail into the Bay and sink the Turkish
ships ? What specific activities of Ibrahim justified going into the
Bay ? What explanations had been made by Ibrahim, and what
protests had been made to him of his activities in the Morea ? [62]

Sir John Gore was sent post-haste across France to put these
and other questions to Codrington in person. It was early
January before he returned with the answers to them, and had a
conference with the Ministers, which he reported to Codrington
as follows : [63]

I saw them again yesterday ; the same objections and queries — the
same question — except that Lord D. asked me 'why you did not
anchor further off from the Turks ?' I explained that the English ships
had to go near because of the water, and could not anchor further off
lest the French and Russians think they were afraid. . . . If they could
they would throw you overboard, and save themselves ; but you are
above their reach.

It is quite clear, then, that the information the Government was
able to collect during November, December and early January
had not established a very effective defence of Codrington's
decision to move into the Bay.

Information regarding Goderich's state of mind on this subject
is not available, but a note from Huskisson to Harrowby on 22

November probably reflected the attitude of many members of the Cabinet : [64]

> I am afraid the explosions at Navarino will dispel all the Speaker's pleasing dreams of an easy and short session. No man could feel so anxious as myself that it should be both short and easy. . . . But this precipitate act of Codrington's (to give it no harsher description) almost makes me despair. With an utter disregard of his instructions, he has taken upon himself to strike a blow in order to bring the business to a close. Should it have that effect, the scrape may not be quite so serious ; but if it should not (as I fear) it will be only *le commencement de la fin*.

When this was written the Cabinet was still waiting hopefully for news that the Turks had come to terms, a hope that faded gradually as the days and weeks passed. Feeling as he did about Codrington's action, how could Huskisson defend him in Parliament? To a sympathetic audience, Codrington's act could be defended on the ground of necessity, as the only means of separating the combatants, but the opponents of the Government, who had long been seeking an issue to be used against them, were not likely to constitute such an audience when Parliament opened.

In the upper circles of the political world, all sorts of rumours and opinions were circulated during these weeks of futile waiting. Some blamed Navarino on Lord Dudley. 'Ld. Dudley ought to be,' Mrs. Arbuthnot quoted Wellington as saying, ' & might be, impeached for this Navarino affair.' [65] But the information-leaks from the Government did not discredit specific individuals, but the Government as a whole. In early December William Holmes told Harriet Arbuthnot that the Government was 'at *sixes & sevens*, some for peace, some for war, and all despised and derided by every body'.[66] Herries spread the story that Dudley, Huskisson and Lansdowne wanted to permit Russia to occupy Moldavia and Wallachia as a means of coercing the Turks, but that he and Tierney opposed. 'He said Ld. Goderich was laughed at & despised by every body,' the report continued, 'never of any opinion, changing from one side to the other, thinking of nothing but jobs and patronage.' [67] One of the more persistent rumours was that Goderich led the peace party in the Cabinet, and that Huskisson was for war.[68]

N

Few members of the Cabinet, save for Goderich himself, had
had much experience in high office, and they no doubt had looked
forward to the meeting of Parliament, even before Navarino, with
trepidation; and, once they had decided against calling Parliament in November, they exposed themselves to the nerve-racking
suspense of anticipation, while observing the growth of increasing
hostility in the political circles opposed to them. It is only
against this background of general fear and nervousness that the
extraordinary events preceding the fall of Goderich's Government can be properly understood and evaluated.

Whatever may have been Goderich's views of Codrington's
actions, he regarded Navarino as a great British naval victory,
of which he was proud. Looking ahead, Codrington was to be
recalled by Wellington in 1828, and he received a chilly reception
in England. In 1831, however, he paid a visit to Russia, and
there his victory was acclaimed. 'I cannot help being the more
strongly impressed with the contrast in England,' Codrington
wrote to a friend. 'I know scarcely anyone, except Lord Goderich,
who has shown me any extra attention since my striking my flag.'[69]

The first bitter fruit of the post-Navarino atmosphere in the
Cabinet was the quarrel between Huskisson and Herries over the
membership of a finance committee to be established after Parliament opened. In mid-November Tierney casually mentioned
Lord Althorp, an impeccable Whig, to Goderich, who agreed that
he should be on the committee, and said he would accept as its
chairman any individual upon whom the Cabinet members in the
Commons would agree.[70] Later Goderich mentioned the suggestion to Huskisson, who was at first unenthusiastic about the
appointment, but after hearing Tierney's views on 19 November,
Huskisson told him he was 'inclined to the arrangement'.[71] His
attitude encouraged Tierney to sound out Lord Spencer, Althorp's
father, regarding his son's attitude toward the appointment.

About a week later Goderich discussed the appointment with
Huskisson, and, on learning that Herries had not yet been advised that Althorp was being considered, he told Huskisson to
contact him, which he did on 28 November. Huskisson told

Herries that Althorp might be a fit candidate for the chairmanship, and Herries replied that 'so far as his own personal feelings
were concerned, such an appointment would by no means be
unsatisfactory to him.' [72] About this time Tierney entered the
office, and all three discussed both the Althorp appointment
and the composition of the committee as a whole. 'Some
remarks . . .', Herries wrote later, 'conveyed the impression of
something like a final agreement with Lord Althorp.' [73] But he
did not then make an issue of the appointment.

The following day Colonel Frederick Trench, a close friend
of the hostile Duke of Rutland, called on Herries and told him
that he had heard Althorp would be chairman of the finance
committee, and that some members had already been told they
would serve on it. Probably Trench warned him that Althorp,
as a member of the reforming party, was not acceptable to the
Old Tories; at any rate, Herries decided to make an issue of the
procedure that Huskisson had followed in this matter. He wrote
a formal letter of protest to Huskisson, which concluded with the
remark : 'What can now be done to set matters right, I do not
know.' [74]

On learning of Herries's real or feigned indignation, Huskisson
quickly wrote to Tierney, urging him not to hold out expectations
to any of the individuals they had discussed for the finance committee ; [75] and the following day, he wrote Herries : 'I must
admit that both Goderich & I must take some blame to ourselves
for not having sooner informed you of what Tierney had mentioned to Goderich on the subject, but I am sure you will acquit
both of us of anything intentional in the delay.' [76] Tierney
replied to Huskisson that Althorp would accept the chairmanship if it were offered to him, but that the Government was not
committed to Althorp by any agreement whatsoever.[77] Huskisson
showed Herries the letter, and the affair seemed to be ended.[78]
Certainly it should have been, for Huskisson and Tierney had
been guilty of nothing worse than investigating whether or not
Althorp would take the chairmanship if it were offered to him,
and Herries already had received what amounted to an apology
for their having done this.

The Navarino incident and the quarrel between Herries and
Huskisson over Althorp turned Goderich's thoughts to strengthening the Government through the distribution of patronage and
favours. Although he had worked this field intensively before,
the results had not been too impressive. Church appointments
had been made to satisfy several interests, and a close study of
the correspondence reveals that the Bishop of Rochester was a
Lansdowne candidate,[79] the Bishop of Winchester, the King's
candidate,[80] the Bishop of Llandaff,[81] Goderich's own appointee,[82]
and Soder and Man had been agreed upon between the King
and Goderich.[83] An attempt had been made to win over the
Scottish Representative Peers by making the Duke of Gordon
the Governor of Canada,[84] but the Duke of Wellington, by coincidence or design, gave Gordon the Governorship of Edinburgh
Castle, and thus thwarted Goderich.[85] Lansdowne then suggested that the Canadian position should be given to Lord
Rosslyn in an effort to conciliate Lord Grey,[86] but some soundings
evidently indicated that such an offer would be ill received. In
November Goderich attempted to win over some of the Old
Tories by offering the Garter to Lord Clive, but the honour was
refused, due to Clive's loyalty to Wellington.[87] Thus, the attempts
to extend the Government's influence among the Old Tories, Old
Whigs and Scottish Representative Peers had all failed, and the
only Old Tory who accepted a favour was the Duke of Wellington,
who applied to and received from Goderich a peerage for his
brother, Sir Henry Wellesley.[88]

The distribution of peerages and baronetcies rewarded some
supporters, but did not bring much added strength to the
Government. John Lambton was created Baron Durham in
the hope he would help neutralize Grey in the Lords,[89] and the
Earl of Rosebery was made Baron Rosebery in the English peerage to curry favour with the Scottish Peers. Otherwise, Sir
Charles Stuart, who became Baron de Rothesay, was one of
Goderich's 'connections'; Sir William A'Court, who became
Baron Heytesbury, was a recommendation of Lord Dudley, who
secured an earldom for himself in September; and the creation
of Viscountess Canning was a mark of respect for the late Prime

Minister. The distribution of baronetcies and knighthoods repaid past favours, or recognized merit, but did not add significant new strength to the Government.*

By and large, Goderich's patronage projects added up to failure, but he refused to reopen the subject of Cabinet additions, which might have secured new strength for his Government. Late in September the Duke of Portland had asked to be allowed to resign because of his wife's health,[90] but Goderich had replied: 'I have felt from the beginning that the best chance the Govt. had of being able to maintain its ground, was by making as few changes as possible.'[91] Portland did not insist, but the King, knowing his desire, suggested in November that he be permitted to retire in favour of Wellesley, who might be expected to neutralize somewhat the influence of his brother in the Lords. 'I should like the Lord Wellesley scheme very much', Goderich wrote on 6 November, 'if I did not fear it would again

---

* Goderich submitted a list of thirteen candidates for baronetcies in November, and a request that the baronetcy of Sir Isaac Collins be continued in his nephew. Memorandum — Baronetcies Proposed to be Made in November (BP). Almost all of them, as well as two later recommendations, were accepted by the King. Those created, together with their sponsors, are as follows: Sir Richard Hussey Vivian (Lord Anglesey); Robert Tristram Ricketts (Elizabeth Lawrence); Francis Hastings Doyle (Lord Moira); John Forbes Drummond (Lord Dudley). Henry Wakeman was recommended by a Member of Parliament from Worcestershire; George Philips was an influential Member of Parliament; Henry Chamberlain was a fairly distinguished foreign-service officer. Charles William Taylor, Richard Bulkeley Philipps Philipps, and John Hutton Cooper were Members of Parliament; Uvedale Price was a writer; and Edward Marmaduke Joseph Vavasour was a landowner. William Henry Fremantle was granted a knighthood for his services. Goderich did not neglect the interests of his own relationship. Lancelot Shadwell, knighted and made Vice-Chancellor of England, was a close friend of Elizabeth Lawrence. Sir Galbraith Lowry Cole, brother of Lady Grantham, was made Governor of the Cape of Good Hope. 'The Blubberer has got a warrant signed for his £3000 a year pension,' Londonderry reported in October, 'and so has Huskisson.' Londonderry to Burghersh, 20 Oct. 1827, in Weigall, *Burghersh* (London, Murray, 1912), p. 262.

raise that foolish question about Lord Holland.' [92] This was
written just four days before the news of Navarino reached
England.

On or after 3 December, when the Cabinet reassembled after a
weekend vacation, Goderich suddenly changed his mind about
admitting new members into the Cabinet, and the only knowledge
of the circumstances surrounding this decision comes from a
letter written by Huskisson about a week later. Someone
'pressed' him to take Wellesley into the Cabinet as President of
the Council, and this once again opened the question of Cabinet
expansion.[93] After talking the matter over with Huskisson, who
feared an Old Tory plot was in the making, Goderich was encouraged to insist that Holland be added at the same time as
Wellesley, as a means of keeping Lord Grey in check.[94] Goderich
evidently broached the idea of bringing in both Wellesley and
Holland to Lansdowne on 5 December, for the latter wrote the
following day : [95]

> I will not delay . . . telling you that the arrangement you have
> suggested, of which I have been thinking ever since we met yesterday,
> has my entire concurrence, both as to the thing itself, the time & mode
> of carrying it into operation. . . . Of course it should be understood
> that the appointments whatever they are should be simultaneous.
> Whether you & Huskisson make the representation at once to the K.
> or whether you arm yourself first with the opinion of the cabinet (of
> whose general concurrence I think there can be no doubt) must be
> for yourself to judge.

Goderich, acting on a precedent set by Lord Liverpool when he
brought Canning into the Cabinet without consulting some of
its members,[96] decided that they should not tell the others until
later. Charles Grant was later somewhat put out about this
secrecy, but, after thinking the matter over, wrote : 'I ought at
once to have admitted that this was a strong & decisive precedent
& completely in point. I was unjust in not doing so at once.' [97]

Although Lansdowne, Huskisson, and Goderich were all responsible for the plan, it was Goderich who had to face the testy
King alone, and it seems to have been a very disagreeable experience. All that is known of the interview of 8 December is that

Goderich insisted that Wellesley could not come in without Holland, and that the King refused to entertain the proposition.[98] So the three were faced with the problem of their next step — to insist, or not to insist? By 11 December Huskisson wrote that Goderich was 'in a most pitiful state', his 'spirits are worn out', and he had lost his powers of decision.[99] Huskisson traced his condition not to the new Cabinet crisis, but to 'the constant worry in which he has been kept by his all but crazy wife'. It was finally decided that they should insist on the inclusion of both Wellesley and Holland, and that Goderich's resignation should be the consequence of the King's refusal.

So the three drew up a lengthy letter to the King on 11 December, which stressed the need of more 'solid and united support' because some members of both parties, previously at odds with each other, 'are now united in a determined opposition to the Government'.[100] This sentence apparently refers to a current rumour that Lord Bathurst and Lord Grey had not only reached an agreement to oppose the Government, but perhaps even had decided upon the membership of the Cabinet to replace it.[101] If so, it runs counter to Huskisson's fear, expressed in a letter of the same date, that there was an Old Tory plot against the Government,[102] and the scholar is left to interpret the sentence as best he can. Whatever was exactly meant, this was used to justify the demands which followed — that the Duke of Wellington or Lord Hill receive the Ordnance Department, that Wellesley be made President of the Council, and that Holland be brought into the Cabinet, presumably without portfolio. The alternative was resignation.[103]

How the Duke of Wellington's name found its way into the demands is another unsolved mystery. One possible interpretation, which rests on mere surmise, is that Goderich was frightened at this attempt to coerce the King, and insisted that the Duke's name be included in a weak attempt to make the admission of Holland more palatable. This would also explain why he added, unbeknown to the others, the following paragraph to the letter:[104]

Lord Goderich cannot conclude this statement without venturing to add, how deeply he feels his own inadequacy to discharge the great duties of the situation to which your Majesty's far too favourable opinion called him. His own natural infirmities have been aggravated by a protracted state of anxiety during the last two years ; his health is enfeebled, and above all he fears that the health of one dependent upon him for support and strength, is still in a state of such feebleness and uncertainty as to keep alive that anxiety to a degree not easily compatible with the due discharge of duties which require the exertion of all the energies of the strongest mind.

This was simply a statement of inadequacy, not unlike one attached to his letter when he accepted office,[105] and the purpose of bringing in his health and domestic difficulties was probably to awaken sympathy in the King's mind and to cause him to become more co-operative about the appointments. There is not a shred of evidence that Goderich considered it — as the King was to do — as a resignation of his office.

The result of this letter was to cut communications between Goderich and the King for almost a week following the latter's reply, which was dated 12 December : 'Can Lord Goderich satisfy the King's mind, that the Duke of Wellington will accept a seat in the Cabinet with the present members ? . . . The King can only regret that Lord Goderich's domestic calamities unfit him for his present situation, but over this the King unhappily has not control.'[106] Goderich acknowledged receipt of the King's letter, and requested an audience for the following day ; and at the same time he wrote to Huskisson : [107]

Upon reflecting on the letter, I do not think that it amounts to an absolute rejection, but that it adds as a *condition*, the introduction of the D. into the Cabinet as a more effective pendant to H. If I refuse to try that, he will then be able to say that I refused to try what would have reconciled him to the rest of the proposition. If I try it, & fail, then he will be able to say that it is not his fault, for that the introduction of H. was deemed by me to require a 'pendant', & that if that pendant cannot be got he is fairly entitled to say that after my own [?] reasoning the other part of the arrangement would not do. It ought now at all events to be persisted in. I think it would be as well, under any circumstances, if I write to him tonight, in a civil tone, that he might be in better humour tomorrow.

There is neither fright nor panic in this letter, nor any suggestion that he thought he had resigned ; it is the letter of one fencing with the King, hoping to secure an advantage. Huskisson replied that the King's answer had 'haunted me all night', and correctly predicted that the King would not discuss other appointments until the question of a fit head for the Government had been settled.[108] There is nothing to indicate, however, that Huskisson regarded the paragraph added by Goderich as a resignation.

Before sending his reply to Goderich, the King had shown Goderich's letter to Herries and Lyndhurst, probably to warn them that the Holland question had arisen again, but his principal adviser during this crisis seems to have been Knighton. His first reaction seems to have been 'great anger against Goderich . . . great doubt what is to be done & an Idea of Wellesley'.[109] As Knighton had persuaded Herries back in August to make an issue of the Exchequer position as a means of embarrassing the Whigs, it seems probable that he now encouraged the King to resist Holland's appointment, and to assert his authority by regarding Goderich's letter as a resignation. This last decision was to doom the Goderich Administration.

On 13 December the King made this decision known to Lyndhurst and Huskisson, who had audiences with him, and Knighton conveyed it to Herries, who replied: 'I take it for granted that the political objects which have been recently pressed upon the King will at least be suspended under the present circumstances.'[110] There was no remorse in his letter at the fall of Goderich — merely satisfaction that Holland had been excluded. On his arrival home, Huskisson found a letter from Goderich, which revealed that his friend realized for the first time that he had been excluded, and that he was anxious to mend the error if he could. He had talked to Lansdowne that day, and found he would be satisfied with merely a specific assurance that Holland would eventually be admitted to the Cabinet. 'This might perhaps be obtained,' Goderich continued, 'and if it could, and that after all that has passed *you* could be reconciled to such a termination, I can say that at whatever risk to myself . . . I would go to the fight at the opening of the Session, and leave the ultimate decision of our fate to the voice of Parlt.'' [111] His willingness to abandon the Holland–Wellesley project so quickly might indicate that Goderich really had not much faith in it in the first place. Huskisson did not comment on his offer to continue without Holland, but merely reported to Goderich the unsatisfactory nature of his interview with the King.[112]

Huskisson returned to the palace on 14 December, and mentioned Goderich's promise both to Lyndhurst and the King, but it did not change the latter's decision to offer the Prime Ministership to Lord Harrowby, a strange selection, indeed, when one considers that he had retired from the Cabinet for reasons of health. On returning home that night, Huskisson found a letter from Lansdowne, who mentioned the Grey–Bathurst plot as follows: 'I am assured from a quarter on which I think I can rely . . . that a compact has been concluded between Ld. Grey – Ld. Bathurst & going the length of the compleat arrangement of a Govt. First article being that Ld. Grey is to be at the head.'[113] Huskisson quickly wrote a long letter to the King, begging permission to inform Goderich that Harrowby would be sent for, and warning him that otherwise Goderich might not consent to serve in a Harrowby Government. He also sent Lansdowne's account of the Bathurst–Grey plot, which he thought 'is, perhaps, not altogether unfounded'.[114]

Goderich spent 14 December waiting for some word from somebody. His letter to the King of that date, recommending John Forbes Drummond for a baronetcy, indicates that he did not consider his powers in abeyance, and that he continued to act as the King's principal adviser.[115] The following day, after receiving the King's permission, Huskisson wrote to Goderich, revealing that Harrowby had been called in, and adding: 'Now let me entreat of you to keep your own counsel and mine, to wait quietly — to get all the strength and spirit you can — and, above all, not to decide upon anything hastily.'[116] The crestfallen Goderich replied that Lord Harrowby probably would not accept the commission, and promised to do whatever would cause the least embarrassment to everyone.[117] Then, dejected and rejected by everyone except Huskisson, he went to Wrest, where he planned to remain until 19 December.

Harrowby arrived in London on 17 December, conferred with

Huskisson, and then went to the Royal Lodge for an interview. 'The King is evidently divided between his dislike to give his government a stronger Whig tinge', he reported later, '& his fear of returning under the yoke of his old government, with their new connection, which fear seems strong.' [118] He declined the Prime Ministership, and advised the King to retain Goderich at least at present, and if possible through the next parliamentary session ; he further advised that Holland should be added to the Cabinet after the opening of Parliament, and perhaps Wellesley also.[119] His advice — and probably a growing fear that Lord Grey might be forced upon him — had a magical effect upon the King. He was now ready to return the Government to Goderich, and to admit Lord Holland before Wellesley.

Huskisson was now faced with the problem of restoring some order to the shadow Government, and he went about the task in a thoroughly businesslike manner. On 17 December he told the King that Goderich should not be sent for until Lyndhurst, Lansdowne, and Dudley had all agreed to his restoration, and the following day they all assembled at the Lodge. Huskisson reported this meeting to a friend : [120]

> They all gave their opinions that there was nothing left but to see how far Goderich having everything at stake, would strain every nerve to recover his position ; that he has nothing left between success and absolute ruin must be admitted, and they are willing to believe that this feeling may carry him through. At any rate to fall in the attempt and for us to fall with him, will be less disgraceful than to abandon the King on the very day on which he was advised to hold a Council to fix the meeting of Parliament.

There was some talk of Wellesley as a possible alternative at this meeting, but Lansdowne, Lyndhurst, and Dudley all agreed to Goderich's return and thereby bound themselves to stand by him to the bitter end. The only objection came from Lyndhurst, who warned that Herries might resign when he learned Holland was to be brought into the Cabinet.[121]

Huskisson, by following this procedure, strengthened Goderich's position enormously, and the same day he wrote to Goderich, asking him to return to London immediately.[122] 'I shall be in town this afternoon,' Goderich replied. 'Perhaps you could call upon me in the evening. You are right in urging that I have much at stake. I do not believe my sense will hold out.' [123] Huskisson took advantage of the invitation to discuss the Cabinet meeting to be held the following day.

The protracted, wearying chain of events which had begun on 11 December came to an end with the Cabinet meeting of 19 December. One observer described it as follows: [124]

Lord Goderich, at the Cabinet yesterday, made a statement of the circumstances which had led to its being considered by the King that he had resigned, and he professed his willingness to remain in office at present, and provided his colleagues should be of opinion that his remaining would tend to relieve them from the difficulty which had arisen from his proposed retirement. They are understood to have intimated their acquiescence in his proposal.

Huskisson recorded that all members, save Herries, pledged their 'entire support and confidence', and that Herries, following an explanation on a minor point, 'gave his complete concurrence and promise of cordial support'.[125] The point mentioned by Herries had nothing to do with the chairmanship of the finance committee.

Shortly after this meeting some arrangements were made to assure the Prime Minister of a modicum of domestic tranquillity as he faced his tasks in the difficult future. Huskisson explained them to Granville: [126]

G. promises fair. The Lady is now all anxiety he should remain where He is, and promises too, to sacrifice herself to the public cause. A House, I understand is taken for her at Brighton — there I hope she will go soon, and remain long. I have given fair notice that should Goderich collapse, I shall resign and make his Infirmity the ground of my resignation. This I have done through speaking to [one] who has undertaken to keep Lady Goderich to her present intentions.

Huskisson, in most of his correspondence during this period, traced Goderich's difficulties mainly to his eccentric wife.

With these events, arrangements, and rearrangements the Goderich Administration entered its final phase, the twilight zone of its existence. The date for the meeting of Parliament was set for 22 January, and Huskisson sought advice from Lord Binning as to who should receive their circulars.[127]   He also made an unsuccessful attempt to secure a Member to move the Address in the Commons.[128]   Goderich, for his part, sent out summons to his supporters in the House of Lords on 29 December :

As Parliament will certainly meet for the Despatch of Business on Tuesday, the 22nd of January next, and as it is desirable that there should be as full an attendance as possible upon that occasion, I trust it will not be inconvenient to Your Lordship to be present personally in the House of Lords on that day.[129]

But the Ministers went through the motions as spiritlessly as the actors in a theatrical flop the night before closing.

At the time he wrote his circular letters, Goderich had two resignations in his pocket.

If the events of 11–19 December had been kept secret, the Government, which experienced no internal changes, would not have made any explanations in Parliament, and would not have been deeply affected by them.   But *The Times* gave an account of them during 15–19 December which was so garbled and similar to that found in Greville's diary, that he was probably their 'most respectable' source of information.   Frederick Lamb and William Holmes leaked a good deal of information to Wellington, most of it accurate ; [130] Lord Brougham gave some of the facts to Lord Rosslyn ; [131] Lady Holland provided an account of sorts to Lord Lauderdale ; [132] and Lansdowne sent accurate information on the subject to William Lamb.[133]   Information thus found its way into both friendly and unfriendly hands, but, so far as the general public was concerned, they only knew that Goderich had been temporarily suspended from the Prime Ministership, and that it had been offered to Lord Harrowby.   How this news affected the position of the Government it is impossible to gauge, for it had been wobbly ever since Navarino,[134] but it seems probable that the events tended to discredit Goderich, who many believed had tried to run away from his responsibilities, rather than the Government as a whole.

That its opponents fully expected Goderich to meet Parliament is clear from the preparations being made to upset him. One point of attack was the Lord Shaftesbury question. Shaftesbury, who was Chairman of Committees in the Lords, had voted against the Corn Bill back in May, and rumour had it that the Government intended to replace him. Just before Christmas Bathurst wrote to Lord Lauderdale on the subject of retaining Shaftesbury in his position, and Lauderdale, who had already contacted Lord Grey on the subject, replied : 'I think he will go right from what he said to me at Howick, but Auckland is the man he would least like to oppose.' [135] Lauderdale promised that Lord Melville would use his influence among the Scottish Representative Peers, but he wanted Wellington to contact some others in the same group, the Duke of Gordon, Baron Saltoun, and Baron Forbes, and to send a blank proxy to the Marquess of Tweeddale.

Although Wellington had long before expressed a desire to retain Shaftesbury, it is clear from Bathurst's letter to him of 30 December that he was not one of the original projectors of the current combination. He stressed that this was a personal, not a political question, and hence one on which Wellington could take a stand against the Government.[136] Bathurst also advised the Duke that Lord Ellenborough was preparing an amendment to the Address, and expressed his doubts as to the wisdom of such a course.

These letters indicate that the Bathurst–Grey rumours had not been altogether unfounded, but at the same time show that their co-operation was still in an incipient state. If the Government had gone on, they would probably have faced an attempt by Ellenborough to amend the Address on the Navarino question, which just as probably would have failed ; but, if they had attempted to replace Shaftesbury, they would certainly have been snowed under in the Lords. But the chief importance of these plots is that by their very existence they show that the opponents of the Government expected Goderich to persevere even after the events of 11–19 December.

The beginning of the final complex chapter in the history of the Goderich Administration took place the evening of 19 December when Huskisson, who had been a tower of strength during the preceding week, collapsed completely. Only hours after the

Cabinet meeting at which he announced his intention to go on, Huskisson read the following memorandum to Goderich : [137]

> I feel it necessary to request leave to resign, and in taking this step to state, first, what are not my motives. 1st I have certainly not experienced any want of kindness or confidence on the part of the King . . . 2nd. Whilst I feel the difficulties of the approaching Campaign in Pt. I am under no great apprehension that, with fair play, we cannot successfully meet them. . . . 3rd Tho' my health is not strong, it is as good now as when I accepted the Seals in September. But my reason for wishing to be relieved is simply and solely this : I can no longer conceal to myself that Councils which ought to be and which the K. specifically directs should be, held most strictly secret, are not so kept.

Under these circumstances, he felt he could not successfully conduct business in the Commons. What could the newly-reinstated Prime Minister do under these circumstances, but listen and hope for the best? The resignation was not accepted.

Herries waited until the next day before violating completely the promise he had made to Goderich on 19 December of cordial support. He told Lyndhurst that he and Bexley would shortly ask to resign because of the Holland arrangement, and the Chancellor, who seems to have given his promise in good faith, immediately wrote to the wrong man — Knighton — begging him to stop their resignations.[138] The King's physician obediently talked with Herries, and, as a result, the latter decided to bring up the finance committee question.

Huskisson's attempt to resign might be considered as a sort of temporary aberration brought on by excessive fatigue from which, if matters had gone smoothly, he would have recovered but Herries's conduct points to a deliberate attempt to break up the Government, and substantiates Palmerston's characterization of him as a 'live shell' in the Cabinet ready to blow them all up.[139] Out of a clear blue sky he wrote Goderich on 21 December that, unless 'all political views of the narrower kind' were discarded in forming the finance committee, the Prime Minister could have 'my most ready and cheerful resignation'.[140] How he could reconcile this with his own opinion of the fitness of Althorp for the position as chairman, and with his promise to give cordial support to the Government, it is impossible to say. At any rate, he probably desired to raise an issue between himself and Huskisson, and that is exactly what occurred.

Goderich replied that he could not conceive of a case in which he would want Herries's resignation,[141] and forwarded a copy of the letter to Huskisson with the comment: 'Were it not for *recent* events, I should consider Herries' letter more as a pretext than anything else; but as matters stand, it is very doubtful.'[142] This new difficulty unnerved Huskisson still further, and he replied: 'I should be most thankful to anyone that would get me out of it [his situation], without the discredit of appearing to run away, and I am not sure that this letter does not go towards helping me to such an escape.'[143] Nothing was done until after the Christmas recess. Goderich — now completely convinced that they must meet Parliament — either consciously or unconsciously adopted a policy of delay, to let this present quarrel run its course in the hope that the growing imminence of the session would force a compromise.

The past five months had seen many strange and unusual events take place within the Government, but none were more so than those involving Huskisson on the fourth and fifth days of Christmas. He called on Goderich on the morning of the fourth, and, after an extended discussion of the finance committee quarrel, concluded: 'That many circumstances . . . had created in my mind a very decided apprehension . . . that there was an influence elsewhere which wd. be constantly employed in aggravating . . . difficulties and in traducing me in the highest quarter.'[144] He warned the Prime Minister that he was about to take the 'only step by which I cd. protect myself' — resignation. At two in the afternoon, Huskisson saw Lord Anglesey, who asked: 'Are you aware that you are assailed in every way by a secret & powerful enemy having the ear of the K. & possessing the greatest influence?' When Huskisson replied he had suspected as much, Anglesey said it was beyond all doubt, and noted that the Herries matter was 'part of the whole system' to traduce and betray him. Much shaken by this information, Huskisson returned to the Colonial Office, where he had a visitor who warned him that the information printed in *The Times* regarding the events of 11–19 December 'had been furnished from Windsor', which seemed like further evidence of the 'influence' at work against him. Just before leaving the office that evening, Lord Howard de Walden arrived, and warned Huskisson that the King had desired to invite him to a dinner for the Infanta of Portugal, but the 'influence' had ruled him out, and 'that this intended insult had been enforced by insinuations calculated to prejudice my perl. character'.[145]

The next morning Lord Howard de Walden visited him again, and 'stated to me some other proceedings which had been resorted to in order to prejudice my character wi. the K. into which I forbear to enter, not that I have any doubt of their truth, but they are so perfectly fiendlike that I am unwilling to retain the recollection of them even in this shape'.[146] This series of warnings, which may or may not have been coincidental, reduced Huskisson to a frightened shadow of a man, who resembled the description he had given of Goderich on 11 December. At noon he went to Goderich, and told him that his previous suspicions had been confirmed, that a 'baneful & secret influence' was working even harder than he thought to destroy him. The Herries matter was part of the general plot, and that 'the only safe & honourable course for me was to resign at once'.[147] The same day he handed Goderich a formal letter to the King resigning his office,[148] and he refused to attend the Cabinet meeting that afternoon.

So, as of 29 December, Goderich had three resignations in his pocket — two from Huskisson, and one from Herries. If he had sought to avoid meeting Parliament, he could have sent them all to the King, along with his own, but nothing was further from his mind. Instead he had another conversation with Herries, and tried to secure a forthright statement of his intentions, but the Chancellor of the Exchequer merely stated that his resignation was contingent upon Goderich's persevering in a course into which he had been drawn by others.[149] Two facts seemed clear — Herries would resign if Althorp were appointed chairman ; Huskisson would resign — even more than he had already done — if Althorp were not appointed.

o

Huskisson meanwhile considered himself — at times — no longer a member of the Government, and a New Year's Eve party at the Royal Lodge caused him some embarrassment, for Goderich asked him to accompany him there. 'Is there any reason why you shd. not go with him', Howard de Walden asked, when Huskisson brought the matter up, 'beyond that of the risk of his opening confidential discussion with you?' Whether or not Huskisson went with Goderich is uncertain, but he certainly came back with him, and Huskisson's later reference to their 'drowsy return' indicates that the Prime Minister had temporarily shelved his multifarious problems by falling asleep.[150]

The semi-resignation of Huskisson meanwhile had started a chain reaction in the Cabinet. Lansdowne, while suggesting that the finance committee question be postponed until after Parliament met, promised to determine his own course by Huskisson's, which would mean, technically, that he, too, was out of the Government.[151] Lord Lyndhurst struck his colours on 31 December, when he informed Knighton that the Government could not go on in its present form.[152] Anglesey was of the same mind by 1 January, if not before.[153]

During those chilly days of early January, Lord Goderich stood virtually alone in his determination to meet Parliament. Herries, who possessed a degree of political prominence wholly new to him, was probably as fearful of meeting Parliament as Chancellor of the Exchequer in 1828 as he was to be in 1851, when his timidity was a factor in Stanley's refusal to take office. Lyndhurst would have gone on, but not without the moral support of his 'Protestant' friends, Herries and Bexley.[154] Anglesey probably was fearful of introducing the Government's conciliatory policies in Ireland without the support of a united Cabinet. Huskisson seemed overwhelmed at the prominent part he would have to play if the Government met Parliament. They all needed strength at the top to lean on — and this Goderich could not provide. But, in fairness to the Prime Minister, it must be added that they were well aware of his character on 1 September, when the Government was finally formed, and on 19 December, when they gave him a vote of confidence.

As Huskisson, Herries, Lyndhurst, and Anglesey waited impatiently for Goderich to end their suspense by resigning, they became increasingly aware that one day they would have to give explanations in Parliament. This thought caused Huskisson's decision not to insist upon his resignation. 'Why should I make myself the scape Goat?' he asked Goderich on 1 January.[155] But Goderich realized that failure to meet Parliament would badly damage his reputation, and he hoped against hope that the Government might still somehow survive.

Fearing that Goderich would not act, Anglesey, who was on friendly terms with the King, asked Huskisson on 1 January if he should on his own initiative inform the monarch about the state of the Government.[156] Huskisson replied that he was bound to advise Goderich of his intentions,[157] and he thereafter informed the Prime Minister of Anglesey's proposal.[158] After talking with Lyndhurst, Anglesey wrote again to Huskisson on 2 January, asking if there were any possibility of Lord Lansdowne and Lord Holland sitting in the same Cabinet with Wellington and Peel: to which Huskisson replied that Anglesey was to tell the King about the present Administration, not to advise him regarding a new one. But he indicated his willingness to sit with those who had worried Canning to his doom by adding: 'I am no Exclusionist.'[159]

Meanwhile Goderich was bombarded with suggestions that he resign, or take steps which would lead to his dismissal. Lansdowne wrote on 2 January that it was better that the crisis come before Parliament met.[160] The same day Planta wrote that Huskisson asked him to point out that Parliament was scheduled to open in eighteen days, that the Treasury was empty, and they still had no Speech. 'He says', Planta continued, 'that if this delay continues longer, there may be good ground for an *impeachment* against the Ministers that caused and permitted it, & he is very uncomfortable about Your, & his own situation.'[161]

Goderich's refusal to resign is the more remarkable when one considers that Lady Sarah had broken her promise, and he had to accompany her to Blackheath. Before leaving, he answered Planta's letter:[162]

I am not insensible of the embarrassment which the present state of things occasions. But it is not just to throw it all on me, as I shall be enabled to shew upon a future occasion. It is clear however in the meantime that all *is* to be thrown upon me, & everybody is to be saved at my expense. Be it so. But it was not my fault that Herries never gave me to understand on Wednesday the 19th when I stated to the Cabinet my readiness to go on if they were disposed to continue their confidence in me, that he intended two days afterwards . . . to send me his resignation founded upon a circumstance that had occurred weeks before. . . . It is not my fault that a new attack of Gout has prevented the King, & still prevents him from attending to business. . . . It will be my fault if I delay any longer, & accordingly I send by this messenger an answer to Huskisson's letter in which I state that I do not see how if Herries resigns & that the Government becomes changed, I can undertake to take charge of the arrangement of a like one.

This was not what Huskisson and the others wanted him to do. 'It is quite wonderful', Huskisson wrote to Granville, 'to see how he clings to his situation now that, mainly by his own inconsiderate act, he has made it impossible to continue in it.' [163]

On 4 January Goderich wrote to Herries to explain that Huskisson would not give up Althorp's nomination, and asked if it were Herries's 'fixed determination' to resign,[164] but Herries, in reply, refused to elaborate on his letter of 21 December. He added that he did not have 'even the shadow of any personal objection' to Althorp.[165] This latter declaration gave Goderich new hope, and he wrote again the following day, begging him to reconsider withdrawing from the Government on this issue, so that they might 'leave it to Parliament' to decide their fate. At the same time, Goderich wrote to Huskisson hinting that they might still carry on even if Herries resigned,[166] but this time he received no encouragement whatsoever from his friend.[167]

Herries now sought the advice of his 'Protestant' friends. Bexley urged him not to resign, but to let the King choose between him and Huskisson.[168] Lyndhurst replied they would cut a 'pretty figure' if, as Goderich suggested, they went on to meet Parliament.[169] The Chancellor's letter is particularly interesting because he later stated that he tried unsuccessfully to persuade

Goderich to meet Parliament [170] — which was a false, baseless, slander of Goderich. On 6 January, Herries dined with Sir Henry Hardinge, and the latter reported to Wellington, 'your Grace can therefore judge of the interior state of a Cabinet where a colleague does not hesitate to use such language'. [171] Whatever Herries said, it must have been hostile to the continuation of the Government.

The reply Herries sent to Goderich's last plea was merely a rehash of his former meaningless communications,[172] so the Prime Minister, unable to solve this relatively minor question of the chairmanship of the finance committee, wrote to Knighton, and arranged to see the King the next day.[173] Lyndhurst wrote later that he attempted to dissuade him from resigning the night of 7 January, but the true account of Goderich's train of thought on the eve of the dissolution of his Government is contained in one of Huskisson's letters: 'Were I to tell you the projects floating in his mind last night for gaining strength (the Duke of Buckingham etc.) I should only make you smile in pity.' [174] There is no evidence, indeed, that Goderich had any intention of resigning the following day.

Just what Goderich expected would result from his interview with the King on 8 January we do not know, for his mission was merely to lay before him the details of the latest impasse in the Cabinet. All that is known of their conference is that Goderich told him about the quarrel between Huskisson and Herries and that the King gave him a message for Lyndhurst, summoning him to Windsor.[175] The King concluded the Government was 'virtually dissolved', and he seems to have been excited and possibly angry.[176] One story says that Goderich wept before leaving the King, and the monarch offered him his handkerchief. Whether or not this actually took place, one might guess that, if the King and Goderich's colleagues had given him reasonable support during his term of office, there would have been no need for such a gesture at the end of it. No principal adviser, however, ever had so many people so consistently reject his advice.

After Goderich left the King he was accosted by a Gentleman of the Bedchamber who asked for a ride back to London. The

gentleman, who knew nothing of Goderich's audience, found the
ex-Prime Minister ‘very pleasant’, and recalled how he joked and
laughed until they reached Hounslow, at which point he fell
asleep.[177] This was the reward of his placid disposition and clear
conscience. During the past five months, Lansdowne, Herries,
and Huskisson had all attempted to resign on one or more occasions, but could not do so — while he himself had never offered
a resignation, yet his resignation had been twice accepted !

8

In the Grey Government

In January 1828, Goderich faced an unusual situation — for the first time in eighteen years he held no position in the Government, and all his time could be devoted to his domestic concerns. On the eve of her husband's departure from office, Lady Sarah, who for some months had imagined she could not walk, and even fancied herself on the point of death in December, suddenly took a turn for the better. In mid-January Emily Eden found her dressed, walking around the room normally, and abusing Huskisson 'in her old eager manner' for having accepted office under Wellington.[1]

Although Lady Sarah had some relapses during the next two years, she once again took an interest in her husband's career, and was determined that he should not be completely elbowed out of political life. Shortly after he left office, they moved to Pembroke House in Whitehall by St. James's Park, which, though not the fashionable resort it had been in the eighteenth century, was an oasis of good air in the capital. It was a convenient location for one interested in politics, being within a stone's throw of Parliament, where Frederick went nightly, and close to Downing Street, where he might some day return.

The change in the social pattern of their lives was as marked as their change of residence. 'Goderich's conduct is most extraordinary,' Lord Morley wrote. 'He and Lady Goderich, having shut their doors and been invisible for years, are both recovered and apparently in the highest spirits.'[2] That May, Goderich attended the Literary Fund dinner, and proposed the memory of Canning in a 'very good and feeling speech'. 'I looked after his health', Hobhouse noted, 'which he told me was now quite good; indeed, he looked happier and fatter than when Prime Minister.' [3]

Lady Sarah was well enough in the autumn of 1828 for them to travel from place to place. In September they went to her favourite residence at Nocton Hall in Lincolnshire, but they had no intention of withdrawing from the swim of social affairs. Many of the important political leaders now went to Brighton, which had wholly eclipsed Bath as the popular watering-place. But the main attraction of Brighton was not so much its water as its air. The mephitic vapours of London, inhaled constantly, were thought to be injurious to health, while the air of Brighton was considered to be mildly medicinal. Gradually the resort, which was only five hours from London by coach, became known as the lungs of the capital.

Brighton in 1828 was still something of a playground, even though the King no longer came there, and his mistress, who stayed on, was more in the background. There an elegant, ostentatious, and hedonistic society enthusiastically followed the horses, wagered on cock- and prize-fighting, and satiated their appetites. 'I confess', Goderich wrote in November, 'that I am by no means fond of the sort of thing, or the mode of life which one *must* pursue here.' [4] Few of his contemporaries were more fun-loving than himself, but the quality of his amusements, like those of many others from the old Alfred Club set, differed considerably from the robust pastimes of the eighteenth-century aristocracy.

Lady Sarah had rented No. 1, Eastern Terrace, a house only recently completed, and considered the finest in the whole area — a substantial, four-story structure with the most magnificent staircase in the town. Certainly it was more graceful than the massive Corinthian Brunswick Terrace where Peel had stayed that same summer, and to which Lord Wellesley and Lord Granville came that autumn. 'We have all the world at Brighton,' Spring Rice boasted in December, and mentioned the Hollands, Dudley, Goderich, Lord Essex, the Duke of Devonshire, Sturges-

Bourne, Lady Lyndhurst, and others.[5] If he took an afternoon drive in a britzka or landaulet, or better, posted along the road, from Kemp Town to Brunswick Terrace, he could hardly avoid meeting someone of political importance, and Goderich found 'numerous acquaintances of all sorts' at the resort.

It is clear that the Goderichs did not participate vigorously in the pastimes of Brighton. 'I think our little boy the better for the Crispness of the Sea air,' Goderich reported. 'Lady G. I cannot say much for ; but she goes out every day, and is told that she is to acquire great strength in due time, & by persevering in staying here for some weeks.'[6] As, on her outings, Lady Sarah was supine and attended by an apothecary, who felt her pulse, and two maids, who administered brandy and water,[7] we may assume that the activities of the Goderichs were a popular topic of conversation during that season.

The Goderichs remained at Brighton for about a month, then went to visit Hardwicke at Wimpole briefly,[8] after which they once again returned to the resort. By chance, one of Lady Sarah's favourite physicians, a Doctor Clarke, happened to be there at the same time, and the Goderichs made full use of his services. Their boy fell ill with fever shortly after Christmas, and it was mid-January before he had fully recovered.[9]

References to Lady Sarah become increasingly fewer after 1828, and the curtain goes down over Goderich's domestic life, save for occasional glimpses here and there. Early in 1828 she had been 'indifferent about her baby', but this transient attitude, under the force of the unusual dialectic of Lady Sarah's character, did not blend with its opposite, but was supplanted by it. Indifference gave way to morbid concern. 'Sister has been at Wrest,' Emily Eden observed in October, 1829, 'where the old stories are going out — doctors sent for in the middle of the night. . . . In the meantime there is nothing really the matter with the child.'[10] Other stories tend to confirm that Lady Sarah's maternal instincts began to draw her attention away from herself, and her most acute hypochondriacal period was in the past.

Fortunately, their son provided few opportunities which permitted luxuriant worry of the type Lady Sarah had previously

sought. A fragmentary letter by Goderich, which probably dates
to 1830, made the following observations: '. . . after Lady
Goderich and our little Boy. The *former* is never very stout,
but the *latter* I am happy to say is become quite an active,
well-grown, & noisy boy.'[11] Although still not 'stout', Lady
Sarah played hostess at a series of dinners late in 1830,[12] and
thereafter she seems to have led a much more normal and useful
life.

'I should . . . be very sorry', Goderich wrote in January
1828, 'that it should be supposed that any circumstances which
have recently occurred, as affecting my situation, have disinclined
me from public life. . . . My great object at this moment is,
that the country should have the benefit of as strong a Government as can be formed upon those principles which I have always
advocated and supported. . . .'[13] This letter was written on
18 January, three days before he formally relinquished his office
to Wellington, and faced the prospect of finding some place for
himself in the confused political system of the time.

The Canning coalition was now completely shattered — Huskisson, Dudley, Palmerston, and William Lamb accepted office
under the Duke, while Goderich and the Whigs received no offers.
Goderich half-expected that the Duke might seek his services,[14]
and it is probable that he would have accepted had an offer been
made, for, unlike many Canningites, he was among those 'who
upon the formation of the Duke of Wellington's Government,
thought that you and the others could honourably accept the
proposition.'[15] This he wrote to Huskisson in May. But he
assumed that the new Government would act upon the principles
of liberal Toryism, and be formed on as wide a base as possible.[16]

Goderich tried to mend as many fences as possible before
leaving office. The Duke agreed to complete the peerages he had
recommended, and even granted him a few additional patronages.
He wrote letters to Huskisson and the Duke of Buckingham,
and also a lengthy letter to the King, which noted that some
mark of 'approbation' might be in order, but the King merely
declared that he sincerely estimated Goderich's past services.[17]

When Parliament opened in January, Goderich made no move to open the vexed question of who was primarily responsible for the fall of his Government.

The silence on this question was broken when Huskisson, in February, alluded to the break-up in a speech to his Liverpool constituents, which brought a protest from Goderich. 'The impression which that report . . . is calculated to produce', he wrote, '. . . is that whilst all was harmony and good understanding in the Cabinet, . . . I nevertheless . . . took upon myself to consider the Government as dissolved.' [18] 'I shall ever assert . . .', Huskisson replied, 'that you laboured, amidst increasing difficulties, to keep the Government together; and that its immediate dissolution was not to be ascribed to any act which it was in your power to avert.' [19] Although his letters to Goderich were cordial enough, Huskisson on other occasions called his conduct 'imbecilic',[20] and called the part of Canning's Government which had not joined the Duke the 'rubbish'.[21]

Explanations flew thick and fast during February, and the confusion which resulted from them is to be noted in contemporary diaries and letters. 'Lord Goderich made a statement of the circumstances which led to the breaking up of the Administration,' Ellenborough noted, 'which he attributed entirely to the difference between Herries and Huskisson, throwing all the blame upon Herries.' [22] 'Lord Lansdowne makes a statement which materially differs from Huskisson's,' Hobhouse noted 'and shows him [Huskisson] to be a rogue. Lord Goderich makes a statement which shows up Herries not a little, and proves Goderich a dupe.' [23] 'Huskisson's explanation was a shuffle', Hobhouse wrote a few days later, 'leaving the material points untouched . . . Herries had apparently a good story to tell. He read letters from "My dear G." to "My dear H." and attempted to throw a great deal of blame on his maker.' [24] George Villiers thought that Herries's statement was 'triumphant', and thoroughly exposed Goderich's lack of capacity; [25] Greville thought Huskisson's and Herries's explanations were 'satisfactory enough till Tierney spoke, who entirely knocked over their cases, or at least that of Herries . . .' [26] The Countess Cowper put her finger on the source of the confusion when she noted that the public 'see a quarrel between Herries and Huskisson, which breaks up the Government, and the effect is that they remain together and the Whigs are dropped out'.[27] As none of the apologists could describe their political motives in detail, confusion was inevitable, and the explanations would have been better left unsaid.

During the session of 1828 Goderich seems to have hoped to rally some sort of following on a programme of support for the Government if it followed Canningite principles.[28] The reaction of one of his former supporters, Lord Grenville, was probably widespread: 'He seems to take, on set occasions, the line of a firm adherent to the present Government, and how he will conduct himself on the Catholic question I have no means, nor, in truth, any interest to concern myself.'[29] In his effort to keep in the swim of things in 1828, Goderich presented himself to the House with great regularity, but none of his efforts was noteworthy. 'He seems to think it necessary he should always speak,' Ellenborough complained.[30]

It was not Goderich's speeches, but the memory of his failure that influenced political affairs during that session. Wellington, in constructing his Government, sought to avoid the Cabinet divisions that had ruined Goderich,[31] but his inclusion of the Canningites accomplished the result he had hoped to evade. Such an air of indecision lingered around the Government that the Duke of Cumberland told the King that Wellington was as weak a Prime Minister as Goderich, and the King repeated the story until it got back to Wellington.[32] He therefore seized upon an opportunity resulting from a minor squabble to accept Huskisson's resignation, and the other Canningites followed their leader out of office. 'I should soon find myself in the same situation as Lord Goderich', the Duke explained, 'and should be under the necessity of going to the King and telling him that his government was *defunct*; and that I was determined that that should not happen.'[33]

Goderich saw in this secession an opportunity to re-establish his leadership of the Canningite faction. Up until that time he had avoided contacting the official Canningites, but, on hearing of the break-up, he wrote to Huskisson for an interview.[34] This was so harmonious that on 1 June he suggested that the Canningites hold a meeting at his house the following day.[35] Although Huskisson paid him the courtesy of a call, he did not co-operate in gathering the others, and it is clear why he did not. 'Goderich has been very anxious to organize some immediate arrangements . . .', Palmerston wrote on 7 June, 'but this has not been relished. . . . it would have the appearance of putting ourselves under his lead, which, considering what an unfortunate display he made last December as head of a party, it would be by no means expedient for us to do.' [36] This opinion is very important, because it was that of an old friend who had been steady during those weeks of crisis.[37] Palmerston, however, in a list drawn up at the time, included Goderich as a member of the Canningite Party.[38]

Gradually the light dawned upon Goderich that the chances were against his being accepted again as a real leader. In November 1828 he received a letter from his original parliamentary intimate, Charles Yorke, who expressed a desire to see him in office. 'You are very good to think that my being in office would be of service to the Country', Goderich replied, 'but I have no reason to suppose that there exists any desire to have me . . .' [39] His moment in politics had passed. He was now a useful and experienced statesman and politician, but the distance between Pembroke House and Downing Street was too far.

Toward the end of 1828 Wellington, who considered Lord Grantham as a possible successor to Anglesey in Ireland, gave up the project because Goderich was then considered as 'not friendly' to his Government.[40] This probably meant no more than that Goderich was classed with the Canningite seceders. In preparation for the session of 1829 Goderich wrote a lengthy letter on political subjects to Huskisson, and to this extent he was a member of a section of Parliament.[41]

At the opening of Parliament in 1829, however, the speeches of Goderich and Lansdowne were so similar that some observers on the governmental side suspected collaboration. 'Evidently', Ellenborough guessed, 'Goderich and Lansdowne had intended

to make Portugal the *cheval de bataille*.'[42] To what extent this
was planned, or merely coincidence, the correspondence does not
make clear, but Lansdowne considered that Goderich had played
fairly with the Whigs when in office,[43] and he and Carlisle had
supported Goderich in his explanations of the break-up in 1828.
So Lansdowne and Goderich remained on good terms, but it is
doubtful that the former looked to the latter for leadership.

The major question before the House in 1829 was Catholic
Emancipation, and Goderich did what he could to associate himself with this reform, which he had advocated for so long. On
learning that Lord Eldon was circulating a petition against it,
Goderich sponsored a counter-petition, which finally bore 22,000
signatures.[44] His speech on the second reading drew from
Harriet Arbuthnot a veritable gem of criticism : 'Lord Goderich
was *beneath* criticism, he ranted and raved like a strolling player,
and someone remarked to me that, if he had not been swamped
before, he had now done it effectually for that he shewed he had
not ballast enough to keep himself afloat on the sea of medio-
crity.'[45] Another source corroborated her account,[46] so it would
seem that Goderich on this occasion proved once again that
he could not speak on a subject in which he was emotionally
in volved.

After wandering in the political wilderness for two years, Goderich emerged again in 1830, when he finally made an impression
on the chilly House of Lords. On 18 February he joined Lansdowne in speaking in support of the Government's policy in
Portugal — an 'excellent speech, the only good one that was
made', Greville called his effort.[47] Then on 25 February he
defended the Government against a hostile motion based on the
current economic distress. Over the economic grounds he walked
with a light, sure step. He lectured the House on the causes of
the present distress and the faults of the banking system ; estimated the surplus for the year and suggested how it might be
used for tax relief ; and, finally, condemned the 'gloomy, miserable and hopeless views' of the mover. For a brief period, he was
'Prosperity' Robinson again, painting the economic picture with
the bold and colourful strokes of a Van Gogh.[48] While the Duke

seemed annoyed that Goderich had delivered a budget speech, and he denied the surplus predicted, by July it was to become clear that Goderich's prognostications had been accurate. In May Goderich scored another oratorical triumph, when he once again reviewed the economic position of the nation,[49] and this time received not only the compliments of the Duke, but of his former tormentor, Lord Ellenborough, who admitted that it was a 'good and useful speech'.[50]

This speech proved to be the high-water mark of Goderich's support of the Wellington Government, which thereafter suddenly began to recede — why, in the the absence of documents, is a mystery. This change is abundantly clear, however, from the tone of his speeches. Those of 25 June and 30 June supported the position of Lord Grey; that of 8 July was critical of Government finances. Then on 20 July he took up the issue which separated him from the more advanced Whigs — Reform. 'He was not a theoretical reformer,' Goderich admitted, 'but he would give his cordial support to the plan for extending the franchise to Birmingham, believing that it would be very advantageous to Birmingham to be represented in Parliament, and to the country in general to have a gradual and practical reform in the representation.'[51]

The Duke vainly attempted to strengthen his Government in October 1830, and sent Lord Clive to talk with Palmerston, who explained he was acting with Melbourne and Grant, but would like to have Lords Grey and Lansdowne also join the Government with him. Clive replied that the Duke would accept Goderich, but Palmerston did not consider him a substitute for the others — indeed, he 'had not lately had any political communication with Goderich'.[52] 'Goderich is an excellent fellow', Palmerston wrote several days later, 'and an able head of a department, and would be a most agreeable colleague, but would the public have seen in him any security for us . . . against a repetition of *May* 1828?'[53] Following the breakdown of this negotiation, Palmerston met some of the Canningites to discuss Reform, and Goderich was not among those present. The untimely death of Huskisson this same year did not transfer the leadership of the Canningites to Goderich, even though he was sometimes reported in company with them.

In view of Palmerston's failure to recommend Goderich to Wellington, it might be assumed that he had no hand in arranging an office for him in the Grey Government. But if not Palmerston — then who did? Lansdowne is a possibility, and so is Hardwicke, but the latter's influence was long since in eclipse. The mystery deepens because Goderich was, according to his own statement, not even well acquainted with Lord Grey, and, despite the aid given him back in July, obviously had not yet joined his following. There is a possibility that Brougham, who had clung to the coalition Government to the last in 1828, spoke for Goderich; at any rate, Goderich continued to correspond with him from this time until his death, and they seem to have been fairly close friends.[54]

Hardwicke knew of and approved the appointment as early as 19 November,[55] but others in the family seem to have been kept in the dark about it for several days. 'My mother says that Ld. Goderich is not to form a part of the new Cabinet', Lord Stuart wrote to Henry Ellis on 22 November, '& she speaks upon your authority.'[56] Goderich explained his acceptance to Yorke in a letter of 21 November:[57]

Pray accept my apologies for not having written to you yesterday to tell you that I had accepted the seals of the Colonial Office. . . . The possession of office in these times is not only not enviable, but involves an awful responsibility. But under the circumstances of the case, I did not feel that I should be justified in declining the offer made to me (and it was in all respects handsomely made) by Lord Grey. We must do our best, with honest intentions, and trust that God will help us and our Country thro' its multifold difficulties.

Two other letters written by Goderich in 1834 shed some further light upon the appointment in 1830. 'I am aware that when the Board of Trade was proposed to me upon the formation of the present government', he wrote to Grey, 'in conjunction with the Mint, I declined it.'[58] In another letter he stated vaguely that he declined it for reasons 'I felt to be imperative.'[59]

These letters leave unanswered the question of why Grey made

the offer to Goderich, but they show how it was done. The Board
of Trade and the Mint were offered and declined, probably because Goderich followed the precedent set by Sidmouth, a former
Prime Minister who later accepted a Secretaryship of State.
Henry Ellis must have then told friends and relatives that Goderich would not be in the Government. But Grey then acceded to
Goderich's point of view, and offered him the Colonial Office,
which was more fitting for a former Prime Minister.

The question of why it was done is a matter for speculation, but
a glance at the members of the new Cabinet reveals a curious
collection of administrative novices. Writing about Goderich,
Brougham later recalled: 'His business-like habits were in-
valuable to the inexperienced and unofficial Whigs — the Whigs
never learned the lesson — the first in business of all kinds —
that a chief in a department must delegate as much as possible
to the best agents possible, else he will be tormented to death,
and do his work ill.' [60] Goderich had delegated tasks to Wallace,
when he was at the Board of Trade, to Herries when at the Exchequer, to Wilmot Horton and Lord Howick when at the
Colonial Office, and to Gladstone during his later term at the
Board of Trade. In most of these cases, there were rumours that
his subordinate had 'superceded' Goderich, which in all probability meant no more than is included in Brougham's observation,
and which would make of Goderich one of the earlier 'modern'
administrators.

It is likely that this knowledge of official life was the main
attraction that Goderich could offer to Grey. While Goderich
still had many political connections, and the correspondence of
this period shows that he was very active in Lincolnshire politics,
he did not lead a section of Parliament, nor did he command
many votes in either House. He had spoken effectively in the
Lords during 1830, but Lord Grey, with Brougham, Lansdowne,
and Holland at his side, was not in pressing need of Goderich's
forensic abilities. These considerations help confirm that the
factor of his experience weighed heavily in Grey's choice of
Goderich as a Secretary of State.

As second-in-command in the House of Lords,[61] Goderich had

P

to concern himself with issues other than those directly related
to the Colonial Office. During the next two years, the most
important of these was the reform issue, and his espousal of it
required a change in his previous position, which pledged him to
piecemeal and gradual reform. In a letter to Harrowby late in
1831, Goderich explained that the previous resistance to all
reform had made a comprehensive change inevitable. 'When
all classes of society think & reason', he wrote, 'every detail of
national institutions *which cannot bear probing, is in great jeopardy
& sooner or later must yield to universal dissatisfaction.* So it has
been in all ages & in all countries, with the great difference in
our times, that the wheel of change goes around faster and involves more extensive consequences than it ever did before. It
is the lot of our poor humanity, but if we do not watch, and strive
in time to *regulate* its movements, all may be swept away before
we know where we are.' [62]   In an undated letter to Yorke, Goderich observed: 'We do live in a strange world, and he is a bold
man who can pretend to see where it will all end.' [63]

His two major speeches on the Reform Bill, made in October
1831, and April 1832, both stressed the expediency of passing the
measure. In the first he traced the revolution in France not to
the reform policies of Necker, but to the insistence of a 'corrupt
court' and a 'degraded nobility' on retaining their exclusive
privileges.[64] In the second he cited the authority of Edmund
Burke of a 'change in time', and warned that the rejection of the
Bill might cause a war of 'no property against property'.[65] Later
Goderich recalled that he had been a 'zealous and honest advocate' of reform,[66] but neither his letters nor his speeches indicate
much real enthusiasm for the project in itself. Brougham placed
Goderich in a class with Palmerston, and ahead of Richmond and
Melbourne, in his support of the measure; [67] and, according to
one source, he was one of the Cabinet members most insistent on
creating, if need be, enough peers to pass the measure through the
Lords.[68] Perhaps the safest conclusion regarding his attitude is
that he was convinced of the necessity of the Bill, but was not
satisfied that the legislature would be improved by its passage.
Unlike some other members of the Cabinet, he realized that the

Bill was a landmark along a journey, rather than a destination in itself; this is clear from his speech of May 1833, when he wondered 'if any question was settled so far, that no change could be made in it'.[69]

Goderich's decision to support a major reform of the franchise is quite consistent with his lifelong attitude toward political problems. As a member of the liberal movement, his advocacy of the major reforms was largely a matter of timing. On the Free Trade and Slave Emancipation questions, he was in the vanguard; on the Catholic Emancipation and the Reform issues, he joined the movement later. As his letter to Harrowby shows, he believed that it was the task of the statesman to guide change into constructive channels, and only rarely did he adopt an attitude of firm opposition to change. His attitude was probably both the result of his congenial personality, and the lessons he thought were to be learned by members of his class from the experiences of the revolutionary period.

Goderich had long been interested in emigration, both as a means of providing a fresh start in life for 'redundant' British citizens, and as a method of relieving the poor rates; and as far back as 1823 he worked closely with Robert Wilmot (later Wilmot-Horton) to further some Government-aided emigration schemes. 'I do not mean that I am friendly to an Emigration scheme upon an extensive scale,' he wrote to Liverpool that year, 'I am satisfied that in order to be useful it must begin upon a very *limited* scale.' [70] As Chancellor of the Exchequer, he found funds to send 268 Irish paupers to Upper Canada in 1823, and to ship 2,024 more by an Act of 1825.

Goderich's enthusiasm for the idea waxed apace during 1823–5, and, as we have noted above, he submitted to the Cabinet in 1826 a comprehensive plan for mass emigration. Using funds secured from his suggested Corn Law, he hoped to transport 8,000 British families a year to Canada, the Australian settlements, and the Cape of Good Hope,[71] but the Cabinet objected to attaching an emigration plan to the Corn Laws, which were supposed to provide protection, not to raise revenue. 'I have never sanctioned any specific plan', he wrote to Peel in 1827, 'beyond that as contained in a paper which I drew up last summer . . . . That plan, however, was founded upon a principle which is now inapplicable, & was much objected to, viz., of accompanying it with the alteration of the Corn Laws.'[72]   Following this failure, Goderich provided funds on a case-by-case basis.[73]

Their pioneering work in this field created considerable interest in emigration both in Parliament and in the country, and by 1830 there was so much voluntary emigration, aided by parishes or individuals, that the problem was not so much finding passage funds, as locating the emigrants once they reached their destinations.   'The Government might perhaps add some assistance upon the *first* arrival of the Emigrants in the Colony,' Goderich wrote to Brougham late in 1830, 'not however with any notion of getting direct repayments, but merely that those people might start fair who carry with them little or nothing but their labour.'[74] But, once again, Goderich was unable to secure funds for his emigration programme.   A note on a despatch from Lower Canada late in 1831 revealed Government policy as of that date : 'It is not intended to give pecuniary assistance to Emigrants except in cases of the most urgent necessity.'[75]

Another problem arising out of the increasing emigration was protecting the emigrants against exploitation.   Lord Howick, the Under-Secretary for the Colonies, presented a Bill in February 1831, which, among other things, was to establish a commission to oversee the emigration programme,[76] but he failed to secure support and the Bill was abandoned.   So in June he established his own committee for this purpose, which included his brother-in-law, Henry Ellis, the Duke of Richmond, and Howick, who checked on the facilities provided by passenger ships.   In March 1832 this committee was dissolved, and this function was taken over by Thomas Elliot, the new emigration supervisor for the Colonial Office.

Employment opportunities for the colonists differed considerably from place to place during these years.   John Bell, in March 1832, wrote from the Cape Colony that employment possibilities were so limited that the place could only absorb a 'few at a time'.[77]

In Lower Canada the difficulty was sending emigrants to places
where they could find jobs; [78] but the Lieutenant-Governor of
Upper Canada reported in July 1832: 'More than 20,000 Emigrants have reached Coburg [?], York, and Hamilton. These
have either been located, or have found employment.' [79] 83,000
people went to the colonies in 1831, and in 1832 the figure rose to
103,140,[80] which represented more than 40 per cent of the natural
increase of the British people at the time. Under these circumstances, with emigration levels far surpassing those contemplated
by his 1826 project, Goderich was not sure that a 'redundant'
population existed any longer in Britain,[81] and in February 1832
he announced he would present no further emigration schemes to
Parliament.[82]

Space permits only brief statements of Goderich's policies as
Colonial Secretary together with a few examples of each. He was
anxious whenever possible to promote the growth of self-government in the colonies. 'The benefits resulting from the election
by the proprietary body, in every country, of the members of the
popular branch of the legislature', he wrote in 1831, 'are too
familiar to require notice, and are so universally admitted as to
preclude all controversy on the abstract principle.' [83] He generally excepted the slave-holding colonies from this rule, but even
in these he made concessions. In 1827 he ordered the Governor
at Cape Town to place two settlers on his Council, to give them
a voice in the administration,[84] and in 1831 he refused to act on
a recommendation that the Cabildo of the Port of Spain be
abolished.[85]

It was in Lower and Upper Canada that the movement for
greater self-government, led by Louis Papineau and William
Lyon MacKenzie respectively, was most strongly in evidence in
1830, when Goderich took office. The advice offered by the
colonial governors, Lord Aylmer and Sir John Colborne, was
sharply contrasting: 'as an individual', Aylmer reported, 'I live
upon good (I may say cordial) terms with Mr. Papineau, whose
private character I much esteem.' [86] Concerning MacKenzie,
Colborne wrote: 'A more unprincipled demagogue could not
have sprung up to disturb a colony.' [87] Aylmer favoured

conciliation ; Colborne preferred a strong hand across the sea.

For the past several years Lower Canada's Assembly had been agitating for control of the Customs revenues, and in 1831 Goderich decided to concede them, provided the Assembly would draw up a permanent civil list ; but he made the mistake of giving up the revenues before the list was established. On 5 February 1832 Aylmer ruefully reported that the Assembly had refused to establish the permanent list, and would pay the officials out of general supply — which meant that the Assembly had secured a powerful new weapon over them.[88] So this concession merely marked the beginning of a continuing and bitter dispute. Goderich also granted Aylmer's request that Papineau, in an effort to secure his co-operation, should be given a seat on the Executive Council, but when the offer was made in March 1832, Papineau rejected it.[89] 'It is very evident', Aylmer wrote in early 1833, 'that Mr. Papineau & his party, have taken new ground . . . their avowed object is now to alter the whole frame of the Constitution, & Government of the Colony . . . .'[90] Goderich's hopes of conciliating Lower Canada, then, had ended in complete failure.

Meanwhile in Upper Canada, MacKenzie, expelled from the Assembly by the Government's supporters, decided to take his case to England. In June 1832 he and a small party arrived in London, and were granted a hearing by Goderich, who thereafter was bombarded by their demands for Church reform, a dissolution of the Assembly, and the recall of Colborne. Although Colborne had advised Goderich to meet MacKenzie 'in a most decided manner',[91] the conciliatory Colonial Secretary must have treated him in a friendly fashion, for MacKenzie thereafter bragged about his influence at the Colonial Office.[92] An undated letter by Goderich in 1832 also shows that he considered some of MacKenzie's complaints well-founded : [93]

But there are one or two points upon which Mackenzie remarks [?] I think might require consideration. I mean the *jury laws*, & the laws respecting local assessments. The Assembly have I believe passed laws upon these subjects, but the Council have rejected them. The

Government ought *not* to *encourage* the Council in rejecting the Bills of the Assembly ; they have a right to an independent exercise of their functions, but I fear they do not understand their relation in terms [*sic*] of the Legislature.

When MacKenzie proved to be 'an admitted rebel and traitor' during the Canadian Rebellion, Goderich found his past connection with him to be embarrassing, and in 1839 he found it necessary to explain his relations with MacKenzie to the Lords.[94] As the Rebellion did not occur until almost five years after Goderich left the Colonial Office, his encouragement of MacKenzie obviously had little to do with it ; but, as in Lower Canada, his attempts to conciliate were less than futile.

Goderich's policy of non-imperialism fitted in with this general era of colonial apathy. When an opportunity was offered in 1827 for Britain to extend her influence in the Gold Coast, he quickly turned it down.[95] During his second term at the Colonial Office, a plan was submitted to secure control of the Niger River, but Goderich replied that the Government had no intention of sending a fresh expedition to Africa.[96] No doubt he believed there was plenty to be done in the areas of white immigration to sparsely-populated colonies, and the Christianization of the aborigines in the settled ones, without adding further territories to the Empire.

The protection of primitive peoples against exploitation was another of his policies while Colonial Secretary. An example of this is found in New Zealand, where, in 1830–1, some unscrupulous whites encouraged inter-tribal warfare. When a Maori chief complained to Goderich of their activities, he named James Busby as British Resident in the islands to control the activities of British subjects there.[97] This technique of on-the-spot supervision seems to have appealed to Goderich, who, as will be noted below, applied it also in the slave-holding colonies. A second example of concern for the natives was his barring the Dutch from areas newly ceded to the Cape Colony in order to keep out their system of forced labour, or slavery.[98]

As Colonial Secretary Goderich did not restrict his interest and supervision to the making and carrying out of high policy.

The frequency of his notations on despatches received from the colonies indicates that he concerned himself also with the details of his work, particularly in the field of colonial finances. A despatch of 7 June 1832 from Lower Canada bears the following observation : 'Is there not some mistake in the figure stated in his despatch? It appears to me that the balance on hand this year is *less* than the balance last year. This should be pointed out to Lord Aylmer. Who is the Revt. Mr. Atkinson who has a salary of 55.11. 1 from this fund?'[99] Goderich evidently tried to manage colonial funds as carefully as he did his private fortune.

Of all the reforms during this period, the one with which Goderich was most closely identified was the emancipation of the slaves in the Empire. His interest in this crusade had begun with his first vote in Parliament in favour of abolishing the slave trade, and it is seen again in 1815 when he secured funds to care for slaves captured by British cruisers.[100] Although he opposed slavery both on moral and economic grounds, Goderich nevertheless retained a strong sense of balance on this subject, and tried to take a comprehensive view of it.

While he evidently knew many of the 'Saints', he did not act as their spokesman in the Government. In 1824, for example, it is clear that William Wilberforce worked through George Canning, not Goderich,[101] and when he took up his colonial duties in 1830 both Lord Howick, the Under-Secretary for War and the Colonies, and James Stephen, the Permanent Under-Secretary of the Colonial Office, were much more receptive to the ideas and demands of the Saints than was Goderich. He listened patiently to all sides — the Saints, the planters, his colleagues, and the King, who feared that the extinction of slavery would mean the loss of the West Indian colonies.[102] One of the most remarkable evidences of his unusual integrity was Goderich's determination, despite his abhorrence for slavery, not to exercise the authority of the mother country to extinguish it as long as the slightest possibility existed that the colonists would do so themselves.

There then existed two types of slave-holding colonies — the

Crown Colonies, and the colonies which had their own legislatures. In the former, the authority of the Home Government was practically absolute, and slavery could have been abolished in them by a stroke of the pen, but Goderich believed that emancipation should take place simultaneously in the legislative colonies. The West Indian legislatures were not recent innovations, but governmental bodies with long histories in many cases. The Assembly in Barbados dated to the early seventeenth century; so did the one in Bermuda. Jamaica, the most important of the West Indian colonies, held its rights of self-government by charter. Although Goderich did not believe that representative government and slavery were compatible, he was determined to work with these legislatures in good faith.

By an Order in Council of 2 November 1831 Goderich tried to carry out a policy, dating to 1823, of ameliorating the conditions of slavery. This order restricted the working hours of the slaves, and empowered officials called 'Protectors' to supervise the colonial plantations to see that the amelioration policy was being carried out. Goderich hoped that the slaves would be able, in their spare time, to earn enough money to buy their freedom, and he later observed that this procedure 'might have been accepted as a settlement of the question'.[103] At the same time he tried to induce the colonial legislature to carry out this order in good faith by promising certain financial rewards.[104]

Alas, for Goderich's hopes! The solution was not to come that easily. The Order of 2 November was coldly received in the slave colonies. His relative Lowry Cole reported that the Order had created irritation and excitement among the Boers, and that it was impossible to enforce many of its provisions in the Cape Colony.[105] The Crown Colonies, in general, avoided its provisions by various devices, and the legislative colonies simply would not enact enabling legislation to carry it out. Their attitude, though misguided, did not spring purely from oppositionism. 'Your Majesty's perfect knowledge . . .', Goderich wrote the King, 'will doubtless enable your Majesty at once to see how delicate is the task of the Government of this Country in endeavouring to effect improvements in the condition of the Slaves without at

once overturning the whole authority of the Master . . .' [106]
Slave insurrections were not unknown — indeed, there was a
major rebellion in Jamaica in December 1831.

The spring of 1832 brought demands in both Houses for committees to study the slave question, and Goderich, though doubtful of the wisdom of such an approach, went along with it, and
temporarily suspended the operation of his Order of 2 November.
'The King cannot help . . . adverting to the opposite Character
of the Circumstances under which the Two Committees are sitting,' the King wrote to Goderich in June, 'that of the Lords
having originated with the Proprietors of West Indian Estates
. . . while the Committee in the House of Commons originated
on the addresses of those who are clamourous for the Abolition
of Slavery . . . .' [107] Save for gathering information, the Select
Committees of 1832, as Goderich predicted, served little purpose,
and increased rather than allayed excitement.

Goderich had warned the colonies at the time he sent out the
2 November Order that British public opinion demanded that
strong action be taken on the slave question, and his despatch of
12 May, suspending the Order, observed that the dilatory tactics
of the colonists were driving many moderates into the hostile
camp. On 1 June, when a member of the Lords called upon the
Government to clarify its intentions toward slavery, Goderich
made a major statement of policy. 'All their recommendations',
he said, 'ought to contemplate the ultimate abolition of slavery,
because it would be quite impossible to maintain it.' [108] His
despatches of 4 June to the legislative colonies declared that the
Government was now working for the substitution of free labour
for slavery.[109] Thus, the Government was committed to abolition,
and all that remained to be settled were the circumstances under
which it was to take place. This decision did not have the approval of the King, but he expressed his objections 'with perfect
good humour'.[110]

Once this decision was made, the Colonial Office had to take
steps to provide for the safety of the colonies during the difficult
and dangerous moments of transition. Sir Charles Colville in
the former French colony of Mauritius requested reinforcements,

and Lord Howick's reaction to his request illustrates the extreme views held by some of Goderich's advisers : [111]

> The slave colonies are totally incapable of opposing the slightest resistance to your measures, if they are vigorously acted upon. Sir C. Colville had at his disposal the means of blowing the town of Port Louis to pieces had this been necessary & to talk of any resistance which the white popn. of the Mauritius, even supposing them to have been supported by the free coloured people, could have offered to 1200 well disciplined British soldiers supported by a large naval force seems to me positively ludicrous.

The blowing-up of towns, and turning British soldiers and the navy against the white populations of the colonies were actions Goderich hoped to avoid by reinforcing the garrisons, and working cautiously with the colonists.

The passage of the Reform Act of 1832, which undermined the West Indian influence in the Commons, paved the way for Emancipation, and the Cabinet as a whole took it under consideration. Sir James Graham was delegated to learn the views of Fowell Buxton, a leading member of the 'Saints'. These turned out to be a strange combination of extremism and conservatism. He wanted to build up a police force of free Negroes strong enough to keep the whites 'in complete submission', a two-year period during which the slaves would work for wages, and then freedom — abridged only by the vagrancy laws, which would force them to keep in employment.[112] The only compensation he offered to the planters was a loan of an unspecified amount. Lord Howick's plan was considered at the same time as Buxton's. Howick proposed that the slaves be freed immediately, and placed under the vagrancy laws ; and as a further means of forcing them to work, a 40s. per acre tax would be placed on all food-producing land, which they could not pay without working on a plantation.[113] He proposed a £15,000,000 loan as compensation.

These plans, and probably others, were discussed by various members of the Cabinet during the autumn of 1832. 'The real difficulty . . .', Goderich wrote to Graham, 'arises not so much from any inherent difficulty in devising a safe and beneficial scheme of emancipation (which is on the contrary rather easy than otherwise) but in devising a safe mode of *enforcing* its *adoption* without violating all the principles of that unfortunate representative system which prevails in the Legislative Colonies.' [114] Even after the West Indian interest had lost its strength in the Home Parliament, Goderich was determined to respect the traditional principles of self-government in the slave colonies, but once again the attitude of the legislatures demonstrated the hopelessness of trying to work through them. Goderich had sent out his friend Lord Mulgrave earlier in the year to try to secure co-operation from the legislature of Jamaica, but Mulgrave had to dissolve it after reaching a deadlock over the question of its powers. Goderich now realized that some of the veiled powers of the mother country had to be unveiled. [115]

Some fleeting glimpses of Goderich's last month at the Colonial Office, during which he endeavoured to secure an Emancipation scheme agreeable both to the Cabinet and the planters, can be obtained from the correspondence of the period. At a Cabinet meeting of 4 February it was decided that the select committees of the previous year might resume their work, but that the Government would be free meanwhile to forward its own measures. They also agreed that the West Indian interest should be consulted before any propositions were submitted to Parliament. [116] We may assume, from later developments, that Goderich thereafter asked the West Indians to submit their plan for Emancipation.

Another Cabinet meeting was held on 22 February, but its decisions are not available. Before the meeting Howick urged that agreement be secured on two propositions — that slavery should be abolished by act of the Home Parliament, and that a loan of money be offered to the colonies as compensation. He believed that, if the Cabinet agreed to these two ideas, Goderich would be in a position to work out the details. [117] It seems probable that Goderich secured the Cabinet's consent to propositions of this nature.

Shortly after the Cabinet session of 22 February, Goderich received an Emancipation plan from the West Indian interest, which stressed not the conditions of emancipation, but the compensation terms. In addition to aid for carrying on their estates, they demanded compensation for their chattel rights in their slaves, whose value would be based on the selling price in 1823, when slaves were expensive. They also sought compensation for their expenses in rearing young slaves. Finally, they asked that the wages of the freed slaves be based on the selling price of a hogshead of liquor, that the freedmen be required to work six days a week, and that their right to sell their labour be restricted.[118] Howick estimated that, under this plan, the compensation cost per adult slave would be £229. 14*s*. 10*d*., which might be compared with that later given. Payments were to range between £19 for an inferior field-hand to £230 for a slave of the supervisory class.[119]

Goderich held his last conference with the West Indian interest on 27 February. He promised its delegates that the Government measure would take 'the interests of all classes in the colonies' into consideration, and, when they expressed alarm that the Government might abolish slavery without compensation, Goderich assured them that the 'pecuniary interest' of all concerned would not be overlooked. He further stated that the Government's measure would take uniform effect in the colonies — that is, that it would apply both to the Crown and legislative colonies. Lastly, he told them they would have an opportunity to comment upon the Government's plan before it was submitted to Parliament.[120]

Although it might be argued that a more positive personality than Goderich might have advanced the cause of Emancipation more rapidly, it is clear that he moved towards that end in an orderly and effective manner. In 1831 he had provided an Emancipation plan in his Order in Council, in June 1832 he had committed the Government irrevocably to Emancipation, and had demonstrated that it must come from the Home Government, due to the inaction of the colonial legislatures. In early 1833 he began the negotiations which were to be concluded by his successor, Lord Stanley. Well might the Reverend William Knibb, one of the most active Abolitionists in Jamaica, say when he heard of Goderich's replacement: 'We have lost a sincere friend in Lord Goderich.'[121]

The troubles of young and rising Edward Stanley, the Irish Secretary, became a matter of deep concern to Lord Grey late in 1832. He had become so unpopular in Ireland that Stanley was ready, rather than to continue there, to resign from the Government, and as early as 6 October the Duke of Richmond suggested that Goderich relinquish the Colonial Office to Stanley in return for the Post Office and an earldom.[122] The implication was clear — Goderich was a useful member of the Government, but Stanley was sorely needed.

In December a change in four offices was projected for a time. Lord Melbourne, the Home Secretary, would replace Lord Anglesey as Lord Lieutenant of Ireland, and Goderich would replace Melbourne, which would leave the Colonial Office to Stanley.[123] Because of its intimate connection with Irish affairs, Stanley would have been inappropriate for the Home Office. Goderich was ready to agree to this 'with great reluctance', but for some reason — possibly Melbourne's refusal — it did not take place, and on 2 February Lord Grey suggested that Goderich replace Graham at the Admiralty. But by this time the abolition question had become so pressing that Goderich was unwilling to comply, and he wrote to the Prime Minister: 'I have no objection to the Admy. . . . but as the matter stands I cannot but fear that the grounds of the proposed change would never be rightly understood & that I should infallibly suffer under the implication of running away [from] the Slavery question.'[124] This direct refusal laid the matter temporarily to rest.

The resignation of Lord Durham from the sinecure office of Privy Seal once again reopened the Stanley question. On 19 March Lord Grey asked Goderich to move to the Privy Seal, but he flatly refused.[125] To this Grey replied: 'The embarrassment in which I find myself is extreme, & at this moment, the only way out of it that I see, is to take the Privy Seal myself, to bring Althorp to the H. of Lords as First Lord of the Treasy. & make Stanley Chanc. of the Excr.'[126] On 25 March Althorp told a friend that the Government was on the 'eve of dissolution'.[127]

Goderich had already rejected an earldom from Lord Grey when Lord Palmerston came to see him on the subject. Just what passed between them is uncertain — Palmerston obviously stressed the desperate condition of the Government, and may have suggested that Goderich would receive the Garter if he agreed to take the Privy Seal. Beset on all sides to co-operate, Goderich reluctantly went to the palace on 27 March to receive the Privy Seal from the King, and it is clear from later events that he had received no bribe to do so. He told the King that the Garter would provide 'flattering testimony' of his approval of his course,[128] and the King replied that Goderich would have to be advanced in the peerage in order to be eligible for that honour.

Upon returning home Goderich presented his demands to Lord Grey. He wanted a written statement attesting to 'my great repugnance' to the changes, the promise of the Home Office or another 'office of business' when one became vacant, a position for his secretary, Sir Charles Douglas, and the removal of the 'personal obstacle' whenever a vacancy in the Order of the Garter occurred.[129] Lord Durham remarked later that Goderich should have presented his requests before accepting the Privy Seal,[130] and, as it turned out, Grey gave him what he did not want — an earldom — and withheld from him the things that he desired — the Garter and a working office in the Government.

Goderich called this 'the most painful sacrifice that I was ever called upon to make', and one can understand his position. He lost his chance to attach his name to the Emancipation measure, and at the same time, as he fully expected — there is evidence of this in a number of letters — his motives were entirely misinterpreted by the general public. 'He shrank from a question embarrassed with such difficulties,' Le Marchant recorded in his diary. 'He disliked his subaltern. The Privy Seal was offered him and he readily accepted it, leaving no pleasant legacy to his successor.'[131] Every statement in that comment was wrong, except that the Privy Seal was offered to him.

The image of Lord Goderich — as the most timid and fearful individual to hold high office in British affairs — was now completed. As Chancellor of the Exchequer he had tried to run away from the depression of 1826 ; as Prime Minister he had run away before meeting Parliament ; as Colonial Secretary he had run away from the slavery issue. He was always on the run whenever a serious difficulty appeared in his path! Assuming as a premiss that such an individual could not have done anything constructive, historians and some contemporaries traced Robinson's financial measures to Liverpool, Canning, or Herries, his trade measures to Huskisson or Wallace, and Goderich was consigned to the limbo of amiable men, who rated neither praise nor damnation.

9

The Twilight of a Career

===

THE decade of the 1830s was for Goderich, now the 1st Earl of Ripon, a new-found period of domestic tranquillity, and it was probably one of the happiest parts of his life. When they were not in London, Lady Sarah and he usually resided at Nocton Hall, where the former, now fairly recovered from her imaginary illnesses, had established an elementary school which trained a small group of children for the fee of a penny a week. This project no doubt had the enthusiastic support of her husband, who strongly favoured mass education. 'The extension of knowledge', he had written Brougham in 1828, 'is the diffusion of moral good & practical happiness amongst all classes of people.' [1]

Lady Sarah was particularly interested in needlework, and hired a teacher named Justinia to teach the young ladies at the school the complexities of that craft. From all accounts their products were of excellent quality, and the children even sewed pictures with their busy needles. In 1832 Justinia's daughter finished her masterpiece, a picture called 'Adam and Eve'. What Ripon's reaction to it was, we do not know, but he no doubt had some humorous quip for the occasion as he had several years later when he and Hobhouse inspected a picture called 'Ulysses and the Sirens', which showed three large women in a state of *déshabillé*. 'Indecorous', he remarked, 'without being attractive.' [2]

Convinced that George was too frail to be sent to school, Lady Sarah made him the central object of the educative programme at Nocton Hall. To teach him a writing style, his father's letters were used as models. The letters selected must surely have been from an earlier period in Ripon's life, for those of the later 1830s and 1840s were so crabbed, due to his illnesses, that they would serve better as puzzles than as models. Similarly, some of his father's poetry of the earlier period might have had educative value, but that produced at this time, if the poem written for his son's thirteenth birthday is a fair sample,[3] would qualify as doggerel. Whatever examples were held up, and methods used, it is clear that George received an excellent education, and read many fine books recommended by his father.

The quiet of Nocton was disturbed in July 1834 by an evil omen and a catastrophe. The omen came on 12 July, when an earthquake opened a fissure twenty yards wide and twenty-four deep near the town of Ripon, and two days later came the great fire at Nocton Hall, which was reported as follows : [4]

The ancient mansion of the Earl of Ripon, at Nocton, near Lincoln, was totally destroyed by fire. Notwithstanding the active assistance rendered almost immediately on the discovery of the fire, only the library, a quantity of wine, some old pictures and furniture were saved. There is nothing left but the naked and tottering walls.

As few of Ripon's private letters in the family collection are dated before 1834, and an enormous collection of them were written after that time, it appears that history, as well as Ripon's private fortune, suffered from the blaze. Possibly the conclusive answer to Robinson versus Huskisson and other questions pertaining to Robinson's career were destroyed with Nocton Hall. Following the fire, Ripon and Lady Sarah remodelled the steward's house at Nocton, and lived there at times while the mansion was being restored. Other parts of each year were spent at their residences in Carlton Gardens and Putney Heath.

After a period of illness in 1834, Lady Sarah had one of her better years in 1835. Thomas Creevey, never an admirer of the Ripons, reported seeing her in the enclosure at St. James's Park one fine May day : [5]

Who should I meet but Bessy Holyoake *alias* Goodrick, all alone, having dismissed her footman at the gate, and we had a charming walk quite around the whole, in the course of which we met, first Rogers and Mrs. Norton arm in arm ; then Goodrick, the Duke of Richmond and Graham ditto . . .

No aristocratic couple of the nineteenth century inspired so many nicknames as did the Ripons. This one evidently sprang from Lady Sarah's religious interests.

A number of old friendships were renewed during this period, and in one case a quarrel was made up. After leaving the Whigs, Ripon resumed his old intimacy with Peel, who invited him to Drayton in 1836. Ripon replied : 'I shall enjoy your shooting very much, for altho' I cannot fag as I used to do, I am as much a school Boy as ever when shooting is in Quest. . . . Altho' she [Lady Sarah] is very literally well just now, her health is at all times much too uncertain to enable her to venture leaving home.' [6] Ripon was then fifty-six, and was addressing a man only six years his junior, while Lady Sarah was still only forty-five, and had almost three decades of life left to her, but Ripon was already in the twilight of his career.

In 1839 Ripon received a letter from the Marquess of Londonderry, who was publishing his brother's letters, and wanted a testimonial from one close to him in 1814 and 1815. Delighted with Ripon's reply, Londonderry wrote : 'Placed as I have been as almost the Sole Depository of my lamented Brother's Character & Fame, I felt . . . I had but one course to pursue, vizt. The strict adherence to His views, Objects & Principles, as far as I was acquainted with them. . . . If my Zeal & Devotion to His Memory led me too far — I could not afford *you* a greater proof of subscribing to your better judgment, than I have done in leaving out that part of My Letter to Brougham more immediately relating to Canning.' [7] Londonderry called this the 'moment of our Restoration to friendly intercourse', and thereafter Ripon corresponded with him on occasion. Ripon's association with former Canningites continued through this period. He described Sir Stratford Canning as 'an intimate friend of mine',[8] and Lord Rosebery, who had received his peerage from Ripon, was numbered in the same class.

There was probably more variety in Ripon's life in the 1830s than during any other period. He was a Commissioner for Chelsea Hospital. In 1830 he became President of the Geographical Society, and he was President also of the Raleigh Club. But the position of which he was probably most proud was the Presidency of the Royal Society of Literature to which he was elected in 1834, as successor to George Agar-Ellis, Baron Dover, who had held the Woods and Forests in the Grey Administration, and had died at an early age in 1833.

Ripon's inaugural address in April 1835 gives some insight into his wide range of intellectual interests, and the wide breadth of his reading. He discussed the difficulties in constructing a chronology for ancient Egypt, translations of oriental literature, and the general progress of literary effort in history, travel accounts, art, geography, and Greek and Roman studies.[9] The Graeco-Roman world he regarded not only as a source of political knowledge, but as an inspiration for poets, historians, and philosophers.

A short section of the speech was devoted to Thomas Robert Malthus, who had died in 1834, but he did not dwell on the ideas and writings of this economist, and merely stated that, though some of his ideas were controversial, his high character was not. The only littérateur to call forth his unreserved praise was Samuel Taylor Coleridge, who had passed away the same year. As a poet, Ripon ranked him with Wordsworth, but he was quite as enthusiastic about Coleridge's prose works, especially *The Friend*, the *Lay Sermons*, and *Aids to Reflection*, the first of which he called the 'noblest exposition of moral, political, and ideal philosophy, which has appeared within a century and a half'. The two others provided a 'school of discipline for all who would learn to think'. Ripon lamented that 'utilitarian America' appreciated these works much more than did the British public.

Ripon thus acknowledged his debt to Coleridge, but if one goes through his speeches and letters in search of influences, beyond the discovery of a phrase like 'be it so', which Coleridge used, he is likely to be disappointed. Endeavours to trace his moral ideas to Coleridge, his economic thought to Ricardo,

Malthus, Smith, or John McCulloch, and his political outlook to Burke might produce interesting reading, and the conclusions, up to a point, would be valid; but they would not reveal the essence of Ripon. He was a practising Christian, whose attitude toward society and his fellow men was shaped by the Sermon on the Mount. Beyond that, he was a pragmatist, who regarded theories as mere outlines which were filled in by specific conditions and needs of the moment. Theories were made for men, and not men for theories.

The events of the fifteen months following his elevation to the earldom of Ripon in 1833 form a dreary, and even painful, chapter in Ripon's life. A few years later, he explained to Brougham: 'I was confident that my public character would be liable to great injury from the impression that was sure to prevail . . . that that [slavery] was the reason why I retired from that office. I must say that my prognostication was speedily realized.' [10] These rumours of cowardice and weakness, so unfair to him, may account for the sad spectacle Ripon made of himself on 25 June when he introduced the Emancipation Bill into the Lords. Twice during the speech he had to sit down and rest in an attempt to recover his composure, and many of his colleagues slept during the performance, possibly to cover their embarrassment.[11] Ripon, after this personal débâcle, did not attempt to speak on the second reading, and thereafter he rose only occasionally to defend certain clauses in the Bill.

Later in the year Ripon discovered to his dismay how little his continued services meant to the Government. Lord Grey had promised him an 'office of business' whenever some Cabinet changes might permit it, but, when Lord Anglesey retired from the Lord-Lieutenancy of Ireland, the Prime Minister overlooked Ripon's claims, considering him too weak for that position,[12] and gave it to Lord Wellesley. In January 1834, following the death of Lord Grenville, Grey broke an agreement he had made with Ripon in 1831 to promote Henry Ellis to the position of Comptroller General of the Exchequer and, instead, abolished Ellis's job as Clerk of the Pells.[13] The same month, when it was

rumoured that Lord Auckland would retire from the Board of
Trade, Ripon tried to combine that position with the Privy Seal
in order to get a working office,[14] but Grey would not commit
himself. In view of Grey's repeated slights, Ripon late in January refused to attend further Cabinet meetings until some
understanding as to his claims could be worked out.[15] Grey
finally put Ripon off with a promise of a more 'efficient office' in
the future, and agreed that Ellis should secure compensation
for the abolition of his patent office,[16] but it was apparent
from the correspondence that Grey considered Charles Edward
Poulett Thomson, who wanted the headship of the Board
of Trade, more important to the Government than Ripon. All
in all, the dispute was a sorry affair, and the bickering involved
seemed quite beneath the dignity of a former Prime Minister
of Britain.

Although in his speeches Ripon continued to stress that any
British Government must be 'in unison with the spirit of the
age',[17] and declared that reforms, if postponed, acquired new
force by compression,[18] he moved steadily away from the Whig
Liberals in 1833 and 1834, and this brought him into company
with three other less-than-enthusiastic reformers — Stanley,
Graham, and Richmond. In May 1834 the Cabinet was split on
the issue of Irish Church reform, and Ripon and the other three
resigned from the Cabinet on the issue. In explaining his resignation, Ripon stressed that the Established Church was universal,
and that its revenues might be 'redistributed' but not diminished,
unless a 'strong and insurmountable necessity' could be proved.[19]
In this he disagreed with Lord John Russell, who believed that
the excess revenues might be used for educational purposes, and
who, to use Stanley's phrase, thereby 'upset the coach'.

Ripon's resignation over this principle of maintaining the
revenues of the Irish Church probably stemmed partly from his
feeling that this attack on Church property was a violation of the
tacit understanding made during the Catholic Emancipation
debates, when it was understood that Church property would be
inviolate.[20] Had he stayed on Ripon undoubtedly would have
been returned to an 'office of business' in the Cabinet reassign-

ments following the resignations of the other three, but he placed his principles before his desire for advancement. It must be observed, however, that Ripon had the knack of sensing political directions — his early association with Liberal Toryism brought him to the Prime Ministership, his switch to the Whigs brought him a Secretaryship of State, and his decision at this time was to bring him back to office with the Conservatives.

Ripon may have considered an immediate junction with Peel, for on 25 July he discussed Irish Church matters with the Conservative leader, but when Peel took office in November, and Grantham became First Lord of the Admiralty, Ripon continued his attachment to the Stanley section, which was later dubbed the 'Derby Dilly'. 'I am delighted by the decision which you announced of your intention to continue to act with Stanley, Richmond and me,' Sir James Graham wrote him in December. '. . . from the present state of affairs . . . I do not anticipate that with us you will find it necessary to separate from your brother's policy.' [21] During the election that month Ripon helped search for Stanleyite candidates to strengthen their small section of Parliament.[22]

When Parliament opened in February 1835, and Peel began his first term as Prime Minister, Ripon called upon the Government to follow the 'well-understood wishes of the intelligent part of the public', and dwelt upon one of his favourite themes : 'The public mind was set upon material and important changes, not involving . . . any mischievous principle of innovation, but upon the safe principle of remedying abuses wherever abuses were found to exist. . . .' [23] As it turned out, the minority Government was too weak to carry measures originating in either its own, or the public mind and in April, Peel resigned.

During the next twenty months, prior to his return to the Conservatives, Ripon and Richmond continued to be the spokesmen of the rapidly dying Stanleyite section. As such, they participated in the interesting battle of the Lords, described in Turberville's recent work,[24] to recover some of the prestige they had lost during the struggle over Reform. The more violent followed Lyndhurst ; the more cautious took their cues from Wellington.

Ripon, who feared Lyndhurst's tactics might lead to a 'reform' of the Upper House,[25] sometimes supported, sometimes opposed the Government, and behaved like an independent statesman with a strong bent toward moderate Conservatism.

Richmond, the other Stanleyite spokesman in the Upper House, retained a longing for the Whigs, and Ripon and he often neutralized each other's vote. On the divisions related to the Municipal Corporations Act, Richmond supported the Government consistently, while Ripon often voted with the Opposition; but, when a vote was taken on the Government's Irish Church Bill, which contained an appropriation clause, Richmond joined Ripon in his opposition. After watching their activities carefully, Peel reported to Gladstone that Ripon was 'with us', but that Richmond was 'almost as much with the ministers and all but relapsing into their ranks'.[26]

This same pattern of voting characterized the session of 1836, when the Government's measure to establish municipal corporations in Ireland was debated. Ripon expressed his devotion to the principle of 'equal government' for England and Ireland, but he opposed the measure on the ground that the corporations were unnecessary, for their functions were being performed by other bodies.[27] Richmond, on the other hand, gave the Government his support on this measure. But on 25 July they both joined Lyndhurst in opposing and defeating another appropriation clause in an Irish Church measure. At the end of the session of 1836 Lyndhurst strongly defended the right of the Lords to harass and defeat the Government, as they had been doing during the past two years, and Wellington followed him with a speech of 'remarkable moderation', perhaps to offset Lyndhurst's violence. 'When I say *his friends* have expressed the opinions stated above,' Greville wrote, 'I should say that I have conversed with only two — Lords Bathurst and Ripon.' [28] This statement indicates that in late 1836 Ripon was considered to be one of Wellington's friends.

In the autumn of 1836 Ripon accepted an invitation to visit Peel,[29] and the latter in December wrote to Hardinge that Ripon was 'delighted to be . . . received into the bosom of Conservative society'.[30] He took this step a year in advance of Stanley, who did not formally join the Conservatives until December 1837, but Stanley seems, for a time at any rate, to have numbered Ripon among his political friends. Yet Ripon's defection to the Whigs had cost him his place in the Conservative ranks, and, among the peers, Wellington, Lyndhurst, Aberdeen, and Ellenborough, were all ahead of him.

Ripon's declining political influence was evident in a number of small ways. He suggested a plan for the Irish Corporations which would have made a gesture toward 'equal government',[31] but it was ignored by the Conservative leadership. During the elections of 1837, Ripon used his influence at Lincoln, near his family seat at Nocton, on behalf of Henry Ellis, who offered himself to that constituency, but an unidentified 'local bigwig' brought in another candidate.[32] Earlier correspondence shows that back in 1832 Ripon had a very strong voice in the political affairs of Lincoln.[33] In May 1839, when Peel made an abortive effort to form a Government, Ripon was not among those intimate advisers whom he consulted, and Stanley was delegated to inform Ripon that he would have a seat in the Cabinet. 'He said he was quite satisfied', Stanley reported to Peel, 'that he should not have liked to be passed over, but that you would not find him exigent.'[34] Ripon was no longer in a position, as in 1830, to insist upon a Secretaryship of State.

Perhaps to prove his value to the Conservatives, Ripon was very active in the Lords during 1840-1, and made a number of successful speeches on economic affairs. His 'sound money' speech of May 1840, drew high praise from Lord Ashburton, who, as Alexander Baring, had complimented him so warmly almost two decades before on his budgets. His attack on the Government's corn measure in May 1841 drew the following comment from the editor of *The Times*, Thomas Barnes: 'Lord Ripon's was a sharp and clever hit, the point about protection & taxation was cleverly put.'[35] Peel was by no means blind to his old friend's efforts, and in the summer of 1841 he wrote to Ripon that he was uncertain whether or not he had answered his last letter 'but I will prefer the Risk of inflicting upon you a double acknowledgement to that of appearing insensible to the readiness and value of your Communication on the subject of Commercial Policy'.[36]

When the election of 1841 gave the revived Conservatives a majority in the Commons, Peel conferred with his inner circle regarding the procedure in ousting the Government, and this time it was Wellington who informed Ripon of the decisions made. The Duke informed him that a 'no confidence' motion would be made, and added: 'I should think that the resolution will turn a good deal upon Finance, Corn Laws, and Commerce & Manufactures. Have you any objection to undertaking the task?' [37] Ripon had no objections, and presented himself to the House on 24 August. Greville called his speech 'very good indeed', but by this time Ripon had a weakness common to many statesmen with lengthy careers behind them. Members could recall some of his earlier speeches, and could — and did — quote them against him. 'The present Ministers', Lord Lansdowne declared, 'were only humble followers of that great statesman, Mr. Robinson, who now wished to deny his own offspring.' [38] That Mr. Robinson had lived twenty years — and two titles — ago, and he was now an 'elderly gentleman', to use his own phrase, who really had little left to say.

The economic outlook in 1841 was as unpromising as it had been back in 1818, when Ripon had become President of the Board of Trade for the first time. Business activity had reached a peak in 1836, which was followed by severe depression and fluctuations until 1840, and a continuing downward trend which lasted until 1843.[39] Between 1836 and 1843, British exports to Europe and the colonies were fairly stable, but those to the United States fell off sharply. Imports, on the other hand, showed an upward tendency during the whole period. Exports were obviously not keeping up with the increasing production of consumers' and capital goods, and there was serious unemployment. Prices showed a downward tendency, save in corn, which, due to poor harvests between 1836 and 1842, was high in price. A recent work provides a 'Social Tension' Chart, which indicates that social tensions in Great Britain increased whenever food prices and unemployment rose, and the chart for 1837–42 shows tensions were higher than during the post-war depression of 1816–17.[40] Two great national movements, Chartism and the Anti-Corn Law League, gave expression to these tensions.

Aside from the Prime Minister, four individuals at the Board of Trade were involved in the Government's economic reforms of 1841–3. Ripon, as President, was assisted by William Ewart Gladstone, who, at Ripon's request,[41] held the Mint as well as the Vice-Presidency of the Board of Trade. There were two Joint Secretaries — John Macgregor, a Free Trader and friend of Richard Cobden, and George Richardson Porter, who was both his collaborator and rival.[42] Just which of the five should be given credit for a specific idea or plan is difficult to determine in many cases. Gladstone later took credit for the Tariff of 1842,[43] and had a low opinion of both Ripon's and Macgregor's knowledge of economic affairs.[44] Peel in 1841, however, told Gladstone that Ripon was a 'perfect master' of economic subjects,[45] and so, as often occurred in connection with Ripon's career, there was a dispute as to his abilities. Gladstone's part in the economic legislation of this period is described in some detail elsewhere ;[46] Ripon's activities can be gleaned from the abundant correspondence he had with Peel, Gladstone, and Aberdeen.

The four major economic projects undertaken by Peel's Government while Ripon was at the Board of Trade were the adoption of the Income Tax, a revision of the tariffs, a new Corn Law, and the reciprocal trade negotiations with many countries. In all of these undertakings Ripon operated at the policy-making level, and only occasionally became involved in the details, save when the details were of major importance. He co-ordinated policies with Peel as First Lord, and with Lord Aberdeen, who, as Foreign Secretary, was involved in the reciprocal trade negotiations. Rather strangely — especially when one considers that they were intimate friends — Ripon had little correspondence with Henry Goulburn at the Exchequer.

As we have seen previously, Ripon and Herries had planned to make the Income Tax a feature of their budget of 1828 — a budget never presented, much less adopted, and Ripon continued to look on that tax as the means not only of keeping a balanced budget, but as a source of surplus which might be used for tax and tariff revisions. So when Peel suggested the tax at a Cabinet meeting in October, Ripon called the plan 'bold and most judicious'.[47] When the Income Tax Bill had its second reading in the Lords in 1842, Ripon was too ill to attend, and the Government therefore adopted the unusual procedure of postponing its explanation until the third reading, when Ripon made an excellent speech in its defence.[48] As usual, he gave the negative side of the case first, and noted that the tax was open to 'many grave objections', but declared it was necessary to balance the budget, to permit revisions of the tariffs, and because it was the best means of securing additional revenue. His speech, however, did not reveal his own part in deciding upon the specific provisions of the measure, and the only credit that can be claimed for Ripon was passing it through the Lords.

The decision at the highest level to overhaul the system of tariffs was evidently made in October 1841. 'The whole question of intercolonial trade must be looked at in conjunction with that of Foreign Sugar & Coffee', Ripon wrote to Gladstone on 20 October, 'and if we can settle them all, *as part of an enlarged scheme* of policy, it will be the greatest coup that the Government could strike.'[49] Three days later Peel wrote to Gladstone: 'We ought in my opinion to substitute protection for prohibition.'[50] The principle enunciated by Peel drew a distinction which Ripon had stressed as far back as 1816,[51] and which had formed the guideline for his tariff adjustments in the 1820s, as well as Huskisson's revision of 1825.

Ripon also seems to have played a part in determining the limits of the tariff scheme to be presented to Parliament. He explained later that there were 1100 articles upon which duties were charged, and that he thought it best to deal with only 700 or 800 of them.[52] Such a decision was also on the high policy level, and his reasons for limiting the scope of the revisions were given in an undated memorandum of that autumn, in which he enumerated certain imports which could not be changed because they were too important to the revenue, or came under treaties with foreign powers.[53]

Once the general policy had been determined, and the limitations of the tariff revisions had been set, the next step was to establish guidelines for dealing with the individual tariffs. Late in October Ripon wrote to Gladstone that he assumed Macgregor would shortly have a general classification of the articles subject to tariffs, and warned, 'he *must* get some notion of the proportion which the actual duty bears to the price of the article; because reduction may be merely throwing away Revenue for nothing'.[54] After studying the tariff structure for a month, Ripon reported to Peel on 29 November that the Board of Trade proposed a 5 per cent duty, with certain exceptions, on raw materials, a 7–10 per cent *ad valorem* duty on partly manufactured goods, and a 10–15 per cent rate on manufactured items.[55] This plan was generally adopted, save that the tariffs on manufactured goods ranged between 12 and 20 per cent, rather than 10 and 15 per cent.

By that time the general policy had been adopted, the limits to it had been set, and the guidelines for the tariff revision had been laid down. Ripon also played some part in fixing individual rates, but much of this routine work was evidently left to Gladstone and Macgregor. This is clear from a letter Ripon wrote to Gladstone early in April, summoning him to a meeting with Peel. 'If you are not there', he wrote, 'I do not know how we shall get on, as I presume the meeting is to consider the final arrangement of the Tariff, and as I was not there on the day that you considered some points with a view to modifications, I am not sure that I am quite aware of your reason for proposing them.'[56]

When the Bill was making its way through the Commons, Ripon received deputations from both its opponents and proponents, and he evidently convinced some of them at least that the measure was sound.[57] 'You and Gladstone deserve a full share of the credit due on account of the successful issue of the Discussion of the Tariff,' Peel wrote to Ripon in June.[58] On 5 July Ripon explained the measure to the Lords, who were not particularly interested in it,[59] and it passed easily through its various stages. All of this evidence indicates that Ripon played a major role at every stage of the drawing up and passing of the tariff revisions of 1842.

One of the tariff revisions seems to have been of particular interest to Ripon — lowering the duties on cattle. 'I should like to have some information upon the subject of the prices of cattle . . .' he wrote to Gladstone in October. 'The prohibition ought to be removed and a duty substituted.'[60] Three days later he again called Gladstone's attention to the matter, and declared that a relaxation of the tariff would not endanger the British cattle interest.[61] A tariff of one pound per head was subsequently adopted, and Ripon was able to convince the Lords, some of whom were nervous about the proposal, that the increasing population in Britain demanded a revision of this nature.[62]

The third major project of the Government's economic programme was a revision of the Corn Law of 1828, under which foreign corn was admitted into the British market according to a sliding scale of duties. There had been many objections to this law since its passage, and Ripon on numerous occasions had spoken on the general subject of the Corn Laws. In 1833 he had admitted that the law of 1828 was not the 'best in the world', but he warned that if a fixed duty were substituted for the sliding scale, public opinion would 'very soon overturn the fixed duty'.[63] This was his theme again in 1839, when he declared that the alternative to the sliding scale was the withdrawal of Protection from both farmers and manufacturers. Would the woollen manufacturers of Yorkshire, the cotton manufacturers of Manchester and Glasgow, the linen manufacturers of Ireland, and the iron manufacturers of Birmingham agree to a withdrawal of Protection? The adoption of Free Trade, he pointed out, would cause a revolution in the whole revenue system. Once again, in 1841, Ripon held up Free Trade as the only alternative to the sliding scale, and this time he observed that his own support of agricultural Protection was based on a fear of Britain's becoming dependent on other nations for a supply of food, if Free Trade were adopted.[64] Reading his speeches today, one receives the impression that Ripon was torn between his intellectual commitment to Free Trade and a fear of the consequences if the doctrine were applied to agriculture.

According to one authority, Peel at first hesitated about bringing in a new Corn Law, and Ripon was opposed to it.[65] The latter, however, at Peel's request, submitted a memorandum on the subject in early October, which was offered — with typical caution — simply as a basis for discussion. Ripon believed that foreign corn could be brought into Britain profitably for 35s. a quarter, and suggested a sliding scale which would lay a 20s. duty when the averages were at 56s.[66] Peel doubted that foreign corn could be imported that cheaply, and believed that the degree of protection suggested by Ripon was too high.[67] So, in a letter to Gladstone later in the month, Ripon suggested a sliding scale which went from a very high duty when the price was 45s. to the lowest duty when the price was 70s., but he did not suggest specific duty rates.[68] In these exchanges, it was assumed that Ripon's principle, advanced in 1826, of 'intermediate rest' would be adopted in some form.

In November Peel established a committee consisting of Ripon, Sir James Graham, Edward Knatchbull, and — at Ripon's request [69] — the Duke of Buckingham to consider revisions in the method of taking the averages, which were so important to the sliding scale type of Corn Law. Peel also mulled over the possibility of using the contemplated Corn Law as a bargaining weapon to secure trade concessions from Russia,[70] but Ripon pointed out that it would be wise to keep the corn question, which involved the subsistence of the people, entirely separate from other commercial questions.[71] The latter's view was eventually adopted. Ripon visited Peel at Drayton that winter, and during that period and during the Cabinet meetings early in 1842, the plans for the new Corn Law were worked out.

As a result of these meetings, and their study of statistics, the Government decided that the tariffs on foreign corn would be lowered, but that they would be protective, and not revenue, duties. When the averages were at 50s., the duty was 20s.; between 52s. and 54s. the duty was 18s.; thereafter the duty diminished shilling for shilling until the average price was 66s., when the duty was constant at 6s. as the price rose to 67s. and 68s.; then it decreased by one-shilling stages until it became 1s. when the price reached 73s. This represented a liberalization of the Act of 1828, which lay a 34s. 6d. duty when the average was 52s. In 1814 the parliamentary committee had considered 84s. as a fair price per quarter; in 1826 Lord Liverpool had aimed at 60s.; while in 1842 a fair price was considered to be 56s. These figures tend to follow the declining pattern of prices, which was marked just after the war, and less so in the 1830s.

Ripon had charge of the measure in the Lords, and defended it there on 18 April as a modification of the existing law. 'If I could be persuaded by fair argument', he said, 'that the people could be fairly and cheaply fed by the withdrawal of the protection now given to agriculture, I should not be found amongst those who would continue the restrictions on foreign corn.' [72] There was some uneasiness among the Lords regarding the measure, and the Duke of Cleveland wanted Ripon to declare that this act, like the Reform Act of 1832, would be a 'final measure'. 'All he could say for himself was this,' Ripon replied, 'that if he brought forward the measure, intending or wishing it not to be final, he would say so. He had never said that with respect to the measure. He hoped it would be final. He thought it would be a good thing if it were, and that it would not be his fault if it were not.' [73]

Although the Act of 1842 embodied Ripon's principles of non-discrimination among nations in its application, and intermediate rest, he was hardly an enthusiastic supporter of it. 'A scheme may be proposed which ought to satisfy all reasonable Men,' he had written to Gladstone in October, 'and [?] that ought to be the point to which our labour should tend.' [74] So the measure was produced as a reasonable compromise among conflicting interests, and its chief virtue was as a pragmatic solution to a difficult problem. One might doubt, however, that Ripon expected it to be final.

Ripon's work on the averages committee had similar results. There was no way of securing the system against fraud, nor was it possible to satisfy the Protectionists, on the one hand, and the Free Traders, on the other, that the markets selected for average-taking would provide an accurate measure of corn prices in Britain as a whole. Protectionists wished to exclude the London average because it was very high; Free Traders objected to including agricultural towns, where corn prices were low. As a compromise, the Government increased the number of towns consulted in compiling the averages, and included manufacturing and maritime towns as well as agricultural centres. This system probably provided more accurate averages than the one previously in use. The 'intermediate rest' feature of the Corn Act gave some limited protection against fraud.

Another project related to the revision of the Corn Laws involved the admission of Canadian corn at a preferential rate. Ripon strongly favoured this concession to Canada, and discussed it in two letters as early as October 1841.[75] Peel's first reaction, when the project was broached to him, was one of caution,[76] but a month later he was in favour of it.[77] The major difficulty confronting the plan was the possibility of American grain finding its way into Britain via Canada at the preferential rate, and the details were left for Lord Stanley, rather than Ripon, to work out.

The fourth major economic project of Peel's Government was an attempt to negotiate reciprocal trade treaties with a number of nations. Some of these projects had been begun by the previous Administration; others were initiated by the Board of Trade in an attempt to increase exports. Ripon, in a letter of 29 November 1841, to Peel, outlined both the policy and his hopes regarding it:[78]

At all events it would be the establishment of a great principle if we were able to say that *our* doors shall be opened, if other nations will assent to open theirs. We have tried ineffectively to induce them to open their doors by the partial openings which from time to time we have made; *mere example* has not operated, but offers of *conditional* advantages may have a very different effect, and if we can get some one important State to come to an understanding with us, others will be obliged to follow.

R

The usual procedure seems to have been, first, for the Foreign Office to sound out another nation on the subject of commercial negotiations, and, if the nation proved to be receptive, a secretary at the Board of Trade would draw up a 'project' under the supervision of Ripon or Gladstone, who, because of the revenue involved, would have to co-ordinate the plan with Peel or Goulburn; and, finally, the negotiations would be carried on through normal diplomatic channels, or a special negotiator would be appointed.

There can be little doubt that Ripon was referring to France in his letter of 29 November, for he had stressed the importance of this negotiation in an earlier letter to Gladstone. 'I attach great importance to this Treaty,' he wrote. 'I believe it will draw after it other important arrangements of the same kind with other Countries; & then do more for the benefit of Trade, Commerce and Manufacturing than all the Dogmatics of Free Traders, and will remove anti-Corn law agitation.' [79] The problem involved in this negotiation was to legalize a contraband trade which was already in existence,[80] which involved the exchange of French wines, brandies, and silks for British woollens, cottons, and linens.

The project in this case was created by George Porter under Ripon's supervision, and the negotiations were carried on by Bulwer-Lytton. During this period Anglo-French relations, due to the intimacy between Lord Aberdeen and Guizot, were excellent, but France was reluctant to repeal her ordinances against foreign linen, to lower her export duty on raw silk, and to remove her prohibition against British cottons; while Britain hesitated to reduce her duties on French silks, brandies, and wines without substantial 'equivalents'.[81] While Ripon was anxious to have the treaty, he was a firm bargainer, and the negotiations were therefore protracted and were still going on at the time he left the Board of Trade.

It is not clear from the correspondence just who at the Board of Trade drew up the project for a commercial treaty with Portugal, but the negotiations in this case were carried out by Lord Howard de Walden under the careful supervision of the Foreign

Office, which had a special interest in Portugal. Portugal wanted Britain to lower her duties on white and red wines, Madeira wine, brandy, and citrus fruits, which would cost the British Exchequer £300,000; so Britain demanded, in return, substantial Portuguese reductions on woollens, cottons, linens, hardware, and other manufactured goods. The negotiations resulted in a 'most-favoured-nation' treaty being ratified by the two countries in August 1842, but the lowering of duties continued to encounter obstacles. On 12 December, Aberdeen sent a strong protest to Ripon, noting: 'I fear that in some respects our conduct has not been liberal, and I am certain that it has been impolitick.'[82] This charge of illiberality seems to have nettled Ripon, who defended the position of the Board of Trade in two letters, which charged, among other things, that the Portuguese offer regarding woollens amounted to a prohibition. 'I am sure I do not see how we could face the Yorkshire Clothiers if we agreed to such an arrangement,' he replied.[83] But his answers still did not satisfy the Foreign Secretary, who observed: 'You may be as close-fisted as ever you please toward France, Russia, Naples, & even Spain, without a word of remonstrance from me. But I really consider our relations with Portugal as of a character entirely different from those of any other country.'[84]

In December 1842, Ripon and Aberdeen discussed their differences with Peel during a visit to Drayton, and the Prime Minister seems to have sided with Ripon. But Ripon — apparently on his own[85] — suggested a few alterations which impressed Aberdeen as eminently satisfactory.[86] But even these concessions proved unavailing, and by February 1843 Peel was ready to bring the talks 'peremptorily to a close'. The signing of the most-favoured nation treaty with Portugal seems to have been a tactical blunder, for the Portuguese, aware that Britain was negotiating with France a reduction of her wine and brandy duties, anticipated that they would have the benefits of such reductions under their treaty without having to make concessions in return.[87] Before leaving the Board of Trade, Ripon drew up a memorandum on the Anglo-Portuguese negotiations for the information of the Prime Minister.[88]

The Government had inherited from its predecessor a commercial negotiation with Brazil, in which the Foreign Office was deeply involved. Anglo-Brazilian relations had reached a state of the utmost complexity during these years, and so large a number of other considerations affected the commercial negotiations between the two states that space does not permit more than a superficial coverage of the situation. The interested reader seeking further details might refer to an article by this writer on the subject.[89] The general plan was to reduce British tariffs on Brazilian sugar and coffee in exchange for lower Brazilian tariffs on British manufactured goods, and an agreement to regulate the slave trade.

Ripon had a strong personal interest in these negotiations. In September 1841 he asked Lord Aberdeen to permit Henry Ellis to head the special British delegation to Brazil, and added the following revealing sentence: 'I do so, in reliance upon an old friendship of forty years; and as I owe so much of my actual position in the world to the generosity of his Father, I have always felt myself bound to do what I could to help him in his course thro' life.'[90] Aberdeen readily approved Ellis,[91] and thereafter Ripon, Aberdeen, Goulburn, Gladstone, and Macgregor all had a hand in drawing up the Brazilian project. The negotiators, who left for Brazil in the late summer of 1842, found upon their arrival that the Brazilian Government was in no mood to negotiate a treaty, due largely to British attempts to interfere with slavery in that country. In April 1843 Ripon received a letter from Ellis, who advised that the hopeless enterprise be terminated, and the former, in describing the failure to Aberdeen noted: 'We had little tempting to propose.'[92]

Projects of various types were drawn up and discussed during these years. There was some hope of securing an agreement with Holland to exchange lowered rates on Java sugar for concessions in favour of British manufactures,[93] but this one was postponed pending the outcome of negotiations with Brazil. They hoped to secure a share of the carrying trade to Naples in exchange for concessions on Neapolitan wines, but could not go ahead until the negotiations with France had been concluded.[94] Ripon spent considerable time on a project with Spain, which involved British reductions of her duties on Spanish alcoholic beverages, and a crack-down on the smuggling between Spain and Gibraltar, in exchange for a 20 per cent tariff on British cottons.[95]   By February 1843 Peel had lost hope for any comprehensive agreement with Spain, and was ready to accept even the most modest treaty.[96]

There were fears that Belgium was falling under Prussian economic influence, and some thought was given to a treaty with that country, but, as Ripon put it, Britain had 'nothing of real value' to offer Belgium.[97]   The growth of the Prussian *Zollverein* was also regarded in Britain with some alarm because that organization had erected a tariff wall against British goods which in some cases was as high as 100 per cent.   The Government thought about negotiations with the *Zollverein* and Austria, but the only item they had to send to Britain in quantity was corn — 'which I fear to touch in the way of negotiations', Ripon observed.[98]   Some ineffective negotiations were carried on with Hanover in an attempt to regulate the Stade Duties, which were collected at a point on the River Elbe north of Hamburg, and were both vexatious and an impediment to trade in the area, but no settlement was reached during Ripon's term at the Board of Trade.[99]

While these reciprocal trade projects created great billows of smoke, there was little fire under them.[100]   Many years later, Gladstone recalled these negotiations and observed : 'We failed in every case.   I doubt whether we advanced the cause of free trade by a single inch.'[101]   In so far as results were concerned, his conclusion was undoubtedly correct, but the repeated failures demonstrated the impossibility of carrying out seemingly sound ideas and gave Britain a clearer insight into her commercial position in the world.   Furthermore, Britain had shown that her doors were open to any nation which would pay the admission price in the form of reciprocity.

10

The Last Years

'I FIND myself suddenly entered into a new world', Ripon wrote in June 1843, 'where nothing is familiar to me, and where everything presents itself in a new and complex form.'[1] The late President of the Board of Control, and former member of the Alfred Club set, Lord Fitzgerald and Vesey, had died on 11 May, and Ripon, whose illnesses had virtually installed Gladstone as head of the Board of Trade for the past five months, had been promoted to the last Cabinet position he ever was to hold. Due to his lack of experience and knowledge of India, and his frequent incapacitations, Ripon was in this case what he had wrongfully been accused of being in some others — the mere nominal head of the department.

The dual system of authority over India exercised by the Home Government through the Board of Control and the East India Company through the Court of Directors was one of the complexities faced by Ripon in his new position. The Company paid the Governor-General of India, but he received his instructions from, and submitted his reports to, the Board of Control, which passed on such information as it chose to reveal to the Chairman and Deputy Chairman of the Court. The result was that the Government often possessed information of a secret nature which was unknown, or partially known, to the Court of Directors.

The first incident of importance during Ripon's term of office was the recall of Lord Ellenborough, then Governor-General of India. He had been sent there in 1841 to restore British prestige in India, which had been badly damaged by the tragic defeat of the British forces in the First Afghan War, and he did this triumphantly, but in 1842 he became involved in the troubled affairs of Sind. That Indian territory had been ruled by the Amirs, descendants of a Moslem conqueror of the area, but they had been forced to accept British protection at the beginning of the Afghan War. In 1842 Ellenborough sent Sir Charles Napier to Sind to investigate rumours of disaffection, and his aggressive attitude led the Amirs to make a foolish attack upon the British residency in February 1843, which was followed that same month by Napier's brilliant victory over their forces at Miani. In August the Amirs were deposed and exiled, and Sind was annexed to British India. Napier, in addition to building his military reputation, meanwhile secured a very substantial share of the prize money. The activities of Ellenborough and Napier were bitterly denounced by Sir James Outram, who returned to England in 1843 to plead the cause of the deposed Amirs.

The Home Government and the East India Company wanted peace and repose in India, not further annexations, which might prove costly and involve them in future wars; and in his first despatch to India, in June 1843, Ripon cautioned Ellenborough 'to avoid as much as possible *committing us* to any course of policy affecting territorial possession and extension'.[2] But Ellenborough, who knew that British forces were the only power factor of real importance in India, visualized the annexation of the Punjab, Peshawar, and Kashmir, and even had his eye on Egypt.[3] His imperialistic attitude, indeed, had 'half killed' Ripon's predecessor, Lord Fitzgerald, with 'nervousness and apprehension'.[4] The Government and the Governor-General, then, looked at Indian affairs from entirely different standpoints, and the attitude of the former was reinforced by the indignation of the Court of Directors, and a sizeable section of the British public toward the events of early 1843.

Ripon's first impulse was to approve much that had taken place, save for the deposition of all of the Amirs and the confiscation of their property, and on 29 May he had a medal designed for the soldiers in Napier's campaign.[5] The Court of Directors and Wellington, however, were still uncertain in June as to the wisdom of bestowing the medals, and their issue was temporarily held up while the Government considered its policy. On 9 June Peel wrote to Ripon that Wellington did not think they should propose a vote of thanks in Parliament that year — that it would be premature previous to the publication of the Sind papers, and very questionable after their appearance.[6] Ripon, therefore, obediently held up the medals and the vote of thanks until his colleagues could decide upon the Government's policy.

The crux of the difficulty was the summary deposition and despoliation of the Amirs, and it occupied the attention of many members of the Government that June. The Secret Committee of the East India Company wanted the Amirs' property restored to them; Major Outram wanted the same, and, with some restrictions, the restoration of their sovereignty.[7] Among the members of the Government, Lord Stanley thought each case should be decided on its own merits, and that the Amirs should have both their property and sovereignty restored;[8] Peel was ready to restore both, if it would not undermine British rule in India;[9] Wellington feared that restorations would lead to Ellenborough's resignation.[10] Ripon, whose opinion did not carry as much weight as the others, despite his position, sought a compromise which would conciliate the Court of Directors.[11]

The outcome of these deliberations was two letters to Ellenborough, one from Wellington, and the other from Ripon. Wellington, in his letter of 5 July, warned Ellenborough that the Opposition, the Press, and some of the 'best supporters' of the Government were critical of the Sind policy, but he assured him that he was working with Ripon and that the Government would not withdraw its support.[12] In his letter of the following day, Ripon noted that the 'public mind' was uneasy about the deposition of the Amirs, and asked him to consider their 'suggestions' that some worthy Amirs have their property and partial sovereignty restored.[13] Later that month Ripon received permission to strike the medals for Napier's forces,[14] but the vote of thanks was not proposed during the 1844 session.

In July and August Ripon and the other interested members of the Cabinet had to assemble the so-called 'Sind Papers' for study by the Court of Directors and Parliament. As these documents began, at Lord Auckland's request, as early as 1836, their very number caused delay, but even more time-consuming was the process of deciding which to include, and which to withhold. 'General G. Pollock's last letter we cannot give,' Ripon informed Ellenborough, 'for it throws blame upon Nott's army, and would stir up endless strife.' [15] But there were more weighty matters than personal rivalries to consider, and the Government evidently decided that the safety of British rule in India might be jeopardized by the publication of some of the papers most vital to the defence of Ellenborough. Later Peel noted that the Board of Control was 'in possession of information which, if known to the Court, might completely alter their views'.[16] This meant, then, that the Court of Directors had to arrive at their conclusions as to the wisdom of Ellenborough's Sind policy without having all of the pertinent facts at their disposal, and the case presented to them by the Government was a weak one. This was bound to lead to trouble.

The chain of events which led ultimately to Ellenborough's recall began with Peel's letter to Ripon on 19 August. The Prime Minister had just read a letter from an officer in charge of the imprisoned Amirs, which led him to observe : 'The treatment of the Ameers is really disgraceful to the Character of this Country. . . . It makes one ashamed of Indian policy when one reads such an account as the enclosed.' Then he added : [17]

Tell the Chairs — that it would be infinitely more creditable to the Court to recall Lord Ellenborough — and manfully to take upon themselves the responsibility of a Change in the Indian Government — than to paralyze that Government both at Home and abroad by acts demonstrating distrust, and dissensions among the chief authorities who have to conduct the Administration.

Ripon carried out this instruction verbally, and informed Peel on 31 August: 'I did not fail to place before the Chairs in the strongest manner the view of the case suggested by you . . . that they should take upon themselves the responsibility of exercising their power of recalling the Governor General rather than to do any act which by demonstrating distrust & differences between the different parties . . . at home & abroad would impair the strength & weaken the authority of both.' [18]

If Peel and Ripon had hoped that this presentation of the alternatives — to support or recall Ellenborough — would frighten the Court, they were mistaken. On 29 August the Secret Court of Directors passed a resolution noting that 'the proceedings adopted towards the Ameers of the Scinde have been unjust and impolitic, and inconsistent with the true interests and honour of the Indian Government'.[19] They then waited hopefully for the Government to recall Ellenborough, but instead Peel told Ripon to write them an expression of 'regret at the possible consequences of this policy', and, without becoming partisan in the quarrel between Ellenborough and the Court, to express their hope to Ellenborough that he would remain in India.[20] So an impasse was reached — the Government would not recall Ellenborough, and the Court, which had no confidence in him, feared to take on the responsibility of doing so themselves.

When Parliament met in February 1844 much of the public excitement over the unfortunate Amirs had died down, and the Government defeated Lord Ashley's motion on their behalf. Ripon then went on to move a vote of thanks to Napier and his men for their military successes in India, and he called one of Napier's tactics 'one of the most brilliant of its kind ever performed'.[21] But he avoided in his speech the questions of whether or not taking the Sind was a wise move, and if the Amirs should have been deposed or retained. Under these circumstances, the resolutions passed easily.

Meanwhile Ellenborough had become increasingly restless and dissatisfied with the support he had received from the Home Government. Peel considered his attitude 'unreasonable and unjust'. 'Whose fault', he asked in a letter to Ripon, 'is it that the Court of Directors, which hailed his appointment with unanimity and satisfaction . . . has been alienated from him? Certainly not ours.' [22] The Governor-General was even more critical of the Court. 'Ellenborough's conduct and language to the Directors', Aberdeen was quoted as saying, 'had been such as it was impossible for them to endure. . . .'[23] Smarting under what they considered insubordination, the Chairs told Ripon in April that the Company planned to recall Ellenborough, and though Ripon, acting on Peel's suggestion, told them this was 'inconsistent with justice and sound policy',[24] they went ahead with the recall.

Peel sought to mitigate Ellenborough's chagrin at this unfortunate termination of his Governor-Generalship by granting him an Earldom and the Grand Cross of the Bath,[25] but Ellenborough, seeking someone to blame for the recall, charged that Ripon had not defended him vigorously enough before the Court.[26] He was so vocal on this subject on his return to England that Ripon protested to Peel : [27]

You know the great difficulties with which I had to contend . . . in consequence of the hostile relations between the Court and the Governor General. I found that hostility in full vigour when I came to office ; I saw at once all the evils that might follow from it, and used my utmost efforts to avert or at least mitigate them.

All of the available correspondence bears out this interpretation of Ripon's conduct with respect both to the Court and Ellenborough. Ellenborough's imperialism and cavalier treatment of the Company's officers were responsible for his recall. Interestingly enough, a year or so after his return to England Ellenborough was to criticize his successor, Lord Hardinge, for being too aggressive in dealing with the Sikhs,[28] which indicates how a change of geographical situation altered his views !

Several factors prevented Peel and Ripon from giving Ellenborough stronger support. Both of them privately disapproved of his treatment of the Amirs, and regarded the Sind as a potential financial liability. They evidently also believed that their function was to mediate in disputes between the Company and the Governor-General, rather than to be partisans of one or the other. Both realized the difficulties and inefficiencies of the dual government then existing, but neither of them, nor anyone else in the Cabinet, was ready to undertake the onerous task of changing it. Finally, it is clear that neither Peel nor Ripon was

particularly interested in Indian affairs. Once when Ripon suggested that Sir James Graham replace Ellenborough, Peel replied
significantly that Graham was needed at home, and that the
Home Office was more important than India.[29]

Ripon's relations with the conqueror of the Sind, Sir Charles
Napier, form a decidedly unpleasant chapter in his life. Back
in 1831, while Ripon was at the Colonial Office, Napier, then
administrator of Cephalonia in the Ionian Islands, became involved in a bitter dispute with his immediate superior, Sir
Frederick Adam, and, rejecting Ripon's attempt to compromise
it, quit his office with a grudge against both men.[30] In an effort
to re-establish friendly relations with Napier, Ripon, on 5 July
1843, wrote to the testy general, advising him of a promotion and
the award of the Grand Cross of the Bath for his battles in Sind,
and expressing the hope that the past would be forgotten.[31]
Napier made a conciliatory reply, but, as events proved, the past
was not forgotten.

Napier blamed Ripon for the delay in the vote of thanks in
Parliament, and the tardy arrival of the medals bestowed for the
Sind campaign. The vote of thanks was delayed by Wellington
and Peel, and the former was responsible for the indecision about
the medals, so Ripon could be blamed, at most, for the delay in
sending out the medals once they had been approved. This
probably was due, however, to causes over which he had no control, for nothing in the correspondence, or in his parliamentary
speeches, hints that Ripon ever wanted to withhold from Napier
the honours due to him or his men.

A more important source of friction between Napier and Ripon
arose in consequence of the former's campaign against the hill
people, who had been raiding Sind out of the Punjab. In July
1844 Ripon declared in Parliament that a rumour that Napier
planned to attack the Punjab was entirely false,[32] and in his
letters to Napier, he tried to minimize the importance of the
raids of the hill people. 'You give too much importance by your
order to the little affairs of robbers against an outpost', Ripon
wrote, 'which I fear will be made a handle of.' [33] Early in 1845,

acting on a rather vague authority given to him by Ellenborough before his departure, Napier launched a brilliant and successful campaign against the hill people, and settled back to receive again the thanks of a grateful nation. But Ripon, fearing that the charges of imperialism would be revived, delayed publishing the details of the campaign. Perhaps to atone for this — to his way of thinking — unavoidable oversight, Ripon in March 1846, while speaking on an entirely different campaign in which Napier had not participated, called the general 'as gallant a hero as ever wore the soldier's uniform'.[34]

Napier's reaction to Ripon's treatment of his latest victory is indicated by the following letter to a friend : [35]

the least Lord Ripon could do was to say those men did well ; but he attempted to burke my despatch ! It was not till Lord Ellenborough threatened to ask him in his place, why my despatch was not published, that it appeared in the Gazette ; the excuse was 'Indeed, he had forgotten it.' Can you then be surprised at my saying the hottest day in Scinde never made my blood boil as this man did . . . that weak creature, lolling in his easy chair, thrusting the despatch into his drawer — and forgetting it ! The poor creature is afraid of the Court of Directors, that is the secret.

Like Ellenborough, Napier looked upon the East India Company with contempt, and he numbered the Court of Directors among his many enemies and detractors.

For Ripon and Peel's Government, Napier's most vexing quarrel involved his brother, William Napier, and the so-called 'Bombay Faction', led by Sir George Arthur, the Governor of Bombay. The *Bombay Times*, reflecting the attitude of the Government there, was frequently critical of the 'Autocrat of Scinde' or the 'Scinde Czar', as they called Napier, and the latter was not one to overlook reflections cast upon him. Using information which Wellington believed was provided to Charles Napier by Ellenborough,[36] William Napier, who in turn received it from his brother, published a book in 1844, which defended Charles, and attacked both the Court of Directors and Colonel Outram of the 'Bombay Faction'. Some of the information in the book had been classified as secret by the Government, and its publication was therefore a breach of security regulations.

Ripon warned Napier that the book had 'attracted a great deal of attention, and no small degree of uneasiness has manifested itself in Leadenhall Street'.[37] Napier insisted that there was 'nothing injudicious' in the book, but promised to tell his brother not to publish further criticisms of the Indian Government. With that curious blindness arising out of his partisanship for his own cause, Napier refused to admit that his brother had erred, and that Ripon had a right to complain about it. He wrote to his brother that Ripon had written him a 'very silly letter', and that he was angry about William's mention of the 'Adam business'.[38] The question was thus reduced to one of personalities.

Colonel Outram was not one to overlook the charges made against him in the book, and he wrote a strong letter which was published — without his consent, he said — in the *Bombay Times*. This letter was not a breach of secrecy, but one of discipline, for Outram had thereby attacked his superior officer. This letter had two important results. Outram received an official rebuke from Sir George Arthur, and William Napier replied to Outram in a newspaper article, which used classified information furnished to him by his brother.[39] So, by October 1845, a 'paper war' had developed between the Napiers and the 'Bombay Faction'. Sir George Arthur was 'much hurt' by the statements made against himself and his colleagues; Outram was nursing the rebuke he had received; and Napier was in high dudgeon from the attack of a military subordinate. The last finally sent an official letter to the Governor-General demanding that Outram be punished under the articles of war.

The aspect of the quarrel which most concerned the Home Government was the breach of security regulations by the Napiers on two occasions. As in dealing with Ellenborough, Ripon did nothing without the advice and consent of Peel and Wellington. The latter demanded that Napier discontinue all correspondence with his brother;[40] and Peel suggested that Ripon stress the inconvenience to the service arising out of the situation.[41] Ripon thereupon drew up a draft despatch to the Governor-General, which stressed the 'extreme impropriety' of the publications, and suggested that Napier be given an opportunity to deny any connection with his brother's second literary effort.[42]   On reading the draft, Wellington suggested a more 'positive approach' to prevent leaks in the future ; [43] and Peel observed : 'You deal more tenderly with the offence of disclosing official and really secret intelligence — than I should be disposed to deal with it if I had to take cognizance of it.' [44]   The reactions of Peel and Wellington are important in clarifying Ripon's attitude toward Napier.   Far from seeking to embarrass the General, Ripon was doing his utmost to smooth the matter over, and to avoid ruffled feelings.

After the rejection of his first draft by Peel and Wellington, Ripon drew up a second one with the advice of Peel and Wellington in which all parties were held to share the blame for the present situation.[45]   But, like the first despatch, it was never sent. The Chairs of the East India Company asked Ripon to drop the matter, and he decided — probably with the consent of Peel and Wellington — to do so.[46]   Therefore, on 21 November he wrote a third despatch to the Governor-General, in which he said that the Chairs wanted the controversy to 'sleep'.[47]

Ripon then undertook the difficult task of soothing Napier, who was waiting impatiently for Outram to appear before a court-martial.   In his letter Ripon pointed out that attacks of various kinds were part of the price one paid for prominence in official life.   This straw broke the camel's back.   'Your lordship must excuse my saying', Napier replied with deadly calm, 'that I did not require a lecture on that subject at my time of life.' [48] Thoroughly angered and frustrated, Napier penned a veritable treasury of vituperative gems against Ripon during these months. In one letter he appeared as the 'pack-ass' for the Directors, and an 'imbecile'.   'I detest Ripon,' he wrote in March, 'I could not do so more if he was a rascal ; his good-natured drivelling is worse than if he spit in one's face.'   Then on 30 June : 'Lord Ripon is not a rascal by nature, but he is so weak of intellect that rascals do what they please with him, and make him act like one of themselves.'   More than a year later, he wrote : 'Lord Ripon has been my evil genius for sixteen years.'

Despite the cool and often starchy replies he received, Ripon
continued to correspond with Napier until his farewell letter in
July 1846; and, when he learned in 1849 that Napier had been
appointed Commander-in-Chief in India, he wrote him a warm
letter of congratulations.[49]   When the saga of Ripon and Napier
was concluded, the sum total of Ripon's sins were four in number
— his failure to side with Napier against Adam, his refusal to
bring Outram before a court-martial, the delay in delivering the
Sind campaign medals, and his tardy notice of Napier's victories
over the hill people. On the other hand, Napier had been promoted and given the Bath, had been permitted a free hand to
carry out his policies in the Sind, and had been generously supplied with men and material for his wars. And his military merits
had been acknowledged before Parliament and the world on more
than one occasion by the man he insisted on regarding as his
'evil genius'.

A third individual who figured prominently in Indian affairs
during these years was Sir Henry Hardinge, who had met Ripon
during his visit to Paris in 1814, and who had been a member of
the Castlereagh faction after the war. When he set out for India
to replace Ellenborough in June 1844, he carried instructions
to keep the peace from a Government and a Company who had
complete confidence in his abilities. But the situation in the
Punjab since the death of its pro-British ruler, Ranjit Singh, in
1839 had been anarchic, and the third of the territory, called the
cis-Sutlej states, south-east of that river was left to Hardinge's
discretion by the Home Government. Its political future was in
his hands.

Trouble was not long in coming. In the summer of 1845
Hardinge personally inspected the territory, and thereafter
despatched reinforcements, which he hoped would help keep the
peace along the frontier. This led to the strengthening of the
Sikh forces across the river. The Sikh princes then offered
Hardinge a subsidiary alliance, but the Governor-General, in
obedience to his instructions not to become involved in the affairs
of the Punjab, rejected the offer. On learning of this, Ripon

wrote : 'I own that I should look upon the conquest and possession by *ourselves* of the Punjab, as a great misfortune . . .' [50] But the military build-up along the Sutlej had created a tense situation, and on 11 December the Queen Regent of the Punjab, seeking an outlet for the restlessness of the Sikh princes, ordered their armies across the river, and the First Anglo-Sikh War was on.

The British forces, under the command of Hardinge and his military superior, Sir Hugh Gough, neither of whom was a tactical genius, gave battle on 18 and 21 December, and, although the British were triumphant, the battles were costly ones indeed. On 10 February, however, they managed a much better-planned battle at Sobraon, and the Sikh armies were crushed. Acting on the only instructions then in his possession, Hardinge on 9 March signed the Treaty of Lahore with the defeated Sikhs, which ceded the territory up to the Beas River to British India, created an independent state in the hill country under a loyal Sikh named Ghulab Singh, cut down the size of the Sikh army, and provided for a fairly stiff indemnity.

In those days news from India reached Britain by one of two routes. Usually reports were sent by sea via Alexandria–Malta–Marseilles, after which they were carried overland, or — a very recent innovation — were telegraphed from France to England.[51] Some news, however, went from Alexandria to Trieste, where a *Times* courier picked it up, and carried it across Germany and so on to England. Hardinge's accounts of the war, which came over the first of these routes, were delayed due to the breakdown of the ship conveying them, so the initial news of the war reached England via *The Times* route, and was published on 5 February. The official despatches did not arrive in England until 23 February, almost a fortnight after the last battle had been fought.

Although the Government became feverishly active as soon as they learned of the outbreak of hostilities, almost everything that they did went wrong. Wellington, Peel, and Ripon all wanted Hardinge to have charge of military affairs, but there were many technicalities which prevented their commissioning Hardinge, so, in the end, Wellington simply wrote a letter to Gough, asking

s

him to serve under Hardinge.[52]   As the fighting was over before
Wellington's letter arrived, Hardinge, to spare Gough's feelings,
tried to suppress it, but Gough eventually learned of the plan,
and was offended.

As Hardinge was to command the forces, the Government also
had to provide for the contingency of his being killed in battle.
They eventually selected Sir George Arthur, who was on very
cordial terms with Ripon, to be acting Governor-General in the
event of Hardinge being incapacitated. As Hardinge survived the
war, all this precaution did was to give 'mortal offence' to another
British official, who thought his claims were superior to those of
Arthur.[53]

The Government expected victory in India, but did not anticipate that it would come so soon. The day after the Treaty of
Lahore was signed, Ripon wrote to Peel: 'Altho' it may seem
premature to be writing to the G. G. upon the subject of the
future disposal of the Punjaub . . . I nevertheless think that
we ought to convey to Hardinge some general notion of the view
which we are disposed to take of that most important subject.' [54]
Ripon had in mind the Ravi River, well to the north-west of the
Sutlej, as a possible boundary. Peel confessed he did not know
whether the Ravi would make a good boundary or not,[55] so Ripon
secured the 'best map' he could find at the India House, and
discussed the boundary with Wellington.[56]   They realized at
length that they were in no position to make a decision on this
question, and contacted the Chairs, who proved to be divided,
one wanted only the cis-Sutlej territory, the other wished to
annex all of the territory up to the Indus River.[57] Faced with
all sorts of conflicting advice, Ripon at length submitted his Ravi
project to Hardinge together with some general comments by
Ellenborough.[58]

Hardinge eventually received these instructions long after he
had signed his treaty, which, following previous instructions, had
only ceded the cis-Sutlej territories along the Sutlej–Beas line.
He thereafter replied in that wounded tone sometimes employed
by Governors-General who believed that their best efforts had
come to naught: 'I see my course will be considered in-

sufficient . . .' [59] The Cabinet, however, quickly approved the Treaty of Lahore when it arrived, and Ripon hastily assured Hardinge : 'My opinion never varied as to the establishment & maintenance of a Sikh Government being the best solution of the business.' [60]

The Government also expressed its approval in a much more concrete form. Ripon in March moved a vote of thanks in Parliament for Hardinge, and helped secure for him both a peerage and a rich pension. Shortly thereafter Peel's Government fell, and Hardinge, upon hearing this news, wrote to Ripon : 'And now my dear Lord allow me to express what I sincerely feel — the satisfaction and happiness of having served under a Minister & friend, whom I respect as a Public man, & to whom for his personal virtues & kindness to me during 2 years, I am affectionately attached.' [61] Thus, on the subject of Lord Ripon, the conqueror of the Sikhs and the conqueror of the Sind differed sharply, and the former's opinion makes a pleasant flourish on which to end an account of Ripon's term at the Board of Control.

Even after he had been removed to the Board of Control, Ripon continued to be the chief spokesman for the Government on economic affairs in the Lords, and he was on more than one occasion politely chided by the Free Traders for his views on the Corn Laws. Back in 1834 he had tried his best to prove that the 1828 Corn Law was not a 'landlord's Bill',[62] and he spoke on the same subject again in 1839, noting this time that he disliked the very word 'aristocracy'.[63] In 1842 a Free Trader, Lord Kinnaird, quoted back to Ripon a poem he had recently recited at a formal dinner : [64]

> O weel may the boatie row,
> And better may she speed ;
> O weel may the boatie row,
> That gains the bairn's bread.

How long — Kinnaird asked — would Ripon continue in a Government which prevented the 'boatie' from earning half enough bread for the 'bairns'? Lord Monteagle in 1844 taunted

Ripon again on the subject of Free Trade and the Corn Laws.[65]

No doubt the taunts of the Free Traders in the Lords stung Ripon the more because they touched a very sensitive spot — his public image. Since his first appearance in Parliament, he had presented himself as a friend of freedom, as one who put the general welfare before the interests of any class, and — above all — a man with a heart. The Anti-Corn Law League could sting far more effectively than the self-interested Manchester businessmen of 1815.

As of 1845 the only substantial argument, to Ripon's way of thinking, in the way of repeal was that it was unwise to depend upon foreign nations for a food supply, and with the mushroom growth of the British population between 1815 and 1845, this argument seemed stronger rather than weaker as time went by. As was not unusual, therefore, he was immobilized intellectually when the Cabinet met in November 1845 to discuss the threatening potato famine in Ireland. During the first phase of the Cabinet crisis, Ripon doubted the wisdom of Peel's plan to remit the Corn duty to one shilling by Order in Council, and to pledge a modification of the Corn Laws at the next Parliament. He seems to have accepted Stanley's view that this would not help the Irish, who needed absolute means of purchasing food, rather than lower prices for it, and he pointed out that a suspension of the laws would condemn the principle of the system, and make its future re-enactment impossible.[66]

On 29 November Ripon wrote a lengthy letter to Peel in which he stressed the granting of some financial boon to the agricultural interest to compensate the farmers for the loss of their Protection. 'I am not prepared to say what equivalent or compensation could be found which would be at once desirable and practicable,' he observed. 'It would probably only be found in some new adjustment of special burthens upon agriculture. . . .'[67] By this time, however, the wisdom of preserving the Conservative Party in power loomed large in his thinking. 'The crisis is one of immense magnitude', he added, 'and, although, as far as I am personally concerned, I am very indifferent as to the mode in which it may affect itself, I cannot look without the greatest apprehension upon the evils which may fall upon the Queen and the country if you are withdrawn from the guidance of public affairs.' [68]

Unable to carry a united Cabinet with him on his economic proposals, Peel resigned early in December, but the Government continued to function pending the creation of its replacement by Lord John Russell. When he wrote Wellington on an Indian matter at this time, Ripon thanked the Duke profusely for his aid in the past, and asked that he be permitted to consult him on political affairs in the future, which shows that Ripon had no intention of retiring from politics at this time.[69] Russell's failure to form a Government became known before the Duke replied to Ripon's letter, and he therefore did little more than acknowledge it.

Ripon gave Peel his unequivocal support after the latter was restored to power on 21 December. Upon the Prime Minister's request, Ripon contacted Viscount Mahon, then a Secretary of the Board of Control, and Viscount Jocelyn, who had replaced Ripon's friend, Stratford Canning, for King's Lynn, regarding their views on the corn question, and Ripon reported on 22 December that Mahon would accept a modification of the laws, but would resign if the measure called for repeal. He had not yet seen Jocelyn, but he assured Peel that Jocelyn would support the Government unless his constituents forced him to adopt another course.[70] As it turned out, both of them in the end supported the repeal of the Corn Laws.

Although Ripon wrote many letters during early 1846, he maintained in them that discreet silence regarding the Government's corn proposals that had so often characterized his letters in the past. So his thoughts during this period are concealed from the historian. Just before the Bill went to the Lords in May, however, Peel asked his colleagues about the wisdom of using proxies there, and Ripon replied : [71]

I think we must not suffer the Bill to be lost by abstaining to use Proxies upon the Report, in order to get rid of any amendment that would be fatal to the Bill. In 1827 I moved the Report of the Committee on the Corn Bill of that year to omit a clause introduced in the Committee. Proxies were called, but the Government was unable . . . to throw out the clause . . .

Ripon thus recalled one of the most trying incidents in the most difficult year of his life. Wellington had had the proxies in 1827 ; he was still to have them in 1846.

When the Bill had its first reading in the Lords on 18 May, Ripon still had not been assigned to move its second reading, but he took it upon himself to answer the Duke of Richmond, who protested against the first reading. Noting that he expected censures to be cast in his direction, Ripon quoted : 'There is no terror, Cassius, in your threats, for I am arm'd so strong in honesty, that they pass by me as the idle wind, which I respect not.' [72] This quotation seems to have made some impression on the House, for Lord Ashburton mentioned it in a letter to an ageing member of the former Alfred Club set, John Wilson Croker.[73]

The following day Wellington asked Ripon to move the Second Reading. He was very reluctant to do so. This was properly the task of the President of the Board of Trade, Lord Dalhousie, who was a young man without a large catalogue of utterances on previous Corn Bills behind him, and hence might be able to present the measure more effectively. But, when urged to do so by both Wellington and Peel, Ripon undertook the task, and reported to Hardinge that it had been 'most unexpectedly' imposed upon him.[74]

We can only guess what went on in Ripon's mind during his three days of preparation for the speech. Thirty-one years before, Frederick John Robinson, hoping to make an impression on the Commons, had made his first speech on the Corn Laws — now ten, twenty or more speeches on the same subject later, a tired, prematurely aged, and sick old man was called upon to move a Bill designed to put the subject finally to rest. Did he feel satisfaction that the problem was to be shelved at last ? Did he feel satisfaction at linking his name to this measure of Free Trade ? Perhaps he did, but probably his main concern was constructing a speech which would do him credit, and not disgrace him as his efforts on Catholic and slave emancipation had done. This was most difficult, for now physical infirmities added to his emotional problems. 'The Earl of Ripon's extreme weakness excited astonishment', Sir John Campbell had written in 1842, 'that he should ever have risen on the death of Canning to the post of Prime Minister.' [75]

In his speech of 25 May Ripon reviewed his previous attitudes toward the Corn Laws. He insisted that Lord Liverpool had prevailed upon him to introduce the Act of 1815 against his wishes. No document presently available proves or disproves this statement. He declared further that he never supported the Corn Laws on the ground of rent, or the special burdens on agriculture, or that he had advocated them as part of a great system of protection for national industry. All these statements are accurate. Then he went on to explain he had shared year after year in measures and arguments to rid Britain first of prohibitions, and then of Protection itself, which injured the country generally, and even the interests of those it was designed to serve.[76] There can be no question regarding his opposition to prohibitions — he had been in the vanguard of this movement, but he had so often spoken of 'fair protection' that his statement that he was working for its abolition must be accepted on faith.

Ripon next turned to the argument he had used so often in support of the Corn Laws — that it was unwise for Britain to depend on foreign states for her food. He proclaimed Malthus's doctrine that population pressed upon the limits of subsistence, and, pointing to the corn imports during the past few years, he concluded that Britain, whether she willed it or not, was actually becoming dependent on other nations for food. Then, rather surprisingly, he rejected also the argument that the repeal of the Corn Laws was necessary because of the failure of the potato crop in Ireland, and, when Richmond pointed out that Peel had stressed this point, Ripon, with an unusual show of independence, declared: 'I do not see, my Lords, that I am necessarily called upon, in enforcing any particular measure, to say that my views of particular arguments are directly coincident with those of anybody else.' [77] The rest of his speech was designed to prove that this measure was not dictated by the exigencies of the moment, but would benefit the nation as a whole without harming agriculture.

On the whole, Ripon's speech attracted little comment.

Richmond attacked him for inconsistency, and another old friend —
and enemy — and friend again — Lord Londonderry, defended
him. Ripon's speech was like a short subject film before the main
feature, which was Lord Stanley's mighty defence of the traditional system of agricultural England. Thereafter Ripon moved
the committee on the Bill on 11 June, spoke against a hostile
amendment on 15 June, and presented it for the Third Reading
on 25 June. On the last occasion Ripon noted that the measures
for agricultural relief would be presented as they served the
general welfare, and not as compensations for the loss of Protection — so in this matter, too, he accepted the decision of Peel.

During June and early July Ripon mentioned the governmental
prospects in letters to Hardinge. '*Party* views on the one hand',
he wrote, 'and *factious spite* on the *other*, have caused a combination which renders it very probable that we may be beat
upon the Coercion Bill . . .'[78] Two days later Peel resigned,
and early in July Ripon explained: 'Peel felt that it would be
impossible for him to carry on the Government situation as it
was in *both houses*, with any chance of success . . .'[79] He urged
Hardinge to continue in India so long as the new Government
showed its willingness to support him.

The 'factious spite' Ripon mentioned in his first letter was
turned upon him by the Protectionist leader, Lord George Bentinck who, in August, charged that Ripon had made a deal with
Lord Lyndhurst to appoint David Pollock Chief Justice of Bombay in exchange for Lyndhurst's support in placing one of Ripon's
friends in a Church living at Nocton.[80] Bentinck quickly re-
tracted the charge, but the accusation of 'trafficking in ecclesiastical patronage' nettled Ripon, who defended himself in the
Lords on 25 August: [81]

I rest my defence here — I stand on my own character — that
character is before the world — it has been before the world for thirty
years, and if it did not defend me from such attacks, then no explanation I can give, no argument I can urge, can have that effect. . . . I
still would rather be the victim of that wrong, . . . I still would rather
carry with me to the grave the sense of that injury, than be the anony-
mous author of that calumny which this accusation has flung upon me.

This defence, which was delivered emotionally, [82] was both characteristic and uncharacteristic of Ripon. The Lords were used
to hearing him defend his character, but the phrase 'to the grave'
was unusual for Ripon, whose forgiving disposition was one of
the most attractive features of his character.

In so far as the general public was concerned, when Ripon left
Parliament that August night, he walked into an oblivion from
which he never again emerged. But there is no evidence that
Ripon realized that his career was finished. In 1847, indeed, he
repeated his performances of 1828 and 1835, and presented himself to the House on five different occasions; and his final speech,
on Irish affairs, was not made until 14 May 1847. But in 1848
he lapsed into silence, and his name is not even recorded among
the division lists of that year.

The available correspondence provides only brief glimpses
into the last eleven years of his life. Lady Sarah in 1848 fell ill
again, and she lost so much weight that Ripon despaired for her
life, and became so melancholy that he criticized himself for the
inadequacy of his religious faith.[83] But she recovered in 1849,
and his moment of despondency passed. So he returned to
Parliament that year, and was active in the Peelite cause. Sir
Charles Wood was anxious to have him speak on the Navigation
Acts, and wrote to Peel: 'It strikes me . . . that if any peer
spoke early in the debate who would be considered as expressing
your opinion, it would tend more to decide votes than anything.
Ripon expressed his wish not to speak.' [84] This indicates the
closeness of his relationship with Peel. In October, Hardinge
wrote a letter of thanks to Ripon 'for the White Water Lily,
which arrived a few days ago in excellent condition'.[85]

Ripon was not in attendance when Parliament opened in 1850,
but sent his proxy to support the Government on the Address,
and Lord Stanley classed both him and his brother among the
Peelites.[86] That year his little group lost their leader, and
Ripon's reaction to this unexpected tragedy can be gleaned from
letters written to him by friends. Sidney Herbert wrote: 'I went
to Drayton to attend the last sad office to our departed friend.

Even now I can scarcely believe in the reality of all that has happened. As you say, it is impossible to measure the loss.' [87] 'I entirely concur in the just observation you make in yr. note,' Hardinge wrote, ' — to us it is a grt. satisfaction that we adhered to the policy of our grt. Conservative leader . . .' [88] All the Prime Ministers under whom he had served — Portland, Perceval, Liverpool, Canning, Grey, and Peel had by now all passed away, not to mention such intimate associates as Castlereagh and Huskisson, and Ripon was fast fading from the public mind.

Like Lord Stanley, Ripon in 1850 was somewhat disturbed by his son's radical political views, and with more cause, for young Goderich was attracted by Charles Kingsley and Christian Socialism. Ripon and de Grey believed he had been led astray by certain unidentified youthful companions,[89] and they were delighted when he decided to marry de Grey's granddaughter, Henrietta Anne Theodosia, the daughter of Henry Vyner. 'I believe', Goulburn wrote, 'that an early marriage would in Goderich's case be most conducive to the formation of his character and to your happiness.' [90] Ripon observed to a friend that Henrietta was about to marry her 'uncle', an observation which the young couple may or may not have found amusing.[91]

In 1851 Ripon corresponded with Londonderry regarding the future of the 'Peel Party',[92] but by now his participation in political affairs was minimal. His name does not appear in the division lists when Derby was in power in 1852, so his attitude toward the Conservatives is uncertain, but he sent his proxy to support Lord Aberdeen's Government on the Succession Tax, and he apparently considered himself a supporter of this Peelite–Whig coalition.[93] When Britain became involved in the Crimean War, Ripon wrote a letter to Gladstone regarding the method used to pay the Allied armies in 1813, which he thought might be of service at the present moment.[94]

The last few years of Ripon's life are almost a void, save for brief references to his parents which Goderich made in his letters. 'My Father', he wrote in 1855, 'is being greatly injured by a variety of doctors pulling different ways, from whose various recommendations my Mother selects the most violent & administers them to him — so the house is gloomy & our Christmas prospects not very cheering.' [95]   In 1857 Goderich noted that his father was 'laid up with a cold & my mother in a terrible state of mind in consequence.' [96]   Lady Sarah seems at this time to have taken over the management of the *ménage* almost completely from her failing husband, and, when she fell ill herself that same year, young Goderich assumed the family responsibilities.[97]   If she had been in a 'terrible state' over her husband's illness earlier in the year, Ripon was equally perturbed by her siege of sickness. 'I dread the probable result', Goderich wrote, 'because of the effect, which it may have upon my father.' [98]   Whatever might be written regarding the quality of the love between Lady Sarah and Ripon, it was certainly uniform — unwavering and abiding. Goderich traced his mother's recovery, interestingly enough, to her strong constitution ! [99]

During 1858 Ripon seems to have been in fairly good health. At any rate, he was well enough to travel, and his last available letter was written to Lord Brougham while on a visit. By coincidence, it recalled the most important political moment of his life : [100]

> You refer to my recollection, as far as it goes, of some circumstances of the year 1827 ; and in reference to the question you ask, I can only say that I do not recollect any dispute as to Lansdowne's retaining the title of the Home Secretary ; there certainly was some *breach* as to Herries appointment as the Chancellor of the Exchequer, but it had no reference to any other matrs. [?] of the new Government, which was formed, as you rightly suppose, almost immediately after Canning's death. This is all I can undertake to say of the details of a transaction which took place nearly 30 years ago ; especially as being from home, I have no means of referring to any papers or memoranda on the subject. Lady Ripon begs to be particularly remembered to you. I know Goderich has certainly much regretted that he was unable to . . .

The writing at this point trails off into illegibility. What specific questions Brougham had put to him is not clear, but, if Ripon's powers of memory were becoming increasingly fuzzy, the old caution about recording his opinions was still there.

Shortly after writing this letter Ripon, like his father before him, went to Putney Heath to live out the small span of life left to him. In November he fell ill,[101] possibly from some pulmonary disorder, and on 10 January Goderich wrote: 'My Father has gotten Influenza at last, which in his state is more serious than with other people.' [102] For a time he rallied, but on 19 January the doctors pronounced his case hopeless. At one o'clock on Friday, 28 January, he died.[103] Lord Clarendon, in sending his condolences, spoke of the 'peaceful termination of his life', which indicates that his last hours were not accompanied by physical pain.[104]

The same might not be said, however, for the earlier periods of his illness. In February 1859 the new Lord Ripon wrote a letter which reflected his religious views, and described his father's decline: [105]

But I have always felt very strongly that we shall meet again with one another. I do not know how or when or where ; but I believe that their spirits are even now hovering around us, that they have not lost their love for us or their interest in our doings. I often think of my lost little one, as near me, free from all her earthly sufferings & knowing what she never learnt here ; and now my Father has gone forth to join her, and to regain the former vigour of his mind & to reap the rich harvest, which his patient suffering has been laying up for him beyond the grave.

Later in 1859 his uncle, Earl de Grey died, and the writer of this letter became the recipient of a solemn shower of honours, wealth, and landed estates that the Robinson brothers had accumulated during their lifetimes.

In its obituary for Lord Ripon, *The Times* observed : 'He now awaits his burial at Putney, and people are asking — "Who was Lord Ripon? What did he do?"' [106] For many of the great statesmen of his era, the answers to such questions might be fairly clear-cut, but in Ripon's case, they are much less so. Who was Lord Ripon? He had been successively, though seldom un-equivocally, a Pittite, a Tory, a Canningite, a Whig, a Stanleyite, a Conservative, and a Peelite. Thus, to link him to any particular political party is obviously impossible, and it would be more accurate to describe him as the follower of certain statesmen — Lord Hardwicke, Charles Yorke, Lord Castlereagh, and then George Canning. During the years between the fall of his own Government and 1834, he was a free-lance politician, who did not acknowledge any one leader in Grey's Government. But thereafter he became a Stanleyite, and finally, a follower of Peel.

Though party labels held no charm for Ripon, no one was a more loyal member of a Cabinet. He was shocked when the rivalry between Canning and Castlereagh helped dissolve the Portland Government; he constantly adapted his opinions in order to keep Liverpool's Government together; he stood by Canning and his reconstruction of Canning's Ministry until it collapsed under him, and his chief concern in 1845 and 1846 was to keep Peel in power. The only exception to this was his break with Lord Grey, which helped momentarily to wreck the Whig Administration.

The Times noted further: '[he was] the most accommodating Minister we ever heard of, ready to turn his hand at a moment's notice to any kind of work.' This willingness to change jobs is further evidence of Ripon's loyalty to the Governments of which he was a member, and it was particularly noticeable in his assumption of the leadership of the Lords in 1827 — probably the major tactical error of his career — his acceptance of the Prime Ministership, and his taking the Board of Control in 1843. The only exception to this spirit of accommodation was in 1833, when he realized quite rightly that leaving the Colonial Office would complete the ruin of his reputation.

Ripon's loyalty extended beyond the acceptance of new assignments, and is strongly in evidence with respect to his views and convictions. Though he doubted the wisdom of the Corn Act of 1815, he introduced it; though he drew up an entirely different Corn Bill in 1826, he quickly supported the one adopted by the Cabinet; he wanted concessions to agriculture to accompany the repeal of the Corn Laws in 1846, but went ahead virtually without them. The Slave Emancipation measure was not the one he had planned; the Reform Act of 1832 probably went beyond what he really wanted. He defended Ellenborough's course in India, even though he had serious reservations regarding certain of its more important aspects. In reading his speeches, one can never be quite certain whether Ripon was speaking for himself, or acting as the mouth-piece of the Cabinet, whose views he did not fully share.

This readiness to compromise his views makes it difficult to classify Ripon in a few words, or to place him in a political category. Was he a liberal? He believed that a Member of Parliament was generally responsible to his constituents; that Parliament must be responsive to public opinion; that the spread of enlightenment rendered widespread reform inevitable. The one word he emphasized again and again was 'freedom' — freedom of trade, freedom for the slaves, freedom for the religious minorities, and freedom of the Press and of speech. Yet, on the other hand, he was a devoted monarchist, a stout defender of the Established Church, and — though he did not like the word — a supporter of the aristocracy. His concept of freedom also had its bounds.

Three quotations late in his political career probably clarify Ripon's political attitude in its most mature form. 'The science of Government,' he declared in 1841, 'whether legislative or executive, was, in fact, neither more nor less than a perpetually recurring struggle with difficulties.' [107] Why were difficulties continually arising? His answer is found in an 1843 speech in which he discussed the ill-effects of the introduction of machinery: [108]

He did think that there were evils in it. There was no one good in this life that had not with it some concomitant evil. Whether it arose from men's passions, or was to be attributed to the inherent weakness of nations, there was no one good that was not accompanied by some evil.

This curious mixture of good and evil in an imperfect world was also discussed by Ripon in a letter to Gladstone of 1842 regarding a recent strike: [109]

We must hope, however, that whatever grievous injury it has inflicted upon thousands of the labouring class, the result will be to show the fruitlessness & cowardly treachery of those who have been stimulating them to so dangerous a course, & that so, good may (as it usually does) come out of evil.

The Janus-nature of all changes and reforms meant that no problem could be finally settled, and that statesmen would always be involved in political struggles.

This attitude of mind helps to explain Ripon personally, and illuminates the most serious flaws in his statesmanship. It immobilized him all too often when decisive action was needed. Although he believed in Free Trade, he advanced toward that goal so cautiously that the first large-scale tariff reduction waited for Huskisson; although he believed in Catholic Emancipation, he was so unwilling to cause a governmental crisis over that issue that the reform was carried by Wellington. No one wanted more to free the slaves than he did, but he hesitated, and the honour fell to Stanley.

This intellectual stasis was evident also in his speaking. An excellent example of this was his Free Trade speech of 1839,[110] in which he outlined so many difficulties in the path of its adoption that the average listener might well conclude the cause was hopeless. While such an approach afforded pleasure to the more enlightened statesmen who heard him, it was hardly compatible with political leadership. Ripon could stimulate intellectual curiosity regarding a problem, but he could not call forth that strong feeling of political partisanship, which — in an imperfect world — is necessary to the successful projection of reforms and changes.

Ripon was inclined to be passive, and seemed willing to wait for the spread of enlightenment to bring about reforms. A biographer of Lord Melbourne who took note of this in discussing Sir Anthony Hart, whom Goderich had recently appointed to an important position in Ireland: [111]

Hart personified, in point of view, the principle of negation on which the Cabinet was founded. Neither hot nor cold, aggressive or obstructive, progressive at the full pace of public opinion, or subservient to the crapulous bidding of a despotic Court, he tried honestly, but unavailingly, to let wrong die out, without daring to call right into existence.

The author noted that a similar criticism might be made of Ripon himself. But it should be added that Ripon's passivity was comparative, rather than absolute, and that his constant, if mild, opposition to evils had an erosive quality in it.

There remains the question — what did Ripon do? In the sphere of economics, with which his name is usually associated, he was undoubtedly an advocate of greater freedom of trade from 1812 onwards, and constantly stressed the necessity of making trade patterns beneficial to all nations involved. In the Free Trade movement, he has much greater claims to being the father of the 'no prohibitions' approach, than of Free Trade itself. His outstanding contribution to freeing trade while at the Board of Trade was his Acts of 1822, which represented the first serious attack upon the mercantile system.

Ripon's advocacy of reciprocal trade agreements pointed towards what was to become the standard operating procedure among nations at a later date. From his views on international trade, he passed easily to a conciliatory position on international relations as such. He must certainly be placed in the direct line of British statesmen — Lord Grantham, Lord Castlereagh, Lord Aberdeen, Lord Ashburton, William Ewart Gladstone, and the 2nd Earl de Grey, all of whom sensed, if they did not fully understand at all times, the importance of Anglo-American solidarity.

As Chancellor of the Exchequer Robinson must be associated with several ideas and accomplishments. He understood the importance of tax reductions in stimulating business, and removed a large number of war-time taxes, some to encourage trade, and others to end nuisances. His budgets demonstrated that tax reductions, properly applied, might result in greater returns to the Treasury than when taxes were at a higher rate. With Addington, Herries, and, later, Peel, he must be classed as an early advocate of the Income Tax, which was to be the chief economic project of his Administration. As 'Prosperity' Robinson, he responded enthusiastically to the increasing business activity, and, even when business slumped, he continued to stress the basic soundness of the economic system. The effect of his optimism upon the nation's prosperity is impossible to measure.

As Colonial Secretary, Ripon displayed a scrupulous regard for the rights of self-government acquired by the colonists, and observed them not only to the letter, but in spirit. This attitude possibly retarded briefly the emancipation of the slaves, and led to embarrassments later in Canada, but his concern for the colonists could not but in the end redound to the credit of the mother country. Three-quarters of a century ago, when public opinion supported empires, his administration would have been regarded in a rather different light. Then he would have been something of a failure; today he may be held up as an example of an eminently fair and enlightened administrator.

At various times during his political career, Ripon supported such reforms as Catholic Emancipation, the Reform Act of 1832, and the Municipal Reform Act, but he has no claim to being the father of any of these. Nor can his influence upon such leaders as Castlereagh, Canning, Wellington, or Peel be precisely identified. Certainly Castlereagh, Canning, and Peel gave him their confidence, and looked upon him as a highly competent departmental head. His policy of assigning important tasks to trusted subordinates — approvingly observed by Brougham — was, through sheer necessity, to be followed by later adminis trators.

Perhaps Ripon deserves to live in history for his character as much as for anything he accomplished. He and Lady Sarah were the actors in one of the forgotten love stories of the century. His careful regard for the views and feelings of other people, his continuous effort to apply the Golden Rule in his relations with his fellow men, his studied effort to purge all resentments and ill-feelings from his mind, and his anxiety at all times to avoid conflicts, set him apart from the overwhelming majority of other men who have made their mark in Western politics. Few countries would choose to have a man like Ripon at the helm of government in times of stress, nor can we well visualize what a society made up exclusively of Ripons would be like. But of this much we could be certain — it would be an intellectualized world, perhaps, but one strongly tempered with good feeling and goodwill.

T

Abbreviations

AP	Aberdeen Papers (1)	HUSP	Huskisson Papers (1)
B.M.	British Museum	HYP	Heytesbury Papers (1)
BP	Buckinghamshire Papers (2)	LAP	William B. Lawrence Papers (5)
BRP	Brougham Papers (3)	LCP	Lady Castlereagh Papers (4)
CLP	Clay Papers (5)		
C.O.	Colonial Office Papers (6)	LONP	Londonderry-Camden Papers (4)
COLP	Colchester Papers (6)		
CP	Castlereagh Papers (4)	LOWP	Lowry Cole Papers (6)
CPP	Castlereagh Private Papers (4)	LP	Liverpool Papers (1)
		MP	Morley Papers (1)
EP	Ellenborough Papers (6)	MRP	Marquess of Ripon Papers (1)
F.O.	Foreign Office Papers (6)		
GHP	General Lord Hill Papers (1)	NP	Newcastle Papers (11)
		PLP	Pelham Papers (1)
GOUP	Goulburn Papers (8)	PORP	Portland Papers (11)
GP	Gladstone Papers (1)	PP	Peel Papers (1)
GRNP	Grantham Papers (1)	P.R.O.	Public Record Office
GRP	Graham Papers (9)	PRP	Perceval Papers (1)
H.O.	Home Office Papers (6)	RP	Ripon Papers (1)
HP	Hardwicke Papers (1)	SDGB	State Department (Great Britain) (7)
HRP	Harrowby Papers (10)		
HSP	Sup. Hardwicke Papers (1)	WLP	Wellesley Papers (1)
		WP	Wellington Papers (12)

The above papers are located as follows: (1) British Museum. (2) Aylesbury Public Record Office. (3) University College, London. (4) Mount Stewart. (5) Library of Congress. (6) Public Record Office. (7) National Archives. (8) Kingston upon Thames Public Record Office. (9) Netherby. (10) Sandon Hall. (11) Nottingham University (12) Apsley House.

Notes

CHAPTER 1. THE AMIABLE ROBINSONS

1. W. S. Cole, 'Brief Account of the Family of Robinson'. RP, B.M. 43644, and Arthur Collins, *The Peerage of England* (London, 1768).
2. Lord Ilchester, *Henry Fox, First Lord Holland* (London, Murray, 1920), i. 158–9.
3. Ibid. ii. 125.
4. Lord Macaulay, 'William Pitt, Earl of Chatham' in F. C. Montague, *Critical and Historical Essays by Lord Macaulay* (London, Methuen, 1903), ii. 31–33.
5. Maud M. Wyndham, *Chronicles of the 18th Century* (Boston, Houghton, Mifflin, 1924), ii. 186.
6. *Gentleman's Magazine* (1833), ii. 79.
7. Secret Instructions to Lord Grantham, 23 May 1771. GRNP, B.M. 24157.
8. Grantham to the Earl of Richford, 22 June 1771. GRNP B.M. 24157.
9. Shelburne to the King, 12 July 1782, in Sir John Fortescue (ed.), *The Correspondence of King George the Third* (London, Macmillan, 1928), vi. 82.
10. King to Shelburne, 13 July 1782. Ibid., p. 83.
11. Grantham to Harris, 22 Feb. 1783, in Lord Malmesbury, *Diaries and Correspondence of James Harris, First Earl of Malmesbury* (London, Bentley, 1845), i. 502.
12. Grantham to Harris, 20 Feb. 1783. Ibid., p. 501.
13. Ibid., p. 505.
14. Pelham to Grantham, 24 Jan. 1783. PLP, B.M. 33099.
15. Lady Grantham to Hardwicke, 15 Oct. 1784. HP, B.M. 35623.
16. Lady Grantham to Hardwicke, 4 Dec. 1783. HP, B.M. 35621.
17. Lord Grantham to Hardwicke, 17 Aug. 1785. HP, B.M. 35624.
18. Ibid.
19. Lord Grantham to Hardwicke, 3 June 1786. Ibid.
20. Lord Grantham to Hardwicke, 6 July 1786. Ibid.
21. Hardwicke to Yorke, 9 Jan. 1830. HSP, B.M. 45034.
22. *Gentleman's Magazine* (1790), i. 479 ; ibid. (1797), i. 83. G. E. Cokayne, *The Complete Peerage* (London, St. Catherine's Press, 1926), vi. 307.

23. *Gentleman's Magazine* (1845), ii. 420–3.
24. Lady Grantham to Hardwicke, 19 Nov. 1784. HP, B.M. 35623.
25. Lady Grantham to Hardwicke, 9 Oct. 1783. HP, B.M. 35621.
26. H. T. Ryall, *Portraits of Eminent Conservatives and Statesmen* (London, Virtue, n.d.) (de Grey) ; *Morning Post*, 29 Jan. 1859.
27. Sir Denis Le Marchant, *Memoir of John Charles Viscount Althorp, Third Earl Spencer* (London, Bentley, 1876), p. 44.
28. Ryall, *Conservatives*, ii. 2–3.
29. *Translations from the Oxford and Cambridge Latin Prize Poems* (2nd ser.) (London, Longmans, 1833), pp. 72–80.
30. Lady B. to G. L. G., 12 March 1798, in Countess Granville (ed.), *Lord Granville Leveson Gower, Private Correspondence, 1781–1821* (London, Murray, 1917), i. 205.
31. William Lamb to Lady Melbourne, 4 Apr. 1800, in Lloyd C. Sanders (ed.), *Lord Melbourne's Papers* (London, Longmans, 1889), p. 30.
32. Lady B. to G. L. G., (?) Jan. 1802, in Granville, *Gower*, i. 320.
33. William Jerdan, *Men I Have Known* (London, Routledge, 1866), pp. 356–8.
34. Boringdon's Diary, 1802–3. MP, B.M. 48246.
35. Lady B. to G. L. G., Tuesday and Dec. 1802 and 6 Jan. 1803. Granville, *Gower*, pp. 372, 379, 392.
36. Goderich to Wellesley, 15 Dec. 1836. WLP, B.M. 37311.
37. Lady Grantham to Lord Pelham, 5 Aug. 1801. PLP, B.M. 33107.
38. Lord Grantham to Hardwicke, 7 Sept. 1803. HP, B.M. 35696.
39. *Hansard* (2nd ser.), ii. 417.
40. Hardwicke to Charles Yorke, 13 Feb. 1804. H.O., 100/122.
41. Abstract of Monthly Reports of General Officers Commanding in Ireland for Jan. 1804. Ibid.
42. Sir Evan Nepean to John King, 24 Mar. 1804. Ibid.
43. Marsden to John King, 21 June 1804. Ibid.
44. Hardwicke to Robinson, 5, 7, 8 Feb. 1805. HP, B.M. 35756.
45. Hardwicke to Robinson, 19 Feb. 1805. Ibid.
46. Robinson to Yorke, 24 Mar. 1806. HP, B.M. 35706.
47. *Hansard* (1st ser.), x. 1071–9.
48. Kearney to Hawkesbury, 31 Aug. 1805. H.O., 100/131.
49. Rev. L. V. Harcourt, *The Diaries and Correspondence of the Right Honourable George Rose* (London, Bentley, 1860), ii. 251–3.
50. Malmesbury, *Diaries*, iv. 350.

CHAPTER 2. THE ALFRED CLUB SET

1. Malmesbury, *Diaries*, iv. 375.
2. Yorke to Hardwicke, 10 June 1807. HSP, B.M. 45034.
3. Malmesbury, *Diaries*, iv. 379–80.
4. *Hansard* (2nd ser.), xvi. 1192.
5. Malmesbury, *Diaries*, iv. 388.
6. L. Horner, *Memoirs and Correspondence of Francis Horner, M.P.* (Boston, Little, Brown, 1853), i. 429.
7. Lord Colchester, *The Diary and Correspondence of Charles Abbot, Lord Colchester* (London, Murray, 1861), ii. 121.
8. *Hansard* (1st ser.), ix. 451–3.
9. Anon., *Random Recollections of the House of Lords* (Philadelphia, Carey & Hart, 1836), p. 196.
10. Ryall, *Conservatives*, ii. 6.
11. Perceval to Robinson, 26 Dec. 1808. RP, B.M. 40862.
12. Robinson to Perceval, 28 Dec. 1808. Ibid.
13. Canning to Perceval, 31 Dec. 1808. PRP, B.M. 49185.
14. Robinson to Hardwicke, 2 Jan. 1809. HP, B.M. 35648.
15. Anon., *Recollections*, p. 195.
16. Ibid. 194.
17. *Hansard* (1st ser.), xii. 30–35.
18. Ibid. 190.
19. Malmesbury, *Diaries*, iv. 410.
20. Robinson to Hardwicke, 18 Apr. 1809. HP, B.M. 35648.
21. HSP, B.M. 45041, *passim*.
22. Castlereagh to Robinson, 27 Apr. 1809. RP, B.M. 40862.
23. Castlereagh to Stewart, 12 May 1809. CPP.
24. Robinson to Wellesley, 13, 15, 16 May 1809 ; Robinson to Crauford, 31 May 1809 ; Robinson to Horse Artillery, 31 May 1809. CP.
25. Robinson to Yorke, 26 Aug. 1809. HSP, B.M. 45036.
26. J. Bagot, *George Canning and His Friends* (London, Murray, 1909), i. 317.
27. Robinson to Hardwicke, 19 Oct. 1809. HP, B.M. 35648.
28. Robinson to Hardwicke, 8 Oct. 1809. Ibid.
29. Hardwicke to Yorke, 7 Oct. 1809. HSP, B.M. 45034.
30. Robinson to Hardwicke, 8 Oct. 1809. HP B.M. 35648.
31. Robinson to Yorke, 7 Oct. 1809. HSP, B.M. 45036.
32. Robinson to Yorke, 5 Oct. 1809. Ibid.
33. Violet Dickinson, *Miss Eden's Letters* (Macmillan, 1919), p. 24.
34. *Hansard* (1st ser.), xv. 315.

35. *Hansard* (1st ser.), xv. 317.
36. Robinson to Hardwicke, 4 June 1810. HP, B.M. 35648.
37. *Hansard* (2nd ser.), v. 526.
38. Ibid. (1st ser.), xxii. 374–93.
39. Ibid. xxiii. 750.
40. Notation by J. W. Croker. *A Sketch of the Campaign in Portugal* (London, Murray, 1810).
41. *Hansard* (1st ser.), xv. 445.
42. Ibid. xxiv. 210.
43. Ibid. xxi. 1009.
44. Ibid. 1017.
45. Unfinished Autobiography. GOUP.
46. Ibid.
47. Ward to Dudley, 16 May 1820, in Bishop of Llandaff, *Letters of the Earl of Dudley* (London, Murray, 1841), p. 251.
48. Edmund Phipps, *Memoirs of the Political and Literary Life of Robert Plumer Ward* (London, Murray, 1850), i. 438.
49. *Hansard* (1st ser.), xxiv. 360.
50. Robinson to Madam, 16 June (?) 1813. RP, B.M. 40862.
51. Hon. Mrs. Robinson to Lord Fitzharris, 13 May 1812, in Malmesbury, *Diaries*, ii. 280.
52. *Hansard* (1st ser.), xxiii. 174.
53. Robinson to Peel, 29 Jan. 1813. PP, B.M. 40224.
54. Lord Brougham, *The Life and Times of Henry, Lord Brougham* (New York, Harper, 1871), iii. 254.
55. *Hansard* (1st ser.), xxxiii. 488.
56. Robinson to Peel, 18 Oct. 1812, in Charles S. Parker, *Sir Robert Peel* (London, Murray, 1899), i. 61.
57. Croker to Peel, 21 Sept. 1812. PP, B.M. 40183.
58. *Hansard* (1st ser.), xxvi. 972.
59. Ibid. 241.
60. Robinson to Peel, 18 Oct. 1812, in Parker, *Peel*, i. 61.
61. Robinson to Peel, 23 Sept. 1813. PP, B.M. 40230.
62. Parker, *Peel*, i. 56.
63. Robinson to Peel, 18 Oct. 1812, in Parker, *Peel*, i. 61.
64. Croker to Peel, 28 Sept. 1812. PP, B.M. 40183.
65. Robinson to Yorke, 27 Aug. 1813. HSP, B.M. 45036.
66. Croker to Peel, 18 Dec. 1813. PP, B.M. 40183.
67. Robinson to Yorke, 25 Dec. 1813. HSP, B.M. 45036.
68. Croker to Peel, 24 Dec. 1813. PP, B.M. 40183.

CHAPTER 3. FROM PARIS TO OLD BURLINGTON STREET

1. Montagu to Goulburn, 7 Jan. 1814. GOUP.
2. Ibid.
3. Robinson to Grantham, (?) 7 Jan. 1814. LOWP, P.R.O. 30/43–6.
4. Montagu to Goulburn, 7 Jan. 1814. GOUP.
5. Montagu to Goulburn, 9 Jan. 1814. Ibid.
6. Castlereagh to Lady Castlereagh, 15 Jan. 1814, in C. K. Webster, *The Foreign Policy of Castlereagh* (London, Bell, 1931), p. 404.
7. Robinson to Grantham, 15 Jan. 1814. LOWP, P.R.O. 30/43–6.
8. Robinson to Grantham, 18 Jan. 1814. Ibid.
9. Ripon to Londonderry, 6 July 1839, in Marquess of Londonderry, *Correspondence, Despatches, and Other Papers of Viscount Castlereagh* (London, Shoberl, 1851), i. 125–9.
10. Robinson to Yorke, 28 Jan. 1814. HSP, B.M. 45036.
11. Robinson to Grantham, 18 Jan. 1814. LOWP, P.R.O. 30/43–6.
12. Robinson to Lady Grantham, 26 Jan. 1814. Ibid.
13. Webster, *Castlereagh*, p. 216.
14. Montagu to Goulburn, 21 Feb. 1814. GOUP.
15. Memorandum by the Hon. Mrs. Robinson, 27 Feb. 1814. LOWP, P.R.O. 30/43–6.
16. Marchioness of Londonderry, *Robert Stewart, Viscount Castlereagh* (London, Humphreys, 1904), pp. 53–54.
17. Montagu to Goulburn, 22 Mar. 1814. GOUP.
18. Robinson to Hon. Mrs. Robinson, 29 Mar. 1814. LOWP, P.R.O. 30/43–6.
19. Montagu to Goulburn, 4 Apr. 1814. GOUP.
20. Robinson to Hon. Mrs. Robinson, 29 Mar. 1814. LOWP, P.R.O. 30/43–6.
21. Grantham to Hon. Mrs. Robinson, 14 May 1814. Ibid.
22. Robinson to Grantham, 12 Apr. 1814. Ibid.
23. L. A. Bourrienne, *Memoirs of Napoleon Bonaparte* (New York, Scribner & Welford, 1885), iii. 173.
24. Robinson to Grantham, 3 May 1814. LOWP, P.R.O. 30/43–6.
25. Robinson to Grantham, 18 Apr. 1814. Ibid.
26. Robinson to Grantham, 3 May 1814. Ibid.
27. Robinson to Grantham, 5 May 1814. Ibid.
28. Montagu to Goulburn, 23 Apr. 1814. GOUP.
29. Robinson to Peel, 23 Apr. 1814. PP, B.M. 40235.
30. Liverpool to Castlereagh, 9 Apr. 1814, in Webster, *Castlereagh*, p. 532.

31. Liverpool to Castlereagh, 29 Apr. 1814, in ibid., p. 539.
32. Memorandum by Hon. Mrs. Robinson, 19 May 1814. LOWP, P.R.O. 30/43–6.
33. Hon. Mrs. Robinson to Fitzharris, 12 June 1814, in Malmesbury, *Letters*, ii. 418.
34. Hon. Mrs. Robinson to Fitzharris, 16 June 1814, in ibid., p. 423.
35. Ship Manifest, 18 May 1813. LP, B.M. 38474.
36. Buckinghamshire to Liverpool, 17 May 1813. Ibid., B.M. 38253.
37. Robinson to Grantham, 18 Jan. 1814. LOWP, P.R.O. 30/43–6.
38. Croker to Peel, 4 Aug. 1814. PP, B.M. 40183.
39. Dickinson, *Miss Eden*, p. 113.
40. Ibid., p. 18.
41. Robinson to Liverpool, 4 Nov. 1814. LP, B.M. 38260.
42. Peel to Goulburn, 11 Nov. 1814. GOUP.
43. Robinson to Grantham, 18 Apr. 1814. LOWP, P.R.O. 30/43–6.
44. Liverpool to Castlereagh, 12 Jan. 1815, in Londonderry, *Castlereagh*, x. 239.
45. *Hansard* (3rd ser.), lxxxvi. 1086.
46. Robinson to Hardwicke, 20 Jan. 1815. HP, B.M. 35651.
47. *Hansard* (2nd ser.), xvi. 1046.
48. Ibid. (1st ser.), xxix. 988–9.
49. *The Courier*, 17 Feb. 1815.
50. *Hansard* (1st ser.), xxix. 987–8
51. Ibid. 799.
52. Ibid. 800–1.
53. Ibid. 1031.
54. Ibid. 802.
55. Ibid. 804.
56. Ibid. 1237.
57. *Edinburgh Annual Register* (1815), p. 84.
58. *Hansard* (1st ser.), xxix. 995.
59. *Edinburgh Annual Register* (1815), p. 83.
60. *Hansard* (1st ser.), xxix. 1117.
61. Ibid. xxx. 68.
62. Ibid. xxix. 1041.
63. Ibid. 1242.
64. Ibid. xxx. 30.
65. *Edinburgh Annual Register* (1815), p. 79.
66. William Hone, *The Report at Large of the Coroner's Inquest on Jane Watson* (London, William Hone, 1815), *passim*.
67. *Hansard* (1st ser.), xxx. 102–3.
68. Hone, *Coroner's Inquest*, passim.

69. *Hansard* (1st ser.), xxx. 100.
70. *Edinburgh Annual Register* (1815), p. 83.
71. *Hansard* (1st ser.), xxx. 107.
72. *Edinburgh Annual Register* (1815), pp. 84-85.
73. William Jerdan, *Men I Have Known* (London, Routledge, 1866), p. 359.

CHAPTER 4. ECONOMICS WITH A HEART

1. Liverpool to Peel, 23 Jan. 1818. LP, B.M. 38270.
2. Liverpool to Prince Regent, 18 Jan. 1818, in A. Aspinall, *The Letters of King George IV* (C.U.P., 1938), ii. 733.
3. Liverpool to Peel, 23 Jan. 1818. LP, B.M. 38270.
4. Legge to Colchester, 5 Feb. 1818. COLP, P.R.O. 30/9–17.
5. Liverpool to Peel, 23 Jan. 1818. LP, B.M. 38270.
6. Wallace to Liverpool, 22 Jan. 1818. Ibid.
7. Arbuthnot to Liverpool, 12 Jan. 1823, in A. Aspinall, *The Correspondence of Charles Arbuthnot* (London, Royal Historical Society, 1941), p. 40.
8 *Hansard* (2nd ser.), x. 1226–7.
9. Ibid. viii. 200.
10. Ibid. (1st ser.), xxxv. 1049.
11. Ibid. xxxiii. 696.
12. Ibid. xxxix. 68.
13. Ibid. (2nd ser.), i. 641–51.
14. Ibid. vii. 415.
15. Ripon to Gladstone, 25 Oct. 1841. GP, B.M. 44285.
16. *Hansard* (1st ser.), xxxiii. 710–16.
17. Ripon to Gladstone, 25 Oct. 1841. GP, B.M. 44285.
18. *Hansard* (2nd ser.), vii. 1213.
19. Ibid. (1st ser.), xxxv. 1047–8.
20. Ibid. (2nd ser.), vi. 1212.
21. Ibid. (1st ser.), xxxvi. 1295–6.
22. Robinson to Liverpool, 26 Mar., 2 and 19 Apr. 1819. LP, B.M. 38273.
23. Peel to Goulburn, (?) 1815. GOUP.
24. *Hansard* (1st ser.), xxxv, 1050.
25. Ibid. 1044–52.
26. Ibid. (2nd ser.), i. 172.
27. Ibid. 182–5.
28. Ibid. (1st ser.), xl. 338.
29. Ibid. 339–47.

30. Ibid. (1st ser.), xl. 371.
31. Russell to Clay, 15 Oct. 1815. CLP.
32. Unofficial conference, 11 May 1815. F.O. 5–109.
33. Robinson to Castlereagh, 7, 19 June 1815. Ibid.
34. Ibid.
35. Robinson to Castlereagh, 21 June 1815. Ibid.
36. Charles F. Adams, *Memoirs of John Quincy Adams* (Philadelphia, Lippincott, 1874), iii. 238.
37. Ibid., p. 248.
38. Adams to Russell, 10 Oct. 1815, in W. C. Ford, *The Writings of John Quincy Adams* (New York, The Macmillan Co., 1915), v. 416.
39. Adams to Russell, 14 Dec. 1815, in ibid., p. 443.
40. Adams to Gallatin, 22 May 1818, in Ford, *Adams*, vi. 332–3.
41. John Quincy Adams, 30 July 1816. SDGB.
42. Ibid. See also : Adams, *Memoirs*, iii. 345.
43. John Quincy Adams, 22 Aug. 1815. SDGB.
44. Adams, *Memoirs*, iii. 403.
45. Ibid., p. 476.
46. Ibid., pp. 422–3.
47. Ibid.
48. Adams to L. C. Adams, 29 Sept. 1822, in Ford, *Adams*, vii. 310.
49. Adams to Rush, 21 May 1818, in ibid., p. 328.
50. Adams, *Memoirs*, iii. 437.
51. Ibid., p. 471.
52. Richard Rush, 5 Jan. 1818. SDGB.
53. Ibid.
54. *Hansard* (1st ser.), xxxvii, 334.
55. Ibid. 335.
56. Gallatin to Rush, 3 June 1818, in Henry Adams (ed.), *The Writings of Albert Gallatin* (Philadelphia, Lippincott, 1879), ii. 67.
57. Richard Rush, 25 July 1818. SDGB.
58. Richard Rush, 20 Oct. 1818. SDGB.
59. Gallatin to Adams, 9 Nov. 1818, in Adams, *Gallatin*, ii. 86.
60. Richard Rush, 25 July 1818. SDGB.
61. Robinson to Liverpool, 13 Sept. and (?) 8 Oct. 1818. LP, B.M 38273.
62. Adams, *Memoirs*, iv. 321–3.
63. Richard Rush, 17 Sept. 1819. SDGB.
64. Richard Rush, 20 Oct. 1818. SDGB.
65. *Hansard* (2nd ser.), vi. 1424.
66. Richard Rush, 3 Apr. 1822. SDGB.
67. *Hansard* (2nd ser.), vi. 1429.

68. Richard Rush, 10 May 1822. SDGB.
69. Ibid.
70. Ibid.
71. Gallatin to Adams, 9 Nov. 1818, in Adams, *Gallatin*, ii. 85.
72. Richard Rush, *Memoranda of a Residence at the Court of London* (Philadelphia, Carey, Lea & Blanchard, 1833), p. 357.
73. Ibid., pp. 362–3.
74. Gallatin to Clay, 22 Sept. 1826, in Adams, *Gallatin*, ii. 329. See also Gallatin to Clay, 14 July 1827. LAP.
75. Adams, *Memoirs*, iii. 540.
76. Robinson to Liverpool, 19 Nov. 1817. LP, B.M. 38458.
77. Robinson to Liverpool, 5 Mar. 1818. LP, B.M. 38270.
78. *Hansard* (2nd ser.), v. 1065.
79. Ibid. vii. 59.
80. Ibid. (1st ser.), xxxv. 724.
81. Ibid. xli. 1051–4.
82. Robinson to Hardwicke, 14 Dec. 1819. HP, B.M. 35652.
83. *Hansard* (2nd ser.), vii. 1448.
84. Ibid. (1st ser.), xxxiii. 589, 613.
85. Ibid. xxxii. 237 ; xxviii. 1248–9.
86. Banks to Colchester, 28 Jan. 1821. COLP, P.R.O. 30/9–17.
87. Croker to Peel, 25 Aug. 1822, in John W. Croker, *The Correspondence and Diaries of the Late Rt. Hon. John Wilson Croker* (New York, Scribner's, 1884), i. 211–12.
88. Hardinge to Londonderry, 20 Aug. 1822. CPP.
89. Liverpool to Vansittart, 14 Dec. 1822. LP, B.M. 38291.
90. Vansittart to Liverpool, 16 Dec. 1822. Ibid.
91. A. Aspinall, *The Diaries of Henry Hobhouse, 1820–1827* (London, Hume & Van Thal, 1947), p. 95.
92. Liverpool to Peel, 18 Dec. 1818. LP, B.M. 38291.
93. Liverpool to Robinson, 18 Dec. 1818. Ibid.
94. Robinson to Yorke, 20 Jan. 1823. HSP, B.M. 45036.
95. Vansittart to Robinson, 23 Dec. 1822. RP, B.M. 40862.
96. Robinson to Liverpool, 19 Dec. 1822. LP, B.M. 38291.
97. Huskisson to Canning, 14 Jan. 1823, in Lewis Melville, *The Huskisson Papers* (New York, Richard R. Smith, 1931), p. 157.
98. King to Liverpool, 3 Jan. 1823, in Percy Fitzgerald, *The Life of George the Fourth* (New York, Harper, 1881), p. 782.
99. Bathurst and Eldon to Liverpool, 5 and 9 Jan. 1823. LP, B.M. 38291.
100. Frances Bamford and the Duke of Wellington, *The Journal of Mrs. Arbuthnot, 1820–1832* (London, Macmillan, 1950), i. 194.

101. Wynn to Buckingham, 20 Jan. 1823, in Duke of Buckingham and Chandos, *Memoirs of the Court of George IV, 1820–1830* (London, Hurst & Blackett, 1856), i. 412.
102. Fremantle to Buckingham, 27 Jan. 1823, in ibid., p. 420.
103. Colchester, *Diary*, iii. 270–1.
104. Wilbraham to Colchester, 9 Feb. 1823, in ibid., p. 273.
105. Yorke to Robinson, 23 Jan. 1823. HSP, B.M. 45036.
106. Londonderry to Burghersh, 8 Oct. 1832, in R. Weigall, *Correspondence of Lord Burghersh, 11th Earl of Westmoreland* (London, Murray, 1912), p. 272.
107. Londonderry to Lady Londonderry, 29 Dec. 1822. CPP.
108. Hardinge to Londonderry, 24 Jan. 1823. Ibid.
109. Cobbett's *Weekly Political Register*, 27 Mar. 1819.
110. C. R. Fay, *Huskisson and His Age* (New York, Longmans, 1951), p. 100.
111. Huskisson to Canning, 25 Oct. 1822, in Melville, *Huskisson*, p. 148.
112. Robinson to Liverpool, 19 Dec. 1822. LP, B.M. 38291.
113. Wallace to Liverpool, 9 Jan. 1823. Ibid.
114. E. Wood, *English Theories of Central Banking Control, 1819–1858* (Cambridge, Harvard University Press, 1939), p. 82.
115. Arbuthnot, *Journal*, i. 156.
116. W. R. Brock, *Lord Liverpool and Liberal Toryism, 1820–1827* (C.U.P., 1941), p. 173.
117. *Globe and Traveller*, 31 Jan. 1823.
118. *Hansard* (2nd ser.), viii. 199–200.
119. Ibid. 200.
120. Ibid. 210.
121. Ibid. 221.
122. Ibid. 219.
123. Ibid. 224.
124. Aspinall, *Hobhouse*, p. 103.
125. Fremantle to Buckingham, 27 July 1823, in Buckingham, *George IV*, i. 481.
126. Arbuthnot, *Journal*, i. 262.
127. *Hansard* (2nd ser.), ix. 1421.
128. Ibid. x. 323.
129. Ibid. 331.
130. Ibid.
131. Ibid. xi. 804.
132. *Globe and Traveller*, 24 Feb. 1824.
133. Robinson to Huskisson and Huskisson to Robinson, 22 Mar. 1824. HUSP, B.M. 38745.

134. *Hansard* (2nd ser.), xi. 595–6.
135. Ibid. x. 655.
136. Ibid. 1226–7.
137. Minto to Robinson, 23 Apr. 1824. RP, B.M. 40862.
138. *Hansard* (2nd ser.), xii. 722.
139. *Morning Chronicle*, 1 Mar. 1825.
140. *Hansard* (2nd ser.), xii. 1216.

CHAPTER 5. THE BROKEN IDOL

1. Lowry Cole to Lady Grantham, 26 Feb. 1825. LOWP, P.R.O. 30/43.
2. *Hansard* (2nd ser.), xii. 1260.
3. Baring to Robinson, 28 May 1824. RP, B.M. 40862.
4. Palmerston to Robinson, 21 Mar. 1823. Ibid.
5. King to Robinson, 1 July 1823. Ibid.
6. King to Robinson, 27 Mar. 1825. Robinson to Duke of York, 19 Apr. 1825. Ibid. Robinson to Liverpool, 19 Apr. 1825. LP, B.M. 38300.
7. Peel to Croker, 20 Oct. 1815, in Parker, *Peel*, i. 57.
8. Palmerston to Mrs. Arbuthnot, 15 Oct. 1826, in Aspinall, *Arbuthnot*, p. 85.
9. Croker's Note Book, 26 Dec. 1826, in Croker, *Diaries*, i. 305.
10. Jerdan, *Men I Have Known*, pp. 356–8.
11. Marchioness of Londonderry, *Frances Anne, Marchioness of Londonderry* (London, Macmillan, 1958), p. 64.
12. Duke of Wellington, *Despatches, Correspondence and Memoranda of Field Marshal Arthur Duke of Wellington* (London, Murray, 1867), ii. 132.
13. Richard Rush, *The Court of London from 1819 to 1825 by Richard Rush* (London, Bentley, 1873), pp. 367–8.
14. Ward to Buckingham, 4 July 1824, in Buckingham, *George IV*, ii. 99.
15. Ward to Buckingham, 16 July 1824. Ibid., p. 105.
16. Arbuthnot, *Journal*, i. 367.
17. Ibid., p. 392.
18. Wellington to Clancarty, 14 Nov. 1825, in Wellington, *Despatches*, ii. 564.
19. *Hansard* (2nd ser.), xiii. 874.
20. Croker to Hertford, 22 Sept. 1825, in Croker, *Diaries*, i. 258.
21. Arbuthnot, *Journal*, i. 414.

22. Peel to Goulburn, 12 Nov. 1823. GOUP.
23. Arbuthnot, *Journal*, i. 426–9.
24. Sir J. Clapham, *The Bank of England* (New York, Macmillan, 1945), p. 100.
25. Liverpool and Robinson to Directors, 20 Jan. 1826, in *Hansard* (2nd ser.), xiv. 107–9.
26. Directors to Liverpool and Robinson, 25 Jan. 1826, in ibid., pp. 109–11.
27. Ibid., p. 47.
28. Canning to Granville, 10 Feb. 1826, in E. J. Stapleton, *Some Official Correspondence of George Canning* (London, Longmans, 1887) ii. 14.
29. Diary, 20 Feb. 1826, in H. Reeve, *The Greville Memoirs* (London, Longmans, 1875).
30. *Hansard* (2nd ser.), xiv. 707.
31. Arbuthnot, *Journal*, i. 391.
32. *Hansard* (2nd ser.), xiv. 1305.
33. Sefton to Creevey, 12 Feb. 1826, in Sir Herbert Maxwell, *The Creevey Papers* (New York, Dutton, 1923), p. 439.
34. *Hansard* (2nd ser.), xiv. 640.
35. Ibid. xv. 895.
36. Dickinson, *Miss Eden*, p. 113.
37. Hardwicke to Yorke, 11 Nov. 1826. HSP, B.M. 45034.
38. Robinson to Lady Buckinghamshire, 30 Nov. 1815. BP.
39. *Hansard* (1st ser.), xxxiv. 338.
40. Wynn to Buckingham, 11 June 1825, in Buckingham, *George IV*, ii. 261.
41. Robinson to Castlereagh, 25 July 1815. F.O. 5–109.
42. Lady Granville to Lady Morpeth, 14 Oct. 1820, in Hon. F. L. Gower, *Letters of Harriet, Countess Granville, 1810–1845* (London, Longmans, 1894), i. 188.
43. Rush, *Court of London*, p. 252.
44. Miss Eden to Lady Buckinghamshire, 14 Feb. 1819, in Dickinson, *Miss Eden*, p. 30; Goulburn to wife, 19 Feb. 1819, GOUP; Robinson to Hardwicke, 8 Mar. 1819. HSP, B.M. 35652.
45. Croker, *Diaries*, i. 150
46. Lady de Grey to Hardwicke, 5 Jan. 1825. HP, B.M. 35691.
47. Wynn to Buckingham, 20 July 1825, in Buckingham, *George IV*, ii. 272.
48. Grey to Brougham, 12 Aug. 1825, in Brougham, *Life*, ii. 357.
49. Peel to wife, (?) Jan. 1826, in George Peel, *The Private Letters of Sir Robert Peel* (London, Murray, 1920), p. 83.

50. Miss Eden to Miss Villiers, Dec. 1826, in Dickinson, *Miss Eden*, p. 124.
51. Miss Eden to Miss Villiers, 13 Dec. 1826, in ibid., p. 120.
52. Miss Eden to Miss Villiers, 30 Mar. 1826, in ibid., p. 100.
53. Stuart to Clinton, (?) 1826 in James A. Home, *Letters of Lady Louisa Stuart to Miss Louisa Clinton* (Edinburgh, Douglas, 1903), ii. 31.
54. Robinson to Peel, 21 Aug. 1826. PP. B.M. 40388.
55. Robinson's Minute of the Corn Laws, 1826. Ibid.
56. Ripon to Gladstone, 28 Oct. 1841. GP, B.M. 44285.
57. Wellington to Robinson, 20 Oct. 1826, in Wellington, *Despatches*, iii. 432–4.
58. Miss Eden to Miss Villiers, (?) Oct. 1826, in Dickinson, *Miss Eden*, p. 113.
59. Miss Eden to Miss Villiers, 13 Dec. 1826, in ibid., p. 118.
60. Hardwicke to Yorke, 11 Nov. 1826. HSP, B.M. 45034.
61. Miss Eden to Miss Villiers, (?) Nov. 1826, in Dickinson, *Miss Eden*, p. 117.
62. Miss Eden to Miss Villiers, 30 Oct. 1826, in ibid., p. 114.
63. Miss Eden to Miss Villiers, (?) Nov. 1826, in ibid., p. 116.
64. Miss Eden to Miss Villiers, 30 Oct. 1826, in ibid., pp. 114–15.
65. Miss Eden to Miss Villiers, (?) Nov. 1826 in ibid., p. 116.
66. Stuart to Clinton, (?) 1826, in Home, *Louisa Stuart*, ii. 31.
67. Robinson to King, 3 Nov. 1826, in Aspinall, *George IV*, iii. 179.
68. King to Robinson, 5 Nov. 1826. BP.
69. Croker to Robinson, 1 Nov. 1826, in Croker, *Diaries*, i. 298.
70. Robinson to Huskisson, 12 Nov. 1826. HUSP, B.M. 38748.
71. Huskisson to Robinson, 20 Nov. 1826. Ibid.
72. Robinson to Huskisson, 22 Nov. 1826. Ibid.
73. Liverpool to Robinson, 23 Nov. 1826. LP, B.M. 38302.
74. Hardwicke to Yorke, (?) 1826. HSP, B.M. 45034.
75. Miss Eden to Miss Villiers, 13 Dec. 1826, in Dickinson, *Miss Eden*, pp. 118–19.
76. Ibid.
77. Miss Eden to Miss Villiers, 15 Dec. 1826, in ibid., p. 123.
78. Ibid.
79. Robinson to Liverpool, 14 Dec. 1826. LP, B.M. 38302.
80. Liverpool to Robinson, 16 Dec. 1826, in Stapleton, *Canning*, ii. 250.
81. Robinson to Peel, 13 Apr. 1827. PP, B.M. 40393.
82. Liverpool to Arbuthnot, 16 Dec. 1826, in Aspinall, *Arbuthnot*, p. 80.
83. Arbuthnot, *Journal*, ii. 67.
84. *Morning Chronicle*, 17 Oct. 1826.

CHAPTER 6. HOW A PREMIER WAS MADE

1. Robinson to Wellington, 11 Jan. 1827, in Wellington, *Despatches*, iii. 541.
2. Robinson to Liverpool, 13 Jan. 1827. LP, B.M. 38302.
3. Robinson to Huskisson and Huskisson to Robinson, 11 Feb. 1827. HUSP, B.M. 38749.
4. *Hansard* (2nd ser.), xvi. 559.
5. See: Harold Temperley, *The Foreign Policy of Canning, 1822–1827* (London, Bell, 1925) and Arthur Aspinall, *The Formation of Canning's Ministry* (London, Royal Historical Society, 1937).
6. Robinson to Huskisson, 18 Feb. 1827. HUSP, B.M. 38749; Robinson to Peel, (?) 18 Feb. 1827. PP, B.M. 40392.
7. Colchester, *Diary*, iii. 463.
8. Binning to Bagot, 23 Feb. 1827, in Aspinall, *Canning*, pp. 22–24.
9. Mackintosh to Lady Holland, 21 Feb. 1827, in ibid., p. 11.
10. Croker, *Diaries*, i. 336.
11. See: Aspinall, *Canning*, pp. 48–50 and Arbuthnot, *Journal*, ii. 99.
12. Canning to Wellington, 5 May 1827, in *The Wellesley Papers* (London, Jenkins, 1914), pp. 175–6.
13. Wellington to Canning, 6 May 1827, in ibid., p. 180.
14. Arbuthnot, *Journal*, ii. 102.
15. Ellenborough's Memorandum, 14 Apr. 1827, in Aspinall, *Canning*, p. 78.
16. Colchester, *Diary*, iii. 487.
17. Wellington Interview, 16 Apr. 1827, in Wellesley, *Papers*, p. 168.
18. Aspinall, *Canning*, pp. xxxiv–xxxv.
19. Canning to Wellington, 5 May 1827, in Wellesley, *Papers*, pp. 175–6.
20. *Hansard* (2nd ser.), xvii. 474.
21. Ibid. 475.
22. Peel to Robinson, 12 Apr. 1827. RP, B.M. 40862.
23. Robinson to Peel, 13 Apr. 1827, in Parker, *Peel*, i. 476–7.
24. *Hansard* (2nd ser.), xvii. 473–4.
25. Robinson to Peel, 13 Apr. 1827, in Parker, *Peel*, i. 476–7.
26. Granville to Huskisson, 14 Dec. 1827. HUSP, B.M. 38752.
27. *Hansard* (2nd ser.), xviii. 280.
28. Robinson to Canning, 15 Apr. 1827, in Aspinall, *Canning*, pp. 85–87.
29. Canning to Robinson, 15 Apr. 1827, in ibid., pp. 87–88.
30. Canning to Carlisle, 19 Apr. 1827, in ibid., p. 124.
31. Holland to Lansdowne, 21 Apr. 1827, in ibid., p. 146.
32. Granville to Huskisson, 14 Dec. 1827. HUSP, B.M. 38752.

33. Granville to Carlisle, 20 Apr. 1827, in Aspinall, *Canning*, p. 132.
34. Holland to Lansdowne, 21 Apr. 1827, in ibid., p. 145.
35. Hobhouse's Diary, 21 Apr. 1827, in ibid., p. 150.
36. Wellington to Londonderry, 23 and 29 Apr. 1827, in ibid., pp. 165, 200.
37. Londonderry to Arbuthnot, 18 Apr. 1827, in ibid., p. 115.
38. Londonderry to Burghersh, 16 Apr. 1827, in Weigall, *Burghersh*, pp. 258-9.
39. Colchester, *Diary*, iii. 493.
40. *Hansard* (2nd ser.), xvii. 494.
41. Colchester, *Diary*, iii. 493.
42. *Hansard* (2nd ser.), xvii. 549-50.
43. Colchester, *Diary*, iii. 499.
44. *Hansard* (2nd ser.), xvii. 776.
45. Ibid. 808.
46. Ibid. 871-2.
47. Ibid. 1019.
48. Wellington to Huskisson, 24 May 1827. BP.
49. Huskisson to Wellington, 24 May 1827. B.P.
50. Goderich to Huskisson, 31 May 1827. HUSP, B.M. 38749.
51. Goderich to Huskisson, 1 June 1827. Ibid.
52. *Hansard* (2nd ser.), xvii. 1097.
53. Ibid.
54. Huskisson to Goderich, 3 June 1827. BP.
55. Goderich to De La Warr, 4 June 1827. BP; Colchester, *Diary*, iii. 515.
56. Goderich to Canning, 6 June 1827, in Aspinall, *Canning*, pp. 291-2.
57. Wellington to Goderich, 8 June 1827. RP, B.M. 40862.
58. Goderich to Wellington, 11 June 1827. BP.
59. *Hansard* (2nd ser.), xvii. 1227-8.
60. Seaford to Granville, 14 June 1827, in Aspinall, *Canning*, p. 295.
61. *Hansard* (2nd ser.), xvii. 1261.
62. Seaford to Granville, 19 June 1827, in Aspinall, *Canning*, p. 296.
63. Campbell to George Campbell, 14 June 1827, in Lady Hardcastle, *Life of John, Lord Campbell* (Jersey City, Linn, 1881), i. 459.
64. Creevey to Ord, 19 June 1827, in Maxwell, *Creevey*, pp. 462-3.
65. *The Globe and Traveller*, 10 Aug. 1827.
66. *Edinburgh Review* (1828), p. 258.
67. Arbuthnot, *Journal*, ii. 125.
68. Canning to Wellesley, 22 May 1827, in Wellesley, *Papers*, ii. 157.
69. Herries to Arbuthnot, 26 July 1827, in Aspinall, *Canning*, p. 271.
70. Arbuthnot, *Journal*, ii. 127.

71. Lord Broughton, *Recollections of a Long Life* (London, Murray, 1909), iii. 214.
72. Temperley, *Canning*, p. 445, Aspinall, *Canning*, pp. l–liii.
73. Croker to Hertford, 7 Aug. 1827, in Croker, *Diaries*, i. 352.
74. Reeve, *Greville*, i. 103. *Diary*, 9 Aug. 1827.
75. Ibid.
76. Goderich Memorandum on Herries, 17 Aug. 1827. RP, B.M. 40862.
77. King's Memorandum, 8 Aug. 1827, in Aspinall, *George IV*, iii. 275.
78. Goderich Memorandum on Herries, 17 Aug. 1827. RP, B.M. 40862.
79. King to Goderich, 10 Aug. 1827, in Aspinall, *George IV*, iii. 279.
80. Ibid., pp. 279–80.
81. Portland to Goderich, 11 Aug. 1827. BP.
82. Herries Narrative, n.d. in E. Herries, *Memoir of the Public Life of the Right Hon. John Charles Herries* (London, Murray, 1880), i. 154–5.
83. Ibid.
84. Goderich Memorandum on Herries, 17 Aug. 1827. RP, B.M. 40862.
85. Croker Memorandum, 11 Aug. 1827, in Croker, *Diaries*, i. 354–60.
86. Peel to Arbuthnot, 17 Aug. 1827, in Parker, *Peel*, ii. 9.
87. Sturges Bourne to the King, 11 Aug. 1827, in Aspinall, *George IV*, iii. 282–3.
88. Goderich to Lansdowne, 11 Aug. 1827. BP.
89. Lansdowne to Goderich, 12 Aug. 1827. Ibid.
90. King to Goderich, 12 Aug. 1827, in Aspinall, *George IV*, iii. 284.
91. King's Memorandum, 13 Aug. 1827. BP.
92. Goderich Memorandum on Herries, 17 Aug. 1827. RP, B.M. 40862.
93. Hardinge to Peel, 11 Aug. 1827, in Parker, *Peel*, ii. 4.
94. Goderich Memorandum on Herries, 17 Aug. 1827. RP, B.M. 40862.
95. Ibid.
96. Arbuthnot, *Journal*, ii. 129.
97. Goderich Memorandum on Herries, 17 Aug. 1827. RP, B.M. 40862.
98. Lansdowne to Goderich, 14 Aug. 1827. BP.
99. Goderich to Lansdowne, 14 Aug. 1827. Ibid.
100. Goderich to Huskisson, 14 Aug. 1827. HUSP, B.M. 38750.
101. Goderich to King, 15 Aug. 1827. BP.
102. Palmerston to Sullivan, 15 Aug. 1827, in Sir H. L. Bulwer, *The Life of John Henry Temple, Viscount Palmerston* (Philadelphia, Lippincott, 1871), i. 182.

103. Goderich Memorandum on Herries, 17 Aug. 1827. RP, B.M. 40862.

104. King to Wellington, Goderich to Wellington, 15 Aug. 1827, in Horace Twiss, *The Public and Private Life of Lord Chancellor Eldon* (Philadelphia, Carey & Hart, 1844), ii. 187.

105. Goderich to Wellesley, 15 Aug. 1827. WLP, B.M. 37305.

106. *The Globe and Traveller*, 10 Aug. 1827.

107. *The Morning Post*, 11 Aug. 1827.

108. *The Times*, 10 Aug. 1827.

109. Wellesley to Goderich, 19 Aug. 1827   WLP, B.M. 37305.

110. Goderich to Buckingham, 8 Nov. 1827, in Buckingham, *George IV*, ii. 351.

111. Colonel Shawe to Knighton, 15 Aug. 1827, in Aspinall, *George IV*, iii. 287.

112. Londonderry to Wellington, 12 Aug. 1827, in Wellington, *Despatches*, iv. 84.

113. Huskisson to Granville, 31 Aug. 1827, in Melville, *Huskisson*, p. 235.

114. Lansdowne to Brougham, 11 Aug. 1827. BRP.

115. Brougham to Grey, 13 Aug. 1827, in Brougham, *Life*, ii. 368–9.

116. Grey to Ellenborough, 24 Aug. 1827. EP, P.R.O. 30/12–24.

117. Bedford to Russell, 7 Aug. 1827, in Spencer Walpole, *The Life of Lord John Russell* (London, Longmans, 1889), i. 135.

118. Bedford to Holland, 5 May 1827, in Aspinall, *Canning*, p. 213.

119. Grey to Brougham, 19 Aug. 1827, in Brougham, *Life*, ii. 370.

120. Melville to Arbuthnot, 21 Aug. 1827, in Aspinall, *Arbuthnot*, p. 92.

121. Westmorland to Wellington, 18 Aug. 1827, in Wellington, *Despatches*, iv. 99.

122. Londonderry to Lady Londonderry, 13 Aug. 1827. LCP.

123. Arbuthnot to Peel, 17 Aug. 1827, in Parker, *Peel*, ii. 6.

124. Arbuthnot to Peel, 16 Aug. 1827, in ibid.

125. Wellington Memorandum, n.d. in Wellington, *Despatches*, iv. 180.

126. Wellington to Goderich, 17 Aug. 1827, in Twiss, *Eldon*, ii. 187.

127. Bathurst to Peel, 19 Aug. 1827, in Parker, *Peel*, ii. 8.

128. Peel to Wellington, 19 Aug. 1827, in Parker, *Peel*, ii. 8.

129. Arbuthnot, *Journal*, ii. 138.

130. Ibid., p. 140.

131. Ibid., p. 143.

132. Westmorland to Wellington, 8 Aug. 1827, in Wellington, *Despatches*, iv. 74.

133. Planta to Huskisson, 21 Aug. 1827, in Melville, *Huskisson*, pp. 228–30.

134. Herries, *Memoir*, i. 160.
135. Ibid.
136. Goderich Memorandum on Herries, 17 Aug. 1827. RP, B.M. 40862.
137. Herries, *Memoir*, i. 161.
138. Reeve, *Greville*, i. 108–10. *Diary*, 20 Aug. 1827.
139. Goderich Memorandum on Herries, 17 Aug. 1827. RP, B.M. 40862.
140. Ibid.
141. Herries, *Memoir*, i. 162–4.
142. A. Aspinall, *Lord Brougham and the Whig Party* (Manchester, The University Press, 1927), p. 156.
143. Planta to Huskisson, 21 Aug. 1827, in Melville, *Huskisson*, pp. 228–30.
144. Huskisson to Lord Howard de Walden, 27 Aug. 1827. HUSP, B.M. 38750.
145. Huskisson to Goderich, 29 Aug. 1827. RP, B.M. 40862.
146. Lansdowne to Huskisson, 28 Aug. 1827. HUSP, B.M. 38750.
147. Goderich to Huskisson, 29 Aug. 1827. Ibid.
148. Huskisson to Granville, 31 Aug. 1827, in Melville, *Huskisson*, p. 234.
149. Herries, *Memoir*, i. 169–70
150. Ibid.
151. Ibid.
152. Goderich to Huskisson, 30 Aug. 1827. HUSP, B.M. 38750.
153. Huskisson to Goderich, 31 Aug. 1827. Ibid.
154. Huskisson to Granville, 31 Aug. 1827. Ibid.
155. Goderich to Huskisson, 1 Sept. 1827. Ibid.
156. Goderich to Lansdowne, 31 Aug. 1827. BP.
157. Goderich to King, 1 Sept. 1827, in Aspinall, *George IV*, iii. 293.
158. Huskisson to Goderich, 1 Sept. 1827. RP, B.M. 40862.
159. Huskisson to Lansdowne, 1 Sept. 1827. HUSP, B.M. 38750.
160. Lansdowne to Huskisson, 1 Sept. 1827. Ibid.
161. Ibid.
162. Goderich to Herries, 1 Sept. 1827, in Herries, *Memoir*, i. 209.
163. Herries to Goderich, 2 Sept. 1827, in ibid.
164. Brougham to Allen, 5 Sept. 1827, in Aspinall, *Brougham*, p. 283.
165. Reeve, *Greville*, i. 111. *Diary*, 1 Sept. 1827.
166. Huskisson to Warrender, 2 Sept. 1827. HUSP, B.M. 38750.
167. Fremantle to Buckingham, 16 Sept. 1827, in Buckingham, *George IV*, ii. 350.

168. Herries to Bexley, 31 Aug. 1827, in Herries, *Memoir*, i. 208.
169. Holmes to Mrs. Arbuthnot, 13 Aug. and 6 Sept. 1827, in Aspinall, *Arbuthnot*, pp. 89, 93 : Holmes to Arbuthnot, 22 Aug. 1827, in Parker, *Peel*, ii. 13.

CHAPTER 7. HOW A GOVERNMENT FELL

1. Eden to Villiers, (?) July 1827, in Dickinson, *Miss Eden*, p. 129.
2. Eden to Villiers, 12 July 1827, in ibid., p. 132.
3. Eden to Villiers, 11 Aug. 1827, in ibid., pp. 138–9.
4. Eden to Villiers, 12 July 1827, in ibid., p. 132.
5. Eden to Villiers, 1 Sept. 1827, in ibid., pp. 141–2.
6. Ibid.
7. Goderich to Huskisson, 4 Sept. 1827. HUSP, B.M. 38750.
8. Eden to Villiers, 3 Nov. 1827, in Dickinson, *Miss Eden*, p. 152.
9. King to Goderich, 25 Oct. 1827. BP.
10. Horton to Huskisson, 27 Oct. 1827. HUSP, B.M. 38751.
11. Eden to Villiers, (?) Nov. 1827, in Dickinson, *Miss Eden*, p. 154.
12. Eden to Villiers, 2 Dec. 1827, in ibid., p. 155.
13. Ibid., pp. 155–6.
14. Lawrence to Clay, 22 Nov. 1827. LAP.
15. Prendergast to Wellesley, 20 Dec. 1827, in Wellesley, *Papers*, ii. 211–12.
16. Arbuthnot, *Journal*, i. 391, 427.
17. Bathurst to Arbuthnot, 16 Sept. 1827, in Aspinall, *Arbuthnot*, p. 94.
18. Grant to Peel, 22 Aug. 1827, in Parker, *Peel*, ii. 13.
19. Memorandum, 22 Apr. 1827, in Aspinall, *Canning*, p. 157.
20. Londonderry to Burghersh, 20 Oct. 1827, in Weigall, *Burghersh*, pp. 261–2.
21. Herries to Peel, 8 Nov. 1841, in Parker, *Peel*, ii. 506.
22. Arbuthnot, *Journal*, ii. 155.
23. Fremantle to Buckingham, 16 Sept. 1827, in Buckingham, *George IV*, ii. 350.
24. *Hansard* (2nd ser.), xiv. 1317.
25. Huskisson to Harrowby, 22 Nov. 1827. HUSP, B.M. 38752.
26. Wellington to Goderich, 21 Aug. 1827. BP.
27. Goderich to Huskisson, 10 Oct. 1827. HUSP, B.M. 38751.
28. Hardwicke to Yorke, 9 Nov. 1830. HSP, B.M. 45034.
29. Huskisson to Adam, 6 Oct. 1827. HUSP, B.M. 38751.
30. Bennett to Goderich, (?) 1832. RP, B.M. 40878.
31. Palmerston to Lamb, 15 Nov. 1827, in Sanders, *Melbourne*, p. 110.
32. Lansdowne to Lamb, 22 Nov. 1827, in ibid., p. 114.

33. Croker Memorandum, 11 Aug. 1827, in Croker, *Diaries*, i. 359.
34. W. M. Torrens, *Memoirs of the Rt. Honourable William, Second Viscount Melbourne* (London, Macmillan, 1878), pp. 178–9.
35. Lansdowne to Lamb, 3 Oct. 1827, in Sanders, *Melbourne*, pp. 105–6.
36. Lamb to Lansdowne, 19 Sept. 1827, in Torrens, *Melbourne*, pp. 157–159.
37. Lansdowne to Lamb, 22 Nov. 1827, in Sanders, *Melbourne*, pp. 112–114.
38. *Hansard* (2nd ser.), viii. 1388.
39. Dudley to Gallatin, 1 Oct. 1827. LAP.
40. Gallatin to Clay, 28 Sept. 1827. Ibid.
41. *Hansard* (2nd ser.), xxiii. 1048.
42. Lord Colchester, *A Political Diary, 1828–1830 by Edward Law, Lord Ellenborough* (London, Bentley, 1881), i. 36.
43. Goderich to Wellesley, 20 Oct. 1827. WLP, B.M. 37305.
44. Goderich to Huskisson, 20 Sept. 1827. HUSP, B.M. 38751.
45. De Walden to Huskisson, 4 Oct. 1827. Ibid.
46. Dudley to Huskisson, 8 Oct. 1827. Ibid.
47. De Walden to Huskisson, 8 Oct. 1827. Ibid.
48. Dudley to Granville, 9 Oct. 1827. Ibid.
49. Goderich to Huskisson, 10 Oct. 1827. Ibid.
50. Lansdowne to Goderich, 12 Oct. 1827. BP.
51. Dudley to Codrington, 16 Oct. 1827, in Lady Bourchier, *Memoir of the Life of Admiral Sir Edward Codrington* (London, Longmans, 1875), p. 302.
52. Canning to Codrington, 1 Sept. 1827, in ibid., p. 294.
53. General Order to All the Captains, 8 Sept. 1827, in ibid., pp. 295–6.
54. Codrington to Dudley, 8 Nov. 1827, in ibid., p. 395.
55. Goderich to Huskisson, 10 Nov. 1827. HUSP, B.M. 38752.
56. Huskisson to Goderich, 10 Nov. 1827. Ibid.
57. Arbuthnot, *Journal*, ii. 148.
58. Ibid. See also: Gore to Codrington, 14 Nov. 1827, in Bourchier, *Codrington*, pp. 393–5.
59. Palmerston to Lamb, 15 Nov. 1827, in Sanders, *Melbourne*, p. 108.
60. Palmerston to his brother, 27 Nov. 1827, in E. Ashley, *The Life and Correspondence of Viscount Palmerston* (London, Bentley, 1879), i. 117.
61. Draft to Sir Frederick Adam, 21 Dec. 1827. HUSP, B.M. 38752.
62. Memorandum to the Lord High Admiral, *c.* 30 Nov. 1827. Ibid., B.M. 38753.
63. Gore to Codrington, 6 Jan. 1827, in Bourchier, *Codrington*, p. 405.
64. Huskisson to Harrowby, 22 Nov. 1827. HUSP, B.M. 38752.

65. Arbuthnot, *Journal*, ii. 156.
66. Ibid., p. 148.
67. Ibid., p. 149.
68. Ibid., p. 151.
69. Codrington to Captain W. C., 19 Jan. 1831, in Bourchier, *Codrington*, p. 522.
70. Goderich to Herries, 24 Dec. 1827, in Herries, *Memoir*, ii. 23–24.
71. Huskisson Memorandum, 28 Dec. 1827. HUSP, B.M. 38753.
72. Herries's Statement, (?) 1827, in Herries, *Memoir*, ii. 13.
73. Ibid.
74. Herries to Huskisson, 29 Nov. 1827. HUSP, B.M. 38752.
75. Huskisson to Tierney, 29 Nov. 1827, in Herries, *Memoir*, ii. 18.
76. Huskisson to Herries, 30 Nov. 1827, in ibid., p. 17.
77. Tierney to Huskisson, 2 Dec. 1827. HUSP, B.M. 38752.
78. Huskisson Memorandum, 28 Dec. 1827. Ibid., B.M. 38753.
79. Lansdowne to Goderich, 17 Sept. 1827. BP.
80. Goderich to King, 16 Nov. 1827, in Aspinall, *George IV*, iii. 327.
81. Ibid.
82. King to Goderich, 23 and 27 Nov. 1827, in ibid., pp. 334–6.
83. Goderich to King, 28 Nov. 1827, in ibid., pp. 336–7.
84. Goderich to Huskisson, 21 Sept. 1827. HUSP, B.M. 38751.
85. Gordon to Huskisson, 15 Oct. 1827. Ibid.
86. Horton to Huskisson, 27 Oct. 1827. HUSP, B.M. 38751.
87. Arbuthnot, *Journal*, ii. 149.
88. Wellington to Goderich, 1 Dec. 1827, in Wellington, *Despatches*, iv. 162–3.
89. Goderich to King, 19 Nov. 1827, in Aspinall, *George IV*, iii. 330–1 and n.
90. Portland to Goderich, 28 Sept. 1827. BP.
91. Goderich to Portland, 10 Oct. 1827. Ibid.
92. Goderich to Huskisson, 6 Nov. 1827. HUSP, B.M. 38752.
93. Huskisson to Granville, 11 Dec. 1827. Ibid.
94. Ibid.
95. Lansdowne to Goderich, *c*. 6 Dec. 1827. BP.
96. Grant to Goderich, 15 Dec. 1827. Ibid.
97. Ibid.
98. Huskisson to Granville, 11 Dec. 1827. HUSP, B.M. 38752.
99. Ibid.
100. Goderich to King, 11 Dec. 1827, in Aspinall, *George IV*, iii. 345.
101. Lansdowne to Huskisson, 14 Dec. 1827. HUSP, B.M. 38752.
102. Huskisson to Granville, 11 Dec. 1827. Ibid.
103. Goderich to King, 11 Dec. 1827, in Aspinall, *George IV*, iii. 345.

104. Ibid.
105. Goderich to King, 10 Aug. 1827, in ibid., pp. 280–1.
106. King to Goderich, 12 Dec. 1827, in ibid., p. 347.
107. Goderich to Huskisson, 12 Dec. 1827. HUSP, B.M. 38752.
108. Huskisson to Goderich, 13 Dec. 1827. Ibid.
109. Planta to Huskisson, 13 Dec. 1827. Ibid.
110. Herries to Knighton, 13 Dec. 1827, in Aspinall, *George IV*, iii. 349.
111. Goderich to Huskisson, 13 Dec. 1827. HUSP, B.M. 38752.
112. Huskisson to Goderich, 13 Dec. 1827. Ibid.
113. Lansdowne to Huskisson, 14 Dec. 1827. Ibid.
114. Huskisson to King, 14 Dec. 1827. Ibid.
115. Goderich to King, 14 Dec. 1827, in Aspinall, *George IV*, iii. 349.
116. Huskisson to Goderich, 15 Dec. 1827. HUSP, B.M. 38752.
117. Goderich to Huskisson, 16 Dec. 1827. Ibid.
118. Harrowby to Goderich, 18 Dec. 1827. HRP.
119. King to Knighton, 17 Dec. 1827, in Aspinall, *George IV*, iii. 351.
120. Huskisson to Granville, 18 Dec. 1827, in Melville, *Huskisson*, pp. 263–4.
121. Lyndhurst to Knighton, 20 Dec. 1827, in Aspinall, *George IV*, iii. 352–3.
122. Huskisson to Goderich, 18 Dec. 1827. HUSP, B.M. 38752.
123. Goderich to Huskisson, 18 Dec. 1827. Ibid.
124. Somerset to Wellington, 20 Dec. 1827, in Wellington, *Despatches*, iv. 170.
125. Huskisson Minute, 3 Jan. 1828. HUSP, B.M. 38753.
126. Huskisson to Granville, 21 Dec. 1827. Ibid.
127. Binning to Huskisson, 25 Dec. 1827. Ibid.
128. Huskisson to Portman, 22 Dec. 1827. Ibid.
129. Goderich to Wellesley, 29 Dec. 1827. WLP, B.M. 37310.
130. Lamb to Wellington, 14 and 16 Dec. 1827 : Holmes to Wellington, 19 Dec. 1827, in Wellington, *Despatches*, iv. 168–70.
131. Rosslyn to Brougham, 22 Dec. 1827, in Brougham, *Life*, ii. 376.
132. Lauderdale to Bathurst, 24 Dec. 1827, in Wellington, *Despatches*, iv. 174.
133. Lansdowne to Lamb, 20 Dec. 1827, in Sanders, *Melbourne*, p. 115.
134. Peel to Arbuthnot, 5 Dec. 1827, in Aspinall, *Arbuthnot*, p. 95.
135. Lauderdale to Bathurst, 24 Dec. 1827, in Wellington, *Despatches*, iv. 174.
136. Bathurst to Wellington, 30 Dec. 1827, in ibid., pp. 173–4.
137. Huskisson Minute, 19 Dec. 1827. HUSP, B.M. 38752.
138. Lyndhurst to Knighton, 20 Dec. 1827, in Aspinall, *George IV*, iii. 353.

139. Bulwer, *Palmerston*, i. 331.
140. Herries to Goderich, 21 Dec. 1827. HUSP, B.M. 38753.
141. Goderich to Herries, 24 Dec. 1827, in Herries, *Memoir*, ii. 22–24.
142. Goderich to Huskisson, 25 Dec. 1827. HUSP, B.M. 38753.
143. Huskisson to Goderich, 26 Dec. 1827, in Melville, *Huskisson*, pp. 269–70.
144. Huskisson Memorandum, 28 Dec. 1827. HUSP, B.M. 38753.
145. Ibid.
146. Ibid.
147. Ibid.
148. Huskisson to King, 29 Dec. 1827. Ibid.
149. Herries Memorandum, 29 Dec. 1827, in Herries, *Memoir*, ii. 33–35.
150. Huskisson to Goderich, 1 Jan. 1828. HUSP, B.M. 38753.
151. Lansdowne to Huskisson, 30 Dec. 1827. Ibid.
152. Lyndhurst to Knighton, 31 Dec. 1827, in Aspinall, *George IV*, iii. 356.
153. Anglesey to Huskisson, 1 Jan. 1828. HUSP, B.M. 38753.
154. Lyndhurst to Knighton, 20 Dec. 1827, in Aspinall, *George IV*, iii. 353.
155. Huskisson to Goderich, 1 Jan. 1828. HUSP, B.M. 38753.
156. Anglesey to Huskisson, 1 Jan. 1828. Ibid.
157. Huskisson to Anglesey, 1 Jan. 1828. Ibid.
158. Huskisson to Goderich, 1 Jan. 1828. Ibid.
159. Huskisson to Anglesey, 3 Jan. 1828. Ibid.
160. Lansdowne to Goderich, Wednesday, (?) 2 Jan. 1828. BP.
161. Planta to Goderich, 2 Jan. 1828. Ibid.
162. Goderich to Planta, 3 Jan. 1828. Ibid.
163. Huskisson to Granville, 4 Jan. 1828. HUSP, B.M. 38753.
164. Goderich to Herries, 4 Jan. 1828, in Herries, *Memoir*, ii. 25.
165. Herries to Goderich, 5 Jan. 1828, in ibid., pp. 26–27.
166. Goderich to Huskisson, 5 Jan. 1828. HUSP, B.M. 38753.
167. Huskisson to Lansdowne, 5 Jan. 1828. Ibid.
168. Bexley to Herries, 5 Jan. 1828, in Herries, *Memoir*, ii. 53–54.
169. Lyndhurst to Herries, (?) 6 Jan. 1828, in ibid., p. 56.
170. Fitzgerald, *George IV*, pp. 853–4.
171. Hardinge to Wellington, 7 Jan. 1828, in Wellington, *Despatches*, iv. 182.
172. Herries to Goderich, 7 Jan. 1828, in Herries, *Memoir*, ii. 32.
173. Goderich to Knighton, 7 Jan. 1828. BP.
174. Huskisson to Granville, 8 Jan. 1828. HUSP, B.M. 38754.
175. Huskisson to Anglesey, 8 Jan. 1828. Ibid.
176. King to Lansdowne, 20 Jan. 1828, in Aspinall, *George IV*, iii. 371.
177. Dickinson, *Miss Eden*, p. 158.

CHAPTER 8. IN THE GREY GOVERNMENT

1. Miss Eden's Journal, 18 Jan. 1828, in Dickinson, *Miss Eden*, p. 157.
2. Morley to Granville, 26 Feb. 1828, in A. Aspinall, 'The Last of the Canningites', *English Historical Review*, l (1935), 638–69.
3. Broughton, *Recollections*, iii. 263.
4. Goderich to Yorke, 5 Nov. 1828. HSP, B.M. 45036.
5. Rice to Denman, (?) Dec. 1828, in Sir Joseph Arnould, *Life of Thomas, First Lord Denman* (Boston, Este & Lauriat), 1874, i. 229.
6. Goderich to Yorke, 5 Nov. 1828. HSP, B.M. 45036.
7. Dickinson, *Miss Eden*, p. 154.
8. Hardwicke to Yorke, 7 Dec. 1828. HSP, B.M. 45034.
9. Goderich to Huskisson, 12 Jan. 1829. HUSP, B.M. 38758.
10. Eden to Villiers, (?) Oct. 1829, in Dickinson, *Miss Eden*, p. 190.
11. Goderich to Yorke, n.d. HSP, B.M. 45036.
12. Miss Eden to Mrs. Lister, (?) Nov. 1830, in Dickinson, *Miss Eden*, p. 204.
13. Goderich to Buckingham, 18 Jan. 1828, in Buckingham, *George IV*, ii. 358–9.
14. Ibid.
15. Goderich to Huskisson, 28 May 1828. HUSP, B.M. 38756.
16. Goderich to Buckingham, 18 Jan. 1828, in Buckingham, *George IV*, ii. 358–9.
17. Goderich to King, 21 Jan. 1828, in Aspinall, *George IV*, iii. 373. King to Goderich, 22 Jan. 1828. BP.
18. Goderich to Huskisson, 9 Feb. 1828. HUSP, B.M. 38755.
19. Huskisson to Goderich, 12 Feb. 1828. Ibid.
20. Aspinall, 'The Last of the Canningites', *English Historical Review*, l (1935), 638–69.
21. Huskisson to Bourne, 16 Jan. 1828. HUSP, B.M. 39948.
22. Colchester, *Ellenborough*, i. 24.
23. Broughton, *Recollections*, iii. 241.
24. Ibid., p. 246.
25. Villiers to Bagot, 19 Feb. 1828, in Bagot, *Canning's Friends*, ii. 434.
26. Reeve, *Greville*, i. 127. *Diary*, 25 Feb. 1828.
27. Countess Cowper to Frederick Lamb, (?) 1828, in Countess of Airlie, *Lady Palmerston and her Times* (London, Hodder & Stoughton, 1922), i. 152.
28. *Hansard* (2nd ser.), xviii. 281.
29. Grenville to Buckingham, 19 Apr. 1828, in Buckingham, *George IV*, ii. 373.

30. Colchester, *Ellenborough*, i. 84.
31. Wellington to Knighton, 19 Jan. 1828, in Aspinall, *George IV*, iii. 371.
32. Bulwer, *Palmerston*, i. 235.
33. Wellington Memorandum, 20 May 1828, in Wellington, *Despatches*, iv. 455.
34. Goderich to Huskisson, 28 May 1828. HUSP, B.M. 38756.
35. Goderich to Huskisson, 1 June 1828. Ibid.
36. Bulwer, *Palmerston*, i. 248.
37. Palmerston to Goderich, 18 Dec. 1828. RP, B.M. 40862.
38. Bulwer, *Palmerston*, i. 248.
39. Goderich to Yorke, 5 Nov. 1828. HSP, B.M. 45036.
40. Colchester, *Ellenborough*, i. 282.
41. Goderich to Huskisson, 12 Jan. 1829. HUSP, B.M. 38758.
42. Colchester, *Ellenborough*, i. 337.
43. Miss Eden's Journal, 12 Jan. 1828, in Dickinson, *Miss Eden*, p. 157.
44. *Hansard* (2nd ser.), xxi. 614–16.
45. Arbuthnot, *Journal*, ii. 263.
46. Colchester, *Ellenborough*, ii. 4.
47. Reeve, *Greville*, i. 277. *Diary*, 19 Feb. 1830.
48. *Hansard* (2nd ser.), xxii, 944–57.
49. Ibid., xxiv. 430–40.
50. Colchester, *Ellenborough*, ii. 241.
51. *Hansard* (2nd ser.), xxv. 1290.
52. Palmerston Memorandum, undated in Ashley, *Palmerston*, i. 211.
53. Palmerston Memorandum, 12 Oct. 1830, in Aspinall, *Brougham*, pp. 182–3.
54. Goderich to Brougham, 3 Mar. 1828. BRP.
55. Hardwicke to Yorke, 19 Nov. 1830. HSP, B.M. 45034.
56. Stuart to Ellis, 22 Dec. 1830. RP, B.M. 40880.
57. Goderich to Yorke, 21 Nov. 1830. HSP, B.M. 45036.
58. Ripon to Grey, 20 Jan. 1834. RP, B.M. 40863.
59. Ripon to Althorp, 20 Jan. 1834. Ibid.
60. Brougham, *Life*, iii. 254–5.
61. A. Aspinall, *Three Early Nineteenth Century Diaries* (London, Williams & Norgate, 1952), p. 138.
62. Goderich to Harrowby, 19 Nov. 1831. HRP.
63. Goderich to Yorke, n.d. HSP, B.M. 45036.
64. *Hansard* (3rd ser.), vii. 1368–77.
65. Ibid. xii, 383–90.
66. Ibid. xxiv. 262.
67. Brougham, *Life*, iii. 254.

68. Creevey to Ord, 21 Jan. 1832, in Maxwell, *Creevey*, p. 583.
69. *Hansard* (3rd ser.), xvii. 1179.
70. Robinson to Liverpool, 6 May 1823. LP, B.M. 38575.
71. Robinson Minute, 17 Sept. 1826. RP, B.M. 40863.
72. Robinson to Peel, 12 Mar. 1827. PP, B.M. 40392.
73. Ibid. See also Peel to Robinson, 12 Mar. 1827. RP, B.M. 40863.
74. Goderich to Brougham, 28 Dec. 1830. BP.
75. Aylmer to Goderich, 17 Dec. 1831, (notation) C.O. 42–233 (Lower Canada).
76. Todhunter to Goderich, 8 June 1827, in V. Harlow and F. Madden, *British Colonial Developments, 1774–1834* (Oxford, Clarendon Press, 1953), pp. 418–19.
77. Bell to Goderich, 11 Mar. 1832. RP, B.M. 40878.
78. Aylmer to Goderich, 17 Dec. 1831. C.O. 42–233 (Lower Canada).
79. Colborne to Hay, 5 July 1832. C.O. 42–411 (Upper Canada).
80. W. S. Shepperson, *British Emigration to North America* (Minneapolis, University of Minnesota Press, 1957), p. 258.
81. *Hansard* (3rd ser.), iv. 262.
82. Ibid. ix. 1147.
83. Goderich to Grant, 25 May 1831, in Harlow and Madden, *Colonial Developments*, p. 97.
84. Goderich to Bourke, 14 June 1827, in ibid., p. 115.
85. Goderich to Grant, 25 May 1831, in ibid., p. 97.
86. Aylmer to Goderich, 26 Aug. 1831. C.O. 42–233 (Lower Canada).
87. Colborne to Hay, 6 Feb. 1832. C.O. 42–411 (Upper Canada).
88. Aylmer to Goderich, 5 Feb. 1832. C.O. 42–236 (Lower Canada).
89. Aylmer to Goderich, 2 Mar. 1832. Ibid.
90. Aylmer to Goderich, 30 Jan. 1833. C.O. 42–241 (Lower Canada).
91. Colborne to Hay, 5 July 1832. C.O. 42–411 (Upper Canada).
92. *Hansard* (3rd ser.), xlvi. 327–8.
93. Goderich to Howick, (?) 1832. C.O. 42–411 (Upper Canada).
94. *Hansard* (3rd ser.), xlvi. 327–32.
95. Goderich to Campbell, 25 Aug. 1827, in Harlow and Madden, *Colonial Developments*, p. 496.
96. Hay to Read, 9 March 1832, in Paul Read, *Settlements on the Niger in Western Africa* (London, Ridgway, 1840).
97. Goderich to New Zealand Chiefs, 14 June 1832, in Harlow and Madden, *Colonial Developments*, pp. 522–4.
98. Goderich to Cole, 26 May 1831, in ibid., pp. 515–16.
99. Notation on Aylmer to Goderich, 7 June 1832. C.O. 42–237 (Lower Canada).
100. *Hansard* (1st ser.), xxx. 794.

101. Canning to Wilberforce, 4 Jan. 1824, in R. and S. Wilberforce, *The Correspondence of William Wilberforce* (London, Murray, 1840), ii. 477.
102. King to Goderich, 5 June 1832. RP, B.M. 40862.
103. Circular Despatch, 9 June 1832, in Harlow and Madden, *Colonial Developments*, p. 587.
104. Circular Despatch, 10 Dec. 1831, in ibid., pp. 579–84.
105. Cole to Goderich, 21 Mar. 1832. RP, B.M. 40878.
106. Goderich to King, 6 Mar. 1832. Ibid., B.M. 40862.
107. King to Goderich, 5 June 1832. Ibid.
108. *Hansard* (3rd ser.), xiii. 286.
109. Circular Despatch, 9 June 1832, in Harlow and Madden, *Colonial Developments*, p. 587.
110. Taylor to Goderich, 6 June 1832. RP, B.M. 40862.
111. Howick to Goderich, 4 Oct. 1832. BP.
112. Macaulay to Wilberforce, 26 Nov. 1832, in Wilberforce, *Correspondence*, ii. 524–6.
113. W. L. Mathieson, *British Slavery and Its Abolition, 1823–1838* (London, Longmans, 1926), pp. 228–9.
114. Goderich to Graham, 15 Dec. 1832. GRP.
115. Reeve, *Greville*, ii. 352. *Diary*, 2 Feb. 1833.
116. Cabinet Memorandum, 4 Feb. 1833. BP.
117. Howick to Goderich, Sunday, (?) 17 Feb. 1833. Ibid.
118. Howick to Goderich, 24 Feb. 1833 and Howick Minute, 24 Feb. 1833. Ibid.
119. Sir Alan Burns, *History of the British West Indies* (London, Allen & Unwin, 1954), p. 628.
120. Goderich Minute, 27 Feb. 1833. BP.
121. Mathieson, *British Slavery*, p. 230.
122. Richmond to Graham, 6 Oct. 1832, in Charles S. Parker, *Life and Letters of Sir James Graham, 1792–1861* (London, Murray, 1907), i. 177–8.
123. Brougham, *Life*, iii. 160.
124. Goderich to Grey, 2 Feb. 1833. RP, B.M. 40863.
125. Goderich to Grey, 20 Mar. 1833. Ibid.
126. Grey to Goderich, 20 Mar. 1833. Ibid.
127. Broughton, *Recollections*, iv. 295.
128. Goderich to Grey, 27 Mar. 1833. RP, B.M. 40863.
129. Grey to Goderich, 28 Mar. 1833. Ibid.
130. Broughton, *Recollections*, iv. 298.
131. Aspinall, *Diaries*, p. 329.

CHAPTER 9. THE TWILIGHT OF A CAREER

1. Goderich to Brougham, 3 Mar. 1828. BRP.
2. Broughton, *Recollections*, v. 70.
3. Ripon Poem, 24 Oct. 1840. BP.
4. *Annual Register* (1834), 15 July 1834.
5. Creevey to Ord, 5 May 1835, in Maxwell, *Creevey*, p. 647.
6. Ripon to Peel, 3 Nov. 1835. PP, B.M. 40422.
7. Londonderry to Ripon, 13 July 1839. RP, B.M. 40863.
8. Ripon to (?) Maxwell, 23 Dec. 1834. Ibid.
9. *Address Delivered at the Anniversary Meeting of the Royal Society of Literature*, 30 Apr. 1835 by the Earl of Ripon, President. B.M. 11824 dd 39 (2).
10. Ripon to Brougham, 4 Apr. 1838. BRP.
11. Aspinall, *Diaries*, p. 341.
12. Ibid., p. 358.
13. Ripon to Grey, 14 Jan. 1834. RP, B.M. 40863.
14. Ripon to Grey, 20 Jan. 1834. Ibid.
15. Richmond to Ripon, 28 Jan. 1834. Ibid.
16. Draft to Ripon, 31 Jan. 1834. Ibid.
17. *Hansard* (3rd ser.), xxiv. 262.
18. Ibid. xviii. 364.
19. Ibid. xxiv. 262–6.
20. Ibid.
21. Graham to Ripon, 23 Dec. 1834, in Parker, *Graham*, i. 219–20.
22. Ripon to (?) Maxwell, 23 Dec. 1834. RP, B.M. 40863.
23. *Hansard* (3rd ser.), xxvi. 144–7.
24. A. S. Turberville, *The House of Lords in the Age of Reform* (London, Faber, 1958), pp. 333–65.
25. Stanley to Ripon, 13 Oct. 1835. RP, B.M. 40863.
26. Gladstone Memorandum, 20 Jan. 1836. GP, B.M. 44777.
27. *Hansard* (3rd ser.), xxxiv. 910–17.
28. Reeve, *Greville*, iii. 362. *Diary*, 21 Aug. 1836.
29. Ripon to Peel, 3 Nov. 1836. PP, B.M. 40422.
30. Peel to Hardinge, 12 Dec. 1836. *Hardinge Papers*.
31. Ripon Plan, (?) 27 Dec. 1836. PP, B.M. 40423.
32. Ripon to Peel, 4 Aug. 1837. PP, B.M. 40424.
33. George J. Pennington to Goderich, 9 July 1832. RP, B.M. 40880.
34. Stanley to Peel, 9 May 1839. PP, B.M. 40426.
35. Barnes to Delane, (?) 4 May 1841 in Office of The Times, *The History of The Times* (London, 1935), i. 447.

36 Peel to Ripon, 7 Aug 1841. RP, B.M. 40863.

37. Wellington to Ripon, 22 Aug. 1841. Ibid.

38. *Hansard* (3rd ser.), lix. 88.

39. W. W. Rostow, *British Economy of the Nineteenth Century* (Oxford, Clarendon Press, 1948), pp. 17–19.

40. Ibid., pp. 123–5.

41. Ripon to Gladstone, 4 Sept. 1841. GP, B.M. 44285.

42. Ripon to Gladstone, 15 Apr. 1843. Ibid.

43. John Morley, *The Life of William Ewart Gladstone* (New York, Macmillan, 1911), i. 240.

44. Gladstone Memorandum, n.d. in ibid., p. 250.

45. Ibid., p. 240.

46. Francis Edwin Hyde, *Mr. Gladstone at the Board of Trade* (London, Cobden-Sanderson, 1934).

47. Ripon to Peel, 17 Oct. 1841, in Parker, *Peel*, ii. 496.

48. *Hansard* (3rd ser.), lxiv. 3–23.

49. Ripon to Gladstone, 20 Oct. 1841. GP, B.M. 44285.

50. Peel to Gladstone, 23 Oct. 1841, in Parker, *Peel*, ii. 497.

51. *Hansard* (1st ser.), xxxiii, 696.

52. Ibid. (3rd ser.), lxiv. 953.

53. Ripon Minute on World Trade, 1841. PP, B.M. 40497.

54. Ripon to Gladstone, 28 Oct. 1841. GP, B.M. 44285.

55. Ripon to Peel, 29 Nov. 1841 and enclosure. RP, B.M. 40863.

56. Ripon to Gladstone, 2 Apr. 1842. GP, B.M. 44825.

57. *Hansard* (3rd ser.), lxiv. 953.

58. Peel to Ripon, 16 June 1842. RP, B.M. 40863.

59. *Hansard* (3rd ser.), lxiv. 939–54.

60. Ripon to Gladstone, 22 Oct. 1841. GP, B.M. 44285.

61. Ripon to Gladstone, 25 Oct. 1841. Ibid.

62. *Hansard* (3rd ser.), lxiv. 949.

63. Ibid. xvii. 1179–87.

64. Ibid. lviii. 493 ; ibid. lix. 46–47.

65. Hyde, *Gladstone*, pp. 47–48.

66. Peel to Ripon, 19 Oct. 1841. RP, B.M. 40863.

67. Ibid.

68. Ripon to Gladstone, 28 Oct. 1841. GP, B.M. 44825.

69. Ripon to Peel, 26 Nov. 1841, in Parker, *Peel*, ii. 505.

70. Peel to Ripon, (?) Nov. 1841. RP, B.M. 40863.

71. Ripon to Peel, 17 Nov. 1841, Parker, *Peel*, ii. 505.

72. *Hansard* (3rd ser.), lxii. 574.

73. Ibid. 752.

74. Ripon to Gladstone, 28 Oct. 1841. GP, B.M. 44285.

75. Ripon to Gladstone, 20 and 29 Oct. 1841. Ibid.
76. Peel to Ripon, 30 Oct. 1841. RP, B.M. 40863.
77. Peel to Ripon, 22 Nov. 1841, in Parker, *Peel*, ii. 505.
78. Ripon to Peel, 29 Nov. 1841. RP, B.M. 40863.
79. Ripon to Gladstone, 28 Oct. 1841. GP, B.M. 44285.
80. Peel Memorandum, (?) Dec. 1841. PP, B.M. 40497.
81. Aberdeen to Ripon, 12 and 28 Dec. 1842 ; Ripon to Aberdeen, 13, 27, and 29 Dec. 1842. AP, B.M. 43072.
82. Aberdeen to Ripon, 12 Dec. 1842. Ibid.
83. Ripon to Aberdeen, 13 Dec. 1842. Ibid.
84. Aberdeen to Ripon, 14 Dec. 1842. Ibid.
85. Ripon to Aberdeen, 29 Dec. 1842. Ibid.
86. Aberdeen to Ripon, 28 Dec. 1842. Ibid.
87. Ripon to Peel, 9 Apr. 1843. RP, B.M. 40864.
88. Ripon to Gladstone, 8 Apr. 1843. GP, B.M. 44285.
89. Wilbur Devereux Jones, 'The Origins and Passage of Lord Aberdeen's Act', *The Hispanic American Historical Review* (Nov. 1962), pp. 502–20.
90. Ripon to Aberdeen, 7 Sept. 1841. AP, B.M. 43072.
91. Aberdeen to Ripon, 7 Sept. 1841. Ibid.
92. Ripon to Aberdeen, 24 Apr. 1843. Ibid.
93. Ripon to Gladstone, 2 Jan. 1843. GP, B.M. 44825.
94. Ripon to Gladstone, 14 and 21 Oct. 1841. Ibid. ; Ripon to Aberdeen, 16 Nov. 1841. AP, B.M. 43072.
95. Ripon to Gladstone, 21 Oct. and 5 Nov. 1841. GP, B.M. 44825 ; Ripon to Peel, 29 Nov. 1841. RP, B.M. 40863.
96. Peel to Ripon, 13 Feb. 1843. RP, B.M. 40864.
97. Ripon Memorandum, n.d. GP, B.M. 44825.
98. Ripon to Peel, 29 Nov. 1841. RP, B.M. 40863.
99. Ripon to Peel, 2 July 1842 and Peel to Ripon, 4 July 1842. RP, B.M. 40863 ; Ripon to Aberdeen, 30 Sept. 1842. AP, B.M. 43072.
100. Hyde, *Gladstone*, p. 126.
101. Gladstone Memorandum, n.d., Morley, *Gladstone*, i. 267.

CHAPTER 10. THE LAST YEARS

1. Ripon to Ellenborough, 3 June 1843. RP, B.M. 40865.
2. Ibid.
3. Ellenborough to Fitzgerald, 26 June 1843. Ibid. Ellenborough to Hardinge, 15 Apr. 1844, in Parker, *Peel*, iii. 29–30.
4. Reeve, *Greville*, ii. 159. *Diary*, 14 May 1843.

5. Ripon to the Queen, 29 May 1843. RP, B.M. 40864.
6. Peel to Ripon, 9 June 1843. Ibid.
7. Ripon to Wellington, 26 June 1843. Ibid.
8. Ibid.
9. Peel Memorandum, (?) 30 June 1843. Ibid.
10. Wellington to Ripon, 29 June 1843. Ibid.
11. Ripon to Wellington, 21 June 1843. Ibid.
12. Wellington to Ellenborough, 5 July 1843. Ibid.
13. Ripon to Ellenborough, 6 July 1843. Ibid.
14. Ripon to Ellenborough, 24 July 1843. Ibid.
15. Ripon to Ellenborough, 31 July 1843. Ibid.
16. Peel to Ripon, 12 Oct. 1843, in Parker, *Peel*, iii. 13.
17. Peel to Ripon, (?) 19 Aug. 1843. RP, B.M. 40865.
18. Ripon to Peel, 31 Aug. 1843. Ibid.
19. Secret Court Resolution, 29 Aug. 1843, in Parker, *Peel*, iii. 10.
20. Peel to Ripon, 1 Sept. 1843. RP, B.M. 40865.
21. *Hansard* (3rd ser.), lxxii. 1490–7.
22. Peel to Ripon, 9 Dec. 1843, in Parker, *Peel*, iii. 17–18.
23. Reeve, *Greville*, ii. 241. *Diary*, 4 May 1844.
24. Peel to Ripon, 6 Apr. 1844, in Parker, *Peel*, iii. 21.
25. Peel to Ellenborough, 6 May 1844, in Parker, *Peel*, iii. 28.
26. Ellenborough to Peel, 19 Feb. 1844, in ibid., p. 20.
27. Ripon to Peel, 31 Dec. 1844, in ibid., p. 265.
28. Ellenborough to Ripon, 9 Jan. 1846. RP, B.M. 40875.
29. Peel to Ripon, 30 Apr. 1844, in Parker, *Peel*, iii. 23.
30. Sir W. F. Napier, *The Life and Opinions of General Sir Charles James Napier* (London, Murray, 1857), i. 439–40.
31. Ripon to Napier, 5 July 1843. RP, B.M. 40865.
32. *Hansard* (3rd ser.), lxxvi. 701–4.
33. Quoted in Napier to Davenport, 28 Nov. 1845, in Napier, *Napier*, iii. 353–62.
34. *Hansard* (3rd ser.), lxxxiv. 865.
35. Napier to Davenport, 28 Nov. 1845, in Napier, *Napier*, iii. 355–9.
36. Wellington to Ripon, 12 Oct. 1845. RP, B.M. 40874.
37. Napier to Napier, (?) 1845, in Napier, *Napier*, iii. 269.
38. Ibid.
39. Ripon to Wellington, 10 Oct. 1845. RP, B.M. 40874.
40. Wellington to Ripon, 12 Oct. 1845. Ibid.
41. Peel to Ripon, 18 Oct. 1845. Ibid.
42. Ripon Draft of Instructions, (?) Oct. 1845. Ibid.
43. Wellington to Ripon, 29 Oct. 1845. Ibid.
44. Peel to Ripon, 23 Oct. 1845. Ibid.

45. Ripon to Peel, 8 Nov. 1845. Ibid.
46. Ripon to Peel, 14 Nov. 1845. Ibid.
47. Ripon to Hardinge, 21 Nov. 1845. Ibid.
48. Napier to Ripon, (?) 1846, in Napier, *Napier*, iii. 419–21.
49. Ripon to Napier, 7 Mar. 1849. RP, B.M. 40877.
50. Ripon to Hardinge, 7 Nov. 1845. Ibid., B.M. 40874.
51. Peel to Ripon, 31 July 1843 ; Ripon to Ellenborough, 31 July 1843. Ibid., B.M. 40865.
52. Ripon to Hardinge, 20 Mar. 1846. Ibid., B.M. 40875.
53. Ripon to Hardinge, 6 June 1846. Ibid., B.M. 40877.
54. Ripon to Peel, 10 Mar. 1846. Ibid., B.M. 40875.
55. Peel to Ripon, 10 Mar. 1846. Ibid.
56. Ripon to Wellington, 12 Mar. 1846. Ibid.
57. Ripon to Hardinge, 23 Mar. 1846. Ibid.
58. Ibid.
59. Hardinge to Ripon, 9 May 1846. Ibid. B.M. 40876.
60. Ripon to Hardinge, 6 July 1846. Ibid. B.M. 40877.
61. Hardinge to Ripon, 3 Sept. 1846. Ibid.
62. *Hansard* (3rd ser.), xxiii. 409.
63. Ibid. xlvi. 588.
64. Ibid. lx. 974.
65. Ibid. lxxv. 699.
66. Ibid. lxxxvi. 1095.
67. Ripon to Peel, 29 Nov. 1845, in Sir Robert Peel, *Memoirs by the Right Honourable Sir Robert Peel* (London, Murray, 1856), ii. 197.
68. Ibid.
69. Ripon to Wellington, 19 Dec. 1845. RP, B.M. 40874.
70. Ripon to Peel, 22 Dec. 1845. Ibid.
71. Ripon to Peel, 14 May 1846, in Peel, *Memoirs*, ii. 281.
72. *Hansard* (3rd ser.), lxxxvi. 733.
73. Ashburton to Croker, 26 May 1846, in Croker, *Diaries*, ii. 274.
74. Wellington to Ripon, 22 May 1846 ; Ripon to Hardinge, 28 May 1846. RP, B.M. 40876.
75. Hardcastle, *Campbell*, ii. 227–8.
76. *Hansard* (3rd ser.), lxxxvi. 1086–95.
77. Ibid. 1095.
78. Ripon to Hardinge, 24 June 1846. RP, B.M. 40877.
79. Ripon to Hardinge, 6 July 1846. Ibid.
80. *Hansard* (3rd ser.), lxxxviii. 852.
81. Ibid. 999.
82. Bonham to Peel, 28 Aug. 1846. PP, B.M. 40597.
83. Goulburn to Ripon, 6 Dec. 1848. RP, B.M. 40877.

84. Wood to Peel, (?) Mar. 1849, in Parker, *Peel*, iii. 504.

85. Hardinge to Ripon, 3 Oct. 1849. RP, B.M. 40877.

86. Stanley to Malmesbury, 16 June 1850, in Earl of Malmesbury, *Memoirs of an Ex-Minister* (London, Longmans, 1884), i. 194.

87. Herbert to Ripon, 11 July 1850. RP, B.M. 40877.

88. Hardinge to Ripon, (?) July 1850. Ibid.

89. Goulburn to Ripon, 15 Nov. 1850. Ibid.

90. Goulburn to Ripon, 23 Jan. 1850. Ibid.

91. Hardinge to Ripon, 22 Jan. 1851. Ibid.

92. Londonderry to Ripon, 20 July 1851. Ibid.

93. *Daily News*, 29 Jan. 1859.

94. Ripon to Gladstone, 20 May 1854. GP, B.M. 44285.

95. Goderich to Bruce, 24 Dec. 1855. MRP, B.M. 43534.

96. Goderich to Hughes, 4 Feb. 1857. Ibid., B.M. 43548.

97. Goderich to Hughes, 21 Dec. 1857. Ibid.

98. Goderich to Bruce, 19 Jan. 1858. Ibid., B.M. 43534.

99. Goderich to Hughes, 21 Dec. 1857. Ibid., B.M. 43548.

100. Ripon to Brougham, 26 Oct. 1858. BP.

101. Goderich to Bruce, 3 Nov. 1858. MRP, B.M. 43534.

102. Goderich to Hughes, 7 Jan. 1859. Ibid., B.M. 43548.

103. *Daily News*, 29 Jan. 1859.

104. Clarendon to Goderich, 29 Jan. 1859. MRP, B.M. 43621.

105. Ripon to Bruce, 14 Feb. 1859. Ibid., B.M. 43534.

106. *The Times*, 29 Jan. 1859.

107. *Hansard* (3rd ser.), lix. 1100.

108. Ibid. lxvi. 282.

109. Ripon to Gladstone, 31 Aug. 1842. GP, B.M. 44825.

110. *Hansard* (3rd ser.), xlvi, 583–92.

111. Torrens, *Melbourne*, pp. 178–9.

Index

315

Date Due

Demco 38-297